Past, Present, Parallel:
A Survey of Available
Parallel Computing Systems

PAST, PRESENT, PARALLEL:

A Survey of Available Parallel Computer Systems

Arthur Trew and Greg Wilson (Eds.)

Springer-Verlag
London Berlin Heidelberg New York
Paris Tokyo Hong Kong

Arthur Trew, PhD
Edinburgh Parallel Computing Centre, University of Edinburgh,
James Clerk Maxwell Building, Edinburgh EH9 3JZ

Greg Wilson, MSc
Edinburgh Parallel Computing Centre, University of Edinburgh,
James Clerk Maxwell Building, Edinburgh EH9 3JZ

ISBN-13:978-3-540-19664-8   e-ISBN-13:978-1-4471-1842-8
DOI: 10.1007/978-1-4471-1842-8

British Library Cataloguing in Publication Data
Past, present, parallel. a survey of available parallel computing systems.
1. Multiprocessors
I. Trew, Arthur, *1957–* II. Wilson, Greg, *1963–*
004.35
ISBN-13:978-3-540-19664-8

Library of Congress Cataloging-in-Publication Data
Past, present, parallel: a survey of available parallel computing systems /
Arthur Trew and Greg Wilson, editors.
p. cm.   includes index.
ISBN-13:978-3-540-19664-8
1. Parallel processing (Electronic computers)   2. Parallel computers.
I. Trew, Arthur, 1957– . II. Wilson, Greg.
OA76.58.P38 1991
004'.35–dc20   90-27003
                                                         CIP

2128/3830—543210 (printed on acid-free paper)

Foreword

In the mid-1980s, the UK's Economic and Social Research Council set up a Programme on Information and Communication Technologies (PICT). Its dominant remit has been "to conduct social science research on the implications of developments in information and communication technologies for individuals, for organisations, and for economic and social development". This traditional social science focus on the *effects* of technological changes has, however, been complemented by research on their *causes*.

PICT researchers at the University of Edinburgh (principally Eloína Peláez, Alfonso Molina, and Donald MacKenzie) chose to examine parallel computing as a case study in current changes in information technology. The development of parallel architectures is one of the more important of those changes. It promises to change radically the economics of high-performance computing and, accordingly, has been the focus of considerable interest from both existing firms and start-up companies. Government as well as industry has been involved, for example, the US Defense Advanced Research Projects Agency.

Edinburgh PICT commissioned this report because it saw the need for a thorough, up-to-date survey of parallel computing. Most existing surveys date from the mid-1980s, when enthusiasm about parallel computing was at its height. At the start of the 1990s, that enthusiasm is tempered by experience. Some firms have prospered; others have failed; and there have been important new entrants to the market.

The reader will find in the pages that follow a clearly-drawn picture of the current status of the different strands that make up parallel computing. There is also another, more implicit, story being told in these pages, a story about the forces shaping innovation in high technology at the end of the twentieth century.

Donald MacKenzie
Department of Sociology
University of Edinburgh

Acknowledgements and Disclaimers

We wish to thank Donald Mackenzie and the Programme on Information and Communication Technologies (PICT) for funding us to write this report, David Wallace and the management of the Edinburgh Parallel Computing Centre (EPCC) for allowing us to spend more time on it than we should have, and all the people who so freely gave us time and information, without which this book could not have been written. Most of all, we wish to thank Colin Brough, Malcolm Brown, Neil MacDonald, Mike Norman, Sandy Robertson, Rob Scott, Mark Smith, Billy Taylor, and Matthew White for their hard work and their patience.

Because of the rate at which parallel computing is changing, a report such as this cannot be comprehensive or up to date. We have tried to restrict ourselves to companies whose main interest is multiprocessor computers, and we believe that this report does cover most such firms. Vendors of software systems for parallel computers have not been given wide coverage, nor have manufacturers of multiprocessor add-in boards for workstations and PCs. (We have used Caplin Cybernetics as an example of a company producing add-in products because of their close link to DEC; this does not imply that we regard Caplin's products as superior to those of its competitors.)

Our authors have not had direct experience with all of the machines they describe. However, they are each acquainted with that general type of computer and are able to place the information they have received in context. We have attempted to be objective in our review of each company, and, where appropriate, to discuss the relative merits of its competition. While the products of some companies may be referred to more often than others when making comparisons, this is not meant to imply that these companies' products are superior to those of their competitors.

While the factual information presented here is true to the best of our knowledge, PICT, EPCC, the editors, and the contributors do not accept any liability or blame howsoever arising from errors, omissions, or other faults in this document, or any damage or liabilities arising from such omissions, errors or other faults from the use of this document or the information contained herein. Any opinions presented are those of the individual contributor, and do not necessarily reflect the position of PICT, EPCC, or the University of Edinburgh. We have attempted to acknowledge all trademarks, and apologise for any which we have not acknowledged or have acknowledged incorrectly.

Arthur Trew
Greg Wilson

Contents

List of Figures

List of Tables

Chapter 1

Introduction

Since their invention in the 1940s, computers have been built around one basic plan: a single processor, connected to a single store of memory, executing one instruction at a time. Now, at the beginning of the 1990s, it is clear that this model will not be dominant for much longer. Parallelism — the use of many processors together in a single machine to solve a single problem — is the future of computing.

1.1   An Introduction to Parallel Processing

In 1986 Tim Johnson and Tony Durham produced a report for Ovum Ltd. on the state of the parallel computing industry. They began by saying:

> The more successful people are in making use of computers, the more computer performance they find they need. To put some of the new ideas for computer applications into effect, users must have much greater performance available to them at much lower cost. The time is coming when many users will find that parallel processing is the best way of meeting their requirements. (Ovum report pg. 1)

The last five years have proved their prediction correct. What was, in 1986, largely the preserve of academic and industrial research has become a significant segment of the high-performance computing market. More significantly, all of the major actors in supercomputing today acknowledge that parallelism of one kind or another is the only way that they will be able to meet the market's increasing demand for high-speed, low-cost computing. Even in conservative areas such as on-line transaction processing, established firms such as DEC and IBM are facing increasing competition from younger companies whose use of parallelism gives them a significant price/performance edge.

1.1.1   B. P. (Before Parallelism)

Parallel processing is best defined by contrasting it with normal serial processing. At the 1947 Moore School lectures, John von Neumann and his colleagues propounded a basic design, or architecture, for electronic computers in which a single processing unit was connected to a single store of memory. In a von Neumann machine, the processor fetches instructions from a program stored in memory, then fetches operands for those instructions from the same memory, performs a calculation, and writes the results back to the memory.

The von Neumann architecture was popular for several reasons. First, it was conceptually simple: only one thing was going on at a time, and the order of operations corresponded to what a human being would do if he or she were carrying out the same computation. This conceptual simplicity was very important in the early days of computer science, when little or nothing was known about how to write a program for an automatic calculating machine.

Second, von Neumann machines were simple(r) to build than any of the alternatives, since they contained only one of everything. Third, von Neumann machines made economic sense. A rule known as Grosch's Law, which was promulgated at the time, held that the performance of a computer was proportional to the square of its cost. This was because the basic components of computers (vacuum tubes and magnetic drums) were fragile, error-prone devices. The reward in terms of speed and reliability of putting extra effort and resource into the construction of these devices was substantial.

Von Neumann and his colleagues did not ignore the possibility of using many processors together. Indeed, von Neumann was perhaps the originator of the idea of cellular automata, in which a very large number of simple calculators work simultaneously on small parts of a large problem. However, the hardware technology of the time was not capable of creating such machines, and the software technology was not capable of programming them.

Things began to change in the 1960s. On the hardware front, the switch from vacuum tube to solid state components was obviating Grosch's Law. As shown by DEC's introduction of the PDP series of minicomputers late in the decade, big computers were no longer necessarily the most cost effective. According to the Ovum Report, "The $18,000 minicomputer cut right across Grosch's Law by providing price/performance similar to that offered by the new CDC 6600 — even though the CDC machine was regarded as the wonder of its time in that respect." (Ovum report pg. 16).

At the same time, programmers were inventing ways of handling concurrency. The introduction of time-sharing mainframes in the 1960s, such as the IBM Series 360 range, accelerated the development of software techniques for handling interprocess communication, resource scheduling, and memory contention. While such techniques generally receive less press than the hardware developments of the time, they were to be at least as important in the development of truly parallel computers a decade later.

The early 1970s witnessed the development of the first "vector" computer, the Cray-1, a development of the CDC 6600. In a vector computer, the circuitry which carries out arithmetic operations is divided into stages; for example, that which does floating-point addition is divided into separate sections which compare the exponents of the operands, shift one or the other, perform the addition, and then normalise the result. If two long vectors of numbers are being added together, successive additions can be overlapped to increase the overall throughput. The existence of such high-performance computers created a demand for high-speed, low-cost computing which could only increase.

Four things conspired to bring the idea of parallel processing to life in the late 1970s. The first, and most important, was the development of Very Large Scale Integration (VLSI) technology, which allowed tens (now hundreds) of thousands of transistors to be put on a single integrated circuit. This development completely reversed Grosch's Law. Small computers, built around small processors, quickly became more cost effective than large ones, because the pay-off for increased construction effort on a silicon chip was less than linear.

The second major development was in programming methods. By the late 1970s, concurrent techniques such as monitors, semaphores, and signals had become a standard part of the undergraduate curriculum in computer science. As a result, there was a large community of programmers who had been trained to think about concurrency. These programmers were given extra opportunity to practice their skills by the rise of real-time programming made possible by VLSI. As it became economic to dedicate a small processor to managing a piece of laboratory equipment or a missile (or, later, a video recorder or washing machine) methods of co-ordinating several actions at once and handling high-speed communications between different pieces of hardware established themselves[1].

The third development of the 1970s was the actual construction of parallel computers. Pioneering projects such as C.mmp (Computer with multiple mini-processors) begun at Carnegie-Mellon University in 1971, and the Illiac IV, one of the most heroic failures in the brief history of computing, provided valuable lessons for the future of parallel computing. In particular, the Illiac IV showed the danger of trying to combine too many new-wave ideas at once (such as parallelism *and* state-of-the-art components), and the need for usable programming languages and environments.

Finally, the continued development of vector computers, especially the eponymous Cray series, fuelled the growth of computational science. Many scientific problems, such as modelling global weather patterns, analysing the aerodynamic properties of a wing, and simulating the strange sub-atomic world of quantum theory, cannot be solved exactly. Simulation and approximation are the only way in which science can deal with such problems, but for such problems these approaches require enormous volumes of computation. Scientists quickly discovered that they could do more science, and better science, with supercomputers than without, and supercomputers quickly became a *sine qua non* in fields such as meteorology and particle physics.

By the early 1980s, parallel computers were appearing which were intended for use, not for study as things in themselves. ICL, in the United Kingdom, produced six Distributed Array Processor (DAP) machines, each of which contained 4096 single bit processors. In the United States, the group at the California Institute of Technology headed by Geoffrey Fox and Charles Seitz constructed the Cosmic Cube, a 64 processor "hypercube" machine (see below) intended originally for work on planetary dynamics which found much wider application, and spawned several generations of commercial imitators.

Today, the number of companies producing parallel computers, and the number of different computers being produced, is growing rapidly. Proponents of parallelism use two arguments to show that the future of high-performance computing belongs to them. The first is economic: parallel computers tend to be much more cost effective than their serial counterparts. This is primarily because of the economies

---

[1]Real-time programming of embedded systems was one of the major considerations in the design of both the transputer and its "native" language Occam.

of scale of VLSI technology — with any given technology, ten small processors with the same total performance of one large processor almost invariably cost less than that one large processor.

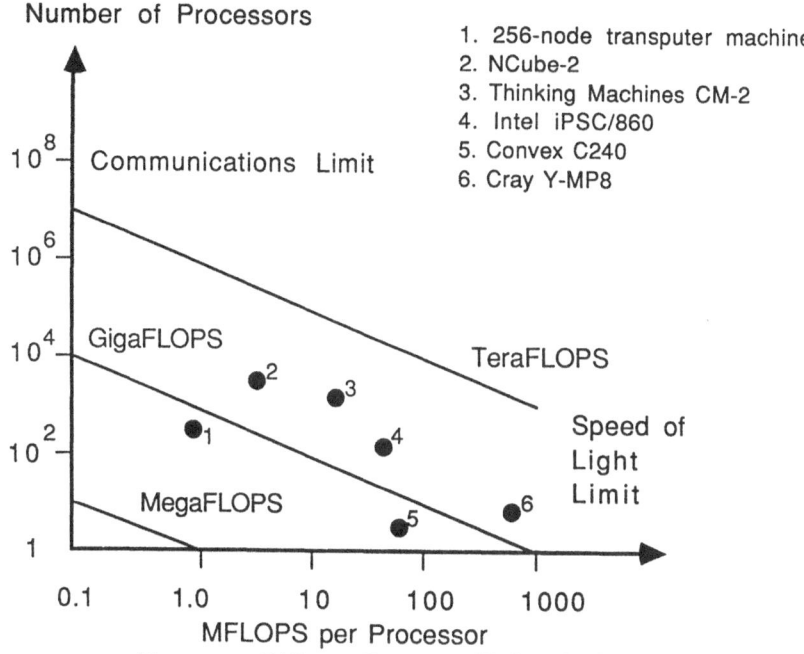

Figure 1.1: Different Routes to Higher Performance

The second argument is based on a fundamental physical law. Because information cannot travel faster than the speed of light, the only ways of performing a computation more quickly are to reduce the distance information has to travel, or to move more bits of information at once. Attempts to reduce distance are eventually limited by quantum mechanics — a computer whose wires are single atoms might be physical realisable, but would have to incorporate enormous levels of redundancy to compensate for quantum uncertainty. Moving more bits at once is parallelism, and this is the approach which is proving successful. Today, every major player in the supercomputing game is building machines which use several processors together in order to solve a single problem. The "only" questions remaining are how many processors should be used, how big should they be, and how should they be organised? As Figure 1.1 shows, one can trade individual processor performance against the number of processors to achieve the same absolute performance in a variety of ways. However, to achieve teraFLOPS performance it is clear that the only practical approach is to use a very large number (at least tens of thousands) of very fast processors (at least tens of MFLOPS each).

1.1.2   Computer Architectures

Michael J. Flynn's 1972 taxonomy of computer architectures is still the most generally used method of classifying parallel computers. Flynn divided computers according to whether they used single or multiple "streams" of data, and (orthogonally) single or multiple "streams" of instructions (Table 1.1).

Table 1.1: Flynn's Taxonomy

	Single Instruction	Multiple Instruction
Single Data	SISD (von Neumann)	MISD
Multiple Data	SIMD (DAP)	MIMD (Sequent, iPSC/2)

An SISD computer carries out one instruction on one datum at a time. This is the conventional von Neumann architecture [2]. An MISD computer, on the other hand, would apply several instructions to each datum it fetches from memory. No computers conforming to this model have yet been constructed.

The third of Flynn's four groupings is SIMD. In an SIMD computer, many processors simultaneously execute the same instructions, but on different data. For example, if the instruction is ADD A B, each processor adds its own value of B to its own value of A.

The three most significant computers of this type produced to date are the now AMT Distributed Array Processor (or DAP), the Connection Machine (CM) built by Thinking Machines, and the MP-1 from MasPar. These machines are built of very simple *processing elements* (PEs) but compensate for this simplicity by using many of them together — up to 4,096 (arranged in a 64×64 grid) in the current generation of DAP, 65,536 (2^{16}) in a full-sized CM, and 16,384 in the MP-1. A single master processor broadcasts program instructions to the individual PEs, which carry out the instructions on their own data. PEs can be disabled temporarily so that operations are only carried out on part of the data; this provides a way of making computations data-dependent, like the IF statement in most languages.

Processing elements can also transfer data amongst themselves. In the DAP, PEs are connected in a square array. Each PE can simultaneously shift one bit in one direction and receive a bit from the opposite direction. Repeated shifts can move large volumes of data from any part of the grid to any other. The communications mechanisms in the CM and MasPar are similar, although they both provide an extra level of random routing between the PEs. One of the strengths of

---

[2]There are very few "true" von Neumann machines around these days; almost all computers use some small-scale parallelism, such as pre-fetching of instructions, but this is usually hidden from the user.

SIMD computers is that as more processing elements are added, so are more inter-processor links, so that the total communications bandwidth of the machine rises in proportion to its size. Such scaling properties are an important consideration in MIMD computers as well.

Experience has shown that SIMD are very good at some things, but inefficient at others. For example, many of the algorithms used in image processing involve performing the same operations on each pixel of the image, such as taking a weighted average of its value and the values of its four nearest neighbours. If each pixel is mapped to a separate PE, an SIMD machine can carry out the calculation for each pixel simultaneously, producing the clean image in much less time than a serial machine would require. On the other hand, when the task is not well load-balanced the SIMD architecture can be inefficient. For example, in ray-tracing some light rays never intersect an object and leave the scene immediately, while others have a very complicated path involving many reflections/refractions. While schemes exist for many applications which may reduce the imbalance, those PEs which are assigned straightforward tasks must still wait for the other processors to finish.

MIMD computers are an evolutionary step forward from SISD computers. An MIMD computer contains several independent (and usually equi-powerful) processors, each of which executes its individual program[3].

There are several different ways of building an MIMD computer with current technology. The primary distinction is between a computer with a small number of powerful processors and a computer with a larger number of smaller processors. Other characteristics, such as the relationship of processors to memory and the way processors are connected, follow on from this initial distinction.

A few large machines have evolved from existing computers; the best example is Cray's Y-MP/832, in which eight extremely powerful vector processors are combined in a single machine. The great advantage such machines have is the large amount of software which can be recycled for them. This is a particularly important consideration for vendors such as Cray Research Inc., whose machines require a very large investment of programming effort to reach their achievable performance. This effort, whether it comes from the manufacturer or the user, inevitably increases the effective cost of the machine, and delays the time at which the application program begins to produce useful results.

A similar approach has been followed by other manufacturers such as Sequent and Alliant. Instead of using very powerful vector processors, however, these designs couple several conventional microprocessors (typically the Intel 80386) to create a machine with mainframe performance at minicomputer cost. These machines allow much existing software to be re-used, as well as many well-understood ideas about managing concurrency.

---

[3]In practice, these processors often execute the same program, but may follow different paths through it or be at different points in the program at a given time.

So long as the number of processors remains small, engineers can connect them all to a single memory store. This leads to a *shared-memory* computer, in which every processor can access any part of the whole machine's memory. (In less extreme examples, processors have some private memory, which may be compared to a private office, but also share some memory, like programmers share a library or a coffee lounge.) Shared-memory computers are attractive because they are relatively simple to program. Most of the techniques developed for multi-tasking computers, such as semaphores, can be used directly on shared-memory computers.

However, computers with physically shared memory have one great flaw: they cannot be scaled up indefinitely. As the number of processors trying to access the memory increases, so do the odds that processors will be contending for such access. Eventually (in fact, very quickly), access to memory becomes a bottleneck limiting the speed of the computer. The use of local cache memory can alleviate this problem by permitting commonly used data to be stored locally on each processor. This approach, when taken to its logical limit, distributes all of the memory between the processors, so reducing the required memory bandwidth. Accessing memory locations on remote nodes then poses a new problem. In the BBN Butterfly, the memory is distributed between the processors which are connected by a high-performance switching network. Here, shared memory is emulated on top of the distributed memory architecture by having a global address space and interprocessor communications are hidden from the user.

However, it is more common in distributed memory machines, such as the Intel iPSC/2, the Meiko Computing Surface, for each processor to maintain its own memory and for the user program to specifically request information from another node. Nevertheless, the problem remains of how to link these processors together. Connecting them all to a single bus, or through a single switch, leads to the same sorts of bottlenecks as discussed above for large numbers of processors. Similarly, linking each processor to every other is not an acceptable solution, because the number of connections (and hence the cost) rises with the square of the number of processors. The only practical solution is to connect each processor to some small subset of its fellows.

The most popular processor interconnection topology today is undoubtedly the *hypercube*. Pioneered by the CalTech group in the early 1980s, and used by Danny Hillis in the Connection Machine, hypercubes are a generalisation of the familiar square and cube; the six simplest hypercubes are shown below (Figure 1.2).

Hypercubes have several advantages. First, the number of nodes in a hypercube grows exponentially with the number of connections per node, so that a small increase in the hardware at each node allows a large increase in the size of the computer. Second, the number of alternative paths between nodes increases with the size of the hypercube, which helps relieve congestion. Third, efficient algorithms are known for routing messages between processors in a hypercube (e.g. random

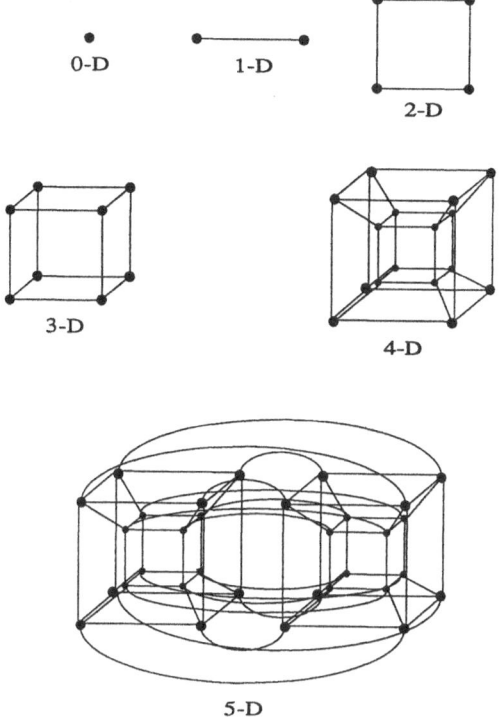

0-D   1-D

2-D

3-D   4-D

5-D

Figure 1.2: 0-D to 5-D Hypercubes

two-phase routing). Finally, and today most importantly, a large corpus of software and programming techniques exists for hypercubes, as exemplified in routing harnesses like Express and discussed in books such as that by Fox et al. [SPCP].

An alternative approach to the MIMD topology question was developed by Meiko in their Computing Surface range. In these machines, processors are connected through switching chips, which allow the user to change the topology to suit his or her program (within certain limits). If the problem seems to require a tree of processors, such a tree can be constructed; if a square mesh is needed, that can be made available; and even hypercubes can be created, albeit of low dimensionality. The development of routing software which can adapt to various topologies [TINY] is now obviating the question of topology.

1.1.3 Computer Software

The two main arguments against the use of parallel computers today are that they lack software, and that they are difficult to program. Clearly, the first is largely a product of the second — if parallel computers could be programmed the same way as serial computers, existing software could be ported to parallel computers as it is routinely ported between different serial computers.

There are basically three groups of computer users today: those who will do whatever they have to in order to get maximum performance, those who just want to program, and those who don't want to use computers *per se*, but do want spreadsheets, statistics packages, word processors, and the like. The first group, made up largely of scientific programmers working in such leading-edge fields as aerodynamics and quantum chromodynamics, feels comfortable working at a low level, and typically resorts to assembly language programming no matter what machine they are using in order to wring the last few operations per second from the hardware. While such people appreciate good programming environments, they are often willing to work without them, and are frequently prepared to write new programs from scratch rather than recycle old ones. This tacit acceptance of an ever-changing regime makes such programmers not so relevant to this discussion.

The third group of people includes 90% or more of today's computer users. With few exceptions, they do not yet need the power of parallel computers (a word processor capable of accepting one million keystrokes per second is not a useful device), and are averse to programming anyway. It is therefore mainly the second group, the applications programmers who could put their programs onto conventional machines but would like to take advantage of the price/performance of parallel computers, which needs to be considered.

To date, parallel computer manufacturers have tried to meet the demands of this group in three different ways. The first is by hiding the parallelism of the machine from the programmer. Vectorising compilers for computers such as the Cray, which can exploit the parallelism present in the small loops which make up much of scientific codes, allow programmers to trade a small amount of performance for a great deal of programming ease. The most extreme attempt to exploit this willingness to trade was made by the now-defunct company Multiflow, who wrote their compiler and then built a machine to run its output.

The second approach, mentioned several times previously, is to allow programmers to re-use what they know about concurrent programming on conventional machines. This is the route taken by manufacturers such as Sequent and Alliant. While programmers must deal with parallelism explicitly on these computers, they can do so using such well-known tools as semaphores. This approach virtually demands that the underlying architecture be shared-memory, and hence it seems that it will have a limited lifespan.

The third approach is to make the user write explicitly parallel programs. This can either be done by adding parallel constructs to existing languages, or by providing entirely new languages for describing parallelism. Enriching existing languages has so far been more successful. Environments like Express and Tiny allow programmers to write in languages with which they are familiar, using tools (especially UNIX programming support tools) which they find comfortable. As will be discussed later, the imposition of special-purpose languages has led to some notable failures, and was largely responsible for the failure of Inmos to capture a significant share of the American computer market. One example of this was the adoption of Occam by FPS for their T series computer in the mid-1980s. This machine made few sales and caused severe problems for FPS (cf. Sections:fps).

SIMD computer manufacturers have largely been able to ignore these issues for two reasons. First, the lock-step nature of SIMD processing means that many of the problems of synchronisation and communication which MIMD programmers have to wrestle with simply do not arise. Second, SIMD computers have, to date, presented an appearance so so radically different from conventional SISD computers, that the opportunity to re-use existing software is small. Consequently, the need to retain traditional languages is reduced. Despite this, all of the major SIMD manufacturers have stayed with conventional high level languages, usually Fortran and C, although the Connection Machine may also be programmed in a variant of Lisp. The advent of Fortran 90, which has integral parallel constructs, may change this situation and allow increased code portability.

The way in which programmers deal with parallelism is largely determined by how deep into the underlying hardware they are willing to go. As noted above, those requiring the highest performance will always have to program at a low level, irrespective of the hardware. The majority of programmers, however, seem to want something a little less gritty.

On some machines, programmers are forced to deal with parallelism as it is found in the underlying hardware. The concurrent constructs in Occam, which was initially the only language provided for the transputer, exactly reflected the capabilities of the underlying hardware. (In fact, compilation from Occam into assembly code was almost a one-for-one translation of instructions.) While this made it a good language for real-time programming, it was very uncomfortable for people who wanted to write large applications.

A more popular approach is to provide the user with the ability to create and place processes which can communicate with one another through function calls. CrOS, the Crystalline Operating System for the CalTech hypercubes, was an early step in this direction; its descendant Express, marketed by Parasoft, is widely used. In the UK, Meiko has recently produced its own CS Tools programming environment which offers much the same functionality. One of the advantages of this approach is that the function calls performing communication can be abstracted from the hardware (Express runs on transputer machines as well as hypercubes) and can be embedded in a variety of languages (primarily C and Fortran). Finally, partial abstraction from the underlying hardware creates a "level of programming" comparable to that encountered by systems programmers.

The final option is to abstract from the underlying hardware completely. Proponents of this route tend to come from a symbolic processing background, and tend to employ ideas first seen in Artifical Intelligence (AI) in their approach to parallelism. Programming environments such as Linda and Strand (described in detail later) seek to provide what the programmer wants, rather than what the hardware will allow. Whether such schemes can be efficiently mapped onto distributed memory computers is as yet unsettled.

1.1.4   Types of Parallelism

One of the simplest ways to use parallelism is the task farm. In this approach, a master process produces a number of independent tasks which are farmed out to slave processes. Once these have been processed, the results are collected by a third process, which writes them to disk or displays them on a graphics board. Typically, the master and each slave reside on different processors. This arrangement provides good load balancing for many types of problem — if one task takes a long time to complete, the other processors in the system can get on with processing other tasks in parallel.

A problem is only suitable for task farm parallelism if it can be broken down into a large number of tasks which can be executed independently of each other. In order to maximise the throughput of a task farm the number of tasks should be much greater than the number of processors available. A typical application is ray tracing on a MIMD machine. The screen is broken up into many small patches, which are then distributed by demand among the available processors. Each slave then draws the part of the image in its patches.

Another effective form of parallelism is grid decomposition. In this case, the application must be based an underlying grid, as in cellular automata and image processing applications. This grid is divided into patches and one patch put on each processor. Each processor updates the values in its part of the grid, then swaps boundary values with its neighbours. This approach yields good results when a local operator must be applied to each point on the grid. The operations on the grid can be carried out in parallel on each of the sub-grids except in the boundary regions.

A third form of parallelism, algorithmic parallelism, is usually more difficult to implement well. In algorithmic parallelism the different functions within the application are put on different processors. For example, the transformation, clipping, shading, and Z-buffering stages of a graphics pipeline can each be put on separate processors. The problem with pipelines of this sort is that they are susceptible to bottlenecks. If one stage of the pipe is more compute-intensive than the others, its performance will limit that of the system as a whole.

Chapter 2

SIMD: Specialisation Equals Success

The paradigm of lock-step parallelism embodied in SIMD computers has proved to be extremely successful at solving a wide range of scientific problems. One reason for this is that many of the problems which arise in more general models of parallelism, such as deadlock, cannot occur on SIMD machines. As a result, there has been greater architectural convergence among SIMD manufacturers, and more progress toward standards such as FORTRAN 90, than anywhere else in the parallel computing field. The increasingly competitive struggle between Thinking Machines Corp. and other manufacturers at the "speed at any price" end of the market, along with AMT's fight to expand its share of the signal and image processing market, have been made even more intense by MasPar's recent entry into this field.

2.1   Active Memory Technology

Relevant Activities Supplier of the DAP, a fine-grained SIMD processor

Location Headquarters, Hardware development and production: Active Memory
Technology Inc., 16802 Aston Street, Suite 103, Irvine, California 92714, USA.
Telephone: (714) 261 8901, Fax: (714) 261 8802. Software design and Euro-
pean sales: Active Memory Technology, 65 Suttons Park Avenue, Reading,
England. Telephone: 0734 661111, Fax: 0734 351395.

Relevant Officers Neil Pearce, Non-executive Chairman; Geoff Manning, Chief
Executive; Ronald McKellar, Finance Director; Bill Terry, VP Sales; Bruce
Alper, VP Corporate Development.

Employees 39 in the UK and 40 in the US.

Financial details AMT is mainly funded by UK venture capital companies. It
has 20% of the equity held by ICL and a further 20% vested with employees.

2.1.1   The Company

Active Memory Technology (AMT) make a range of massively parallel SIMD computers – the Distributed Array Processor (DAP). The company was formed in 1986
as a spin-off from ICL who had at that time been developing fine-grained parallel
machines for nearly 15 years. The original design for these machines as a large
SIMD grid of single bit processors was made by Stewart Reddaway at ICL in the
period 1972 – 1976 and as such was a forerunner for a range of computers, such
as the MPP from Goodyear, the Thinking Machines' Connection Machine (cf. 2.3)
and the MP-1 series from MasPar (cf. 2.2).

   The first generation ICL DAP was not a commercial success largely because of
its reliance on an ICL mainframe as the front-end and general consumer resistance
to new technology. The need for the mainframe host added considerably to the capital and recurrent costs of the machine and only six were placed within the UK and
none abroad. At about the same time as the first generation DAPs became commercially available research was started on a superDAP. This design went through
several iterations and in its final form was to be an array of 4 bit processors and
was projected to have approximately ten to one hundred times the performance of
the DAP for arithmetic operations. This work was shelved in the early 1980s in
favour of a second generation mini–DAP developed for the scientific workstation
and defence signal processing markets. The new machine was to have a 32×32 grid
of processors and be hosted by a PERQ workstation. Unfortunately, this also was
dropped when the development work fell behind schedule and the PERQ did not
continue to command a large market share. Only 13 pre-production mini–DAPs

were made and only a minority were sold. In 1983 the earlier superDAP design was revived in a modified form for a defence funded development known as VDAP. This project was stopped by ICL soon after the formation of AMT. Some of the ideas will finally be embodied in AMT's CP8 coprocessor (cf. 2.1.2 below).

At this time ICL also saw their main market place as the standard mainframe computer and viewed the DAP as an interesting project but one which was too academically and scientifically oriented. ICL, therefore decided that the product did not fit well within their corporate strategy. Coupled with some internal pressure from within the DAP project team it was thought that the best way forward was to float off the effort to a separate company.

Hence, the expertise in the design of fine-grained parallel machines was carried across to AMT. ICL now have a 20% shareholding in AMT in return for the transfer of intellectual property rights and patents. However, they do not have a management role. Sales to the defence sector were the main interest in the DAP by ICL and consequently they are believed to be continuing with some basic software design for this market.

From the outset, AMT was established as a joint UK/US organisation with approximately equal numbers of employees within each country. The decision to split the company was taken for two reasons, firstly it was thought that entry to the US market place would be easier from a supplier which had a US production base. Secondly, at the time when AMT was founded it was believed that more expertise in chip design existed in the US and that it would be faster to produce a new processor chip there rather than in the UK. Consequently, hardware development and production has been based in California while the software effort and, until recently, the top management has been sited in the UK.

However, after Geoff Manning became Chief Executive Officer of AMT in November 1989 he felt that the corporate structure should become more unified, and that the top management should be at one centre. Since the majority of sales were in the US, overall management was accordingly transferred to California.

Clearly, AMT see the US as their major market and are trying to gain acceptance there, though it may be that Europe, after 1992, will be large and open enough to support a specialised manufacturer. It may be supposed that this move towards being seen more as an American company cannot but help to improve the probability of being granted DARPA aid for future projects. There are no plans to move the software effort from the UK because most experience in that field lies here.

The company is capitalised at approximately £15 M, of which over £10 M has been raised from UK venture capitalists.

2.1.2 The Machine

Despite various changes to the processor technology and front-end hosts the DAP
has, until now, remained basically unchanged since its conception in the early
1970s. The DAPs currently being produced by AMT are the third generation of
such machines and have much improved high speed I/O and debugging facilities
over the original ICL models. The first model from AMT was a 32 × 32 array of
processing elements (PEs), this was followed one year later by a 64 × 64 lattice[1].
The computational core of the DAP is this array of PEs which are arranged in a
square two-dimensional lattice. These processors execute the same tasks in parallel
(SIMD parallelism) and gain not from processor complexity but by their numbers.

In comparing the first and third generation DAPs one must not overlook the
improvements which have been made from the original ICL machines in terms of
their size, operational requirements and running costs. The University of Edinburgh
had two ICL DAPs hosted by an ICL 2972 mainframe for about five years in the
early 1980s. It has also had two AMT DAPs for the past two years. On the basis of
this experience it is possible to make a direct comparison of the products. The ICL
DAP was a 64 × 64 processor array with 4 kbit of memory per PE and unlike the
more recent models this had to hold both program and data. It had a volume of
250 ft^3, weighed 2 ton, required three phase electricity, used approximately 20 kW
and needed to be housed in a machine hall with air-conditioning and purification.
The mean time between failures on these machines was 11 days. The AMT DAP
has a minimum memory size of 32 kbit per PE and the present DAP 500 series is
capable of being fitted under a desk. It requires only normal mains electricity, uses
about 300 – 400 W and needs no special cooling or air-cleaning provision. Since
installation there has only been one hardware failure on one of the University of
Edinburgh's DAPs. This record is consistent with the basic aims of AMT which
are discussed below (Figure 2.1.5).

The third (current) generation DAPs are still based upon an array of single bit
PEs. These processor chips have been re-engineered to use CMOS technology but
are still custom designs. A single chip contains 64 PEs. Design studies are underway
to implement the processors using sub-micron CMOS technology. At present all
DAP models have a nominal 100 ns cycle time, although there are plans to reduce
this by a factor of two in the near future. Each PE has direct connection to its
own local memory, while interprocessor communications are via an orthogonal grid
of data highways with, in addition, direct links to each of its nearest neighbours

---

[1]The naming convention for the DAP models is as follows: the series number is the logarithm
(base two) of the edge size of the array ($32 = 2^5$). To this is appended the clock speed in MHz and,
if the PEs have an attached co-processor, the letter c. Finally, the memory size of the machine,
measured in Mbyte, in sometimes added. For example, a 64 × 64 processor DAP with attached
co-processor (see later) and 128 Mbyte of memory running at 10 MHz would be described as a
DAP 610c-128

(Figure 2.1). This high level of connectivity provides very rapid data shifting and broadcast.

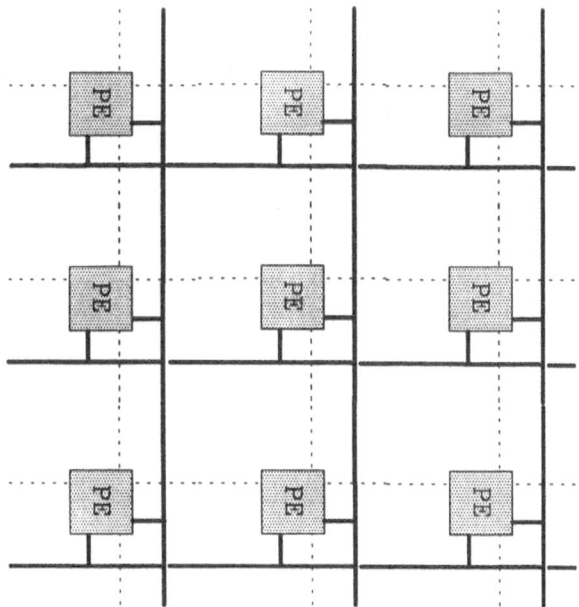

Figure 2.1: The DAP PE Interconnection Strategy

On a single bit processor all arithmetic must be performed in software: the DAPs are, therefore, best suited for applications which involve boolean operations or calculations on low precision numbers, for example image processing of 8 bit data. Nevertheless, much floating-point work has been performed on the DAP especially where the inherent parallelism in the application is well suited to the machine architecture. In order to address this issue an announcement has just been made of an upgraded DAP which includes a co-processor (the CP8) so enhancing its performance on computationally intensive tasks such as floating point and integer arithmetic. It is interesting to note the re-emergence of the concept behind the superDAP a decade after that project was stopped. Each PE will then have a new associated co-processor which is able to access the same array memory. As may be surmised form its name the CP8 co-processor is an 8 bit device. Included in the hardware are a number of features which permit data reorganisation, these additions should speed up arithmetic by a substantial factor over the 1 bit PEs. AMT estimate that for floating point arithmetic the new DAPs will have a performance improvement by a factor of about ten, though this improvement will only be achieved in real applications when communications are not important. It is expected that the first machines to include co-processors will be available towards the end of 1990.

This move towards a hybrid machine containing both single bit and floating point units is similar to the strategy adopted by Thinking Machines with their Connection Machine (CM) (cf. 2.3.2). In this case AMT have chosen to pair every single bit PE with a relatively simple 8 bit processor whereas in the CM a group of 32 single bit processors share a very powerful floating point engine. During the design stage AMT considered the option of coupling a fast floating point processor (e.g. an i860 or Weitek chip) to each row of PEs with the array grid. However, they opted instead for the CP8 solution for three reasons. Firstly AMT wanted to keep control over the hardware technology and this is only possible using custom designed chips. Second, it is a company policy to make all DAPs throughout the range source code compatible, such that it is only necessary to recompile code when porting from one model to another. This would not be possible if some machines had a different architecture which was not transparent to the user. The addition of a co-processor to each PE retains a machine which is logically equivalent to the previous models and the mapping of the code onto the array is performed by low level software not visible to the user. Lastly, and perhaps most importantly, it was felt that there was an imbalance in the CM between the internal bandwidth and the power of the Weitek chips, which limited its floating point performance. AMT, therefore, sought to match the computational power of the CP8 with the internal bandwidth of the machine. The CP8 has registers which permit both data transfer to memory and computation to be performed concurrently. Also, because it is an 8 bit processor it is possible to obtain significant speed improvements on low precision variable types (e.g. 1 byte integers) as well as real numbers.

Program instructions are passed from a code store to the Master Control Unit (MCU) where they are interpreted before being issued to the processor array. Communication between the MCU and PE array is along a 32 bit wide bus, although on DAP 600 models this fans out to 64 channels to permit faster broadcasts. For a clock rate of 10 MHz, therefore, the data transfer rate is thus 40 Mbyte/s.

As with the PEs the MCU is custom designed hardware. In addition to its control role it is also responsible for scalar arithmetic operations and for validation of all calculations performed by the array: each PE has an associated slave PE and both PEs perform the same task, any errors are reported to the MCU. This control structure may be contrasted with the CM (cf. 2.3.2) where all instructions are issued by the front-end host and as such impose an extra load on the internal communications.

There are a range of memory sizes available in the range 4 to 128 Mbyte for the 510 series and 16 to 512 Mbyte for the 610 models. A direct upgrade path exists for memory expansion. Memory sizes of 32, 64, 128 or 256 kbit/PE are available and may be extended in the field. The limit imposed by the architecture is 1024 kbit/PE. In order to achieve the minimum memory access times the array memory is made from static RAM, despite the extra cost of these chips. All data paths and memory in the system are parity checked and tests are also made on all memory accesses by application programs. A schematic diagram illustrating the DAP architecture is shown in Figure 2.2.

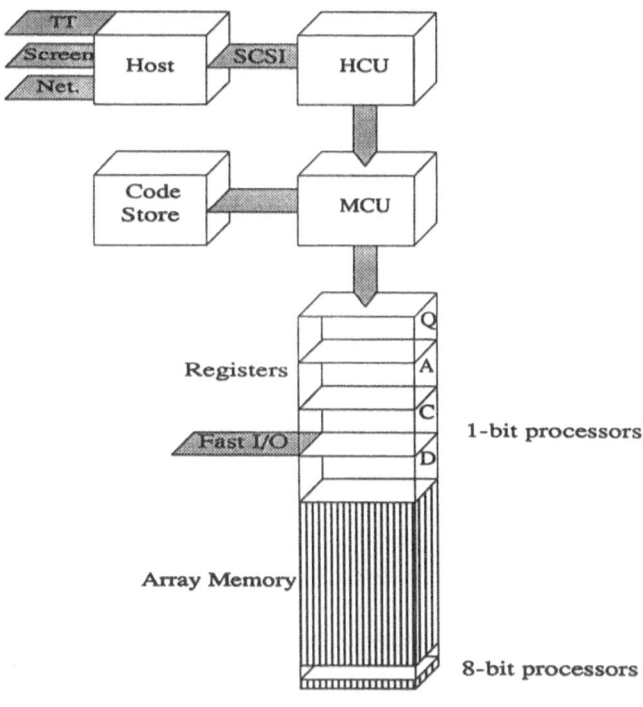

DAP 610c

Figure 2.2: A Schematic Diagram of the DAP Hardware

The connection to the front-end computer is handled by the Host Connection Unit (HCU), this is based upon a MC68020 processor and communicates via a standard interface. For a Sun workstation front end this is a SCSI link which permits data transfer between both machines at approximately 1 – 2 Mbyte/s. Connection to Vax machines is via the integral VME bus to either DR11-W or DRB32 interfaces. These operate at approximately half and double the speed of the SCSI link respectively. While such data rates are acceptable for direct user control of the running of programs on the DAP or for input of relatively small quantities of data they are rather slow for direct disc access. A high speed disc can may be connected directly to the DAP giving data transfer rates of 16 Mbyte/s (measured by the manufacturer).

At a very early stage in the life of AMT an analysis was performed of the fundamental strengths of the DAP. Considering its high internal bandwidth and preference for boolean or short length datatype arithmetic it is not surprising that the study showed the DAP to be best for data parallel problems, such as image processing. It was therefore decided to produce a high speed graphics interface. This is available as an optional board which is used in conjunction with a high resolution monitor (1024 × 1024 pixel) to give fast graphics at approximately 40 Mbyte/s. This board has dual frame buffers and adds only a few percent to the processor CPU overhead. As interactive graphics becomes increasingly important for many user applications this interface has played an essential role in the success of the DAP. AMT view this facility as a major selling point in comparison with the Connection Machine or MasPar MP-1. A similar interface also exists for high speed input.

Learning from the earlier commercial failures of the ICL machines which were seen to be due, at least in part, to the decision to host them from unusual machines, AMT choose to present a product with a well-known user interface. To this end current DAPs are front-ended by either any Vax running VMS or by a Sun work-station. DEC VMS or UNIX are therefore provided as the user environment. This strategy is very much in line with other parallel processing manufacturers (e.g. Inmos, Meiko, Cogent, Sequent and Caplin) who provide users with a standard environment, usually UNIX, to ease the transition to parallel programming.

Although the possibility of porting UNIX onto the MCU has been considered this is now not thought to be an option, perhaps due to the difficulties encountered by other manufacturers such as Meiko (cf. 5.3). What is more likely for programs which do not require real time user interaction is a scheme whereby application codes could be written and compiled on a workstation and then transferred to a PC connected to the DAP through one of the RS232 ports. This PC would then boot the code onto the DAP for execution.

2.1.3   The Development System

Program writing is performed on the front-end host and thus makes use of the editors and other development tools supported on that machine. AMT provide a interactive debugger (called psam) for testing the DAP code which provides most of the functions required of such systems. The features included are the ability to insert break points at run time, to step the program execution one line at a time and query the values of variables. This system may be compared with the similar facilities available for the MP-1 under MPPE (cf. 2.2.3) the major advantage of the latter is the window-based environment which it offers. This may therefore be seen by some as being more user-friendly.

2.1.4   Programming Languages

The DAP may be programmed either in Fortran-Plus (an extended version of Fortran 77), or for optimal CPU performance in APAL (an assembly level language). Plans to implement Fortran 90, when that language standard becomes stable, are underway. The present extensions to the Fortran language standard are the inclusion of a range of data structures designed to match the DAP architecture and the provision of logical masks to block PEs from updating their data if required. A comparison of some of these features with standard serial Fortran code is shown in the program fragment below.

```
          Fortran-Plus                        Fortran~77
C
C  sky**2 comparison                 C  sky**2 comparison
C  with zero-point                   C  with zero-point
C
      real sky(*100,*100)                real sky(100,100)
      real z_p                           real z_p
C                                    C
      z_p = 0.5                          z_p = 0.5
      call evaluate(sky)                 call evaluate(sky)
C                                    C
C  compare; if sky**2 < z_p          C  compare; if sky**2 < z_p
C  then set sky = z_p                C  then set sky = z_p
C                                    C
      sky(sky**2.lt.z_p) = z_p           do 10 i = 1, 100
C                                            do 10 j = 1, 100
                                                if(sky(j,i)**2.lt.z_p)
                                        1           sky(j,i) = z_p
                                    10   continue
```

Clearly, an advantage of such parallel languages is the greater simplicity with which many problems can be coded. As noted in the original report "...one of the biggest attractions of parallel machines could be their capacity for processing algorithms which provide a more simple and direct representation of the real world than those we are used to using" (Ovum report pg. 15). It is also probable that experience with Fortran-Plus had a significant effect upon the deliberations of the standards committee for Fortran 90.

Previous versions of Fortran Plus limited the extent of the parallel matrix dimensions (in the above example $(100, 100)$) to be the edge size of the processor grid, though it was possible to "stack" these arrays using additional array indices. Despite these modifications to the language the machine is still most efficient when the data structures have sizes which are an integral multiple of the edge dimension of the processor array since this ensures the maximum utilisation of each PE.

To date compilers for the DAP have been written in-house. This may change soon with the implementation of a software interface to the DAP known as the Virtual Array Processor (VAP). The VAP is designed to present a stable platform on which external software houses can build compilers. It is possible, therefore, that the range of languages available may soon expand. However, in 1988 a survey was made of the parallel processing community in the UK by Alvey project ARCH001 "The Development and Exploitation of an Active Data Model of Parallel Processing". This showed that a large majority of users expressed a preference for Fortran with, interestingly, the runner up as Occam. In third place came C, with about half the number of votes cast for Occam. It would be interesting to repeat this survey in the light of the current trend on transputer-based machines away from Occam and towards higher level languages.

2.1.5   The Market Niche

As of June 1990 over 80 DAPs have been placed by AMT into various institutions around the world. Table 2.1, below, gives a breakdown of the 74 machines sold to 52 different purchasers before March 1990 by geographical area and by centre.

Table 2.1: Sales of DAPs by Area and by Type

Site	UK	US	Europe	Rest
University/Research Estab.	20	5	3	0
Govt. Laboratory	2	1	0	0
Industry	5	34[A]	3	1[B]

A: Includes sales to US Army.
B: Japan.

When these institutions were asked about their primary projected usage of their machine the answers showed that the single most important area of interest was in image or signal processing (Table 2.2). The numbers now refer to institutions, not to machines.

The range of applications noted in Table 2.2 corroborates the AMT marketing claim that machines are sold for a large variety of uses, rather than as engines devoted very specific niches. The company aim is rather different from that of Thinking Machines (cf. 2.3.5) who strive towards very large installations and ultimately to the teraFLOPS machine. The AMT strategy is to improve the compute power per £, per watt and per in^3 and so hope to become the world leader in

Table 2.2: Major Interest Areas of DAP Purchasers

Application	UK	US	Europe	Rest
Image/Signal Processing	6	11	1	1
Database searching	4	1	0	0
General applications	10	2	1	0
Fluid Flow	2	1	0	0
CAD	2	0	2	0
Other	3	4	2	0

deployable systems. They, therefore, see areas such as defence applications, seismic processing as those offering most opportunity for expansion. In 1985 it was projected that " ...a total market [for "cubes"] which could be worth $5 G a year in sales in the USA by 1992." (Ovum report pg. 28). The estimate by AMT of the size of the current worldwide market is £1 G.

2.1.6 The Competition

Clearly in the SIMD manufacturers' race there are only three real runners at the moment: AMT, Thinking Machines and MasPar. How do AMT see these; as competitors in the same event or not? The answer depends a little upon whether one looks at the US or UK but Manning's view is that the markets for the DAP and the Connection Machine do not overlap significantly: the price differential between the machines is so large that prospective buyers seldom consider both alternatives. With MasPar, however, the situation is rather different: on paper they present an entry level machine which is more powerful and cheaper than the DAP 510 (Summary 2). To combat this threat AMT place great emphasis upon their much longer track record with DAPs, well over a decade if the ICL experience is included, the high speed graphics facility which the present MasPar machines lack and the much larger number of machines already placed. Furthermore, AMT feel that they have progressed further along the road towards a rugged machine for deployable applications than MasPar and that this market is due to expand. The most telling fact, however, is that price cuts may be announced in the relatively near future, especially for large memory machines, which would reduce the cost of the DAP with co-processor to current level of a DAP without one. This enhanced machine would, on paper, outperform the quoted figures for the MP-1. So do MasPar represent a serious danger to AMT? Manning's view is no "MasPar have widened the range of machines available and increased market awareness of SIMD architectures. We expect that this will benefit all."

So, who do AMT view as their main rivals? Again this depends upon the application area: for defence purposes special purpose hardware is seen to provide most competition. Here the argument is between the greater flexibility of the general computer and the exact specification of the custom hardware. There is, apparently, the possibility of increased sales in this direction since on grounds of cost the US Department of Defence now prefer to buy existing products rather than develop new ones.

In the University sector MIMD machines provide the major competition. In the US this usually means NCUBE (cf. 4.2) or Intel (cf. 4.1), while in the UK it is Meiko (cf. 5.3). Despite the difficulties selling to such institutions due to their general lack of funds this market is seen as very important by AMT since it is recognised that these are the prime innovators in parallel algorithm development. This opinion closely mirrors the view that "The development of new algorithms for replacing established sequential solutions to problems with new parallel ones could become a minor academic industry on its own, and a ready source of PhD topics" (Ovum report pg. 36).

Finally, a market which has only recently been attacked but one in which AMT feel that they have a very strong product is for the database searching machine, whether this be for DNA sequence analysis or text handling. Here prospective purchasers tend to be very conservative and prefer mainframes despite the very significant power/£ improvement which is possible from parallelisation. It is to meet the inherent requirement for high speed access to large quantities of data in these applications that AMT have developed the fast disc interface discussed above.

2.1.7   The Future

It is planned to recast the MCU, still mostly using TTL logic, in CMOS technology in order to give a lower power consumption. The same may also happen to the I/O controllers. More significant is the project now under development in joint collaboration with E-Systems and funded by DARPA. This is to make an object code compatible DAP 510 engineered in GaAs with an expected clock speed of approximately 10 ns. Delivery of the first system is anticipated in the middle of 1991. It is accepted however that GaAs is a very young technology and the production costs are correspondingly high, consequently AMT suspected that this machine may never be a commercial proposition but only be of interest for military or space applications. It will be interesting to monitor the market acceptance of such machines and compare this with the 1985 prediction "Perhaps the GaAs supercomputer will prove the electronic equivalent of Concorde, finding a market only with those organisations which can justify paying any price for maximum performance" (Ovum report pg. 18).

In 1985 it was said that "The languages developed for sequential programming are also quite inadequate for gaining the full performance benefits of the new cube architectures. Programmers need tools for expressing and manipulating parallelism directly, and progress in this area so far has been very patchy and uncoordinated. Parallel versions of Lisp, C, and Fortran are proliferating almost as rapidly as parallel processor suppliers." (Ovum report pg. 14). Today ,the situation has not changed greatly and it will be interesting to monitor the three major SIMD manufacturers to see whether any common standards will be adopted for the high level languages.

2.2   MasPar Computer Corporation

Relevant Activities Supplier of the MP-1 Family of Data–Parallel computers.

Location Headquarters: MasPar Computer Corporation, 749 North Mary Avenue, Sunnyvale, California 94086, USA. Telephone: (408) 736 3300, Fax: (408) 736 9560. European sales: MasPar Computer Corporation, First Base, Beacontree Plaza, Gillette Way, Reading RG2 0BP, Berkshire, England. Telephone: 0734 753388, Fax: 0734 313939.

Relevant Officers Jeff Kalb, President; Tom Blank, Director of Architecture; Bill Hogan, VP Marketing; John Nickolls, VP Hardware Engineering; Peter Christy, VP Software Engineering; Jim Peachy, VP Operations; Ralph Mele, VP Sales.

Employees Over 100 in the US, and at present four in the UK.

Financial details $30 M has been raised from venture capital companies, mostly based within the US. The last round of such fund raising has just been completed.

2.2.1   The Company

MasPar was founded in March 1988 by Jeff Kalb, formerly VP of "low-end systems" at DEC. He also had some responsibilities for the development of DEC's new Massively Parallel Processor (MPP). It appears, however, that Kalb saw a possibility for producing a cheaper product more quickly Kalb decided to form a spin-off company: MasPar. Apparently the split was amicable since DEC agreed to the transfer of technology to MasPar for such items as the global router (see below). In return, however, DEC have no shareholding and no intellectual property rights on MasPar products, so how do they gain from the division? The answer seems to be that the MPP, which is expected to appear in a couple of years, is a SIMD machine similar to the MasPar MP-1. It is, however, designed to be a more expensive product, and as such not a direct competitor to the MP-1 series. Moreover, the success of the MP-1 would increase market awareness of SIMD computers and therefore help in attracting initial sales of the MPP.

In consequence of this mutual benefit DEC and MasPar have a close working relationship with the current MP-1 being hosted by a Vax workstation. In addition, a special programme for prospective purchasers has been established which is jointly funded by MasPar and DEC. This arrangement is to last for two years and gives substantial (approximately 35%) discounts to sites buying DEC and MasPar equipment, provided that the application(s) run on those machines are approved by DEC and the results are presented at a DEC sponsored conference and are published in the public domain. To be accepted, the proposed field of research must be one which is likely to promote the use of SIMD parallel processing. While assisting MasPar with sales it is clear that the main reason for DEC sponsoring this initiative is to stay abreast of developments in the parallel computing field and so be better able to target their MPP when this arrives.

The company views itself as being strongly market led and having produced a machine which is not technologically revolutionary but builds upon features from a variety of other SIMD computers: the Connection Machine from Thinking Machines (cf. 2.3); the DAP from AMT (cf. 2.1); and the BLITZEN (a research machine produced by the University of North Carolina). Nevertheless, MasPar spent $10 M out of the $17.6 M raised from the first two rounds of funding on research and development. This has resulted in a number of patents already granted and more still pending.

Using a strategy of employing known technology and only implementing products which are perceived to be in demand by the market MasPar hope to become profitable quickly. This approach may display considerable business acumen but, clearly, any company can only be totally market led if others create the general awareness and demonstrate technological solutions to current problems. In the longer term, therefore, it may be expected that MasPar will have to increase their research and development role by considering new technologies.

It is clear from the staff figures that the company is almost totally based in the US, with both hardware production and software development sited in California. At present, both the UK and European sales offices are placed in the UK, but this might change depending upon the geographical distribution of sales. There do not appear to be any plans to devolve any other responsibilities outside the US at present. MasPar has just finished the third round of fund raising from venture capital companies, most of these are based in the US. All attempts to attract funds have been fully supported and the total capitalisation of the company is now approximately $30 M. It is hoped that all necessary capital for development of the machine and its software has now been raised.

2.2.2   The Machine

The MP-1 family of SIMD processors has certain similarities in basic architecture with the AMT DAP (cf. 2.1.2) but with a different interprocessor communications provision. There are five models within the MP-1 series which is divided into two ranges: the MP1100 and MP1200. The difference between these is the maximum number of boards which can be fitted within the cabinet and hence the largest number of Processor Elements (PEs) in the machine. There is also an increased number of I/O slots on the MP1200 range, so enabling a larger number of peripheral devices to be attached. For the MP1100 range there are three models, with 1024, 2048 or 4096 PEs. A further two machines are introduced at the top of the MP1200 with 8192 and 16384 PEs respectively[2]. The MP1216 computer is the largest which is currently available and which can be supported by the present hardware. It must be noted that since MasPar is still a relatively new company it has not been possible for us to determine the performance of any of these machines and all such figures quoted are therefore taken from the manufacturer's literature.

The computational core of the MP-1 is an array of PEs arranged in a rectangular two-dimensional lattice. These processors execute the same tasks in parallel (SIMD parallelism). This core is tightly coupled to a Vax front-end host and, possibly, also to high speed I/O devices. MasPar are one of a very small number of companies who are permitted direct access to the DEC memory bus.

The PEs are RISC-like processors which have direct connection to their own local memory. The processor chips were custom designed by MasPar, they use 1.6μm CMOS VLSI technology and each chip contains 32 PEs. A change to 1.0μm CMOS is planned within the next couple of years. One consequence of this move to smaller die sizes is that it will then be feasible to produce a 65536 PE MP-1, an upper limit which is imposed by the hardware. The PEs are grouped as clusters of 16 arranged as a 4×4 grid. Each PE cluster also has associated PE memories and connections to the communications network (see later). To reduce the cost of the computer the memory is held on Dynamic RAM (DRAM). At present, the memory is fixed at 16 kbyte per PE but when 4 Mbit DRAMs become cheaper it is planned to offer a version with four times as much memory. This is an interesting contrast to the AMT DAP, in which the memory may be easily extended but only two different PE grid sizes are made, whereas here the memory per PE is fixed but the number of processors may be upgraded in the field.

Each PE provides operations on 1, 8, 16, 32 and 64 bit operands. The PE hardware includes a number of separate functional units: a 64 bit mantissa unit, a 16 bit exponent section, a 4 bit Arithmetic Logic Unit (ALU) and a single bit logic system. The different functional sections within the PE can be active simultaneously during each set of micro-code instructions, for example floating-point operations may require the use of the exponent, mantissa, ALU and logic units together. The internal 4 bit nature of the PE is not visible to the user, which will permit future machines to be produced with larger, or smaller, ALU widths without changing any user code. Learning from the Thinking Machines' experience with the Connection Machine (cf. 2.3.2) MasPar decided not to include fast scalar processors to back up the PE clusters because of the reduction in their performance due to the internal memory bandwidth. It is interesting to note that in upgrading the DAP to include faster processors AMT also chose not to adopt this solution for exactly the same reason.

---

[2]The naming convention for the MP-1 machines is straightforward: the first digit is the series number, the second is the range and finally the number of PEs in units of 1024, hence a 16384 processor machine is known as the MP1216

The floating-point/integer units use more than half of the PE silicon but this is thought by MasPar to be justified by the increased performance over the bit-serial PE within the DAP or the CM.

Instructions are issued to the PEs by the Array Control Unit (ACU), a RISC-like processor based upon standard chips from Texas Instruments. It also contains 128 kbyte of data memory and 1 Mbyte of code store. The clock rate is 12 MHz. The remit of the ACU is to fetch and decode program instructions, compute addresses, perform scalar arithmetic, send control signals to the PE grid and monitor the PE array status. The function of the ACU is, therefore, very similar to that of the MCU in the DAP, though the ACU is, in fact, a more powerful processor. It is expected that the current ACU will be replaced in the "medium term" with a more widely available and faster RISC-based processor. This may obviate the need for a front-end host. The link from the ACU to the PE array consists of two separate connections, one for program instructions, the other for data. The data bus is 48 bit wide, while that for the instructions is 4 bit, these gives transfer rates of about 70 and 5 Mbyte/s respectively.

The design of the hardware provides indirect addressing of PE arrays, which means that individual processors can access variables which lie at different offsets within their memories. This is a very useful feature permitted by the Connection Machine, but not on the DAP. This functionality is available from all languages designed to run on the MP-1.

Interprocessor communications are handled by two separate mechanisms. The choice of which is more appropriate for a given application is determined by the regularity of the data transfer. For situations in which an entire array of data is to be moved across the PE lattice then the X-Net communications mesh is more efficient and should be used. Conceptually, the X-Net mesh is a one bit wide communications network which links each processor with its eight nearest neighbours. In fact, however, each PE has only four interconnects located at its diagonal corners, thus forming an X shaped grid at 45° to the PE lattice. A schematic diagram illustrating this connection strategy is shown in Figure 2.3. There is a three way node at each intersection of the X-Net grid which allows communications to be routed to any of the eight PE's nearest neighbours. The direction for the outgoing message through this tri-state node is set by the ACU at the same time as the PEs are instructed to transmit, so that there is no latency in the connection and hence the communications of a bit between neighbouring processors takes one clock cycle. At the edges of the PE array the interconnects are wrapped around to form a torus, though the user may select planar boundaries in which case any differences between the topologies are handled by software. The aggregate X-Net bandwidth for the MP1101 system is 1.1 Gbyte/s, this increases linearly with system size.

Random communications between arbitrary processors are possible via a three-stage global router which emulates a crossbar switch. Each PE cluster has a con-

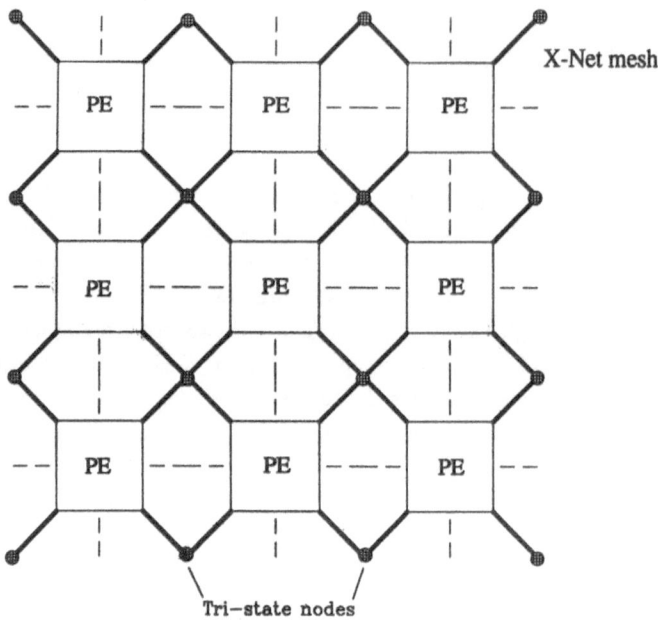

Figure 2.3: A Schematic Diagram of the X-Net Mesh Interconnect

nection to the router stage of the switch and another to the target stage. These ports are shared by all PEs within the cluster. The router and target units of the global switch are connected by an intermediate stage. The address of the target PE is calculated by the originating processor and, if all the links through the router between the start PE cluster and the finishing one are free, then connection is established. Clearly, this may necessitate some PEs waiting, perhaps for some time, for others within the same cluster to finish their data transfer. Once set, the link is bi-directional and on closing the target PE sends an acknowledgement. Data transfer through the links is bit-serial and clocked synchronously with the the PE clock. Since the router ports are multiplexed for each PE cluster arbitrary communications patterns require a minimum of 16 router cycles to complete. A connection through the router takes 40 clock cycles to establish and a further 10 to break, though MasPar claim to be working to reduce these quite considerable overheads. Given the novelty of this form of routing on an SIMD machine it may be unfair to complain about the speed with which connections are made since those applications which require the global router would be more difficult to code on other SIMD computers.

For the smallest of the MP-1 machines, the 1024 PE system, this communications harness acts like a 64 × 64 crossbar switch, thus permitting up to 64 simultaneous connections. The number of poles on the switch grows linearly with the number of processors in the machine. As with the other chips in the MP-1, the router chip was custom designed by MasPar and fabricated using 1.6μm CMOS technology.

It is proposed by MasPar that a fast I/O controller will be attached to a spur from the global router and will, when it and the interfaces are developed, drive a fast disc array, high speed graphics monitor, HiPPI link etc. All devices attached to the I/O controller will compete for its bandwidth with the consequent possibility of reduced performance. The maximum speed of this link is expected to be 200 Mbyte/s, provided that the internal bandwidth of the global router is sufficient to drive it at this rate (this implies that the machine be at least an MP1104). The HiPPI interface is being developed in conjunction with a major US aerospace manufacturer.

It would appear that the plans to implement these fast peripherals and the fact that both the CM and the DAP already have high speed graphics devices and disc farms is a major change for the better over the last few years. In 1985 it was claimed that "They [parallel computers] do not generally have, as yet, the input and output (I/O) channels, the different levels of memory, the language compilers, the programming environments, and many of the other facilities which computer users require to achieve a large throughput of work" (Ovum report pg. 3).

The user interface to the MP-1, known as the UNIX subsystem (USS), is provided by a Vaxstation 3520. This machine runs ULTRIX, an implementation of BSD UNIX by DEC, and handles the program execution and network communications. The USS interacts with the ACU through a VME bus, specifically, there is shared memory between the USS and ACU which permits processes to have common data structures. In addition, DMA is provided for bulk data transfers. Since there is as yet no fast graphics facility to transfer data straight from the PE array to a monitor any images generated by the user's program must be displayed on the X Windows console connected to the USS. The data transfer rate along this link is estimated to be about 1 – 2 Mbyte/s, about the same as a SCSI interface. Obviously, this is much too slow for any applications which require real-time user interaction, especially since this link must carry all communications between the USS and ACU. It is estimated that a fast graphics interface will be produced some months after the fast I/O interface is available, and this is not expected until the end of 1990.

A mechanically strengthened version of the machine is being made by Rugged Digital, a company who specialise in the production of computers for military and mobile applications. Deployable applications have been a major market for AMT and it may be supposed that MasPar wish to attract such sales also.

2.2.3 The Program Development System

A program development system known as the MasPar Parallel Programming Environment (MPPE) runs on the USS. It has been estimated that this is the product of five – ten man years of effort and MasPar place great emphasis on its ease of use. It provides debugging and data visualisation tools to aid the production of user code and is based on top of the X Windows interface. It is not anticipated that users will require this system once their code has been completed and fully tested since it may interfere with other active processes, for example the presentation of graphical output from the PE array. The debugger is broadly similar in appearance to dbx. It has access to special registers on the ACU which are not otherwise available to the front-end host. Apparently, the hardware was designed to ensure that there are no CPU overheads for program execution on the PE array from use of the debugger. However, the increased traffic along the connection between the USS and ACU may have some penalties and there is, of course, an extra CPU load placed upon the front-end host.

While we have not had the opportunity to test out the MPPE in earnest it does appear to be more user friendly than the psam debugger on the DAP (cf. 2.1.3). However, the range of debugging facilities offered by both products are not very different. It is understood that at least one prospective UK buyer chose the MP1101 over the DAP 510 on the basis of the appearance and functionality of the MPPE.

2.2.4 Programming Languages

The only language currently available on the MP-1 is the MasPar Parallel Application Language (MPL). This is based upon Kernighan & Ritchie C (first edition) with a small number of extensions to allow for the parallelism of the machine. It does not hide the computer architecture from the user, who must be aware of such things as the size of the PE array etc. In this respect, and in terms of its power, it is very similar to the earlier versions of Fortran-Plus written by AMT for the DAP (cf. 2.1.4). Although an assembly language also exists it is not released to users, except under special arrangement. The reason for this is to permit MasPar to change the low level software without interfering with user software: only the higher level languages are guaranteed to be backwards compatible. In the case of the DAP AMT have supplied APAL (their assembly language) for a considerable time and, in the MasPar view, this is now a major constraint for software developments on that machine. It is not known whether AMT share this opinion.

A parallel version of Fortran (MPF) is planned for release within a few months. This language adheres to the Fortran 77 standard with array parallel extensions from Fortran 90. With this compiler, unlike MPL, the PE array size is hidden from the user, which should increase code portability between models. Unlike the DAP, the MasPar programmer only has to write one program. The compiler determines which sections are best run on the USS, the ACU and the PE array. Since the ACU is a fast scalar processor it may be expected that most of the non-array work will be performed here.

MasPar's Fortran compiler is being written in association with the independent specialist supplier Compass. This company has produced parallel compilers for Thinking Machines in the past. However, experience with such software shows that these are non-trivial programs and it will be interesting to monitor the development timescale of this compiler.

A parallel version of C may be expected at some point and is expected to be ANSI standard with parallel extensions similar to those within Fortran 90. However, the exact specification of this language is still awaiting the final outcome of discussions with other SIMD manufacturers.

2.2.5 The Market

The close relationship between DEC and MasPar extends into the marketing field where DEC increase the exposure of the MP-1, especially within Europe. This is aided by the current special prices being offered by MasPar and DEC for certain projects, though these are strictly controlled and it is not straightforward for sites to be accepted (cf. 2.2 above). To date only one machine has been sold under this initiative but MasPar, naturally, have hopes that this number will increase substantially in the near future.

MasPar view their machine as a general purpose device with a bias towards the scientific computing market. They have not implemented many specialised libraries on the machine, preferring instead to have accepted packages ported on to the machine by the software producer, perhaps in liaison with MasPar. To this end they attempt to reduce software development times by staying with language standards (eg. Fortran 90) and are keenly looking for new partners. To date it is claimed that five packages have been ported onto the MP-1, though only two of these are yet commercially available: an image processing workbench from Paragon Imaging and signal processing software from Entropic Speech (hopefully ready late in 1990). AMT prefer to stress the length of time for which DAPs have been available and the consequent amount of testing in real applications which has been possible.

The MasPar aim, like AMT (cf. 2.1.5), is not to compete with Thinking Machines (cf. 2.3.5) to produce ever larger and more powerful machines at very high cost but to sell affordable high performance computers which maximise the CPU per $. Since the company is still very young sales are few and statistics on the usage of these have a low signal/noise ratio. It is, therefore, not possible to test MasPar's claim that their machines are primarily used for general purpose computing rather than as single use engines. In Table 2.3 there is a breakdown of the 18 machines sold, each to a different purchaser, in the first six months of operation. To date these sales have been equally divided between the US and the rest of the world.

Table 2.3: Sales of MP-1s by Centre

Site	Number
University/Research Estab.	9
Govt. Laboratory	3
Industry	6

2.2.6   The Competitors

The company produces a range of machines with wide differences in performance and cost. It, therefore, does not always compete with the same set of vendors for all models. Given this situation and the relative youth of MasPar it is difficult to be specific about the major competitors encountered. Generally these are the usual companies one would expect: manufacturers of parallel and super-mini computers. Specifically, the major rivals are AMT, Alliant, Convex and the transputer-based suppliers, most notably Meiko (cf. 5.3).

It is interesting to compare the attitude of MasPar and AMT and the way in which the different perceptions of the market requirements feeds through into the respective products. During the design stage of the DAP 510 AMT decided, on the basis of an analysis of the market, that a very strong selling point would be its ability to perform fast image processing for applications which involved not simply high speed visualisation but a large element of number crunching as well. As a consequence of this it was decided to give priority to the production of a high speed graphics interface. Looking at the market some three years later MasPar have decided that, except for general scientific machines, the most important sector is for database searching; this primarily requires fast, large discs rather than visualisation. The high speed disc interface is therefore, being developed first. It is true that AMT have also been addressing this market for some time and also now provide fast discs connected directly to the DAP, yet their single most important market is still in the image/signal processing area and have not yet sold a machine with a high speed disc which did not also have fast graphics.

An opinion held by some of those at MasPar who were interviewed was that if AMT had expanded the range of models faster and had, for example, developed a DAP 520 soon after the DAP 510 was released, then MasPar would not have been born, or would now be having a much harder time selling machines. It is clear that this is supposition, but it may be surmised that there is some truth in the claim given the close similarity in machine architectures. No statement was forthcoming on MasPar's policy when the DAP with co-processor, perhaps at a reduced price, actually becomes available. It remains to be seen how fast the new DAP 610c will actually run but on the basis of AMT estimates (Table 1) and MasPar's performance figures for the MP-1 (Summary 2) the price/performance ratio may then be tilted in AMT's favour.

2.2.7   The Future

It is clear that in the immediate future MasPar will concentrate on developing the peripherals required to let the machine communicate with the outside world: the high speed disc, graphics, HiPPI interface etc. In the longer term no large changes in the product seem to be agreed upon, though an improvement in the price/performance ratio of the hardware and an increased number of software packages available appear to be the general goals. The prevailing view is that "what the market wants the market will get" – not an obvious recipe for innovation. The hoped for improvements in the system disclosed are very general: a move from 1.6 to 1.0μm (and then sub-micron) CMOS technology; machines both larger and smaller than the current end models; more memory and faster PEs. It is perceived that their market niche will continue to be for machines in the £100 - 600,000 range and that the company will attempt to provide an improved performance/ price ratio. The target is to increase this by 30% per annum.

2.3 Thinking Machines Corporation

Relevant Activities Supplier of the Connection Machine, a massively-parallel SIMD processor.

Location Headquarters: Thinking Machines Corporation, 245 First Street, Cambridge, Massachusetts 02142, USA. Telephone: (617) 876 1111, Fax: (617) 876 1823. European Sales: Tarweakker 10, 39 41 LB, Doorn, Holland. Telephone: 3430 14045, Fax: 3430 14418.

Relevant Officers Sheryl Handler, Founder and President; Dick Clayton, VP Operations; Edward Kramer, VP Sales; John Mucci, VP Marketing.

Employees Approximately 400 in the US and 12 in Europe.

Financial details Total capitalisation undisclosed, most funds raised from private placements but some from venture capital companies and assistance from DARPA for hardware development. Sales in 1989 were approximately $45 M.

2.3.1 The Company

Thinking Machines Corporation (TMC) was formed in 1983 by Sheryl Handler. Unusually, her background was not in computing but rather in biotechnology. Nevertheless, she saw an entrepreneurial opportunity in parallel processing. Originally, it was proposed that the company should produce a computer to satisfy the needs of AI and symbolic processing researchers, rather than a fast general-purpose scientific machine. Consequently, the original Connection Machine (CM), the CM-1, was designed without floating-point performance in mind. It is interesting to note the change in company view on this issue as AI became less fashionable later in the decade and the marketplace looked for increased power. TMC is now aiming for the teraFLOPS computer (cf. 2.3.5).

A number of designs for the original machine were considered before that of Danny Hillis, who was then at MIT, was adopted. This was for a fine-grained SIMD array of single bit processors (known as a data-parallel computer in TMC parlance). The first beta-test machine was delivered at the end of 1985, with commercial sales starting some six months later. In concept, this machine drew upon experience with earlier SIMD computers, such as the ICL DAP (cf. 2.1) and the MPP from Goodyear, though its processor interconnection topology was markedly different. The choice of SIMD rather than MIMD was based upon the belief that the former represented the inherent parallelism in most problems better than the latter, was easier to program and provided the best marketing opportunity. In terms of the number of machines[3] placed worldwide TMC is the second largest

---

[3]Defined by TMC to be those with a sustainable performance in excess of 1 GFLOPS

American supercomputer company (the first being Cray Research Inc.). The higher price of a Cray over that of a CM means, however, that in financial terms TMC is rather further behind. In fact, Fujitsu of Japan has also a larger number of machines installed than TMC. TMC estimates that about 500 supercomputers exist around the world, of which approximately 10% are CMs.

TMC views themselves as company driven by applications and technology, rather than by the market. They are proud of the "academic" atmosphere fostered at their headquarters, where a large proportion of the staff are application scientists. It has been said by TMC of themselves that they have an "unbusinesslike" appearance to which the scientific user community can relate. This emphasis on scientific applications and the affinity with academic establishments is used by TMC to explain its very high profile within the computing world, despite the relatively small number of machines sold. The spread of TMC's reputation is not surprising given the wide range of applications run on CMs at large and influential US centres such as NPAC, Sandia, Los Alamos and NASA. In any case, large and powerful machines always have an allure not shared by their more modest cousins. It is probable that another factor in promoting the CM was the publicity given to it by Hillis's book [HILL] on the development of the machine. This was one of the first popularisation of parallel computing and became widely read.

It must be said, however, that within TMC the influence of the sales and marketing departments is growing and it is not clear that any multi-million pound organisation can be truly unbusinesslike and still survive and flourish. It may be supposed, therefore, that the research department is backed by a commercially aware management. Moreover, the move towards increased floating-point power, as mentioned above, clearly demonstrates that TMC is in touch with, and responsive to, the demands of the marketplace.

At the beginning of 1989 TMC started to expand operations into Europe. To this end, sales offices have now been opened in Germany, France and Holland although only the address for this last office is given above. TMC expects to open a subsidiary in the UK by the end of 1990.

2.3.2   The Machine

The CM is perhaps the best known SIMD computer. It has been extensively publicised for its high performance and has only recently had any rival (the 16384 processor MasPar MP-1, cf. 2.2) for the degree to which massive parallelism has been taken. The smallest CM has 4096 processors and the largest 16 times this number.

Like the other commercially available SIMD machines, the MasPar MP-1 and AMT DAP (cf. 2.1), the CM is hosted by a conventional front-end computer: a Sun-4 workstation, a Vax running ULTRIX (a version of BSD UNIX developed by

DEC) or a Symbolics 3600-series Lisp Machine. This provides a standard operating system for code development and testing.

The original CM, the CM-1, was designed and built in 1983 – 84. A 16384 processor prototype was funded by DARPA, with the first commercial deliveries of a machine taking place in 1986. After approximately a year of experience with the CM-1 the company decided to implement a number of improvements to the machine to remedy defects common to most supercomputers at that time. As reported in 1985 "They [parallel computers] do not generally have, as yet, the input and output (I/O) channels, the different levels of memory, the language compilers, the programming environments, and many of the other facilities which computer users require to achieve a large throughput of work" (Ovum report pg. 3). Consequently, the basic concept of a SIMD computer with single bit processors arranged as a hypercube and hosted by a standard front-end was retained, but high speed visualisation, fast disc farms and more memory per processor were introduced.

The revised CM was unveiled at the end of 1987 and is now the only version sold. The new model range is divided into two: the CM-2a and CM-2. The CM-2a may have either 4096 or 8192 processors while the CM-2 contains 16384, 32768 or 65536. These machines are described in more detail below and a schematic diagram of the CM-2 architecture is shown in Figure 2.4.

The processor array is the computational core of the machine and consists of a large number of identical processors. These are very simple bit-serial devices which are directly connected to their own local memory. The processors are custom designed and were modified from the CM-1 originals in order to increase performance. They are made using 2.0μm CMOS technology and are packed 16 to a chip. The clock speed is 8 MHz (4 MHz on the CM-1).

Processor memory is implemented in standard, commercially available dynamic RAM (the CM-1 used faster static RAM, but this was limited to 4 kbit per processor). The size of the memory is now in the range 64 kbit to 1 Mbit. This gives the largest CM an upper memory limit memory of 8 Gbyte. Both the number of processors and memory per PE may be increased in the field.

In addition, every pair of single bit processor chips (32 processors) may, optionally, be supported by a floating-point accelerator unit. Two versions of the accelerator chip are available, for single or double precision. The hardware in the floating-point unit is based upon a Weitek 3132 chip and a memory interface unit (the SPRINT chip). The latter is necessary because the memory access of the Weitek chip is orthogonal to the direction in which the data are stored on the single bit processors. Therefore the memory interface unit transposes the 32 bit words for the floating-point accelerator. The SPRINT chip also provides hardware support for indirect addressing. The floating-point and memory units are driven by firmware and are transparent to the user.

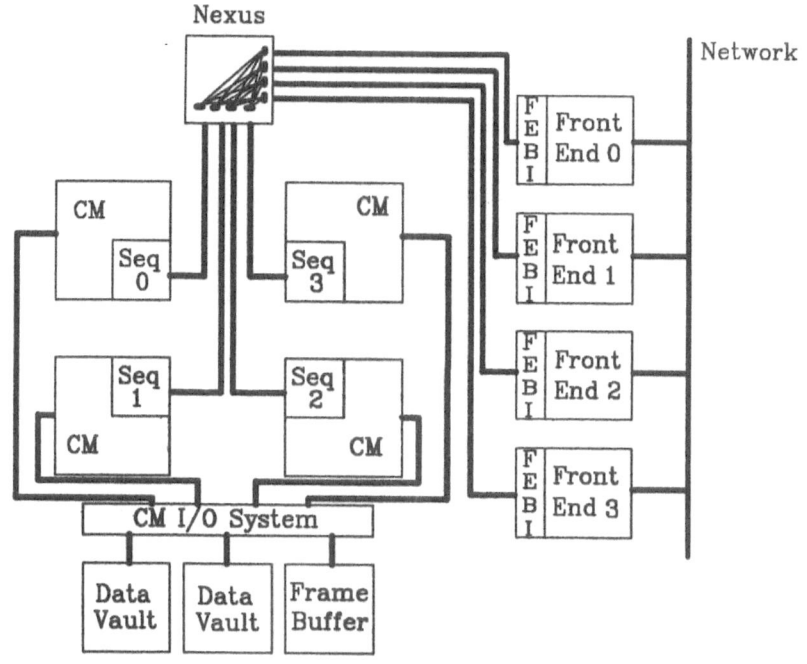

CM−2 Architecture
Figure 2.4: A Schematic Diagram of the CM-2 Hardware

There are similarities in basic design between the CM and the DAP (cf. 2.1.2) since both are based on the concept of an SIMD array of single bit processors, though those in the CM are significantly slower than their DAP counterparts. However, TMC led the way with the provision of floating-point accelerators to enhance the machine's performance. This development is only now being introduced by AMT (but was implemented from the start in the new MasPar MP-1 cf. 2.2.2). It is very interesting to note, however, that both AMT and MasPar have taken an approach similar to each other but which differs markedly from that of TMC. AMT chose to provide each single bit processor with its own, relatively slow, co-processor, while MasPar effectively incorporated this into the processor by giving each of these a wider data path. This is very different from the solution of having 32 sharing one very fast floating-point engine.

Why did they not follow the TMC lead? The answer is that TMC's implementation is inherently inefficient: the Weitek 3132 chip has a peak speed of 14 MFLOPS and has a single 32 bit wide data path from the local memory. Now, if one considers the typical performance of this chip when fitted in the CM-2 it is clear that the internal bandwidth provides a severe bottleneck: at a clock rate of 8 MHz only 8 Mword (1 word equals 32 bit) may be transferred to or from the Weitek per second. Since a typical floating-point operation will require the transmission of about 1 to 3 words, then the typical sustainable rate of calculation will be 8 to 8/3 MFLOPS, or 60 to 20% of its peak performance. Unpalatable as these conclusions may be for TMC, they are borne out by the performance figures derived from their own publications (Summary 3). In the DAP and MP-1 the floating-point processor is simpler (and hence cheaper), thus more closely matching the communications bandwidth.

Given this obvious problem, why did TMC choose to link the CM with the Weitek chip? The answer seems to be simply that at the time when the CM-2 was being designed the 32 bit Weitek chip was thought to be the most appropriate. Consequently, TMC decided to develop the SPRINT chip to translate the memory mapping of the CM into that of the Weitek. This considerable investment of effort, combined with TMC's view that they could not keep pace with the rest of the semiconductor industry in designing its own floating-point hardware, has restrained them from replacing the Weitek with custom hardware. Given the analysis above, however, it would seem that it is not necessary to produce state of the art processor designs, but rather to develop either a simpler, and hence cheaper, floating-point chip or, better still, to increase the interprocessor bandwidth of the CM so as not to waste the computing power already available. It may be supposed that the reason that the former approach has not been adopted is because TMC do not wish to incur the necessary development costs.

In fairness it should be pointed out that such an imbalance between floating-point performance and memory bandwidth is not unusual. A number of developments in compiler design for the CM are anticipated which would enable high level languages to manipulate the registers on the Weitek chip, rather than just memory addresses. This will have the effect of making more accessible the maximum sustainable performance of the machine, which to date has required some degree of assembly language programming. Reports from users show that it is currently possible to gain an improvement by a factor of 10 in speed, by programming the Weitek chips in microcode rather than relying on the standard routines. The main reason for this is that when performing floating-point operations on the Weitek chip it is normal to transpose the data by passing it through the SPRINT chip. However, it is possible to store the data already transposed and transfer it to the floating-point accelerator with microcode, thus saving the conversion overheads.

The combination of two single bit processor chips and one Weitek is the basic building block of the CM-2. Sixteen such blocks form a board and 16 boards make one octant (8192 processors). A full CM-2 is composed of 8 octants. Each octant has two I/O channels which may be connected to either a graphics monitor or disc farm, although only one of these may be operational at any one time. The 4096 processor CM-2a has two I/O channels also. Each channel can support peak data transfer rates of up to 50 Mbyte/s, though in practice this may be reduced by slow peripheral devices or software. The provision of equivalent I/O facilities on each octant means that it is possible for a large CM-2 to be subdivided (see below).

Each processor chip contains a router node, in addition to its 16 single bit processors. These nodes are wired together in the form of a hypercube to produce the complete network. The router nodes forward messages to the next appropriate node and perform some simple dynamic load balancing. Without resorting to use a costly global switch, the hypercube topology minimises the number of intermediate processors which must be traversed in order for a message to propagate across the machine. On the CM-1 two separate interprocessor communications networks were supported: the router and the News grid. The former was based upon the hypercube wiring and provided point to point communications. Each originating processor calculated the address of the recipient and then sent the message to that site. Hardware was provided to pipeline traffic going to the same processor as well as to buffer and route messages. The News grid connected nearest neighbours on a two-dimensional Cartesian grid. Since with this system all processors passed data in the same direction it is not necessary to specify destination addresses and there is no possibility of messages being blocked. Consequently, this mode of transmission was about 6 times faster than using the hypercube router.

Interprocessor communications on the CM-2 are basically the same as implemented on the CM-1 except that the News array has been redesigned to use an n-dimensional grid (where n may be in the range 1 – 31 and may be selected from software), rather than be restricted to two dimensions. This is now implemented on top of the hypercube network rather than using its own hardware. It is difficult to give precise figures for the bandwidth of the News grid because this depends upon the size of the data set being moved (see below). However, typical values of 2.5 Gbyte/s are quoted by TMC for the 65536 processor CM-2. Since this should scale linearly with system size we may deduce that the appropriate value for the 4092 processor CM-2a is 160 Mbyte/s. Although more flexible, the strategy behind the News grid is similar to that used in the DAP or on the X-Net mesh network in the MP-1. We may, thus, compare its bandwidth with those for the equivalently sized DAP 610 and MasPar 1104 of 5.2 and 4.5 Gbyte/s respectively. It is clear that the ratio of processor power to internal bandwidth is therefore much larger in the CM-2. How important this is will depend upon the user's requirement for data transfer between processors.

The bandwidth of the router depends both upon the message lengths and access patterns (i.e. the number of potential network clashes). TMC suggests that for a random set of connections on a 65536 processor CM-2 the aggregate throughput without collisions is approximately 250 Mbyte/s. The hardware communications limit for the hypercube network is actually approximately 7 Gbyte/s, very much larger than the value quoted above. There are two reason for the discrepancy, first random interprocessor communications take an average of about 6 steps and hence reducing the throughput by this factor. Second, before it is transferred, the data must be copied out of memory and onto registers on the SPRINT chip, thus lowering the effective bandwidth further.

In order to talk to the CM the host computer must have specialised hardware connected to its memory bus, this device is known as a front-end bus interface (FEBI). In the case of a Vax host the speed of this link is approximately 1.3 Mbyte/s, while for the Sun it is around 3 Mbyte/s. If the host machine is a Vax or Sun-4 workstation then up to four FEBIs may be mounted within the one machine, thus allowing several users access to the CM at one time. Since the Symbolics Lisp machine is a single-user workstation only one FEBI may be fitted to it. A maximum of four FEBIs may be used with the CM-2. These are connected to a bi-directional 4×4 crossbar switch called the Nexus. In the case of the CM-2a only two FEBIs may be connected and the Nexus is a 2×1 switch. The Nexus may be reconfigured in a few seconds using utilities provided to permit the CM-2 to be repartitioned.

The FEBI is connected through the Nexus to a sequencer within the CM which decodes the commands from the front-end and forwards them to the processor array. A CM-2 may contain up to four separate sequencers (only one in the CM-2a), these may be connected to any of the front-end machines, or alternatively be ganged and controlled as a single unit by one host. This allows a CM-2 to be split into sections of either 8192 or 16384 processors and means that it may be shared by up to four users running different applications. In the CM-2a it is not possible to subdivide the processor array.

As described in Section 2.3.4 the conventional way to program the CM has been to write code to be executed on the host. This contained calls to routines which were run on the PE array. Originally, when the front-end was a dedicated host (the Symbolics 3600) then it was easy to keep the slower CM-1 busy. With the hardware upgrades over the past few years the possibility of a reduction in throughput caused by the CM having to wait for program instructions from the host has increased. Consequently, TMC is now making provisions to alter this system. The sequencer contains 128 kbyte of scratch RAM, which until now has not been used. The plan is to develop the compilers such that they can output execution modules in CM microcode. These will be transferred at run-time to this RAM on the sequencer which can then issue instructions along its high speed link to the PE array. This is similar to the programming method on the AMT DAP, with the sequencer playing the role of the MCU in that machine.

In order to facilitate high speed data visualisation and disc I/O each 8192 processors have an I/O controller which communicates via an I/O bus to a number of possible peripheral devices. The controller allocates access to the various devices which may be connected and performs all multiplexing functions necessary during the data transfer. The I/O bus is 80 byte wide (of which only 64 are data, the remainder being used for error checking etc.). There are two standard types of attached device: a disc farm and a high speed graphics monitor. Normal discs cannot sustain the I/O rates from CM and so a number of discs are connected together. The CM disc farm is known as the Data Vault and consists of 39 separate drives (another 3 are held in reserve in the event of a failure). This gives a total storage of 20 – 40 Gbyte and a transfer rate of 40 Mbyte/s. Up to 8 Data Vaults may be operated in parallel, one for each octant. Graphical visualisation is achieved by connecting a 1280×1024 pixel 24 bit frame buffer to the I/O bus.

As with the DAP and MP-1, the number of physical processors is not an upper limit for the size of grids which may be modelled. In the language of the CM, the machine simulates an array of virtual processors (VP), the size of which is determined by the problem. When the number of VPs exceeds that of physical processors more than one VP is mapped onto a single processor. This has effects in two areas: usage of the floating-point accelerator and the News network. First, pipelining is implemented on the Weitek chips, which gives an approximately 60% increase in throughput for large VP sets. Second, consider the News network, when data are to be moved in a given direction many originating and target VPs will lie on the same physical processor. In these cases it is only necessary to reorganise processor memories to effect the shift. The remaining data transfers are passed through the hypercube network as before. This strategy of mixing memory relocations with communication results in the large increase in throughput seen in the transfer rates quoted above. The process is handled by system software and is, therefore, transparent to the user.

2.3.3   The Development System

Programs for the CM are written on the front-end host and the user therefore has access to the editors and other development tools supported on that machine. TMC also provides a debugger for testing the parallel sections of code, called cmdbx. This is an extension of the standard UNIX dbx with facilities for examining parallel data structures on the CM. It provides the usual functionality expected from dbx, for example to set breakpoints interactively, change variables and step execution.

The CM libraries also are compatible with the UNIX profiler gprof. This allows users to time sections of their code in the normal manner.

2.3.4   Programming Languages

At present, a CM program is actually executed on the front-end computer, the code is interpreted and the parallel sections converted into calls to routine for the CM, though changes to the compilers may soon alter this.

Three languages are currently available on the CM-2; *Lisp, C* and CM Fortran. The first two are standard Lisp and C with parallel extensions to accommodate the parallelism of the machine. This is accomplished by the introduction of new data types for parallel variables. However, in the case of Fortran an implementation of Fortran 90 allowed the standard array data structure to be used. All three languages make use of an underlying library of subroutines known as PARIS (PARallel Instruction Set), which supplies the functions required to distribute data around the CM.

Fortran is seen by TMC as the major language for scientific parallel applications. To this end they have implemented a version of Fortran 90 for the CM in conjunction with a specialist compiler provider, Compass. A number of other array processing extensions have been provided, though there are also restrictions. Examples of this are that EQUIVALENCE, pointers, and structures are not supported. At present, there is also the constraint that Fortran is only available for those machines with a Vax front-end. However, a beta test version of the CM Fortran compiler running on a Sun-4 does exist and should be commercially available soon. Object modules generated by the Vax Fortran compiler may be linked into the CM code without recompilation, though these, of course, will only run on the host but do extend the range of functions available.

Early versions of the C* compiler had a number of problems and attracted a considerable amount of criticism from users. Although the functionality was reasonable the efficiency of the generated code was very poor. These faults were accepted by TMC and a new C* compiler has been written by Compass and TMC, which will be shipped soon. TMC expects this release to compete with CM Fortran in terms of performance. It is also understood that a new common definition of parallel C for SIMD machines is under discussion and may be introduced in the longer term.

The C* compiler is implemented as a translator to standard C with embedded calls to PARIS routines. This intermediate code may then be compiled using the standard C compiler on the host. Following the C++ example, C* features a single new data type to support the machine parallelism, together with a small number of extensions to the language. In C* the program is divided into two sections: parallel and serial. These are differentiated by syntactic context (a new structure exists within C* to define those routines to be executed in parallel), but once that context has been established the contained code is standard C.

While C and Fortran are principally used for numerical work, Lisp is more suited for artificial intelligence and symbolic processing applications and was the first language to be implemented on the CM. The CM *Lisp is based upon Common Lisp with extensions to take advantage of the parallelism of the CM. In effect, each processor executes a subset of Common Lisp with a single thread of control existing on the host computer. Although the system software is written in micro-code the primitives of the Lisp language are very similar to the instruction set of the CM thus making the production of very efficient code possible. Given the original *raison d'être* of the CM as an engine for AI researchers it is interesting to note the close relationship which still exists between Lisp and the current machine. This is in spite of the fact that the usual range of applications which TMC emphasises as suiting the CM typically involve large amounts of floating-point work.

The implementation of *Lisp consists of both an interpreter and compiler, which are themselves written in Common Lisp. It may, therefore, be mounted on any host which supports this language.

Indirect addressing is permitted by the hardware and thus this functionality is provided by all of the high level languages. This feature is essential for many applications and while available on the MasPar MP-1 is not on the AMT DAP (cf. 2.1.4).

2.3.5 The Market Niche

When the first CM was being designed and produced, the AI and symbolic processing field was very active and the computer was aimed at this market. A few machines were sold for this purpose but it rapidly became clear that most scientific and industrial customers were more interested in Fortran and the floating-point potential of the CM, rather than in its novelty value as an interesting architecture. Consequently, TMC felt that it was necessary to diversify and changes were made to produce the CM-2 with improved floating-point performance and fast I/O facilities. Now, while TMC sells machines for both symbolic and numeric applications, it is now the latter which attracts most sales. It is clear that TMC is aiming for the high ground in parallel computing with a drive towards ever faster machines and are willing to leave the low-end market to others. This drive gives the CM-2 a status not shared by cheaper computers.

The aim of TMC is to become the largest supplier of very powerful supercomputers in the world. Their goal for the CM-2 was to provide such power while retaining the ease of program development enjoyed by users of conventional machines and it is their belief that this combination is the key to their success. "If you have a problem which can't run elsewhere, then come to us" is a summary of their attitude. Although the CM is cheaper than a Cray it is recognised that the latter still has the advantage of a larger software base, though TMC believes that this is changing (cf. 2.3.6). Most sales are now made on the basis the floating-point performance of the CM-2 to scientific computing institutions. To date over 55 machines have been bought by about four dozen different purchasers, of which five are in Europe. TMC believes that traditionally the market in the UK and Europe is as large as that in the US and Japan. Consequently, it is expected that the rate of future sales in Europe will gradually increase to become similar to that in the US.

Marketing in Europe started some two years after that in the US/Japan, despite their assessment that the prospects in UK/Europe are as good as those on the other side of the Atlantic. The reason given for this is that, initially, TMC felt unable to provide an adequate level of support for European customers (each CM site has an on-site TMC application engineer to provide local assistance). TMC has announced no plans to devolve software or hardware effort into Europe, though they accept that it would be consistent with company policy so to do.

In 1988 TMC had sales totalling approximately \$30 M, while by 1989 this had risen to about \$45 M.

2.3.6   The Competition

Despite making basically the same type of machine as AMT and MasPar, TMC does not view these companies as competitors because of the large price differential between the products. This an opinion shared by AMT and MasPar. TMC seems to regard these companies with benign interest since SIMD is seen by all three as the technology of the future and there is no direct commercial conflict. It is true that the CM is much more expensive than either the DAP or MP-1 but TMC believes that this can be an advantage. In addition, they claim that it is unfair to compare the relative prices of the hardware since most purchasers will also incur the extra costs of software conversion. Clearly, this will be a larger proportion of the total cost for the cheaper machines. For applications which do not need computers with the highest performance it is relatively easy for a buyer to find a conventional architecture which will fulfill their requirements. Indeed, it may be cheaper to take this route after consideration is given to the effort of program conversion. At the upper end of the performance scale, however, TMC claims that this is not so true, since the relative costs of parallel and conventional solutions become very different and purchasers may thus be more willing to expend effort to convert existing programs. There is clearly some truth in this argument but it does not take account of the fact that more establishments have the funds necessary to buy an MP-1 or DAP than can afford a CM-2. It may be supposed, therefore, that these other companies will generate a larger volume of sales.

The major competition is perceived by TMC not to be a specific machine, but the conservativeness of prospective purchasers and the amount of code which must be converted. As discussed above parallelisation of existing programs is not always a straightforward process and may require a large investment of effort on behalf of the buyer to convert such code. If that commitment is lacking then TMC concedes that the sale will probably go to a conventional computer or, for example, to Cray, despite the higher cost of these options.

In the US, NCUBE (cf. 4.2) and Intel (cf. 4.1) also provide competition, though the differences in machine architecture apparently keep these "conflicts" relatively rare. The transputer-based machines from, for example, Meiko (cf. 5.3) or Parsytec (cf. 5.5) are also in a different price bracket and are not serious rivals, except at the low end of the CM range and to universities or other cost-conscious purchasers. When any such competition does arise it is, apparently, always within Europe. This situation may change when the Meiko i860 machine becomes available, this will be capable of speeds in excess of 1 GFLOPS at a cost comparable with that of the CM-2.

In 1989 TMC won the IEEE Gordon Bell Award[4] in both the raw performance and best price/performance categories. To win the former, a seismic modelling program running on a 65536 processor CM-2 gave a sustained performance of 5.6 GFLOPS. Although this is only 20% of its peak potential, TMC points to the fact that the peak rating of an 8 pipe Cray Y-MP is only 3 GFLOPS. When taking the higher cost of a Cray Y-MP into account the price/performance advantage rises to about 12. This award, TMC believes, heralds the end of the era in which vector supercomputers can be regarded as providing the ultimate in computing power.

2.3.7 The Future

It is common knowledge that TMC is striving towards the production of a ter-aFLOPS machine. TMC accepts that they have been funded by DARPA to build the components of such a computer, but it is the policy of TMC not to comment further on unannounced products. Apparently, a number of developments are being investigated and a CM-x will arrive, though its relationship to the CM-2 is still secret. Clearly, the teraFLOPS computer will require either more or faster processors (or as is most likely a combination of the two). Even if the internal bandwidth bottleneck were removed to allow the Weitek floating-point accelerators to operate at full speed this would only give the 65536 processor CM-2 a top speed of 28 GFLOPS – less than 3% of the desired value. Distinct improvements will also have to be made in interprocessor communication rates if these peak rates are ever to be realised in real applications.

New versions of the Fortran and C compilers are under development, these will have a common back-end and provide support for a number of features to enhance the performance of the CM-2. The first is to permit manipulation of the registers on the Weitek chip from high level languages. The increased use of these registers will reduce the dependence of the floating-point unit on memory bandwidth which as discussed in Section 2.3.2 can be a bottleneck. Second, the new compilers will be able to produce execution modules which can be copied to RAM on the sequencers, thus eliminating the possibility of any delay being introduced because of the relatively slow link to the host.

---

[4]An annual prize given to machines which are deemed to have made significant advances in scientific and engineering computing.

Company Summary 1: Features of the AMT DAP

Source	Active Memory Technology Ltd.
Type	Fine grained SIMD array.
Availability	First site delivery in October 1987. Over 80 machines now placed.
Price	£87,000 for a 1024 processor system (4 Mbyte memory) to £420,000 for a 4096 PE configuration with co-processor (128 Mbyte memory).
Processing nodes	Single bit processors (optionally with attached 8 bit co-processor) arranged in a square grid and driven by a DEC Vax or Sun workstation.
Processors	Single bit processor: 2μm CMOS semi-custom cell based proprietary design with 12,000 gates per chip. CP8: 0.8μm CMOS semi-custom data path design, approximately 50,000 gates per chip.
Memory	Between 32 to 1024 kbit per PE.
Communications	PE to PE connections along nearest neighbours links and orthogonal data highways. The internal bandwidth (data memory to PEs) is 1.3 Gbyte/s (DAP 500) or 5.2 Gbyte/s (DAP 600).
I/O connections	Host connection via SCSI or DEC link at approximately 2 Mbyte/s. Video input/output from/to graphics device at 80 Mbyte/s (DAP 500) 160 Mbyte/s (DAP 600) for concurrent input and output. Direct disc connection at 16 Mbyte/s.
Performance	1130 MIPS for integer*1 add, 3.1 GIPS for logical AND, 28 MFLOPS for real*4 multiply, 108 MFLOPS real*4 saxpy. All figures measured in real applications on DAP 610 (without co-processor) using Fortran-PLUS. Manufacturer's estimate for the DAP 610c is 20 GIPS for integer*1 add and 560 MFLOPS for real*4.
Host system	Front end may either be Vax or Sun workstation. Connection of terminals or PC to integral RS232 ports in also possible.

Operating system	As provided by the front-end host; either Vax VMS or UNIX.
Programming languages	Either Fortran or C on the host and Fortran-plus or APAL on the DAP. There are plans to introduce an extended version of C for the DAP.
Physical configuration	DAP 600 series: $52.3 \times 23.7 \times 35.5$ inches. Weight 110 lb. DAP 500 series: $25 \times 17 \times 31$ inches. Weight 325 lb. Dimensions are exclusive of host machine.
Power dissipation	< 1.0 kW (dependent upon model). Cooling is provided by an internal fan.
Sources	Publicly available material plus interviews with AMT staff, most notably Geoff Manning and Stewart Reddaway.

Company Summary 2: Features of the MasPar MP-1

Source	MasPar Computer Corporation.
Type	Fine grained SIMD array.
Availability	First site delivery in January 1990.
Price	Under a DEC initiative, the MP1101 sells for £71,500 for specified projects, while the MP1216 costs approximately £400,000. These figures represent an approximate 35% discount on the retail price.
Processing nodes	The PE hardware includes a 64 bit MANTISSA unit, a 16 bit EXPONENT unit, a 4 bit Arithmetic Logic Unit (ALU) and a single bit LOGIC unit. These are arranged on a square grid in clusters of 16.
Processors	Custom designed chips contain 32 PEs implemented in two-level metal 1.6μm CMOS. Each chip has 450,000 transistors.
Memory	A fixed memory of 16 kbyte/PE.
Communications	Nearest neighbour communications via the X-Net mesh: 1.1 (18) Gbyte/s, global router 80 (1300) Mbyte/s. Figures refer to MP1101 machine, those in brackets for the MP1216 model (Manufacturer's figures).
I/O connections	Nearest neighbour connections via the X-Net mesh, the internal bandwidth is 1.1 (18) Gbyte/s for the MP1101 (MP1216). Global communications through the Global Router, the bandwidth depends upon required connection pattern with a maximum of 80 (1300) Mbyte/s, figures for machines as above (Manufacturer's figures).
Performance	26 GIPS for integer*4 add, 1.3 GFLOPS for average of real*4 add and multiply. All figures are manufacturer's estimates and relate to the MP1216 model.
Host system	Vaxstation 3520.
Operating system	The Vaxstation 3520 front end provides ULTRIX, and a special system based on X Windows for software development and execution (MPPE).

Programming languages An extended version of Kernighan & Ritchie (first edition) C is currently available. Parallel version of Fortran and C are planned.

Physical configuration MP1200 series: $55.5'' \times 23.5'' \times 32.5''$. Weight less than 800 lb.
MP1100 series $42'' \times 18.5'' \times 32.5''$. Weight less than 800 lb.
Vaxstation 3520 $27'' \times 21'' \times 18''$.

Power dissipation < 3.7 kW, depending upon configuration. Cooling is provided by an internal fan.

Sources Publicly available information together with interviews with the European office personnel and in consultation with top management in California.

Company Summary 3: Features of the TMC CM-2

Source	Thinking Machines Corporation
Type	Fine grained SIMD array.
Availability	First commercial delivery of the CM-1 in mid 1986, the CM-2 followed approximately 15 months later.
Price	A CM-2a with 4096 processors, FEBI board, 128 Mbyte memory, frame buffer and graphics monitor, but excluding front-end host: $\sim$ £350 k A typical 65536 processor CM-2 costs $\sim$ £5 M, including a Data Vault.
Processing nodes	Single bit processors with optional floating-point accelerator shared between blocks of 32. Arranged as a hypercube and driven by a Vax, Sun or Symbolics 3600-series Lisp machine.
Processors	Proprietary single bit processor fabricated using $2\mu m$ CMOS with 14,000 gates per chip. Floating-point accelerator: Weitek chip plus memory interface.
Memory	Between 64 and 1024 kbit of memory per processor.
Communications	Provision is made for regular communications on a grid of dimension < 16 and also for a router. Both are based upon the hypercube communications network. The former has an aggregate bandwidth of 2.5 Gbyte/s, the latter 250 Mbyte/s for a 65536 processor CM-2. (Manufacturer's figures.)
I/O connections	Each octant has two I/O connections which may be linked to a disc farm (the Data Vault) or high speed frame buffer. Data transfer rates of up to 50 Mbyte/s are possible, though only one channel per octant may be active at any time.
Performance	TM quote a peak performance for the largest CM-2 with Weitek floating-point accelerators of 28 GFLOPS. In practice, it is accepted by TM that sustained rates are $5 - 10\%$ of this value, the highest sustained speed recorded is 5.6 GFLOPS.
Host system	Sun 4 workstation, a Vax running UNIX or a Symbolics 3600-series Lisp machine.

Operating system
: As provided by the host system: either UNIX or Lisp.

Programming languages
: Fortran 90, C* and *Lisp are supported. A new version of parallel C may be released shortly.

Physical configuration
: CM-2a series: $26'' \times 26'' \times 43''$. Weight 375 lb.
CM-2 series: $56'' \times 56'' \times 62''$. Weight $1,200 - 3,000$ lb.
Dimensions are exclusive of host machine, Data Vault and other peripherals.

Power dissipation
: The smallest CM-2a requires 3.5 kW, while for a full 65,536 processor CM-2 the power requirement is 28 kW. The CM-2 range also uses 3-phase electricity. The machines are air-cooled.

Sources
: Publically available documentation together with discussions with users and interviews with TM staff.

Chapter 3

Shared Memory Multiprocessors: The Evolutionary Approach

While some advocates of parallelism believe that a complete break should be made with computing's past, many others have built successful companies by adopting an evolutionary approach to parallelism. It is no great step to move from a computer whose operating system gives each user the illusion of having his or her own independent processor, to one which actually provides such processors, along with an operating system which knows how to use them. By retaining a model of computing with which the majority of users feel comfortable, these firms hope to become computing's mainstream in the 1990s.

3.1 Alliant Computer Systems

Relevant Activities Manufactures a range of parallel supercomputers and visualisation systems.

Location Corporate Headquarters: Alliant Computer Systems, 1 Monarch Drive, Littleton, MA 01460, USA. Telephone: (508) 486 4950. European Headquarters: Alliant Computer Systems UK, Ltd., 10 Heatherley Road, Camberley, Surrey, GU15 3LW, UK. Telephone: 0276 682881. Far Eastern Headquarters: Nihon Alliant Computer Systems, Diamond Plaza Building, 25-Ichibancho, Chiyoda-ku, Tokyo 102, Japan. Telephone: 03 222 1766.

Relevant Officers Ronald H. Gruner, Chairman; Craig Mundie, President; John M. Harte, VP Sales and Customer Services; Rich McAndrew, VP Hardware Development; Jay Torborg, VP Technology; George Tranos, VP Manufacturing; Dan McCoy, VP Human Resources.

Employees 450 worldwide

Financial details In the financial year 1989 Alliant made a gross profit of $35.2 M, and had total assets of $93.4 M.

3.1.1 The Company

Alliant Computer Systems Corporation manufactures parallel and visualisation computers, which integrate parallel computing power with parallel graphics capabilities. The company has based its products on three fundamentals: parallel processing, 3-D visualisation, and industry standards.

Alliant was founded by Ron Gruner, Craig Mundie, and Rich McAndrew in May 1982. All three founders had backgrounds in electrical engineering, with Gruner having had much success in the 1970s at Data General. In the early 1980s it became clear to the founders that the major computing firms had become very distant from their origins in the science and engineering market. This apparent market niche together with the rise of parallel computing lead to the foundation of Alliant. The challenge of parallel processing was a key factor in this start-up with the founders choosing not to produce a powerful uni-processor which would nibble at Cray's heels, but instead to develop a parallel machine.

Alliant was established, with funding of more than $26 M from American investors including Hambrecht & Quist, Kleiner Perkins Caufield and Byers, and Venrock Associates. In December 1986, Alliant completed a $30 M initial public offering of its common stock and in May 1987, secured a further $50 M in funding. In 1988, it acquired Raster Technologies, a supplier of high-performance graphics systems. However, after this take-over Alliant went through a time of falling profits and losses, because of the take-over, poor international marketing and a congested market place. In response to this Alliant integrated Raster Technologies into the company much more quickly than planned, and so incurred further losses, but they were in a stronger position as a result and the balance sheet returned to profit in 1989, and has stayed so since. As a result of close links forged with Intel while formulating the PAX standard, $3 M of Alliant stock was purchased by Intel. In March 1990 Gruner claimed that Alliant had $40 M of cash to spend, so clearly the problems of 1988 have been overcome.

The first Alliant machines were announced in 1985, and since then a number of machines based on custom designed processors have been released. However, the current product line consists of the FX/2800 series which unlike its predecessors uses a third party supplied processor, the Intel i860. The FX/2800 sells in the range of £350 k to £1.5 M, and has performance which is claimed to be at the low end of the Cray Y-MP product line (Summary 21).

Alliant are heavily involved with setting and using industry standards for parallel computing, this is exemplified by the FX/2800 series. Together with Intel Alliant are developing the Parallel Architecture Extended (PAX) standard, which comprises of the Intel i860 processor, AT&T UNIX, and Alliant's parallelising software. Standards are good for users and application developers who have a stable base to work from but can be difficult for hardware manufacturers since they can't gain an advantage over the competition by offering new, and unique systems. However, Gruner does not see this as a problem since Alliant have a head start with their parallelising technology. Also, adopting standards cuts the development time for new products.

3.1.2   The Hardware

All of Alliant's machines are based around the same basic design which is shown in Figure 3.1. The architecture is based on a number of high-performance processors linked through an interconnect and cache system to a shared memory. The access to the memory is through caches which provide improved performance. These high-performance processors are time shared between the jobs by the operating system, and can work together as a truly parallel machine when necessary. The processors are linked by the concurrency control bus which is used to coordinate the processors. As well as the high-performance processors the machine has a number of interactive processors which run the UNIX operating system and execute interactive user jobs. The split in processor classification reflects the dual aims of achieving high-performance numerical processing and responsive interactive processing. Alliant produce visualisation variants of all their machines which have graphics sub-systems to provide high-performance graphics capabilities.

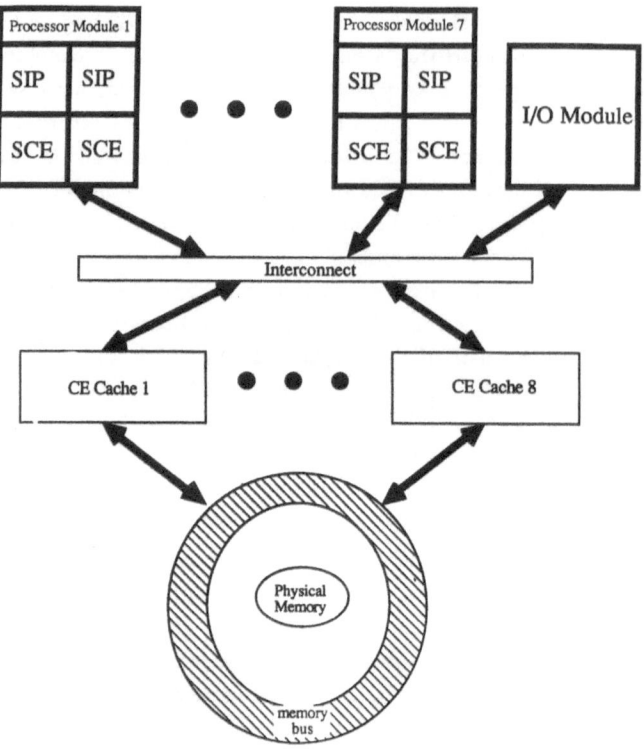

Figure 3.1: The Architecture of the Alliant FX/2800

All Alliant machines have similar architectures, so it is not a difficult task to upgrade to a new and more powerful computer. The earlier Alliant models, the FX/40 and FX/80, were binary-compatible, but the latest machine the FX/2800 uses a different processor technology and so recompilation is necessary before porting applications to it.

The FX/2800 has become the basis of Alliant's product line since its introduction in early 1990. This machine is labelled the "standards-based supercomputer" by Alliant, since it is based on the Intel i860 processor. The FX/2800 can have up to seven processing modules each with four i860s, giving a maximum of 28 i860s and a peak performance of 1.1 GFLOPS. The four i860s in a processing module are arranged as two Super Computational Elements (SCEs) and two Super Interactive Processors (SIPs). The SCEs in the system provide the compute power and can be configured into a parallel resource for larger tasks. The SIPs carry out most of the operating system tasks, interact with the users, and perform some graphical functionality. The I/O module containing one SIP connects to the outside world via two 20 Mbyte/s channel interfaces. Unlike its predecessors the FX/2800 does not have a separate graphics sub-system, instead the visualisation is performed by the SIPs and SCEs.

Alliant have used an interleaved distributed cache design to overcome the memory bottleneck problem for their machines. The physical memory, which is not distributed, is connected to a memory bus which serves a number of computational processor caches (CPC). The CPC provides a four way interleaved 512 kbyte cache with a maximum bandwidth of 376 Mbyte/s. In the FX/2800 there can be eight cache modules which serve up to seven processing modules, as well as the I/O module. Alliant chose to use a shared, interleaved cache as opposed to a distributed cache, as used by Sequent (Section 3.7) because they felt that improved performance could be gained for the following reasons:

- In loop parallelism there is a strong likelihood of several processors needing to access the data in one block, and so by storing these data in a shared cache there would be less cache invalidations.

- There will be reduced contention for the memory bus, since the caches are shared and so there are fewer entities competing for the bus.

- Fast communication between processors, since several processors can share a cache they can communicate via shared memory without having to load a block from memory.

The CPCs are connected to the SCEs by a 16×8 crossbar switch which can connect up to seven processing modules to the eight cache ports. The memory data bus consists of a 72 bit wide data-path which has a maximum bandwidth of 640 Mbyte/s.

3.1.3 The Visualisation Machines

The machines described in the previous section all have visualisation variants which have special parallel graphics hardware. The high speed graphics sub-system shares the same memory as the other processors and so can access results quickly.

The graphics sub-system consists of a display list board with display management processor, one or more image memory units (IMUs), and one or more Z-buffer memory units (ZMU). This system's parallelism is controlled by hardware which allows the system to be very efficient. The SCEs and SIPs provide front-end processing of high-level commands while the ZMUs and IMUs provide low-level high speed graphics support.

Initial processing on the graphics commands are performed by the SIPs and SCEs, including: lighting models, rendering surface properties, smooth shading, clipping etc. These are achieved by using the programmers hierarchical interactive graphics standard (PHIGS). In the FX/2800 PHIGS functionality is provided by software, whereas in its predecessors custom graphics hardware performed PHIGS tasks.

3.1.4   Software

The Concentrix operating system is based on Berkeley 4.3BSD UNIX, and is responsible for the usual UNIX tasks as well as controlling the parallel hardware. A Concentrix kernel runs on each processor in the system, and a locking mechanism is used to ensure consistency between these multiple kernels. The scheduler will transparently assign jobs to processors to keep as many of the processors busy as possible. If a task requires parallel resources then Concentrix will group a number of processors into a complex and assign the whole task to it. The scheduler can be adapted dynamically to adjust it to the local needs. The user can explicitly code for program parallelism by using either a UNIX-like fork utility, or a loop level function. This latter option, CNCALL, specifies that each iteration of a loop should be carried out in parallel.

Alliant supply an environment for use in real time systems. This package, the FX/RT executive provides strict constraints on system response and scheduling to allow real time applications to be developed. The FX/RT package features the following: priority scheduler; process memory resident; asynchronous event handling; and symbolic naming.

The Alliant Fortran compiler automatically produces code for the parallel vector hardware. The compiler is optimized for extracting loop parallelism from the Fortran code. The compiler also allows users to direct the optimising process so that their knowledge of the code can utilised in the parallelisation process. Profiling tools are provided which allow the programmer to analyse the parallelisation of the code. The compiler generates code for five modes of operation:

- scalar

- vector

- scalar concurrent, each iteration in the loop is potentially executed in parallel with hardware synchronising to ensure that the dependencies are maintained between iterations

- vector concurrent, a loop is broken up into chunks which can be executed in vector mode

- concurrent-outer-vector-inner, where the innermost loop is executed in vector mode while the outer levels are used for parallelisation.

The Fortran compiler analyses the source code for data dependencies then it looks for possible areas of concurrency and vectorisation, and finally it optimises the scalar code. Feedback on the optimisation process is provided by messages, listings, and profilers and the programmer can insert directives into the code to guide the compiler if the automatic optimiser is unsatisfactory.

Alliant also supply similarly optimised C and Ada compilers. A number of standard maths libraries are available on the Alliant machines, including: parallel versions of Eispack and Linpack; NAG; and IMSL.

Alliant provide graphical support through PHIGS and PHIGS+, as well as X Windows. The Visedge package helps users to visualise and interpret 3-D data. Graphical objects can be edited, moved, changed etc. by the package.

More than 150 application packages currently run on Alliant's FX/Series, including windowing systems (X Windows, NeWS, SPIDER etc.); electronics packages such as SPICE-FX, an analogue circuit simulator; mechanical engineering applications, including MSC/NASTRAN, and a finite element analysis program.

3.1.5 The Market Niche

Alliant see themselves as supplying the demand for cost effective computing for scientific and engineering users. Also they see a demand for high performance visualisation platforms. The Alliant range of machines has clearly been targeted at these areas as shown by their approach to parallelism. Engineers can achieve the benefits of parallelism, to a degree, without having to write explicitly parallel code. Thus it would be hoped that existing applications would run efficiently without modification. Alliant have in the past chosen not to address the data processing market, although this is changing and a number of database packages including Ingres are now available on their systems.

The area of high-speed visualisation is very important to Alliant. There is a demand for systems which allow the huge amounts of data generated by supercomputers to be displayed graphically, and at a pace which can keep up with these powerful machines.

The location of installed systems is approximately 50% USA, 25% Europe, and 25% Japan. Alliant have supplied machines for use in the following areas:

- Solid and fluid mechanics. Applications include automotive crash simulation, air flow over an aircraft, and design and testing. Mercedes Benz use an Alliant machine to visually simulate the combustion inside a diesel engine and so allow design engineers to see how different designs behave.

- Computational Chemistry. New drugs, polymers, and other molecules can be modeled in real time, thus allowing the scientists to see their results.

- Simulation and control. Alliant machines are used in real time flight simulators.

- Image/Signal processing. Applications include satellite data analysis and remote sensing.

The key aspect in all these areas is the combination of high-powered numerical processing combined with fast visualisation techniques. Recently, the San Diego Supercomputer Centre chose the FX/2800 as part of a $6 M visualisation laboratory. The machine will serve as a 3-D graphics rendering engine, fileserver, and network server.

Alliant spends approximately 15% of its revenues on R&D projects. This commitment is reflected in new software and hardware developments, such as the Alliant/Intel PAX standard. Another example is algorithms that transparently take advantage of parallelism on particular applications, as in the FX/Ada compiler. In addition, Alliant contributes research funds to institutions to increase the use of parallel processing. Recipients include the University of Southern California's parallel research symposia, and the algorithm research unit of the M.D. Anderson Cancer Center at the University of Texas.

Alliant sells its systems to end-users, VARs, and OEMs. Prior to 1988, Alliant distributed machines internationally through Apollo, but this proved to be a poor decision since Apollo had troubles of their own and so had limited success. The company operates several direct sales and customer support offices in the US, as well as a worldwide network including offices in France, Holland, Italy, Sweden, Switzerland, the UK and West Germany. A wholly owned subsidiary markets Alliant's products in Japan and Asia. In addition, Alliant has distributors that serve Australia and the Far East, including Taiwan, Korea and Hong Kong. A remote diagnostic centre operates out of Alliant's North American and UK headquarters.

3.1.6   The Competition

Alliant are in competition with other minisuper computer manufacturers such as Convex (3.4) and DEC. However, the FX/2800 gives Alliant an advantage over the current range of machine supplied by these firms. Alliant claim that the FX/2800 offers twice the performance of the newly announced DEC Vax 9000 model 440, and two and a half times the performance of the top range Convex C240 (3.4.2).

At the lower bound of their market Alliant are in competition with the top range workstations, while at the other extreme they are in competition with the low range machines produced by Cray Research Inc. (7.1). Silicon Graphics (6.2 are competing to a degree in the visualisation market.

3.1.7   The Future

Alliant see the future as being standard systems. The PAX standard which has been developed in co-operation with Intel is an attempt to define an industry wide standard for parallel processing. If such a standard is adopted then Alliant would be in a strong position because the standard is based on their software. The next processor in the i860 series, which is code named the N11 by Intel will feature Alliant's concurrency instructions in its instruction set, and so will fit more naturally into the Alliant architecture than the i860. Recently, Alliant have become members of the MASS 860 group which includes IBM, Intel, Olivetti, Oki, and Samsung. This group has the objective of providing standards for hardware and software systems based on the Intel i860.

The visualisation capabilities of the Alliant machines is crucial to their future since there is an increasing demand for systems which allow data to be analysed visually. Recently, in Japan at an office furniture exhibition an Alliant system was used to allow people to design their dream office and then "walk" in and look around. This example shows the possibilities for high speed graphics systems.

3.2   BBN Advanced Computers Inc.

Relevant Activities Supplier of the TC2000 – a MIMD processor aimed at the time critical and supercomputing markets.

Location Headquarters: BBN Advanced Computers Inc., 10 Fawcett Street, Cambridge, Massachusetts 02138, USA. Telephone: (617) 873 6000, Fax: (617) 873 3315. European Office: BBN Advanced Computers, Heriot-Watt Research Park, Riccarton, Edinburgh EH14 4AP. Telephone: 031 449 5488, Fax: 031 449 5855.

Relevant Officers Ben Barker, President; David Micciche VP Marketing and Sales; John Goodhue, VP Research and Development; Gary Schmidt, VP Scientific Office; Sarah Long, Director International Operations.

Employees Approximately 60 in the US and representation in Europe and Japan.

Financial details Total capitalisation undisclosed, a wholly owned subsidiary of Bolt Beranek and Newman Inc.

3.2.1   The Company

In 1948 Bolt, Beranek and Newman was founded as a acoustic consultancy company (BBN). Over the years the company expanded and, as the use of computers and communications increased, diversified its interests. BBN have been responsible for such well known communications systems as ARPAnet. In 1989 BBN had a total revenue in excess of \$290 M, though it made an operating loss of \$25 M, mainly due to decreased sales of computing and communications hardware to the US government.

In 1972 BBN first ventured into parallel processing with the Pluribus, a multibus machine consisting of a number of interconnected Lockheed SUE minicomputers, which was designed to act as a node for ARPAnet. Approximately 50 of these machines were built, almost all were bought by the US government for networking applications and some are reported as being still in use.

The direction for the future was, however, set in 1978 when BBN was commissioned by DARPA to produce a new parallel computer. In fact, DARPA's interest was not centred on the computer *per se* but rather in the development of a fast communications switch around which the new machine was to be based. This switch was named the Butterfly because its wiring topology is similar to the Fast Fourier Transform butterfly. Consequently, the computer became known as the Butterfly. In an updated form, this Butterfly switch still forms the basis for the latest generation of BBN computers.

The processors in the Butterfly were built around 68000-series chips from Motorola, each with 500 kbyte of memory. First deliveries of the Butterfly computer were made in 1981, and some 30 – 40 machines were sold, most of which were to universities interested its novel architecture. From the DARPA point of view the project was also a success because of the development of the Butterfly switch. It was not a requirement that the product be a marketable computer. Encouraged by the response to the Butterfly, BBN decided to upgrade the machine. This new computer, the Butterfly Plus, had 4 Mbyte of memory per node and used more powerful Motorola 68020 processors. About 50 of these were sold.

On two previous occasions BBN had chosen to target specific market niches with the establishment of subsidiary companies, and so it was with parallel processing. In July 1986 BBN devolved its parallel computing effort to a new company: BBN Advanced Computers Inc. (BBN ACI). In order to raise the research and development funds it was decided to form BBN ACI in partnership with Paine Weber Development Corporation. Such R&D partnerships are an American concept and until the late 1980s provided a tax efficient opportunity for small investors. Together, Paine Weber and BBN raised $32 M for the development of the new computer and jointly owned the rights to the developed technology.

This redesigned machine was to be aimed at the time-critical and supercomputing markets. At that time the former was estimated to be worth approximately $5 G and growing at 25 – 30% per annum. To emphasise the change in hardware the new computer was rechristened the TC2000 (TC being short for Time Critical). However, it was accepted that some time would be required for the development of this machine and it was decided that as an interim measure a number of changes could be made to the Butterfly Plus to enhance its performance and usability. This computer was to be known as the GP1000 (GP standing for General Purpose).

The Butterfly switch in the GP1000 remained unaltered from that in the Butterfly Plus. The major change, however, came in the way in which the machine was controlled. The previous two Butterfly computers were compute engines, with a front-end host on which the user developed code. For the GP1000 BBN ACI decided to remove this front-end and to implement the operating system directly on the processors. This move was justified on two counts: it would reduce reliance on other suppliers, and the new machine would be more flexible, if the operating system was under BBN ACI's control. In line with the growing trend towards UNIX the operating system implemented was a version of Berkeley UNIX 4.3BSD known as MACH (developed by Carnegie Mellon).

The GP1000 was as successful in attracting sales as the Butterfly Plus (about 60 machines were sold, 75% to universities). In the light of this success BBN decided, in 1990, to buy the technology from the partners. BBN is, therefore, the owner of all the technology related to the TC2000.

BBN are viewed as a technology driven company, though BBN ACI are more market led. It is not surprising, therefore, that after it had been on sale for a few years BBN ACI undertook a reappraisal of the best market for the GP1000.

As a consequence of this study it was decided that the machine could be better directed away from general scientific computing and towards the time critical[1] market. The principal reason appears to have been the amount of money to be made in the respective fields. As described above, most previous sales had been made to universities and research establishments, bodies which are not usually rich. However, time critical purchasers tend to be banks and other large financial companies, defence establishments or large industries, especially aerospace – institutions with much deeper pockets. In 1988 Dataquest, a market research company, estimated that the market for high-performance parallel computers was \$60 M, while that for Online Transaction Processing (OLTP) was \$27 G.

The TC2000 was introduced in July 1989. Although BBN ACI would still consider making and selling a GP1000, the TC2000 is now the only machine actively marketed and is described in more detail below. Sales of this machine have been lower than expected, and BBN ACI have reported operating losses in 1989. They do not expect this situation to change until at least the middle of 1990.

3.2.2   The Machine

The TC2000 is a shared memory, medium-grained, MIMD computer. The individual processors run different tasks as allocated by the user program. Moreover, the machine may be partitioned into autonomous clusters, permitting more than one application to be run concurrently. Cluster allocation and management is dynamic, so that, for example, a pool of "public" processors can be maintained for multi-user use, and a pool of "free" processors maintained for parallel processing. Additional resources may thus be given to CPU intensive processes and returned to the "free" pool when that task is completed. BBN ACI have taken great care to design the TC2000 to be modular, permitting users to add extra hardware as required, in units of one, or more, processors at a time.

The Butterfly Switch

The heart of the TC2000 is the Butterfly switch, the third generation of the design first developed under the original Butterfly project for DARPA. This switch allows each processor to access all memories in the machine, irrespective of their location. Ideally, in order to maximise the throughput of a switch it should have a separate data path between each input and output node (a crossbar). Unfortunately, since the number of connections in such a device rises as the square of the number of processors, its cost rapidly becomes prohibitive. The Butterfly, therefore, builds upon a set of 8×8 crossbar switch modules (upgraded from 4×4 on the GP1000),

---

[1]This is a term used by BBN to encompass traditional real-time simulations and the mission critical applications run by military and defence related establishments

which are connected together as shown in Figure 3.2. This solution gives inferior bandwidth to a crossbar because of switch contention. However, the cost of the Butterfly grows more slowly as the number of nodes increases than a full crossbar. Also, for a reasonable number of processors it gives better throughput than a bus-based system which may be fast (have a wide data path) but can only connect two points at any one time.

Input   Output

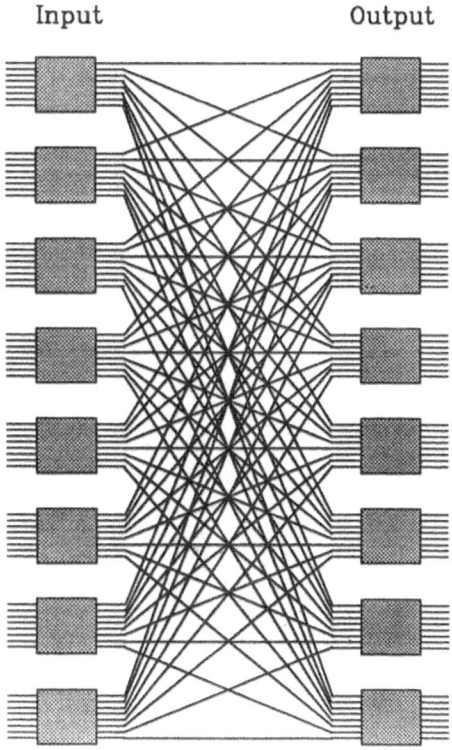

Figure 3.2: A Two-Column Butterfly Switch. The shaded boxes are 8×8 crossbar switch modules.

Each switch module connects up to eight processors, which can link any of their inputs to any of their outputs. In machines which contain more than eight processors, the output links from the switch modules are grouped together to form a multi-stage switch. Two versions of the Butterfly switch are available, which have either two stages (as shown in Figure 3.2) or three stages. The maximum number of processors allowed with the former is 64, while the maximum with the latter is 512. Message routing through the switch is based upon network packet switching techniques originally developed by BBN for the US government. Messages contain three bits of routing information for each stage in the switch. These tags permit one of the eight output nodes on the switch module to be selected, thus routing the message to the next stage.

As mentioned above, each processor may access the memory of any processor in the system and so the TC2000 may either be thought of as either a shared memory or local memory computer, depending upon the method used to decompose the application onto the machine. The major difference is that accesses to local memory are typically 3 − 4 times faster than those to remote locations (after allowing for memory contention). The process of remote access is transparent to the user on the TC2000 and is one of the main advantages of the Butterfly design. In order to be able to access remote memory this must be declared as shared, otherwise it is private to that process. These declarations are made by the user from software and because of the faster access rate it usually makes most sense to have private memory as local to the processor running the process.

When a processor references a remote memory location the requested address is sent out from the CPU as normal. It is then picked up by the switch interface and converted into a switch message and routed through the Butterfly switch to the interface chip on the appropriate function card. At this point the switch message is reconverted into a memory reference and sent to the memory location. The contents of that location are then sent back through the switch by the reverse of the original route. To the processors (and hence the user) the process of interrogating remote memories is, therefore, identical to that for accessing local memory, the only penalty is the extra time taken to negotiate the switch.

It is obviously possible for several processors to try to access a given memory location at the same time. In this situation one of the colliding requests is permitted to continue, while the others are returned to the originating processors. These automatically retry to make the connection after a random, short delay. While a memory access is active that processor memory is locked to all others. In order to reduce contention for memory, commonly used data should and can be distributed across the memories of several processors.

The hardware for the current Butterfly switch is custom designed by BBN ACI and made from ECL gate arrays. Each path through the Butterfly is 1 byte wide and, as the switch hardware is clocked at 38 MHz, the maximum bandwidth is 38 Mbyte/s per channel. This is a factor of 10 improvement on the throughput of the switch in the GP1000 and gives a maximum interprocessor bandwidth for a 64 processor TC2000 of 2.4 Gbyte/s.

The Processors

The processor cards in the TC2000 are built around the Motorola 88000-series RISC chips; each of these processor cards are designated as a TC/FPV. At present, these processors have a 20 MHz clock speed. However, BBN ACI believe that since the clock rate of the Butterfly switch is significantly faster than this it will be straightforward to upgrade the TC2000 to accommodate faster processors as these appear.

The first of the 88000-series processors is the 88100. This chip is rated by Motorola as having a peak floating-point performance of 20 MFLOPS (single precision). One of these is mounted on a function card, together with three 88200 cache/memory management chips and a Butterfly switch interface. Two 88200s are used for program instructions for the 88100, the other for data. These can be accessed simultaneously by the processor. The use of cache memory is a relatively cheap method for improving overall memory access rates since the storage of frequently used data in cache reduces the number of accesses to the slower system memory. Each 88200 contains 16 kbyte of four-way associative cache memory and supports both write-through and copy-back schemes to keep the system memory up to date.

The switch interface is a custom design from BBN ACI and is implemented as a pair of CMOS gate arrays. It converts signals between the function card and the Butterfly switch and buffers data transfers. Decoupling the switch clock from that of the function card is necessary to permit the use of different clock rates within the machine. Why did BBN ACI not design their own floating-point hardware? The answer is threefold: first buying commercially available chips gives economy of scale and removes all development costs. Secondly, the large chip manufacturers, eg. Motorola and Intel, have the experience, resources and facilities with which it would be nearly impossible to compete. Finally, adopting a *de facto* industry standard design permits the use of third-party software.

All physical memory in the TC2000 is distributed amongst the function cards. Currently, there are two types of these, with either 4 Mbyte or 16 Mbyte of memory. These are implemented using standard, commercial 1 or 4 Mbit DRAM chips. Not all function cards in the machine need contain the same amount of memory and may be upgraded in the field.

The Communications System

When the TC2000 was developed from the GP1000 two hardware changes were made to cater for the new targeted market. These were an increase in the number of I/O interfaces and the provision of a high precision real-time clock. Each function card has its own real-time clock. These have a resolution of $1\mu s$ and are synchronised globally to maintain their times to within $1\mu s$.

The VME I/O interface is on the TC/FPV function card. Each TC2000 has at least one VME interface to support attached graphics devices, discs etc. However, up to 5 VME interfaces can be used on each switch module, a bandwidth increase important to many time critical applications. As the bandwidth of a single VME I/O channel is 8 Mbyte/s the maximum I/O rate for a 64 processor machine is 320 Mbyte/s. Disc access is through standard SCSI discs connected to the VME bus.

All components of the function card: the processor, memory, Butterfly switch and VMEbus, are connected together by a BBN designed bus – the Transaction bus (Tbus). This bus is 32 bits wide, is clocked at 20 MHz and so has a maximum bandwidth of 80 Mbyte/s. All memory references, whether local or remote, are made across the Tbus and it is designed to prevent deadlock which could occur if two devices tried to read data from each other simultaneously. In these circumstances, one device is selected and its request satisfied, while the other waits until the first transaction is completed.

Despite not having a TC2000 with which to measure its sustainable performance for a real application, we may estimate this from the speed of the Tbus. For a typical single precision floating-point operation 3 words of data must be passed to and from memory, the maximum rate at which this can be accomplished is $80 \times 10^6/(4 \times 3)$ s^{-1}. This gives a sustainable performance of approximately 7 MFLOPS. Clearly, cache memory may increase this figure, while the use of remote memory accesses will decrease it. BBN ACI suggest that the somewhat higher figure of 12 MFLOPS is sustained in some real applications.

A final component on each function card and switch module is not directly connected to the Tbus, nor is it accessible by users, this is the Test and Control System (TCS) slave processor. This device is implemented using the Motorola 68HC11 chip and checks the function card or switch module for correct functioning. It monitors board temperature, voltage levels and tests for the presence of key signals, such as the clock and processor activity register. These slaves communicate via their own diagnostic bus to a master TCS processor, which is, in turn, connected to a console and private disc drive. In the event of hardware failure, the appropriate TCS slave reports the location of the fault to the master which produces an error message. TCS system software permits the isolation of the malfunctioning component, while allowing the rest of the machine to run as normal. BBN ACI claim that many faults can be anticipated by noting small changes in board voltage levels and that as a consequence suspect components can be replaced before total failure.

The TCS processors have the additional task of loading the bootstrap program onto the function cards at load time from their private disc. This obviates the need for specialised bootstrap ROMs.

3.2.3   The Development System

Many other parallel computers have a host to shield the user from the machine and provide a standard environment within which to develop code. Although previous versions of the Butterfly did make use of a front-end computer, BBN ACI decided that extra flexibility could be obtained by providing operating systems to run on the processor clusters directly. Two operating systems are available, nX and pSOS^{+m}. The former provides a POSIX standard multi-user operating system and is based upon Berkeley UNIX 4.3BSD, while the latter is designed for real-time applications. In addition, there is a symbolic debugger and performance analyser in the Xtra Tool Set and a run-time library (known as the Uniform System) provides a parallelisation paradigm.

The nX operating system is a development of MACH, which was run on the GP1000, and is reputedly much faster. It provides both Bourne and C shells and will support up to 512 processing nodes. In its simplest form, nX assigns each newly created process to different processors so as to effect some level of load balancing. In addition, it permits users to bind those modules within a program which may be executed in parallel to different processors.

Two disadvantages of running the operating system on the same processors that are used for the computation are that an extra CPU overhead is thereby introduced, and data memory must be allocated to the kernel. The percentage of CPU time lost to nX is not known, but the operating system does require 1 Mbyte of memory, a significant fraction of that available on the smaller memory TC/FPV function card.

pSOS^{+m} is designed for use in real-time or time-critical applications and is virtually an industry standard in the US. It was written by Software Components Inc. and has been ported to the TC2000 by BBN ACI. Whereas nX is designed to have considerable functionality and will allocate tasks for execution with some degree of "fairness", pSOS^{+m} is written to be fast and provide predictability of execution. To this end, it is a small kernel with a limited number of commands. It supports a priority-based, preemptive scheduler for multi-tasking.

Both nX and pSOS^{+m} can share memory, execute simultaneously and interact together. This lets users run different parts of an application under the operating system most suitable for that purpose.

BBN ACI have developed a tool set, Xtra, which lets the user monitor and analyse program execution. It utilises a standard X Windows interface and thus requires the use of a X Windows terminal or workstation connected to the TC2000 by an Ethernet. There are two main products within Xtra, TotalView and Gist.

TotalView in a menu-based debugging system, which may be used with programs running under either nX or pSOS^{+m}, which provides interactive symbolic support for code written in Fortran, C, or a mixture of these. It is possible to set conditional and unconditional breakpoints and evaluation points within each process interactively. The CPU overhead is estimated to be less than 5%.

Gist is designed to give the user a picture, in real-time, of the state of all processes running in parallel. It is used to discover bottlenecks in the code, whether these arise because of synchronisation problems due to processes awaiting data, or caused by sections of the program which are especially CPU intensive. Gist is a separate program from TotalView but the two are closely interlinked, so that each may be called from within the other.

3.2.4 Programming Languages

Fortran, C and Ada compilers are available for the TC2000. Of these, Ada is the most recent addition and illustrates BBN ACI's interest in attracting military applications. An assembler is also provided and can give speed improvements in CPU intensive routines. Normally, it is difficult to code RISC processors in assembly language because of problems synchronising data fetches and arithmetic. However, BBN ACI claim that because the 88100 uses a register scoreboard system (as used in the Cray, cf. 7.1) to handle instruction synchronisation this process is relatively straightforward here. Fortran, C and assembly language can cross-call procedures and all languages can also access system calls in either nX or pSOS^{+m}.

The current Fortran compiler for the 88000 was produced by Green Hills Software Inc., with a number of additions written in-house by BBN ACI. This compiler contains a number of optimising features, which includes the ability to exploit the fast register accesses possible in the 88100 RISC processor. It has been developed with the intention of code portability between machines, though given the dependence upon the underlying machine architecture it is not clear how truly portable real programs written for the TC2000 can be. In this, of course, it is no different from other parallel computer. The compiler adheres to the Fortran 77 standard but is enhanced to include most Vax/VMS extensions. BBN ACI expect that it will conform to the Fortran 90 standard, when this finally becomes established. Great emphasis has been placed upon the development of this compiler by BBN ACI, due to considerable user pressure. This is in line with many other supercomputer manufacturers (eg. Thinking Machines, cf. 2.3.4) who find that Fortran is the most commonly used language for parallel processing.

Parallelism may be expressed within Fortran programs in one of two ways. The Parallel Computing Forum[2] standard extensions to the language definition have been included to permit sections of code to be executed in parallel. Alternatively, calls can be made the Uniform System run-time library which enables processor activity to be initiated and controlled.

As with Fortran, C was written for the 88000 by Green Hills and modified by a compiler team within BBN ACI. It shares common code generation software with the Fortran compiler and as such implements the same set of optimising functions. It is a superset of the Kernighan & Ritchie standard C and includes many ANSI and Berkeley extensions. The C compiler is supplied as standard with the TC2000, while the other compilers are available at extra cost. The reason for this is that BBN ACI recognise that it is necessary to include a compiler with the basic system, but as the TC2000 Fortran is a more polished product it can more easily be sold as a separate item. Green Hills C++ is expected to be available soon.

---

[2] A group a computer manufacturers including Cray and IBM who have produced a standard for parallel constructs in Fortran

The Uniform System library was designed especially for C, though as noted above it may also be called from Fortran. Unlike implementations of C on some other parallel computers this compiler does not include extensions to reflect the parallelism of the machine but relies totally on calls to the Uniform System. In relation to Fortran, C is rather less efficient.

A version of the TeleGen2 Ada written by Telesoft has been ported onto the TC2000. This includes an integral development and execution environment which is run under nX, though Ada code may also be executed under pSOS^{+m}. Since this is, effectively, a standalone system it is not possible to use the standard TotalView debugger with Ada, although the software development tools available under nX may be employed. This language is designed primarily for large codes and the compiler is implemented in three stages.

The development and execution system which is supplied with Ada includes a source-level debugger, library manager and toolset, and a number of language tools. Ada is designed for very large applications and program development by teams, such facilities are therefore much more important than normal for software consistency. It is claimed to be as efficient as C on the TC2000.

3.2.5 The Market Niche

As discussed above, after a couple of years selling the GP1000 as a general scientific parallel computer, BBN ACI decided to change its target to attack the time critical market. At that point there were few competitors in the field and the market leader, Gould, was in the process of being taken over by Encore (cf. 3.5). Consequently, Gould users felt uncertain about their future directions, this state of flux was compounded by the merger between Concurrent (cf. 3.3) and Masscomp. BBN ACI felt that they could capitalise on this situation and that there was a lucrative market niche for a parallel time critical computer. This move influenced the hardware development of the TC2000 as discussed in Section 3.2.2.

Unfortunately, the basic design of the TC2000 is not particularly well suited for all segments of the time critical market. BBN ACI claim that the full advantages of the Butterfly switch are only realised in relatively powerful (and hence expensive) systems with over 12 nodes. Apparently, prospective clients wishing to purchase machines for flight simulation are typically interested in those within the $225 - 275 k range and there is keen competition within these limits. This is approximately the cost of a three – four node TC2000, and it is unlikely that foreseeable extensions in aeroplane design will require the computer to be extended beyond eight processors. In response, BBN ACI point to the flexibility of their (modular) machine, nevertheless it is to the upper-end of the time critical market which they must look for most sales.

In the first year since its release, about 12 TC2000 machines have been sold, mainly in the US and Japan, though at least one sale was in Europe. The majority of these systems are relatively large (a minimum of 16 nodes). Table 3.1, below, shows the distribution of the first ten of these divided by type of purchasing body.

Table 3.1: Sales of the TC2000 by Centre

Site	Number
University/Research Estab.	4
Govt. Laboratory	4
Industry	2

A number of these machines are being used for real-time processing applications, such as signal processing, and several for parallel processing research.

3.2.6   The Competition

BBN ACI see different competition in the three main markets which they are now targeting. In the time critical market, special attention is given to flight simulators, in which they are in direct competition with Gould, Concurrent (cf. Section 3.3) and Harris. For supercomputing sales the major competitors are Intel (cf. 4.1), Alliant (cf. 3.1), NCUBE (cf. 4.2) and, in Europe, Meiko (cf. 5.3).

In the OLTP market the major competitors are the large mainframe manufacturers, DEC and IBM, who have the advantages of a range of database software already available. In an effort to counter this BBN ACI spent about 18 months of preliminary exploratory work in a joint project with Oracle to port the Oracle database software onto the TC2000. Although good initial results were obtained, it was decided not to continue with the project. Nevertheless, BBN are still interested in forming such links, if a suitable partner could be found. BBN ACI believe that without such recognised database software available on their machine, any hardware manufacturer is unlikely to make a great impact on this market.

Sales to the above markets take a considerable length of time to complete (6 - 12 months). In an effort to increase the number of machines sold, BBN ACI are making renewed efforts to woo scientific purchasers. Although, in fact, BBN ACI would claim that they had never really forsaken this market, in which they have considerable experience. Given the price of the TC2000 the competition is what one might expect. In the US, this principally comes from NCUBE, Intel and Alliant. While in Europe, it is usually Meiko, AMT (cf. 2.1) and Parsys (cf. 5.4).

3.2.7 The Future

BBN ACI have just announced their intention of developing an enhanced version of the TC2000 for delivery in 1992. This new machine will support up to 2,000 processors, each with an estimated 100 MFLOPS peak performance (64 bit). New techniques should permit a four-fold improvement in packing density of the chips. BBN ACI also anticipate improvements to the compilers, the Butterfly switch and the possibility to support 32 to 128 Mbyte of memory per processor.

In the longer term, BBN ACI intend to produce a much more powerful system which should be ready around the middle of the decade. The basic concept is to provide "3T" performance: over one TFLOPS power, one Tbyte of main memory and one Tbyte/s of memory bandwidth. The system will use concepts developed by BBN during the Monarch project, but still use commercial chip sets and adhere to industry standards.

3.3   Concurrent Computer Corporation

Relevant Activities Manufacture multiprocessors for real-time and fault-tolerant applictaions.

Location Corporate Headquarters: Concurrent Computer Corporation, 106 Apple Street, Tinton Falls, NJ 07724. Telephone: (201) 758-7000.

Relevant Officers Dennis R. Brown, President and CEO; Dean W. Freed, Chairman; Coenraad Stork, Marketing Manager; Don Bradbury, Director of Customer Services; Michael Baker, European GM; Gerry Crook, UK General Manager.

Employees 2800 employees worldwide.

Financial details Annual sales currently exceed $240 million.

3.3.1   Background

The organisation now operating as Concurrent Computer Corporation has been around in one form or another for a long time. Its first incarnation was as Interdata Inc., a computer firm founded in 1966. Interdata was acquired by Perkin-Elmer in 1974, and became that company's Data Systems Group. In 1985, the group was spun off as Concurrent, and in 1988, it merged with Masscomp (the Massachusetts Computer Company). Concurrent now has a worldwide manufacturing, sales and service organisation, with a presence in 34 countries and an installed user base of over 30,000 machines.

During the past decade, Concurrent has concentrated on producing computers for use in areas such as transaction processing and flight simulation, in which very fast response times and robust fault tolerance are important. Their systems have employed multiple processors both to improve response time (by having several processors handling interrupts and running tasks simultaneously) and to provide seamless backup in the event of component failure. Because Concurrent has often provided complete systems, rather than just computing platforms, the company has not felt the need to move towards standards such as UNIX as quickly as other firms.

3.3.2   The 3200 Series

Concurrent currently supports two distinct product ranges, the older 3200 Series, built around a proprietary LSI processor, and the more recent 8000 Series which uses the same MIPS R3000 chip used by Silicon Graphics and Stardent.

The 3200 series of multiprocessor systems was launched in 1982, and aimed at the high performance, real-time market. The 3200 series machines are asymmetric, in that different memory and I/O resources can be allocated to each processor to tailor machines to particular applications.

The addition of I/O processors and better Fortran support resulted in the medium grained Model 3260 MPS. Later models in the 3200 Series were the Model 3230 MPS and the Model 3280 MPS, which was at one time Concurrent's high-end system. Application-managed parallel processing was available, and a performance of between 6 and 33 MIPS was quoted on Whetstone benchmarks.

The newer 3280E MPS uses the architecture of the 3280 MPS to provide, tightly-coupled, asymmetric parallel processing. From a minimal configuration of 2 processors — one CPU plus one auxiliary processing unit (APU) — incremental growth can result in a full configuration supporting six processing units. All of the 3280's processors use Shottky TTL, MSI and LSI technology, and contain eight sets of 16 general-purpose 32 bit registers, eight 32 bit floating point registers, and eight 64 bit floating point registers. The primary system data highway is provided by a 256 Mbyte/s ECL memory bus (E-Bus). This bus contains two separate paths: one for read operations from memory and the other for write operations. Each path has a maximum bandwidth of 160Mbyte/s. Real memory, which consists of 1 Mbyte CMOS dynamic RAM chips with an 80 ns access time, can be two-way or four-way interleaved, and is available in increments of 16, 32 or 64 Mbytes up to a maximum of 256 Mbytes.

Each processor includes 16 kbyte of 45 ns cache memory, 8 kword of writable control store and integrated floating point hardware, and supports a full 32 bit address range. A four-stage instruction pipeline is used to complete instructions in 400 ns. All memory access, including access to shared memory, is via set associative caches, one each for instructions and data.

Concurrent's concentration on the real-time market is shown by their advertising brochures, which quote interrupt response time before mentioning processor performance. This low response time, which is guaranteed to be no more than 15 μs, is coupled with the ability of the 3200 Series machines to keep one processor on "hot standby" to replace another if the latter fails to produce a highly fault-tolerant system.

The Control/Diagnostic System (CDS) is the sole facility for controlling and monitoring the 3280E MPS. It is used to configure dual ported E-Bus interfaces (EBIs), which can be connected either to processors or through bus-to-bus interfaces to an I/O bus. Each of these I/O buses supports up to three direct memory interface channels, offering a total throughput capacity of up to 120 Mbyte/s. A full 3280E MPS configuration occupies three cabinets, one of which is dedicated to the E-Bus and memory system, while another supports I/O and houses 6 3280 processors with I/O bus connections. The third cabinet houses two processor chassis, each supporting four processors.

Concurrent's proprietary OS/32 operating system controls the tightly-coupled system, and runs ready tasks on any available processor. Languages supported include Fortran 77 and C³ Ada, both of which can exploit the machine's parallel architecture, as well as Cobol, C, Pascal, BASIC II and CAL/CAL MACRO assemblers.

OS/32 is a proprietary real-time interrupt-driven operating system which, after controlled concurrent memory access, attempts to eliminate another major bottleneck in multiprocessor system, namely the scheduling of activity across processors. OS/32 provides users of the 3200 Series systems with the ability to control individual APUs.

3.3.3   The 8000 Series

In February 1990, Concurrent announced the Series 8000, its first new product line since its merger with Masscomp. The 8000 Series machines are based on the R3000 RISC from MIPS Computer Systems. Three incarnations are currently available: the 8300, a single or dual processor system including 6 VMEbus channels and between 8 and 64 Mbytes of RAM; the 8400, which has a peak performance of 160 MIPS and supports up to 12 VME slots; and the 8500, which can support up to four dual CPU boards and 128 Mbyte of RAM. The minimal 8500 unit comprises one dual CPU board, eight Mbyte of RAM and a single I/O system.

At the same time as the 8000 Series was announced, Concurrent released Version 6.0 of its Real-Time UNIX (RTU) operating system. Originally developed for the 3200 Series, RTU is a System V compatible operating system which contains extensions to support real-time programming. For example, RTU services all interrupts on one processor, but dispatches tasks to other available processors for execution in order to ensure predictable response times. Similarly, CPUs may be dedicated to running a single process, to ensure that process is always ready to execute, or may be made available to run whatever processes are presently in the run queue. These facilities are supported by a kernel which contains pre-emption points, so that high-periority processes can actually interrupt the kernel at non-critical moments. Two other features of RTU which are particularly useful to real-time programmers are its provision of Asynchronous System Traps, which are queueable, prioritisable software interrupts, and contiguous files, in which a single area of a disk is allocated in advance to hold a file to improve access time.

3.3.4   The Market

Concurrent has always focused on solving time critical applications. Their major product in this area is the Simulation (SIM) Package System Group, which provides for military and commercial training simulation applications, covering weapons systems trainers, power plant simulators, avionics development, and flight simulators.

In this field, BBN, Gould and Harris have traditionally provided the most direct competition.

The 3200 Series is in use in a variety of other situations, including a large number of on-line transaction processing systems. However, throughout the 1980s an increasing number of users were unhappy with the proprietary nature of Concurrent's software, such as its Reliance relational database package, and began to migrate to more widely supported systems. While Concurrent believes that its future lies with its installed base of 3200 Series system, and there are no plans to abandon OS/32, its small systems division hopes that RTU will be able to attract real-time customers away from DEC, Harris and Encore/Gould.

The Series 8000 is aimed at transaction processing, training simulation and the military. Concurrent believe that these superminicomputers offer the fastest real-time Unix processing currently available.

3.3.5   The Future

Concurrent is already exploring areas such as GaAs and ceramic superconductors for high-speed computation, and research is continuing into vector processing for advanced scientific applications, automatic decomposition techniques for faster parallel program execution, and AI. With their guaranteed user population of 3200 users, and the development of a Unix-like operating system for Concurrent's systems, Concurrent are confident that they will be offering competitive, real-time, parallel processing power for some time to come.

3.4 Convex Computer Corporation

Relevant Activities Designs, manufactures, and markets high-performance multiprocessors for scientific and engineering applications.

Location Convex Computer Corporation, 3000 Waterview Parkway, PO. BOX 833851, Richardson, Texas 75083-3851, USA. Telephone: (214) 447 4000.

Relevant Officers Robert J. Paluck, Chairman; Peirre R. Lamond, President and Chief Executive.

Employees Approximately 1000 people worldwide.

Financial Details 1989 operating income $16 M; total capitalisation $150 M; net income $4 M.

3.4.1 The Company

Convex designs and manufactures computers for scientific and technical users. Formed in 1982, the company aims to satisfy the increasing demand for fast, affordable supercomputers.

Convex shipped its first product, the C1, in March 1985. At first, a conscious decision was made against using parallel processing, since Bob Paluck, the company president, felt that building a fast single pipelined vector processor would provide the the company with a marketable product in a shorter time than a new parallel architecture. This was justified on the grounds that uniprocessor hardware was simpler to design and that the UNIX operating system, which Convex intended to offer, was already well developed for such machines. Furthermore, Convex designers believed that it would be possible to build upon the existing vectorising compiler technology for uniprocessors.

While this strategy sufficed in the short term, eventually Convex's competitors began to produce systems which outperformed the C1. Also, Convex learned that there were applications which could be parallelised more effectively than vectorised, and gradually sales were lost. Customers were unwilling to buy hardware which could become rapidly redundant.

To address these problems, Convex chose to make its second generation machine, the C2, a multiprocessor. Convex's approach differed from that of startup multiprocessor companies, such as Sequent (section 3.7), in that they chose to couple a few fast processors together, rather than build their machines around many slower ones. They felt that programming a coarse-grained machine with shared memory would be easier than for any other configuration, and that ultimately the most easily programmed architecture would prevail. Also their coarse-grained approach allowed loop parallelism to be utilised efficiently and this meant that sequential programs could be transparently parallelised.

The C2 was introduced in 1988, it was designed to provide both high performance and a good time-shared environment. To manage the parallelism of the machine Convex invented a hardware mechanism called Automatic Self Allocating Processors (ASAP). Before 1988, most attempts to achieve parallelisation employed a static method of scheduling tasks to processors, a simple, but often inefficient method. ASAP was intended to eliminate the possibility of idle processors by using hardware schedulers to assign tasks to available processors as long as there was work to do, and so maximise CPU utilisation.

Currently both the C1 and C2 are still marketed by Convex and are discussed in more detail below.

3.4.2   The Hardware

The C120, essentially a uniprocessor with the potential of being configured as a dual processor machine, is Convex's smallest production machine. It has a high-performance 64 bit custom designed CPU which has integrated scalar/vector functional units built out of 8k gate CMOS gate arrays. This machine is based on the original C1 which had no scalar floating-point hardware; instead, it sent operands to the vector processor. Each processor is coupled to its own memory and can produce up to 40 MFLOPS (manufacturer's figures). In 1984 the C1 was upgraded to be the C1-XP by adding a 20 kgate add and multiply unit. At that time Convex favoured relatively slow, low cost memory systems, based on memory cards with four-way interleaving and a single 80 Mbyte/s memory path. There was also a physically addressed 64 kbyte "P-Cache" designed to speed up memory accesses. The C1 CPU executed a single instruction stream, which was accelerated by a 4 kbyte instruction cache. The main locus of control was the address and scalar processor, which was microprogrammed using a writable control store. A further improvement in bus bandwidth utilisation was provided by a small 1 kbyte data cache with a simple write-through update policy. The C1 memory system had 4 Gbyte of virtual memory and 1 Gbyte of physical memory. The six year old C1-XP, with only minor changes, became the C120 upon when the C2 series was announced in 1988.

The C201 and C202 are mid-range machines which provide entry into Convex's parallel computing systems. Coupled to a 145 Mbyte/s memory bus, their 64 bit vector/scalar processors can generate 36 MFLOPS and 80 MIPS maximum throughput. Convex's fastest products, the C210 – C240 machines, have either two, three, or four processors each coupled to a shared memory by a 200 Mbyte/s system bus. All the C2 series machines use ASAP technology to manage parallelism. The architecture of the Convex C240 is shown in Figure 3.3.

There were several problems with the C1 series. Benchmark analysis showed that the two-level cache system exhibited thrashing — memory blocks were often copied into a cache set only to be replaced by other memory blocks. This happened

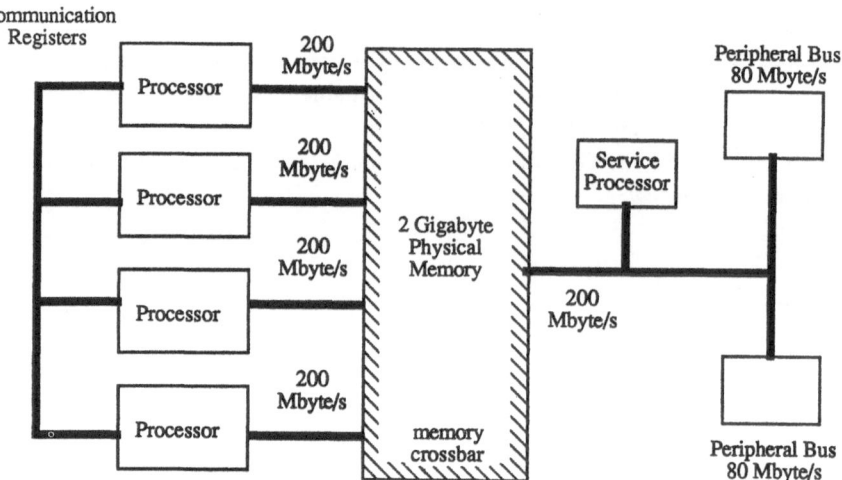

Figure 3.3: The Architecture of the Convex C240

most frequently when vector operations were executed on arrays with more than four million elements. The heavily pipelined architecture could not cope with this behaviour, so the C1 series did not deal gracefully with overloaded time-shared environments. Even the instruction set was restrictive, and was eventually extended to include trigonometric functions, square roots and vector convert instructions.

However, during the design stage of the C2, Convex was short of resources, and so decided to re-use as much of the C1's technology as possible. As a result the C2 uses the C1's I/O system, not only because it was robust but also because it was considered to have been over-powered for the that machine. The most important changes were in the cache design. The two level P-Cache system was replaced by an instruction cache, address cache and a data cache. All are direct mapped and support a single level write-through update scheme with a hardware invalidation policy between processors to enforce cache coherency. Thus, if two processors share data in their caches and one processor updates its version, the other processor automatically invalidates its "dirty" data. Vector instructions are written and read directly to and from main memory, avoiding caches. Convex's architects chose a direct-mapped cache because the associated fast access time outweighed the possibility of thrashing. While the write-through update policy can load the memory bus, this was not a problem with the C2 since it had a 200 Mbyte/s bus bandwidth for vector processing and so this extra bus load could be tolerated.

The design of the C2 was accompanied by the development of the ASAP hardware scheduling system. ASAP provides a constant supply of process instruction streams, or *process threads*, to the processors until all threads have executed to completion, or until there are no idle processors. ASAP works in three phases: forking, scheduling and joining. First, the compiler divides the program's process into multiple threads and requests that scheduling take place by having a fork request written to the communication registers which are shared by all processors. The scheduler polls the communication registers until it finds a fork request. It then checks for an idle processor and immediately assigns it to the communication register with the impending fork request. This hardware scheduling mechanism takes eight clock ticks, rather than the 10,000 cycles it would have taken from software.

After the thread is executed the processor returns the result to the communication register, where it is joined with other process threads. The threads forked and scheduled by ASAP communicate via global shared memory. As with most tightly coupled shared memory architectures locks are provided for mutual exclusion, and to protect the critical section of activated threads. There is no master/slave concept in ASAP, instead, the scheduling algorithm is dynamic and symmetric; each processor executes the same scheduling algorithm and comes up with the same decision about which process to schedule next.

In addition to a large bank of communication registers the C2 was designed with a larger, more expensive and more sophisticated memory system than the C1. The C2 has the same virtual memory space as the C1 but has 2 Gbyte of physical memory, which is organised as pairs of 39 bit memories rather than a single 64 bit memory. There are five ports into the memory system; the C2's crossbar feature allows CPU and I/O functions to access memory simultaneously. The total CPU/memory bandwidth of the four processor system is 800 Mbyte/s.

3.4.3   Software

Convex's operating system is an enhanced version of Berkeley UNIX which shares resources amongst CPUs. The operating system uses the hardware scheduler and ASAP mechanism, and provides semaphoring techniques which allow operating system functions such as scheduling, memory management and interrupt procedures to occur in parallel on the CPUs in a multiprocessor system. The scheduler selects new processes to execute from a queue of ready-to-run processes and threads from the process's list of ready to run threads. Because ASAP is symmetric, CPUs do not wait for other CPUs when work is available for processing.

The Covue environment provides a Vax/VMS-like environment to ease the transition to UNIX from DEC's VMS operating system. This allows engineers and scientists to utilise the Convex family of machines without having to learn a whole new operating system. Covue includes:

- Vax/VMS command language compatibility.

- DECnet compatibility.

- EDT compatible text editor.

- VMS compatible job batching system.

- Fortran extensions compatible with Vax Fortran.

Languages supported by Convex include C, Fortran 77 and Ada. The emphasis is on providing fast languages for scientific applications; there hasn't been a bias towards business applications to date. Convex's compilers recognise constructs within programs that lend themselves to vectorisation and parallelisation and generate appropriate machine-level vector and parallel instructions. The compilers can detect both instances in which serial code can be executed on separate processors, and instances in which processors can be forced to assist in the execution of a program. In either case the parallelism is transparent to the user, so that programs can run on upgraded machines without change and achieve increased performance. The Convex compilers can automatically parallelise: loops with long vectors; outer loops of nested loops; loops with inter-dependencies. They also parallelise independent scalar regions and loops with subroutine calls if directed to do so through compiler directives.

The Convex C compiler conforms with the ANSI C standard, and automatically vectorises and parallelises standard C code. Users are informed which parts of their programs were vectorised or parallelised and why other parts were not. Users are also permitted (and encouraged) to perform minor reconstruction and to add in-line directives to gain further performance improvements.

The mechanism for extracting parallelism and vectorism is similar for all three compilers. To vectorise, the compiler simply searches for operands which require the same operation. Parallelising code is more difficult to detect, and is done by allocating threads from a loop whose iterations are independent to different processors. Typically, vector code is generated for the inner loop, which runs on a single processor.

3.4.4   The Market Niche

In the last five years Convex has installed 600 systems with 375 customers in 33 countries. The market for their machines splits as shown in Table 3.2.

Recently, a contract has been secured with the NASA Ames research centre for machines for use in a broad range of aeronautics programs. The National Institutes of Health are using Convex equipment for protein and DNA sequence analysis and molecular modeling. In the UK, Convex have installed a machine at the SERC Daresbury laboratory.

Table 3.2: The Markets for Convex Machines

Area	%	Example Uses
Emerging markets	6	environmental applications, linear programming, real-time simulation, and visualisation
Advanced research	7	computing resources for research establishments
Petroleum industry	10	oil exploration, seismic analysis, and reservoir mapping
Computational Chemistry	15	chemical reaction simulation, and new drug design
Government and aerospace	23	research, signal processing, and simulation
CAE	32	development and testing of new cars, aircraft, and semiconductors
other	7	

Convex is expanding. In 1985 its total revenue was $11 M, which represented a net loss $5 M; in 1986 revenues increased to $40 M with a profit of $10 M. Three years later, in 1989, there had been a rise of 92% in the operating income from $9 M to $17 M. Convex is particularly eager to pursue the Japanese demand for its products; there are presently 100 systems installed in that country.

Convex have channelled their marketing efforts overseas to Europe, Malaysia, Indonesia, Turkey and Algeria. By staying at the low end of the supercomputer market Convex hopes to be able to supply a broad range of users throughout the world.

3.4.5 The Competition

In 1984, Convex nearly lost its market niche, because of the threat possed by the introduction of the Alliant FX-4 (Section 3.1.2). Convex managed to leapfrog the next series of Alliant machine with the introduction of its C2 series, particularly the C240. Convex likes to compare itself with Cray (7.1); the C240 is said to be as fast as the Cray-XMP (7.1.2), but at a fraction of the cost. Today, there is fresh competition from Alliant's i860 system and the IBM RS/6000.

3.4.6 The Future

Convex's next machine, the C3, will have to have a performance at least double that of the C2 in order to compete. The C3 will be based on Gallium Arsenide technology which will result in a very fast machine. However, they will continue to design their own processors while almost all other manufactures are adopting standard based processors produced by third party vendors such as Intel and Motorola. While custom designed processors can be tailored to the system architecture to give performance benefits, they take significantly longer to bring to the market, and so allow competitors to get to the market first.

Convex has continued to enhance its products by introducing Enhanced Scalar Products, which deliver substantial application performance gains, and the Integrated Disk Channel, which supports corporate-wide database servers and file systems. Convex's goal in the near future is to maintain compatibility with all its previous machines. This suggests that the next generation of Convex supercomputers will use a few tightly coupled, heavyweight processors, rather than rely on the "many hands make light work" approach of its rivals.

3.5 Encore Computer Corporation

Relevant Activities Supplier of the Multimax and Encore 91 shared memory MIMD computers.

Location Headquarters: Encore Computer Corporation, 6901 West Sunrise Boulevard, Fort Lauderdale, Florida 33313, USA. Telephone: (305) 497 5430. UK Head Office: Encore Computer (UK) Ltd., Marlborough House, Mole Business Park, Randalls Road, Leatherhead, Surrey, England. Telephone: 0372 363636.

Relevant Officers Kenneth G. Fisher, Chairman, President and CEO; Daniel O. Anderson, Executive VP; William L. Avery, VP and General Manager Product Operations; T. Mark Morley, VP Chief Financial Officer; Rowland H. Thomas, Executive VP, Chief Operating Officer; Robert A. DiNanno, VP Customer Services; J. Thomas Zender, VP Marketing.

Employees Approximately 1900 employees, mostly based in the US.

Financial details Public limited company quoted on the New York Stock Market. Total assets at the end of 1989 were $185 M.

3.5.1 The Company

Encore was formed in May 1983 by Kenneth Fisher. He had previously held senior positions in Honeywell and Prime, and has been credited with building Prime into a major company. However, he decided to leave after an internal dispute. For the first three years Encore was primarily concerned with research and development of its Annex terminal server, which was subsequently sold to Xylogics, and with the Multimax UNIX machine. Early versions of the Multimax were not a great success because a number of hardware problems resulted in poor reliability. This delayed the launch of the machine and a number of OEMs decided to withdraw from their marketing agreements. However, Encore managed to rectify these faults and within a year the problem had been solved.

Encore view themselves as a company responding to both market demands and new technological possibilities. They feel that it is important to maintain such a balance, but accept that in reality the latter is more important as most decisions within Encore are made by scientists and engineers. They describe their objective as the creation a family of shared memory, multiprocessor computers, based upon standard commercial chip sets in order to reduce development times and costs. These advantages are now widely recognised and the use of proprietary chips is becoming standard for many computer manufacturers, for example Intel (cf. 4.1), BBN (cf. 3.2), FPS (cf. 3.6) and all of the transputer-based companies. Encore is aiming its machines at the the commercial data processing/database and the real-time markets. To a lesser extent they also target the the scientific computing sector. To date, the company is best known for its Multimax range but it has recently announced the Encore 91, the first in the new Encore 90 series. Both these machines are described in more detail below.

In 1986, Encore received orders for the Multimax from DARPA and also a three year contract to produce a more powerful parallel processing computer by linking a number of Multimaxes together. This technology was delivered to DARPA, but it was not a requirement that the product be a marketable computer and it has not, as yet, been made commercially available. However, Encore do say that at some future date a derivative of this machine may be released.

Their largest change in fortune came in April 1989 when Encore took over the Computer Systems Division (CSD) of Gould. Gould had been bought in September 1988 by the Nippon Mining Company, a Japanese metals conglomerate, who wished to devolve the computing sector of Gould and started negotiations with prospective purchasers. Some eight months later CSD was sold to Encore. This increased the total assets of the company roughly sevenfold and increased revenues five-fold. However, the acquisition cost Encore more than the $180 M price tag for CSD because the new company has had to undergo some restructuring to lower costs and increase efficiency.

In 1989 total sales were $157 M, the majority of which ($138 M) came from CSD. This represented a considerable decline from the two companies' combined sales figures of $280 M in 1988. This reduction is attributed to three factors. First, considerable customer uncertainty was engendered during the protracted take-over negotiations for CSD. Furthermore, the original acquisition of Gould by a non-American company caused problems with sales to the US government and to a number of major companies. Second, there was a fall in US sales of the Multimax multiprocessor, which Encore attribute to the redirection of management effort from sales towards the take over of CSD and the subsequent restructuring. Third, a number of CSD products (the Powernode and NP families of computers) are nearing the end of their effective lives and this has resulted in a decline in sales. Encore hopes to revitalise these with an acceleration of the development schedules for new machines.

As a result of the restructuring process Encore has moved its headquarters and transferred its San Diego product development facility to Fort Lauderdale, previously the home of CSD. It has also closed manufacturing plants in Ireland and Puerto Rico and cut about 430 staff. Integration of CSD and Encore facilities and personnel are thought by Encore to be important, not only to reduce costs but also to improve customer confidence in the stability of the new company. Encore has taken this latter point seriously and has held meetings with major customers to convince them of the company's future strategy. Encore returned to profit in the first quarter of 1990 and pointed to an upturn in sales in the last quarter of 1989 which, if maintained, would give an annual revenue only slightly less than that in 1988. Nevertheless, Encore does not expect to pay a dividend on its shares for the foreseeable future.

At the time of the take over Gould was in legal dispute with IBM over alleged infringements of patents held by IBM. While this could have repercussions for Encore, Gould has agreed to indemnify them for five years from the take-over. If during that time sales exceed those made by CSD in 1988 by a factor of 8.75, then 1% of all such revenues will be paid to Gould.

Due to their acquisition of CSD, Encore have a large number of distributors and sales and service offices around the world: 33 in the US and another 32 in the rest of the world, about half of which are within Europe. Of these, only the address for the London office is given above. Within the US the sales force has been divided into three sections, each of which covers a different market sector: real-time, information systems and federal. In addition, Encore place great stress upon a new customer support scheme, designed to sell users a "total solution" rather than just a computer. While not as comprehensive one can see a similarity between this and the policies of the large conventional suppliers, such as DEC and IBM, who have a considerable presence in the commercial database market at which Encore are aiming.

3.5.2   The Machines

Multimax

The Multimax was first designed in 1983 – 86 and is now produced in two ranges: the 300 and 500[3]. In order to provide ease of use, they have a shared-memory design, which effectively hides the parallelism from the user. They are based upon a bus designed by Encore and known as the Nanobus. The Multimax is designed to be modular, so that it may be extended as users' requirements increase. Although similar in design, there are a number of differences in the specifications of the two Multimax models. In the subsequent description the details given apply to 300 series and, where these differ significantly, the appropriate information for the 500 series is in parentheses.

The Multimax is controlled by a processor which provides general monitoring and diagnostic facilities. Called the SCC, it is based upon a National Semiconductor NS32016 and runs at 10 MHz. It can support four serial lines, one for the system console, one for a remote console/modem and the other two, not generally accessible, are for diagnostic purposes.

---

[3]There are two series within these ranges. One has a bus which can support up to ten processors, the other 20. These numbers are added to the range number to give the three Multimax series available today: 310, 510 and 520.

The CPUs in the Multimax are designed around conventional, commercially available chips, the National Semiconductor NS32332 (NS32532). Each of these CPUs has an associated NS32081 (NS32381) floating-point accelerator. Two processors are mounted on a card, known as an Advanced Processor Card, or APC (Extended performance dual Processor Card, or XPC). The processors are clocked at 15 (30) MHz and the manufacturer claims a performance of $\sim$ 4 (8) MFLOPS per FPU. Up to five APCs (ten XPCs) may be fitted into the Multimax.

Optionally, on the 310 each APC may contain a Weitek 1164/1165 vector unit which is controlled by a chip custom designed by Encore. This interface chip makes the Weitek appear like a standard FPU, so that no special compilation is required. This is not available for the 500 series because of problems interfacing the Weitek and National Semiconductor chips. As a consequence, it is commonly accepted that the Multimax 500 has a good integer performance but its floating-point power is disappointing.

Each APC (XPC) also has two 64 (256) kbyte cache memories, one for each CPU. In the Multimax 300 range, memory management is implemented by a NS32382 chip, but on the 500 this is incorporated within the CPU. System memory is provided by a separate board, the Shared Memory Card (SMC). Each SMC has 16 or 64 Mbyte of memory implemented in standard 320 ns DRAM and between one to five (two to ten) of these may be fitted with the machine. This gives a maximum of 320 (640) Mbyte of shared memory.

The core of the Multimax is the system bus. This was designed by Encore in the initial phase of their development. It is implemented in Schottky technology and has a nominal clock rate of 12.5 MHz. It is, in fact, not one but three parallel buses: a 32 bit address bus, a 64 bit data bus and a 14 bit vector bus. In addition, each bus has an extra bit wide channel for parity checking. In the Multimax 310 and 510 the Nanobus has 11 card slots, while in the 520 there are 20.

This combination of clock speed and width of data-path gives a total memory bandwidth of 100 Mbyte/s. One problem with all bus-based parallel architectures is that this aggregate bandwidth must be shared by all the processors, and can cause severe interprocessor communications problems for large machines. It may be instructive, therefore, to consider a Multimax with ten processors: the memory bandwidth per processor is then 10 Mbyte/s. A typical single precision floating-point operations requires about two to three words to be passed to and from memory. This shows that the maximum floating-point performance of the processor is thus approximately 1 MFLOPS. Only at the low-end of the Multimax range, therefore, does the memory bandwidth appear not to be a bottleneck. While this imbalance is a problem experienced by many other machines it is especially severe in a bus-based architecture where the memory bandwidth is fixed. Clearly, the use of cache memory on the APC (XPC) boards will decrease the call made on the Nanobus. However, the addition of a Weitek vector processor will compound the problem as the extra bandwidth allocated for it is small compared to its performance, a problem also faced by the Connection Machine (cf. 2.3).

Connection to external devices and discs is provided by two different cards: the Ethernet/Mass Storage Card (EMC) and the Mass Storage Card (MSC). These boards are the same for all Multimax models. The former gives one I/O channel with a bandwidth of 1.5 Mbyte/s, while the latter has three independent channels with an aggregate bandwidth of 12 Mbyte/s. As with the rest of the processors in the Multimax these cards are designed around National Semiconductor chips. All Multimax models can support between one and four EMCs, while the 310 and 510 models can have up to two MSC cards, and the 520 has a maximum of four.

The Encore 91

The Encore 91 is the first in a new range of parallel machines recently announced by Encore. Beta test releases are expected in the autumn of 1990 with the first commercial deliveries at the start of 1991. The Encore 91 is similar to the Multimax being based around standard chips and is designed to be modular, so that users can upgrade with ease. The processors, however, have been upgraded to the 88000 series of chips from Motorola. In this, Encore have chosen the same technology as BBN (cf. 3.2.2), although they have adopted a slightly newer version of the chip with a 25 MHz clock rate. The reasons given by Encore for choosing the 88000 family of chips are very similar to those of BBN, namely the range of third-party software available and the potential upgrade path. A simplified picture of the architecture of the Encore 91 with two CPUs is shown in Figure 3.4

The first of the 88000-series processors is the 88100. This chip is engineered using Motorola's HCMOS technology and are rated by the manufacturer as having a peak floating-point performance of 20 MFLOPS (single precision). Either two (Encore 9102) or four (Encore 9104) of these are mounted on a single board, together with two, or four, 88200 cache/memory management units (CMMU) per 88100. Each CMMU contains 16 kbyte of four-way associative cache memory and supports both write-through and copy-back schemes to preserve consistency between cache and system memories. One CMMU is used for program instructions for the 88100, the other for data. Both of these can be accessed simultaneously by the processor. The use of cache memory is a relatively cheap method for improving overall memory access rates since the storage of frequently used data in cache reduces the number of accesses to the slower system memory.

Each board also contains 16 Mbyte of shared memory implemented in commercially available 1 Mbit DRAMs. This may be extended by adding up to four memory cards, each having 64 Mbyte. This gives a maximum memory in the Encore 91 of 272 Mbyte.

Communications within the processor board are handled by a bus (the Local Bus) with a bandwidth of 100 Mbyte/s designed by Encore. At first sight this does

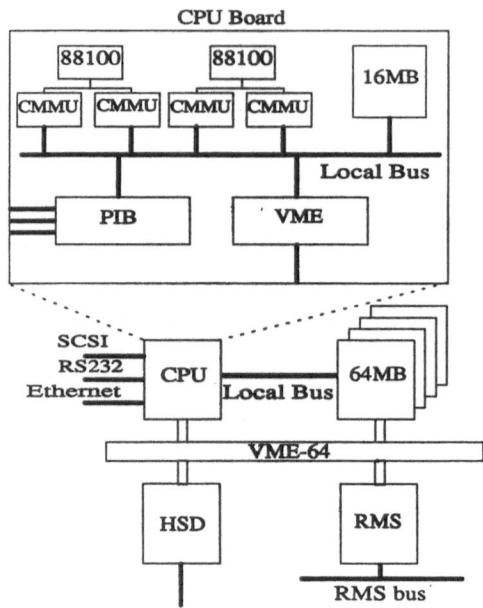

Figure 3.4: The Encore 9102

not appear to be different from Encore's proprietary Nanobus. However, the Local Bus is actually an extension of Motorola's hypermodule. This route was chosen because it provided a simple method for launching the Encore 91 on to the market as quickly as possible, rather than having to redesign the interfaces between the Nanobus and the processor chips.

Communication between the processor card and the extra memory boards is via an extension of the Local Bus. A VME 64 bus (8 byte wide) is also provided. Encore claim that the VME 64 is capable of block transfers at a sustained rate of 55 Mbyte/s (peak 80 Mbyte/s). We may apply the same argument as in Section 3.5.2 above to consider the ratio of processor performance to memory bandwidth. For the 9104, this gives a typical single precision floating-point performance of each 88100 of only about 3 MFLOPS, much less than is claimed for it. Only applications which can make extensive use of the CMMUs will achieve much more than this value.

At present, the maximum number of processors in the Encore 91 is four. However, it is possible to create a larger system by connecting a number of machines together through a custom designed interface. Known as the Reflective Memory System (RMS), this permits up to eight Encore 91s to be interconnected. It was developed by Encore (then Gould CSD) for a UK company who contributed to the design and is targeted directly at the real-time market. It has a throughput of 26.6 Mbyte/s and the maximum distance between machines is approximately 50 m along copper wire, or about 3 km via optical fibre.

Connection to other instrumentation, graphics devices or one other Encore 91 may be made through a slower interface known as the High-Speed Data (HSD) link. This is a VME-based 32 bit bus which is becoming an industry standard connection. It has a bandwidth of 3 Mbyte/s.

3.5.3   The Development System

For the Multimax, Encore developed two varieties of UNIX: UMAX 4.3 and UMAX V. The former is based upon Berkeley UNIX 4.3BSD and the latter is an implementation of the System V UNIX from AT & T. Berkeley UNIX is primarily used in the educational/research sector, while System V is more frequently chosen by commerce. In addition, under contract from DARPA Encore have implemented a parallel version of MACH, a derivative of UNIX from Carnegie-Mellon University. This has the advantage that it runs rather faster and has extensions which make it easier to support parallel architectures. Support for the development work necessary to implement MACH on a parallel architecture has been given to Encore by both DARPA and the Open Software Foundation (OSF). OSF have selected Encore's version of MACH as the basis of their new OSF/1 operating system, which is to be the next generation of UNIX.

On the Encore 91 the only version of UNIX currently supported is UMAX V. However, Encore have developed μMPX from the MPX-32 operating system written by CSD for the CONCEPT/32 range of real-time computers. μMPX is a small kernel which conforms to POSIX standards. It is designed to be fast and to provide predictability of execution. Applications programs can be developed using the standard tools provided with UMAX V and then run under μMPX. Not all processors in the Encore 91 need execute the same kernel, though at least one must run UMAX V. The others may be dynamically switched by the user between the two operating systems, though UMAX V cannot take over a processor until control is relinquished by μMPX.

Encore provide a non-interactive debugger, called Parasight, to aid program development. It runs under a standard X Windows environment on attached workstations.

3.5.4   Programming Languages

Fortran, C and Ada are provided on both the Multimax and Encore 91 computers. In addition, Lisp, Cobol and Pascal are supported on the Multimax. Encore are clear that Fortran is the most popular language for most purchasers, mainly due to the large amounts of code already in existence, although Ada is now becoming increasingly popular. Commercial customers are usually not very interested in languages and are more concerned with the relational database software supported. Interestingly, Encore claim that while most people expect a good C compiler to be provided, few wish to use it for anything other than tailoring systems code. It is unpopular for applications programming.

The Encore Fortran compiler meets the Fortran 77 standard and includes a number of the most popular Vax/VMS extensions. The compiler is available in two versions, one to produce standard sequential code for running on a single processor, the other permits parallel code to written. In order to support the parallelism of the machine this compiler has been extended to include a number of Fortran 90 features. Parallelisation of programs may either be done manually or automatically by a parallel optimiser. This optimiser is implemented as a preprocessor to the compiler. It analyses a serial program and performs a number of code transformations which include loop reordering and parallelisation. If required, the programmer may take the output from the precompiler to perform further parallelisations.

3.5.5   The Market Niche

The acquisition of CSD has caused Encore to reconsider its marketing policy. In a review which is still underway, they have decided to target specific industry niches, most of which are in the real-time and information systems markets. They see their aim as the creation of a family of shared memory, multiprocessor machines which will be able to compete with conventional computers running dusty-deck Fortran but with an improved price/performance ratio.

In 1988 a market research organisation, Dataquest, estimated that the real-time market worldwide was worth $1.4 G, of which 85% was for flight simulation, range/telemetry and energy management applications. The remaining 15% was for industrial and building automation and Encore does not, at present, compete in this sector. It is projected that the lower end of the real-time market will grow by 15% per annum over the next five years, while sales of more powerful machines are expected to increase by 26% per annum over the same period. Encore are targeting the revamped CONCEPT/32 towards these market sectors. However, the newer Encore 91 series discussed above is seen as complementing the CONCEPT range. It may be supposed that this machine will eventually take over from the aging CONCEPT design.

Similarly, Dataquest expect that the technical information systems market, which was worth approximately $2 G in 1988, to grow by 34% per annum to $6.3 G by 1992. The commercial information systems market is just as lucrative and growing even more quickly: $1.4 G in 1988 to $8.1 G in 1992. Encore believe that this expansion reflects the increasing standardisation of database software around Oracle and Ingres and the fact that UNIX has now become a *de facto* standard in government and commercial information systems markets. Encore hope that with the improved price/performance ratio offered by parallel processing, the ability of the Multimax to run Informix, Ingres, Unify and Oracle, and its standard UNIX operating system they will take a increased share of this market.

The Encore 91 is a few months away from volume shipments, and so any analysis of its success, or otherwise, will have to wait. However, the Multimax has been available since 1985 and to date over 1,000 machines have been sold. Approximately 75% of these are for technical applications, the remaining 25% to the commercial market. Relatively few machines are sold with fewer than four to six processors, or more than 10. However, purchasers still prefer to buy the Multimax 500, with its extra backplane space, to allow for future expansion.

The vast majority of these sales have been to the US. Until 1989 only some 25 machines had been placed within Europe, mostly in France. Over the last year, however, the rate of sales in Europe has grown rapidly with about 100 machines placed. This expansion has been largest in those countries in the north and west of Europe: the UK, Holland, Germany and France. There is, as yet, little exposure in Italy or the Iberian Peninsula.

3.5.6 The Competition

Approximately 75% of Multimax sales were to technical purchasers. Even here, buyers were generally not interested in parallelism *per se* but rather in the machine's general ability to support a number of users. Therefore, Encore do not usually find that they are competing with the highly parallel manufacturers, such as Thinking Machines (cf. 2.3) or NCUBE (cf. 4.2), although in the US Intel do sometimes provide competition when floating-point performance is important. Similarly, the transputer-based companies are not often seen as opposition. In Encore's opinion, these companies are still only of real interest to the most technically minded and demanding of customers, usually in the research field. Therefore, although some Multimax sales were made on the basis of the novelty of its architecture, the vast majority have been for running general applications.

The main competition in the technical market comes from DEC and IBM (with the RS/6000). To a lesser extent, Concurrent also provide competition, especially for repeat business, as do Convex (cf. 3.4) and Alliant (cf. 3.1). Unusually, Encore report that custom-built arrays of micros constructed by OEMs are also competitors on occasion. This is especially true for the more technical purchasers. Until about one year ago, Harris were also a major force in the US real-time market, although they have never had a great exposure in the UK and Europe. Nevertheless, they remain a potential threat for the new Encore 91.

In the commercial field, prospective purchasers are uninterested in the technology; they really only care about the available software. Consequently, in the UK both Honeywell Bull and ICL are selling well to local government and similar establishments, and provide the main competition to Encore.

3.5.7   The Future

The introduction of the Encore 91, expected in the last quarter of 1990, has already
been discussed. However, the same chip sets used in that machine are also to be
incorporated in the Multimax. Four Motorola 88100 chips will be mounted on a
board and up to eight of these cards can be fitted into the Multimax. This 32
processor machine is projected to have a performance of about 600 MIPS. Prices
have not yet been set for this new Multimax but Encore suggest that these may
not be very different from those at present. They view the new design as a complementary series to the Encore 91. Although at first the new base Multimax model
will be as powerful as the Encore 9104, in the longer term an Encore 91 with two
16 MHz 88100s will probably be made available to reduce the entry level price. Also
for the immediate future, Encore will stay with the Nanobus. Nevertheless, they
are aware of potential memory bandwidth problems and expect to replace this with
a(approximately ten times) faster alternative in the medium term. They claim that
they will be able to fit this new bus to existing machines when it becomes available.

At present, there are no fast graphics on the Multimax and Encore are aware
of this deficiency. They are in negotiations with potential partners to address this
problem, and are investigating a number of possibilities. However, they do not wish
to develop a product on their own.

DARPA have, as part of the teraFLOPS computer programme, contracted Encore to provide both software and hardware. Further details of how this is to be
achieved has still not been announced, but it will obviously involve more and faster
processors.

3.6   FPS Computing

Relevant Activities Manufacturer of vector and array processors.

Location Headquarters: FPS Computing, 3601 S.W. Murray Boulevard, Beaverton, Oregon 97005, USA. Telephone: (503) 641 3151, Fax: (503) 641 4497. European Sales and Support: FPS Computing, Apex House, London Road, Bracknell, Berkshire RG12 2TE, England. Telephone: 0344 56921, Fax: 0344 52412.

Relevant Officers C. Norman Winningstad, Chairman; Howard Thrailkill, President and CEO; Donald McDougall, Senior VP; Stephen Aanderud, VP Finance; Terry Heilman, VP Operations; Stephen Campbell, VP Marketing; Clark Masters, VP Engineering.

Employees Approximately 400 in the US and 20 in the UK.

Financial details Total capitalisation at the end of the 1989 financial year was $29 M. FPS are a publicly listed company on the New York and Pacific stock exchanges.

3.6.1   The Company

FPS Computing was formed in 1970 by Norman Winningstad, previously an employee of Tektronix. Originally, it was called Floating Point Systems Inc. and for about a decade was one of the major supercomputer manufacturers in the world. This fame was built upon three series of array processors which were built into other manufacturers' computers. They sold over 8,000 machines worldwide and FPS claimed that more applications software was written for these computers than all their competition combined.

Then in 1986 came the infamous FPS T Series. On paper, the T Series was to be the most powerful supercomputer ever built. It was a MIMD computer based upon the Inmos T414 transputer, the same chip as used in a variety of other machines, for example the Meiko Computing Surface (cf. 5.3). These were wired together in the form of a hypercube. Unlike the Computing Surface, in which the transputer performed both as compute engine and communications router, in the T series the T414 served merely for communication and control. Calculations were performed by Weitek vector processors, one of which together with a T414 formed a processing node. The vector processor had direct memory access to its transputer. The introduction of the Weitek processor had two effects: it gave a very large floating-point performance (nominally 16 MFLOPS at 64 bit precision) and it raised the cost by a large factor.

The addition of a four-way switch to each transputer link raised the number of interprocessor connections to 16, and set an architectural limit on the number of processors of 16384. Had such a machine been built it would have had a theoretical peak performance of approximately 200 GFLOPS and had a price tag in the region of $70 M.

In principle, this marriage of transputers and more powerful floating-point processors is an attractive one and forms the basis of the new i860-based computer from Meiko. Unfortunately, FPS made two mistakes. The first was to exaggerate the imbalance already existing within the transputer towards processing power over communications by adding a vector processor. These are data hungry devices, yet the transputer had hardly enough bandwidth to keep itself busy. Furthermore, FPS chose a hypercube wiring topology. In order to link more than 16 processor nodes together in this way required the number of interprocessor transputer links to be increased. This was accomplished by switching each transputer link through a four-way switch, which imposed significant connection overheads, thus slowing down interprocessor communications further. Moreover, in the first design only 1 Mbyte of memory was available for each processing node and this caused severe problems. It was rare, therefore, that the potential performance of the machine was realised.

The second error was to align with Occam. Originally, in an effort to wean users away from conventional IBM or DEC computers, Occam was the only language offered, though Fortran and C were added later. While Occam did have advantages for parallel programming, the majority of users, and almost all commercial customers, were unhappy with the idea of having to rewrite existing code and declined the opportunity to embrace the new language. These feelings were strongest in the US. The response of FPS was to plan Occam courses and sponsor research projects into Occam applications. In the last few years all computer companies who once espoused Occam have changed direction to emphasise Fortran and C. The machine parallelism has then been expressed by either introducing extensions to the language definitions or providing run-time libraries to handle interprocessor communications (cf. 9.3 and 9.4).

Transputer-based companies, such as Meiko, who were building relatively cheap computers could survive in the period before these new high-level compilers became available by selling machines to academic establishments. However, the FPS T Series, with its more expensive vector processors, was aimed at a rather different, and largely more conservative market. Most prospective purchasers did not want to have to rewrite existing code or retrain staff and so sales were few. The failure of the T Series is cited by some as having given the transputer a bad name in the US. In 1987 the T Series was taken off the market, at which point it was estimated that at least a further $15 – 20 M was required to complete the development work.

In retrospect, FPS believe that the T Series had a good hardware design which set a trend for future computers by using commercially available chips in order to reduce development times and costs. Unfortunately, they misjudged the conservatism of prospective purchasers and introduced the machine before the software environment and suitable algorithms were ready. This problem was exacerbated by bad management within FPS: the initial hardware design had been contracted to an outside company and beta test versions of the T Series were not available in time for sufficient system software to be developed.

After the massive investment of money and effort into the development of the T Series with little or no return, FPS went through a period of restructuring. This resulted in an almost completely new top management, massive cut-backs in staff, projects were streamlined and the sale of buildings and assets contemplated, though never carried out. First signs of a possible resurgence came in 1988 with the change of company name to FPS Computing and the launch of a new machine, the Model 500. This machine was based upon a design from Celerity: a company which had been founded by ex-NCR staff and which was selling reasonable numbers of UNIX machines to the US and Germany. Unfortunately, they experienced financial difficulties while waiting for a new chip set to be produced, and were taken over by FPS. The Model 500 was the outcome of the merger. It has sold well initially and has recently attracted $14.5 M of new funding into FPS from an institutional investor. It is described in more detail below.

In the era of the T Series FPS saw themselves as a company led by the technology. However, with the advent of the Model 500 it has returned to its traditional home as being market driven, and here it intends to stay.

3.6.2   The Machine

The Model 500 was introduced in late 1988, since when it has undergone a number of hardware and name changes. It was designed to be a modular machine with scalar and vector processors, the numbers of which could be expanded as the user's requirements grew. This modularity is central to FPS's policy, to enable users to upgrade their machines with new hardware as this becomes available without having to change their software or replace the entire computer.

FPS adopted a shared memory design, believing that this made the machine easier to use. The T Series used distributed memory, as do most of today's parallel machines. However, FPS believe that it is difficult to port existing serial code onto such computers. The system memory was (and still is) implemented in commercially available DRAM, and may be extended to 1 Gbyte from a minimum of 32 Mbyte. Access is via a number of 64 bit wide data paths and is clocked at 33 MHz.

Task assignments to the scalar or vector processors are controlled by system software, so that the architecture of the machine is transparent to the user. This allows code to be ported from one Model 500 to any other after a simple recompilation. Both the scalar and vector processors were custom hardware and connected together by a bus designed by FPS.

The design of the machine is centred around the Scalable Interconnect Architecture (SIA). This has remained essentially constant during the last couple of years and despite the other hardware changes implemented. It is basically a bus designed by FPS which connects the various processors to each other and to memory. Two versions are available: one utilises a 64 bit wide data path clocked at 33 MHz, giving a bandwidth of 267 Mbyte/s. The faster alternative uses four of these buses in parallel, giving a total bandwidth in excess of 1 Gbyte/s.

The first upgrade came in November 1989, when the vector processor was improved. This new unit was based upon the Bipolar Integrated Technologies (BIT) ECL floating-point chip set with custom designed memory management hardware from FPS to allow it to be interfaced to the rest of the machine. The new machine was called the Model 500EA (EA is short for Expandable system Architecture). Various different models within the 500EA range had up to four scalar and two vector processors, though the total number of processors is limited to a maximum of four.

In June 1990 FPS unveiled an agreement with Sun to include the ECL version of the SPARC chip (actually manufacturered by BIT) as the scalar processor in a new range to be known as the System 500[4]. This machine will not be commercially available until the beginning of 1991 and in the interim full details of its construction are not available. It is clear, however, that FPS believe that it represents their greatest hope for the future. This new range can only be supported by the faster SIA.

The SPARC is a RISC based chip with an 80 MHz clock speed, though in the System 500 it will probably be run at about 67 MHz. Nevertheless, it is estimated that it will enhance the performance of scalar operations within the System 500 by a factor of two. Since the SPARC chip is to be clocked at approximately twice the rate of the SIA, buffering is included in the interface hardware. In addition, the SPARC chip is smaller than the previous hardware and this has permitted FPS to increase the maximum number of scalar processors in the machines to 8. It also permits the use of a large range of third party software.

At the same time as the decision to use the SPARC was made known, a matrix co-processor was announced to complement the scalar and vector units. This matrix co-processor has the power to lift the System 500 into the realm of true supercomputing. It is designed around an array of Intel i860 chips, which were chosen because FPS felt that they represented the best opportunity for a clear future upgrade path. The i860 is a 40 MHz RISC based CPU which includes 4 kbyte code and 8 kbyte data caches. It has a peak floating-point performance of 40 – 80 MFLOPS (manufacturer's figures). Each matrix co-processor may contain between four and 84 i860 processors (PEs). These are arranged along a seven buses, or

---

[4]One extra benefit of this to FPS was a joint marketing agreement with Sun.

vectors (Figure 3.5), and interfaced to memory through an 8×8 crossbar switch. To supplement the system memory the matrix co-processors have their own 32 or 64 Mbyte Matrix Registers. These are designed to provide high-speed, temporary storage for frequently used data. This memory is implemented in SRAM and has eight independent ports which may be accessed concurrently. Up to two matrix co-processors may be fitted into the System 500 architecture. This gives an estimated peak performance of 13.4 GFLOPS for the top model in the range.

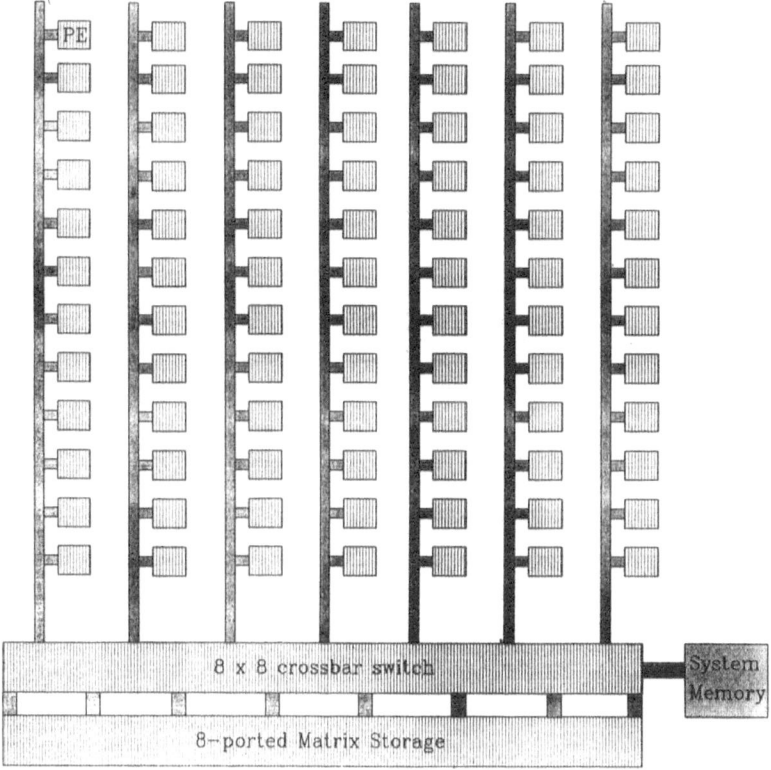

Figure 3.5: The System 500 Matrix Co-Processor

A little thought will show that in order to realise the full benefits of the co-processor the tasks must have a very high ratio of computation to data transfer. The maximum bandwidth between PEs and memory along each vector is 160 Mbyte/s. Tasks are distributed amongst the vectors and pass along the bus until taken by the first free PE. If we take 60 MFLOPS as the peak performance of the i860, and we know that for a full 84 node system the bandwidth per processor is ~ 13 Mbyte/s then, for a full vector of 12 PEs, each processor must perform about 15 floating-point operations for every single precision word received, if all are to be kept busy. Such a large ratio is unusual and it, therefore, restricts the range of applications which can be efficiently ported on to the matrix co-processor. This imbalance between floating-point performance and memory bandwidth is, unfortunately, not unusual.

Also connected to the SIA is an I/O controller to which may be connected a number of I/O devices, the aggregate bandwidth of which is 80 Mbyte/s. In common with the design of the rest of the machine, FPS claim that the I/O controller is implemented in a manner which allows its hardware to be replaced when better alternatives become available. Standard bus interfaces, such as VME and Multibus are provided and it is planned to introduce HiPPI and FDDI in the near future. Ethernet, X.25 and the usual serial line drivers for up to 16 devices are also supported. However, it is not possible to connect high speed graphics monitors directly to the System 500. Until now, FPS have offered fast visualisation on a range of FPS graphics engines which communicate directly with the Model 500/500EA through a dedicated channel. However, in order to preserve binary compatibility the use of SPARC-based Sun workstations with graphics accelerators is now being advocated for the System 500.

Provision has, however, been made for fast disc access since this is seen as central for many of the applications areas targeted by the System 500. A new disc subsystem, the IPI-2, has recently been announced with 6 Mbyte/s disc transfers which can be striped to give $\sim$ 20 Mbyte/s. The largest discs have a 16 Gbyte capacity.

Apparently, all Model 500 machines sold have now been upgraded to the Model 500EA. FPS do not anticipate an imminent halt to the production of the Model 500EA in favour of the System 500, but expect that users will tend to prefer the software environment and power of the latter. They do expect, therefore, that sales of the older model will gradually decline.

3.6.3   The Development System

For the Model 500EA FPS designed FPX, an implementation of Berkeley UNIX 4.3 or 4.4BSD. Now, with the introduction of the System 500, they have moved to SunOS running on the SPARC chips. FPX will not be upgraded in line with future developments, although it will continue to be the only operating system available on the Model 500EA. FPS expect that in time the ever-widening differences between FPX and SunOS will influence purchaser's choices. The provision of UNIX on the scalar processors means that users have the availity to develop code in a standard environment with the commonly used editors and other such tools available.

To aid code debugging and profiling FPS have extended the scope of the normal UNIX tools. Parallel versions of dbx have been written to provide symbolic and assembly language debuggers, called dbxp and adbp respectively. Similar extensions to gprof are also provided to permit users profile parallel codes.

3.6.4   Programming Languages

Fortran, Pascal and C compilers are available for the scalar and vector processors. Assignments to specific types of processors (i.e. scalar, vector or matrix as available) is made by the compiler on the basis of the size of the data structure used. Although users can access the different processors directly, they are not encouraged to do this, as this reduces code portability. Rather it is suggested that compiler directives and calls to the appropriate run-time libraries are used to implement the parallelism in a transparent manner. FPS provides versions of most libraries, optimised for the Model/System 500, including the FPSMath library, which includes 300 routines, including FFTs, matrix and vector manipulations.

The concurrent Fortran compiler, conFORm, is ANSI Fortran 77 compatible and includes most of the more popular VMS extensions. It provides parallel functionality for systems with multiple scalar and/or vector processors and implements a number of optimising features, for example loop reordering and peeling. The compiler was written by FPS in conjunction with Pacific Sierra (for the vectorisation) and Kuck and Associates (for parallelisation). Vectorisation of an application program is achieved by first passing it through conFORm and performing a vectorisation pass. This automatically generates Fortran 90 vector notation to replace scalar constructs wherever possible. Parallelisation is achieved in a similar manner. Normally, this is hidden from the user who simply compiles the code with vector or parallelising options as appropriate. However, it is possible to perform further vector/parallelisations manually on intermediate output files.

The compiler has not been validated for the i860-based matrix co-processor. Work is underway in conjunction with The Portland Group (a company founded by members from the FPS array processor compiler team) to produce this software. The major problem is efficiency: no compiler for the i860 has yet produced code which achieved more than 10% of its peak performance. Consequently, it has been necessary to code CPU intensive code for the i860, such as the FPSMath library, in assembly language. In this, of course, FPS are not alone, the identical problem has been faced by all other i860 users, including Intel (cf. 4.1) themselves. FPS do, however, have an advantage that they have considerable experience with compilers and libraries for their array processors, which had a similar architecture the the i860.

3.6.5   The Market Niche

FPS are very specific about their marketplace. They see themselves as producing high performance computers for scientific and engineering establishments who are interested in running established codes, rather than developing new programs. This usually means that the machine must be capable of coping with dusty-deck Fortran. Consequently, FPS have produced a computer in which the parallelism is hidden from the user, and thus appears to have a standard architecture. This apparent conventionality is a keystone in FPS's strategy to provide a computer targeted at the general computing market. Those portions of the application which are CPU intensive may be coded using calls to run-time library routines. In this attitude one may perceive that the lesson of the T Series has been well learnt and FPS are now offering to commercial customers an apparently conventional number cruncher. The adoption of UNIX as the operating system is regarded by FPS as simply a recognition of the demands of the market, which have been accepted by almost all other manufacturers.

The principal areas targeted for sales are computational chemistry, finite-element calculations, computational fluid dynamics and seismic analysis. They believe that the major algorithms used by these customers which can benefit from the System 500 are FFTs and dense matrix manipulations. Large packages, such as NASTRAN and ABAQUS, containing many hundreds of thousand of line of code, were written in the days of serial machines and rely upon a few CPU intensive and tightly coded routines. It is claimed that few fully understand the operation of these sections and that this has hampered parallelisation of such packages. Much time was spent by FPS on trying to parallelise molecular modelling code for the T Series, without conspicuous success. However, with the more conventional architecture of the System 500 it is possible to port large packages with a minimum of effort.

Table 3.3, below, shows the distribution of the sales of the earlier Model 500EA divided by type of purchasing body.

Table 3.3: Sales of the Model 500EA by Centre and Geography

Site	No.(US/Canada)	No.(Europe)	No.(Far East)
University/Research Lab.	13	6	1
Govt. Laboratory	3	1	1
Industry	10	3	8

The major application areas for these machines are shown in Table 3.4 below. The numbers now refer to institutions, rather than machines.

3.6.6 The Competition

With their move away from the T Series, FPS are clear that the massively parallel manufacturers, such as TMC (cf. 2.3) and NCUBE (cf. 4.2), are no longer in the same marketplace. Most competition comes from the other minisupercomputer makers, such as Convex (cf. 3.4) and Alliant (cf. 3.1), as well as the large conventional machines made by IBM and DEC. The spread of prices means that at the top end of the product range low-end Crays (cf. 7.1) are also possible opposition.

Table 3.4: Major Interest Areas of Model 500EA Purchasers

Application	No.(US/Canada)	No.(Europe)	No.(Far East)
Computational Chemistry	9	1	1
Petroleum/Seismic	7	1	0
Design Engineering	6	2	4
Signal Processing	2	1	3
General Scientific	2	5	2

When the System 500 with matrix co-processor becomes commercially available it is anticipated that competition with Cray Research Inc. may increase.

At present, FPS accept that purchasers, especially those with substantial budgets, are more likely to be attracted to machines from IBM, DEC or Cray than from FPS because of the greater level of system integration and management services offered by these companies. It is hoped, however, that this situation will change as the technology develops and the price/performance advantage offered by companies such as FPS who use standard chip sets increases. FPS state that they have developed a machine as powerful as the projected Convex C3 in a third of the time by their use of commercially available chips. These chips have the added advantage of having a range of third party software available. Furthermore, they believe that, today, only IBM and DEC have the power to forge their own standards and that Cray may soon have problems if they persist with custom designed hardware.

3.6.7 The Future

The T Series was meant to be a teraFLOPS computer, but FPS now state that they would not design such a machine in that fashion today. Moreover, they believe that the world is not ready for the teraFLOPS machine, because the software hurdle is still too high. Furthermore, FPS do not believe that it represents a worthwhile marketing opportunity. Future developments will, therefore, concentrate upon upgrading the performance of their heterogeneous architecture as newer processors become available from commercial suppliers.

3.7   Sequent Computer Systems

Relevant Activities Designs, manufactures and markets high performance general purpose computers.

Location Software design and European sales: Weybridge Business Park, Addlestone Road, Weybridge Kent KT15 2UF. Telephone: 0932 859833. Headquarters: Beverton, Oregon. Hardware development and production: Beverton, Oregon, USA. Telephone: (503) 626 5700

Relevant Officers Karl C. Powell Jr, Chairman and CEO; C. Scott Gibson, President and Chief Operating Officer; Dr Larry L. Evans, VP of Manufacturing; Robert S. Gregg, VP of Finance, Treasurer and Chief Financial Officer; Walter L. Mayberry, VP of Systems Engineering; Michael D. Simon, VP of Marketing; Robert M. Tanner, VP of Worldwide Sales.

Employees 130 (Europe), 70 (UK), 1295 (US and Canada)

Financial details Total revenues have risen to $237 M in the last four years. Net earnings are predicted to double to $12 M in 1990. Total capitalisation in 1990 is $100.7 M. Unisys, Prime and Siemens have signed long-term agreements to buy and resell Sequent machines. Matsushita has chosen Sequent as its partner for high-end business computing.

3.7.1   The Company

Sequent make a range of high performance general purpose computers based on a multiprocessor architecture. Through the concurrent operation of up to 30 microprocessors, Sequent systems deliver the price/performance advantages of microprocessor technology to applications that require computational power previously available only from mainframe systems.

The company was founded in 1983 when Karl C. Powell persuaded 16 fellow Intel (cf. Section 4.1) engineers and marketers to resign and each set aside $98,000, for Sequent's $1.6 M startup capital. Powell resigned from Intel because he could not persuade Intel to develop multiprocessor systems instead of concentrating only on microprocessor design and fabrication. Intel did not have Powell's confidence in his belief that he could design an efficient multiprocessor with the microprocessor technology currently available. The scenario is similar to the creation of Meiko from Inmos. When Powell left Intel 32 bit microprocessors were just starting to appear on the market. They predicted, like many others, that this new technology would have a dramatic impact on the architecture of fast computers. They felt that by exploiting parallelism they could use this technology to compete with the "big boys" selling mainframe and minicomputers.

Building a bus-based multiprocessor computer is not difficult; the challenge is getting an increase in speed proportional to the number of processors. Historically, if there were more than four processors bus arbitration and cache coherency became such an overhead that adding more processors did not improve overall speed. Many computer manufacturers attempted to build a multiprocessor computers and failed. Burroughs, now part of Unisys, spent millions of pounds developing large multiprocessor machines that never really worked.

Whilst most of these manufacturers had tried to build new high-speed components, Sequent built their machine from standard chips, which allowed them to bring their product to market in only two years. Sequent's design team knew that using microprocessors together effectively depended on ways to coordinate them, which was more a question of software than hardware assuming technology could provide a fast enough bus. Where Sequent succeeded and others failed was in developing a version of UNIX which allowed different resources to be allocated simultaneously. In effect, Sequent divided up the main operating system into many small operating systems, each capable of allocating resources, so that each processor does not have to wait to have its resource request filled.

Sequent introduced its first product in 1984 at the annual Cowen & Co. technology conference in Boston. Sequent claimed that in its UNIX based computer, powered by two to 12 microprocessors, it had solved the problem of getting several processors working together efficiently on a single problem. At the time, DEC founder Kenneth Olsen dismissed Sequent's technology as an 'academic curiosity'. In the context of the multiprocessor technology market in the early 1980's, this was an acceptable comment; today, his opinion has changed.

Powell is quoted to have said, "We have to get big fast or we're going to get stuffed." Sequent is certainly trying to get big, and it is doing it by targeting the commercial market in the same way as Sun chased the technical sector. Sequent has commercial accounts with firms like Coca-Cola, Enterprises West, Dollar Rent-A-Car, Reebok Shoes and Apple Computer. In 1988 Sequent expanded its strategic partnerships with the leading relational database software companies: Informix, Oracle, Progress, Relational Technology, and Unify. In December 1988 Sequent and Matsushita formed a joint venture, Pana-Sequent, which is expected to generate $100 M in revenue over the next five years.

3.7.2 The Machine

The Sequent series is an MIMD machine which supports inter-processor communication via shared memory. All processors share a single pool of memory, which allows resource sharing and communication between different processes. The Sequent machine supports both fine and coarse-grain parallelism. The programmer identifies segments of an application that can be broken into multiple concurrent

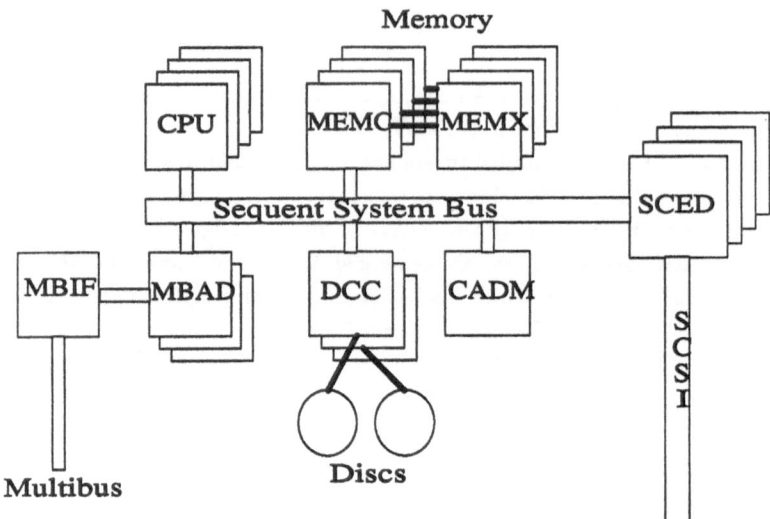

Figure 3.6: Sequent's Multiprocessor Architecture

threads. Using routines from the Parallel Programming Enviroment, the programmer maps his data structures into shared memory for shared access among threads.
The tightly coupled architecture is shown in Figure 3.6.

Sequent currently sells two series of machine, the Balance (B8 and B21) and
Symmetry (S27 and S81). All of these are built around the same high-speed bus.
Different devices can be connected to this bus, so that the family's architecture can
be tailored to a variety of different applications.

The 8 byte wide system bus with a 10 MHz clock rate, yields a channel bandwidth of 80 Mbyte/s. 32 or 64 bit data and 32 bit addresses are time-multiplexed on
the 64 bit bus. Operations are pipelined so that the bus is available following a read
or write request for other transactions before system memory issues its response.

The Balance Series, based on the 32 bit National Semiconductor 32032 processor, has remained unchanged since its conception in 1986. Today, the number of
processors in a B8 machine ranges between two and 12, and in a B21 between four
and 30. A Balance processor card carries two complete CPU subsystems, each of
which contains an NS32032 with a floating point co-processor, 8 kbyte of cache
memory, and all necessary memory-mapping chips. The B8 still features a range
in main memory between 2 and 28 Mbyte, while the B27 offers between 8 and 28
Mbyte. The main difference between the two Balance machine, apart from processor numbers, is main memory and the number of MULTIBUS slots. While the B8
and B21 performance range runs from the MicroVax to three times the Vax 8700,

the Symmetry system's performance peaks at 150 MIPS, well into the supermini and mainframe range. Symmetry machines can support over 1000 simultaneous users.

The S27 and S81 contain two to 30 tightly coupled Intel 80386 microprocessors on dual-processor boards. To maximise performance, the Symmetry architecture permits each CPU to operate at near full speed with a minimum interference from other CPUs. Since the 80386 was not intended for a multiprocessor environment, Sequent designed support circuitry to isolate each CPU from the complications of the multiprocessor environment. This circuitry includes a System Link Controller (SLIC) chip designed by Sequent, which mediates the CPU's communication with other CPUs and subsystems over the SLIC bus. In addition, the CPU can be supported by an optional Weitek floating-point accelerator.

The 10 MHz system bus, takes three cycles to complete a 16 kbyte read or write operation. That is 5.33 byte transferred per cycle, which gives a peak bus performance of 53.3 Mbyte/s. Big caches reduce this bus traffic by 50%. An integral memory management unit supports a virtual address range of 256 Mbyte per process regardless of physical memory size. Common to both series are the two hardware locking mechanisms. The global lock mechanism is used in the Symmetry and Balance series operating with a write-through cache policy. Any four-byte word of system memory can be locked while it is accessed by a special "read-modify-write" operation. An interlock signal is asserted on the system bus during the read, and then removed during the write.

While this signal is asserted other processors or I/O interfaces are blocked from performing locked operations in memory. Blocked processors create no additional traffic on the system bus, so global locking does not degrade system bus performance. However, there is conflict between competing devices that attempt to access the bus simultaneously; this scenario is known as bus contention. Bus contention problems, for both the Balance and Symmetry series are controlled by the "clock/arbitration" board called the CADM board. The board generates the bus clock signals and control arbitration for the other boards on the bus. When contending for the bus, boards in the High-priority slots have priority over boards in the Low-priority slots. Low-priority slots include the dual processor boards, whereas High-priority slots are peripheral controllers: MULTIBUS adapters, SCSI/Ethernet/Diagnostic (SCED) boards and Dual Disc Controllers (DDC). Memory boards can be placed in either high or low priority slots.

The parallel lock mechanism is used in Sequent systems operating under a "copy-back" cache policy. 16 byte regions of processor cache memory can be locked to allow multiple simultaneous locking operations at system level. The most notable technological changes to the Sequent series have been the increases in cache memory size. This has grown from 8 kbyte in 1984, to a 64 kbyte 2-way set associative cache in 1987, to 128 kbyte caches in 1989. A number of peripheral slots have increased as well, emphasising the general purpose nature Sequent set out to achieve. However, Sequent have not upgraded the Intel 80386 microprocessor to one more suitable for multiprocessing.

3.7.3   The Operating System

Sequent provides a multiprocessing operating system called DYNIX, a form of UNIX which has been enhanced to exploit parallel architectures. DYNIX was first designed for the B8 in 1984. It has been so successful that Sequent has formed a new company, called Subsequent, to move the software developed for Sequent's computers to standard single-processor PCs.

In a uniprocessor UNIX system, a process that is ready to run is placed in a "run queue". When the CPU halts execution of one process the CPU moves on to the next process in the run queue. DYNIX uses the same technique, except that more than one CPU is available to dispatch processes from the run queue.

The bottleneck which would occur in a master/slave system is avoided because all processors in the Sequent series are identical. Each processor can simultaneously execute both user code and kernel (operating system) code. Processors automatically schedule themselves so that all are working as long as there are processes to execute. Load balancing can also be controlled explicitly by the user, a type of scheduling algorithm known as prescheduling. In prescheduling, the task division is determined by the programmer before the program is compiled. Prescheduled programs cannot automatically balance the computing load according to the data or the number of processors in the system. Therefore, this method is only appropriate for function partitioning applications, where each process is performing a different task.

While the mechanics of DYNIX have not changed since its release in 1984, there have been several enhancement releases which have included a variety of parallel software development tools. For example, Sequent's Fortran compiler was extended to include a preprocessor to support microtasking, the fine-grained parallelism typically found in program loops or array operations. Sequent claim that with this extension many Fortran programs can be parallelised in a matter of minutes.

To make inter-process communication through shared memory easier Sequent have extended their C compiler to include two extra data types, "shared" and "private", to allow programmers to create and reference variables in shared memory. DYNIX has recently been updated to support both UNIX 4.2BSD and UNIX System V command sets. In the near future performance debuggers will be available, to help resolve speedup problems.

3.7.4   Programming languages

Programming languages supported by Sequent include C, Fortran 77, Pascal, Lisp, and (since early 1988) Ada and Cobol. The presence of Cobol emphasises Sequent's bias towards the business market. DYNIX provides a common debugger for C, Fortran, Pascal, or any combination of these languages. Ada and Cobol include language-specific debuggers.

Different processes can communicate through shared memory using techniques originally developed for uniprocessor computers. DYNIX allows processes to share a common region of system memory. Any process that has access to such a region can read or write in it as it would in ordinary memory. The DYNIX model for parallel programming consists of a virtual multiprocessor running on a physical multiprocessor. The virtual machine consists of N virtual processors which may be assigned to execute the tasks in the parallel application. The kernel is responsible for scheduling fine-grain tasks onto virtual processors, just as the system-wide DYNIX operating system is responsible for scheduling processes onto physical processors. The tasks in a parallel application can communicate with each other and share data through shared memory. The programmer can use the hardware-based mutual exclusion mechanisms to ensure that dependencies between tasks are preserved.

In Fortran programs, most loops are implemented as DO loops, so Sequent has provided a parallel preprocessor that automatically converts selected Fortran DO loops to execute in parallel. To indicate that a loop is to be executed in parallel, the programmer inserts a special comment line in front of the DO statement. For example:

```
DO 100 I= 1,N
  DO 100 J=1,N
    C(I,J) = 0.0
    DO 100 K=1,N
      C(I,J) = C(I,J) + A(I,K) * B(K,J)
100 CONTINUE
```

is converted to parallel code by inserting the line

```
C$DOACROSS SHARE(A,B,C,N), LOCAL(J,K)
```

in front of the first DO statement. To parallize the loop on I, the variables A, B, C, and N must be shared by all processes executing the parallel code, but J and K are scratch variables used locally within the loop.

A recent extension to Sequent's Symmetry model is the KAP/Sequent restructuring preprocessor. This is an optimising preprocessor which identifies potential parallelism within Fortran code and restructures the code for parallel execution on a Sequent system. Its optimisation includes recognition of DYNIX Parallel Programming Library calls. It is not clear how much speedup is achieved after optimisation. Code optimisation also available for C programs, which includes the forking of threads. Sequent emphasise the explicit parallelism of their machine as well as the transparent multiprocessing benefits that increase throughput and multiuser performance, despite being bias towards the commercial market.

3.7.5   The Market Niche

Sequent's management initially thought that their niche would be the technical market targeted by Sun. However, the company is now attacking the much larger business automation transaction processing market. This market involves online transaction processing, which includes accounting and database management programs. By building itself on two new technologies, the microprocessor and UNIX, and taking them into large markets where the competition is selling older hardware and software technology, Sequent have managed to expand from a total revenue of $38.5 M in 1987 to $145.6 M in 1989. Net income per share has increased from 27 to 82 cents in the last three years, while equity per share has increased by about $3 to a current value of about $5.5. Sequent now has installed systems in 28 countries;

Sequent's success in the commercial market place reflects the convergence of major trends in the computer industry. One of these is the growing power of off-the-shelf micro-processors, such as Intel's new 80486. The low cost of these components is reflected in the low cost of the finished product — a fully equipped Sequent Symmetry S81, with 30 Intel 80386 processors, costs around $1 M, 48% cheaper than a comparable DEC Vax 6240. Another is industry's gradual move toward UNIX as the standard operating system for everything from PCs to mainframes. Serious competition in the UNIX world is inevitable, but at this early stage in development there is excellent growth potential for the companies with the right technology and marketing.

However, new hardware architecture only become commercially successful once application software technology emerges to take advantage of that architecture. For Sequent, that software is transaction processing applications utilising fourth generation languages and SQL databases. Companies that sell 4GL and SQL technology, such as Oracle, Informix and Unify are Sequent's most important strategic partners. Most purchasers of Sequent machines buy the machine in order to utilise this new software technology in developing applications.

3.7.6 The Competition

Sequent systems have three advantages: they are fast; they have a clean implementation of UNIX; and they have good transparent scheduling algorithms for parallel processing. But success has bred imitation. Sequent is already confronting other parallel computer makers such as Pyramid and Arix. Another competitor, Icon Systems and Software, are targetting the same business niche as Sequent and are currently building a 128 to 256 user machine running UNIX and MS/DOS on 80386 chips concurrently. Both DEC and IBM are expanding their investment in UNIX systems, while re-sellers such as Unisys and Prime could come out with competing multiprocessing machines.

In response, Sequent is continuing to broaden and improve its product range. The Balance Series has been superseded by the Symmetry Series and shall soon be eliminated from the market. All Balance systems can be upgraded to Symmetry machines. Subsequent, Sequent's newly formed business unit, is attempting to capture the uni-processor market. In January 1990 Subsequent released the S3, which runs DYNIX and can support up to 32 transaction-intensive users. Meanwhile, Sequent expects to incorporate the Intel 80486 into their Symmetry series by the beginning of 1991, and DYNIX itself is currently being upgraded to enhance system performance, make it easier to use, improve its networking capabilities and provide the system security needed for many government and commercial applications. Sequent believes DYNIX will be an important edge as more hardware vendors introduce multiprocessor systems.

3.7.7 The Future

Sequent will focus more sharply on the lucrative commercial computing environment. Sequent's addition of Cobol to the programming environment reinforces Sequent's bias towards business automation machines. In particular Sequent continue to pursue the transaction processing market, which relies increasingly on Relational Database Management Systems. The demand for RDMS is still growing by well over 50% a year. In the future Sequent hope to provide the high performance required by relational database management systems.

Company Summary 4: Features of the Alliant FX/2800

Type	Symmetric vector multiprocessor with shared memory
Availability	Over 550 installations worldwide have Alliant products.
Price	From £350 k for an eight processor FX/2800 system to £1.5 M for the FX/2828 with 28 processors.
Processing nodes	Up to 14 SCEs and up to 14 SIPS per system.
Processor technology	RISC (i860) based. Scalar integer and floating-point, pipelined vector and concurrency control operations.
Memory	4 Gbyte virtual address space. Maximum physical memory 1 Gbyte.
Communications	The processors communicate through shared memory.
I/O connections	Up to 16 VME or Image Memory subsystems, plus Ethernet and other LAN.
Performance	Peak performance: up to 1.12 GFLOPS (64 bit), 24 Mwhetstone per processor.
Operating System	Concentrix (Berkeley 4.3BSD UNIX with parallel extensions). AT&T System V.4 UNIX.
Programming Languages	FX/Fortran – Fortran 77 standard, with Fortran 90 extensions, FX/Ada, FX/C and Assembler.
Physical configuration	System cabinet 29.5″ × 43.5″ × 33.8″, weighing 430 kg. I/O expansion cabinet 24.5″ × 43.5″ × 33.8″, 450 kg.
Power Requirements	8-12 kW for a full FX/2828 configuration.
Sources	Alliant literature, discussions with company staff.

Company Summary 5: Features of the BBN ACI TC2000

Source	BBN Advanced Computers Inc.
Type	Coarse-grained, shared-memory MIMD processor aimed at the time critical and supercomputing markets.
Availability	Commercial deliveries of the first generation Butterfly started in 1981. The TC2000 became available in 1989. The largest machine sold to date is one with 126 processors to the Lawrence Livermore National Laboratory.
Price	The list price for an 16 node machine is approximately $1 M, while that for a "typical" 32 processor TC2000 is about $2 M.
Processing nodes	Each node is a Motorola 88100 RISC processor with three 16 kbyte 88200 cache/memory management chips.
Processors	The 88100 is engineered in sub-micron CMOS and supports a 20 MHz clock rate.
Memory	Each node contains 48 kbyte of cache memory and between 4 and 16 Mbyte of DRAM.
Communications	The Butterfly switch providing point-to-point interprocessor communications is custom designed by BBN ACI and implemented as ECL gate arrays. Each data path is one byte wide and operates at 38 MHz.
I/O connections	Up to 40 VME slots may be configured on a 64 node TC2000. This gives a maximum aggregate bandwidth of 320 Mbyte/s. Provision is also made for either 16 or 32 serial ports and Ethernet connection.
Performance	The 88100 is rated at 15 single precision Whetstone MIPS and 35,000 Dhrystone/s. This gives the 64 processor TC2000 a peak speed of 960 Whetstone MIPS. (Manufacturer's figures).
Host system	None.
Operating system	Both nX, an implementation of Berkeley UNIX 4.3BSD, and pSOS^{+m} for real-time or time critical applications, are available.

Programming languages Fortran, C and Ada. Also a run-time library of routines to support the machine parallelism.

Physical configuration   The 16 processor system has external dimensions of 68.5 × 38 × 65.5 inches, it weighs 1280 lb. Groups of extra 8 processors may be added in expansion modules, these are 68.5 × 38 × 9.3 inches and weigh 333 lb.

Power dissipation   Eight processor TC2000, 5.7 kW; 64 processor model, 34 kW. Cooling is provided by internal fans.

Sources   Publicly available documentation together with discussions with users and interviews with current and past BBN staff.

Company Summary 6: Features of the Concurrent 3280E MPS

Type	Shared memory multiprocessor.
Availability	Several thousand machines installed since 1982.
Price	Tens to hundreds of thousands of dollars.
Processing nodes	From 2 to 12 proprietary 3280 processors.
Processor technology	16 kword microprogrammed, 4 stage pipelined scalar processor.
Memory	CMOS, 256 kbyte or 1 Mbyte DRAM, 2 or 4 way interleaved.
Communications	Common System Bus, 2 independent 32-bit data paths.
I/O connections	Up to 4 I/O buses, and up to 12 direct interfaces; total I/O throughput of 120 Mbyte/s.
Performance	Between 12 and 70 MIPS of scalar processing performance and up to 14 MFLOPS of vector performance.
Operating system	OS/32, real-time, interrupt-driven.
Programming languages	Fortran 77, C^3Ada, Cobol, C, Pascal, BASIC II and CAL/CAL MACRO assemblers.
Physical configuration	Three 71" cabinets.
Power requirements	Max. 8 kW per cabinet.
Sources	Concurrent brochures, conversations with company personnel.

Company Summary 7: Features of the Convex C2

Type	Multiprocessor-tightly coupled, shared memory, highly pipelined with scalar and vector units.
Availability	600 system installed worldwide in 33 countries with 375 customers.
Price	Range between $300 k and $2 M for C1 to C240 machines
Processing Nodes	One to four processors.
Processor Technology	64 bit integrated scalar/vector processors with 40 ns processor cycle time. The scalar unit uses ECL; the rest is CMOS technology.
Memory System	Maximum physical memory 2 Gbtye, 64-way maximum interleaved with a cycle time of 320 ns/40 ns.
Communications	I/O bus ranges from 200 Mbyte/s to 80 Mbyte/s, 64 bit wide.
I/O Communications	Ethernet and DR11-W; networked to workstations from Landmark Graphics and Sun. Supports TCP/IP, FTP, TENET, COVUEnet, NFS and HYPERchannel.
Performance	200 MFLOPS peak on a 32 bit Whetstone benchmark.
Host System	None.
Operating System	Convex UNIX: multi user interactive environment.
Language Support	CCC, Fortran 77, Ada, Vax Fortran, Cray Fortran.
Physical Requirements	System cabinet: 62.5″ × 60.0″ × 39.5″ Weight: 1600 lbs
Power Requirements	C1 Series requires 9.3 to 12.3 kW; C2 Series requires 17.1 to 29.1 kW.
Sources	Company literature and discussions with Convex UK personnel.

Company Summary 8: Features of the Encore Multimax and Encore 91

Source	Encore Computer Corporation.
Type	Coarse-grained, shared memory MIMD processor.
Availability	The first Multimax was delivered in 1985. It is expected that the Encore 91 will be ready for shipping around the end of 1990.
Price	Multimax prices range from $89 k to over $1 M. Prices are not yet set for the Encore 91, but it is expected that the entry level machine will sell for approximately $50 – 60 k.
Processing nodes	The Multimax 300 uses a NS32332 CPU with a NS32081 FPU and a Weitek 1164/1165 (optional). The Multimax 500 uses a NS32532 CPU with a NS32381 FPU. The Encore 91 uses a Motorola 88100 RISC processor with two, or four, 88200 CMMUs.
Processors	The 88100 is engineered using Motorola's HCMOS technology.
Memory	Shared memory implemented in DRAM, up to 80 Mbyte in the Multimax 310 and 510 (160 Mbyte in the 520), 272 Mbyte in the Encore 91.
Communications	Interprocessor communications use a 100 Mbyte/s bus designed by Encore. The Encore 91 also uses a VME bus to connect to extra memory, or to other computers.
I/O connections	Both Multimax and Encore 91 support Ethernet and SCSI interfaces. In addition, both have a VME bus.
Performance	Encore quote the base Multimax 310 (with two CPUs) as providing 4 MIPS, and a 20 processor Multimax 520 as giving 170 MIPS. Similar figures are not given for the Encore 91 but we estimated the 9104 to have a sustainable performance of $\sim$ 12 MFLOPS.
Host system	None.

Operating system   UMAX 4.2 (BSD compatible), UMAX V (AT & T System V) and MACH are available for the Multimax. UMAX V and μMPX are implemented on the Encore 91.

Programming languages Fortran, C and Ada on both the Multimax and Encore 91. Lisp is also available on the Multimax.

Physical configuration   Multimax 300: $52'' \times 28.5'' \times 28.5''$, weight approximately 650 lb.
Multimax 500: $61.5'' \times 42.5'' \times 35.5''$, weight approximately 1100 lb.
Encore 91: Three different cabinets are available, the mid-sized one can accommodate one Encore 91 with a 21 slot VME card cage: $54'' \times 30'' \times 38.5''$.

Power dissipation   Multimax 300: ~ 1.8 kW. Multimax 500: ~ 3 kW.

Sources   Publicly available material plus interviews with Encore staff and users.

Company Summary 9: Features of the FPS System 500

Source	FPS Computing.
Type	A heterogeneous architecture composed of a mix of scalar, vector and matrix processors. The numbers of each may be determined by the purchaser.
Availability	The first System 500 is expected to become available January 1991. Its predecessors, the Model 500 and Model 500EA were introduced in Autumn 1988 and November 1989 respectively.
Price	A Model 500EA with one scalar and one vector processor and 64 Mbyte of main memory costs approximately £300,000. Prices for the System 500 are not yet finalised but are expected to be in the range £400,000 to £2 M, for a machine including an 84 PE matrix co-processor.
Processing nodes	A mixture of scalar, vector and matrix units connected together by a bus. The maximum number of processors in a machine is eight, with no more than two vector and two matrix processors.
Processors	Scalar: ECL based SPARC chip from BIT. Vector: ECL chip set from BIT. Matrix: a number (maximum 84) Intel i860s.
Memory	System memory 32 Mbyte to 1 Gbyte, in addition each matrix co-processor has a 32 or 64 Mbyte cache.
Communications	SIA is a 64 bit wide bus, clocked at 33 MHz. Two versions available, total bandwidth 267 Mbyte/s, or 1 Gbyte/s.
I/O connections	Standard interfaces such as VME, Multibus, Ethernet, X.25 are supported. In is planned to extend this to include FDDI and HiPPI. Currently, the I/O controller has a total bandwidth of 80 Mbyte/s.
Performance	Scalar: 65 MIPS each. Vector: 67 MFLOPS each. Matrix: 320 MFLOPS to 13.4 GFLOPS (4 and 168 i860 respectively). All figures are manufacturer's estimates, work by FPS on a development System 500 indicates

that using i860 assembly language 50% of these peak performances may be realised in applications.

Host system   None.

Operating system   SunOS for the System 500, Berkeley 4.3 or 4.4BSD for Model 500EA.

Programming languages   Fortran, Pascal and C.

Physical configuration   Minimum of two cabinets: one for the processor, the other for I/O peripherals. Processor: $62'' \times 54'' \times 33''$. I/O: $62'' \times 42'' \times 28''$. Maximum combined weight: 3800 lb.

Power dissipation   Between 3.5 and 10.5 kW. The machines use three-phase electricity and are air-cooled.

Sources   Publicly available documentation together with interviews with FPS staff.

Company Summary 10: Features of the Sequent Balance and Symmetry

Source	Sequent Computer Systems
Type	Tightly coupled 32 bit microprocessor, shared memory multiprocessor.
Availability	First machine was available in 1984, and since then 2000 machines have been installed
Price	Prices range from $50,000 to $1 M, for a S27 to an S81. and from $25,000 to $600,000, for a B8 to an B21.
Processing nodes	Processor nodes number from two to 30
Processor technology	The B8 and B27 use NS 32032 chips and the S8 and S81s use 16 MHz Intel 80386s.
Memory	The Balance Series Main memory ranges from 2 Mbyte to 28 Mbyte and has an 8 kbyte on board cache, per processor. The Symmetry Series Main memory ranges from 8 Mbyte to 80 Mbyte and has an 8 kbyte on board cache, per processor.
Communications	The System Bus has an 80 Mbyte/s communication bandwidth and an n to n topology.
I/O connections	MULTIBUS, Ethernet, and a full range of intersystem communications protocols, including X.25, NFS and TCP/IP.
Performance	150 MIPS.
Host system	none
Operating system	DYNIX, based on the UNIX Operating System, supports existing 4.2BSD and System V applications without change.
Programming languages	C, Fortran 77, Pascal, Lisp, Ada, Cobol and assembly language. The PDBX Parallel Debugger is available, as is support for the KAP/Sequent Restructuring Preprocessor and Fortran Parallel Preprocessor Optimisers.
Physical configuration	Each machine in the Sequent Series is self contained in one box.

Power requirements   Max. total DC power for S27 = 750 W. Max. total DC
                         power for S81 = 2 kW.

Sources   Sequent technical literature.

Chapter 4

Hypercubes: A Geometry that Works

Hypercube manufacturers dominated the American market for distributed memory MIMD computers throughout the 1980s for two reasons. First, the seminal work at the California Institute of Technology led by Geoffrey Fox and Charles Seitz showed that a large number of scientific and engineering problems fit well onto hypercubes. Second, this work had provided a base of software, and more importantly of techniques, which saved scientists and engineers from having to think about computer science when what they really wanted to think about was their own subject's problems. While the hypercube architecture may be overtaken in the 1990s by more recent developments, the two companies we describe here have both proved that they are imaginative enough to stay in the parallel computing game.

4.1   Intel Scientific Computers

Relevant Activities Intel Scientific Computers (iSC) design and market low cost
MIMD hypercube machines based on Intel's microprocessor technology.

Location Headquarters: 15201 Northwest Greenbrier Parkway, Beaverton, Oregon, 97006, USA. Telephone: (503) 629 7629. European Headquarters: Pipers
Way, Swindon, SN3 1RJ, UK. Telephone: 0793 696000.

iSC also uses the many Intel offices worldwide.

Relevant Officers Bob Rockwell, General Manager; Justin Rattner, Director of
Technology; David Moody, European Manager.

Employees Currently around 120 (compared to Intel's population of 20,000).

Financial Details Corporate division of Intel.

4.1.1   The Company

Intel invented the microprocessor and is now a leading designer and supplier of
MOS microprocessors and related components. In the early 1970s Intel developed
an 8 bit microprocessor, the 8080, which subsequently evolved into the 8086 16 bit
chip family. One family member, the 8088, was chosen as the CPU for IBM PCs.
The 8086 has since evolved into the 16 bit 80286 and then into the 32 bit version
the 80386, recently followed by the 80486. In February 1989 Intel launched into
the competitive RISC chip market with the 80860, rated at 60 MFLOPS peak.

Intel's interest in parallel processing stems from the iAPX 432 Project started in
1975. The 432 Project was to design a complete microprocessor system with many
radical features for the time including: support for object oriented programming,
capabilities, fault tolerance, and parallelism. The multiprocessing feature was an
early form of bus-based shared memory parallelism. A four processor system was
demonstrated at the 1981 National Computer Conference. For various political
reasons the main thrust of the iAPX 432 Project died soon afterwards[1].

The importance of the 432 Project, however, was not so much the design of a
parallel microprocessor system but that it attracted many talented people to the
Portland area at just the time when microprocessor based parallel machines were
becoming feasible.

In the meantime Intel had been donating chips to various academic projects.
One of these projects was the Cosmic Cube project at CalTech under Charles Seitz
and Geoffrey Fox [COCU]. The main idea behind the project was that off-the-shelf

---

[1]The project did live on under a joint venture between Intel and Siemens named BiiN (cf. 10.1).

microprocessors are cheap and if many of them can be organised to cooperate in parallel then a cheap supercomputer would result.

The Cosmic Cube is a hypercube parallel computer with Intel 8086/7 microprocessors as compute nodes. Various sizes of Cosmic Cube were built with a 64 node version operational in October 1983. Far from being just an academic curiosity, they were put to serious use with significant applications written for them and acquired a substantial user base at CalTech. Early example applications were in the area of quantum chromodynamics and VLSI circuit simulation.

John Palmer, an ex-432 Project member, was the liaison man between CalTech and Intel at the end of 1982. He saw the potential of the Cosmic Cube idea and left Intel taking two other ex-432 Project members, Stephen Colley and William Richardson with him. Together they formed NCUBE (cf. 4.2) in 1983.

In early 1984, Justin Rattner, the chief computer architect on the 432 Project, was sent to CalTech to report on the work there. He was impressed by the achievements of the Cosmic Cube computer and convinced Intel that they should design and market their own version. An Intel Cosmic Cube would give Intel an early foothold in the parallel processing industry, an industry that will surely dominate computing in the future.

In 1984 Intel set up Intel Scientific Computers (iSC) as an autonomous business unit to design and market parallel machines based on Intel's technology and expertise in the microprocessor market. Their first product, the iPSC/1, was announced in February 1985.

4.1.2   The Hardware

iSC have brought out three ranges of hypercube computers to date: the iPSC/1; the iPSC/2; and the iPSC/860. Here we give brief description of the Cosmic Cube since the Cosmic Cube is the father of the iSC computer ranges. Several Cosmic Cubes with from eight to 64 nodes were built from 1982 to 1983. In the largest Cosmic Cube, each node consists of an 8 bit 8086 CPU, 8087 arithmetic co-processor and a small amount of memory. In addition, each node has seven bidirectional communication channels. Six channels are used to connect point-to-point to other nodes, forming a 6-D hypercube architecture, the seventh connects to a global Ethernet bus shared by all nodes. The Cube is controlled from a host machine which communicates with Cube nodes via the global Ethernet bus. Each node runs a small kernel operating system which provides system calls for message passing and handles multiprocessing at nodes. Message passing is achieved by a packet switching store-and-forward technique.

The key behind the design of the Cosmic Cube was the use of standard off-the-shelf tried-and-tested components. The components are a known quantity, so have few teething troubles compared to using new radical specialised architectures.

Buyers are likely to be familiar with the components, since they are already used in many other machines, such as PC compatibles, and already have a sound software base. They are produced in large volume which keeps them cheap.

iPSC/1

In 1986 the Intel Personal SuperComputer range was launched, now known as the iPSC/1. The design of the iPSC/1 was licensed from CalTech and borrowed heavily from the Cosmic Cube research. The most notable enchancement was the use of 80286/7 16 bit chips as node processors. The iPSC/1 consisted of a minimum 32 to a maximum of 128 nodes, connected in a hypercube architecture. Each node consisted of:

- 80286 CPU and 80287 arithmetic co-processor

- 500 kbyte of memory

- 7 communications channels at 20 Mbyte/s peak bandwidth

- 1 global Ethernet channel

- iLBX-II expansion interface with 8 Mbyte/s peak bandwidth

Each node was capable of 1 MIPS peak performance, giving a peak performance of 128 MIPS or 8 MFLOPS (64 bit) for 128 node machine. A complete node resided on a single $9'' \times 11''$ Eurocard. One Computational Unit cabinet measuring $16'' \times 16'' \times 19''$ holds 32 such cards. For a 128 node system, four Computational Unit cabinets are needed.

The cube is hosted by the Cube Manager which communicates with cube nodes via the global Ethernet bus. The Cube Manager consists of: 80286 CPU, 80287 arithmetic co-processor, 2 Mbyte of memory, an Ethernet communications link, and various disc and tape drives.

Each node on the cube executes a small kernel called the Node Executive (NX). which provides multiprocessing and message routing facilities. Message transmission is based on store-and-forward packet switching, undelivered messages begin buffered at intermediate nodes. Programs are developed and compiled on the Cube Manager, under the XENIX operating system, and are transmitted to the nodes of the cube for execution via the Ethernet link.

It should emphasised that the supply of NX operating system as standard with the machine is a major bonus feature. This is possible largely because the regularity of the hypercube architecture means that the packet routing algorithm is simple. This is not true of other manufacturers. For example, Inmos still do not supply message routing software with the transputer, leaving the user to write routing software for each application.

In addition to the standard cube, optional memory and vector extended versions were available. These are achieved by connecting extension cards to nodes via the iLBX-II expansion interface. Extension cards are located in odd card slots in the card rack, main node boards being located in even slots. The number of cabinets is kept the same; so extended cubes range from 16 to 64 nodes. The iPSC/1-MX has nodes expanded to 4.5 Mbyte of memory and is intended for symbol processing applications.

The iPSC/1-VX has nodes extended with Vector eXtension modules. These have 1 Mbyte of memory, for storing vectors, and a user microcodable vector processor. Commonly used microsequences are provided. This boosts node peak performance to 6.6 MFLOPS[2] (64 bit).

iPSC/2

Early 1988 saw the first shipments of the iPSC/2 range, superceding the iPSC/1. The iPSC/2 has a similar architecture to the iPSC/1, but with notable enhancements. Each iPSC/2 node consists of:

- 80386 32 bit CPU and 80387 arithmetic co-processor

- 1, 4, 8, 16 Mbyte memory options

- 64 kbyte memory cache

- eight bi-directional communications channels using a Direct-Connect Routing module

- iLBX-II expansion interface

The use of the 16 bit 80386/7 chip set has boosted peak node performance to 4 MIPS. A maximum configuration machine of 128 processors has a peak performance of 512 MIPS or 27 MFLOPS (64 bit) with 1 Gbyte of aggregate memory (8 Mbyte per node max. in this configuration).

The Direct-Connect module was developed from research at CalTech. It operates eight bidirectional communications channels at 2.8 Mbyte/s peak and implements a hybrid of circuit switching and packet switching, called *wormhole routing*. When a message is sent from one node to another the initial part of the message is sent in packet switching mode. The rest of the message follows the same route through intermediate nodes as the initial message portion without the need for store-and-forward delays. Message latency is improved by 3–10 times over the iPSC/1 store-and-forward technique.

---

[2]One VX node has virtually the peak performance of a 128 node basic iPSC/1!

Only seven of the eight links are used for connecting to other processor nodes, the remaining link is left for I/O expansion. The system-wide Ethernet link is no longer provided with the iPSC/2. The Systems Resource Manager (alias Cube Manager) communicates with the Cube via the I/O link of one of the compute nodes. Programs are distributed to the Cube by the Systems Resource Manager through its 'client node' using a spanning tree algorithm. Node processors run a smaller and faster kernel than NX called NX/2. The Systems Resource Manager consists of: 80386 CPU, 80387 arithmetic co-processor, 8 Mbyte of memory, Direct-Connect Routing to one node on the cube, external communications via Ethernet link, and various disc and tape drives. The Systems Resource Manager runs under AT&T UNIX, Version V, with a windows interface.

Compute nodes support multiprocessing under NX/2 as long as the processes on a node are owned by the same user. An added enhancement over the iPSC/1, however, is that the Systems Resource Manager can allocate subcubes of the Cube to different users allowing the Cube to be 'space shared'.

The basic model has scalar and vector expansion options. Scalar expansion is in the form of a module based on the Weitek 1167 arithmetic accelerator which boosts node performance on floating point operations by three times. Vector extension is in the form of the same Vector Extension module as used in the iPSC/1, boosting peak node performance on vector operations to 6.6 MFLOPS (64 bit). This gives the iPSC/2-VX the same peak MFLOPS rating as the iPSC/1-VX of the same node count. Since a scalar entension module sits piggy-back on a main node board, nodes can be both scalar and vector extended.

4.1.3   The Concurrent I/O facility

Launched in October 1988, the Concurrent I/O facility is an extension to the iPSC/2 to provide high bandwidth I/O and mass storage capabilities. Each node on the iPSC/2 has eight communications links, seven of which are used to form the hypercube architecture. The 8th link is for connecting to I/O nodes. An I/O node consists of:

- 80386 CPU and 80387 arithmetic co-processor

- 4 Mbyte of memory expandable to 16 Mbyte with 64 kbyte memory cache

- single bidirectional communications channel compatible with Direct-Connect

- SCSI bus interface with 4 Mbyte/s peak transfer rate

- support for up to seven disc drives

Various disc drives are available, the largest being 574 Mbyte. An I/O node can be adapted to support VME bus or Multibus. I/O nodes execute the NX/2 kernel augmented with the Concurrent File System (CFS). The CFS presents a single UNIX-like hierarchical file system and automatically distributes files over the discs transparently in 4 kbyte blocks. UNIX compatible calls are available to read/write blocks to the file system.

What happens when 128 nodes are all trying to read/write data? The CFS provides two solutions to this problem. The first solution is to have all nodes access the same file but read/write different file blocks. A lseek() call is provided that enables a node to read/write every N^{th} file block. The second solution is to access separate files. The CFS provides the facility to read/write to a common file name with the processor number appended, eg. node 0 would write to *fred000*, node 127 would write to *fred127*.

Again it should be stressed that the regularity of the hypercube architecture is largely responsible for the simplicity of the CFS. Computer systems with potentially irregular architectures, such as transputer based machines, make files services harder to implement.

Compute nodes can offload their I/O jobs to I/O nodes increasing compute throughput. In addition, the CFS has calls that allow compute nodes to compute at the same time as reading or writing data to I/O, further increasing throughput.

iPSC/860

In January 1990, the latest generation of hypercubes, the iPSC/860, was launched. This is an iPSC/2 with the CPU and co-processors replaced Intel's latest microprocessor the 80860. The 80860 is a RISC processor with an on board floating point unit. With a 40 MHz clock frequency, the 80860 performs at 60 MFLOPS peak, since it can fetch and process more than one instruction per clock cycle though the use of pipelining and instruction caching. Each iPSC/860 node consists of:

- 80860 CPU

- from 8 Mbyte to 16 Mbyte of memory

- Direct-Connect module controlling eight bidirectional communication channels (2.8 Mbyte/s peak)

Each compute node executes the NX/2 kernel. However, the multiple processes per node feature is not supported. This is because during a context switch, the instruction pipeline and cache need flushing which degrades performance substantially. That should not hinder the marketability of the iPSC/860; users are likely to be more interested in raw speed rather than the niceties of NX/2. Getting anywhere near peak speed is likely to be more of a problem. RISC microprocessors rely on advanced compiler technology to make full advantage of their architecture. The 80860 is no exception. iSC recently quoted a figure of around 1 GFLOPS for a kernel application on a 64 node iPSC/860. This may sound impressive but represents only 26% efficient use of the machine. Hopefully better compilers will improve this position.

Currently, only Fortran and C compilers are available for 80860 compute nodes. For continued support of the symbol processing market, iPSC/2 80386 nodes supporting the Lisp and Ada languages can be mixed with 80860 compute nodes in the same machine, producing heterogeneous parallel machine. The 80860 and 80386 nodes cooperate, as one would expect, by message passing.

The iPSC/860 comes with at least one Concurrent I/O node and the Concurrent File System as standard. The minimum system consists of eight 80860 compute nodes each with 8 Mbyte of memory and one I/O node with a 650 Mbyte hard disc. The maximum size system of 128 nodes, has a peak performance of 7.6 GFLOPS (64 bit), aggregate memory of 2 Gbyte, and eight I/O nodes with a total of 165 Gbyte of disc storage. The Systems Resource Manager is the same as that used for the iPSC/2.

4.1.4   The Software

Neither Intel nor iSC produce much in-house software for their products. Exceptions to this are the NX node operating systems and the Concurrent File System. Most software is developed by specialist software companies with some involvement from iSC. iSC do not favour any one operating system or set of software standards arguing that the industry is too young for that and such things should be user driven, not supplier driven. Many operating systems for iPSCs available through third parties vendors although they are not supported by iSC. Such operating systems include MACH, Express (section 9.1), and CrOS III.

Languages

All iSC hypercube systems come with Fortran 77 and C to meet the needs of the scientific/research markets. These are full standard languages with added subroutine call to NX facilities for message passing. The supply of user familiar languages like Fortran and C from the beginning is crucial to the take up of a new computer product, especially in parallel computing. The transputer was a near failure because of the insistence of Inmos to supply only Occam, a language with which users had no familiarity and little desire to learn.

Use of the nodes with Vector Extension modules is via the Pacific Sierra VAST-2 Fortran preprocessing package. VAST-2 preprocesses DO and IF loops replacing then with vector extension calls. Also supplied is VECLIB, a library of common vector functions, such as Fast Fourier Transforms, which can be called directly from Fortran, and execute on the Vector Extension module.

Optionally available is Concurrent Common Lisp (CCLisp). This is a full common Lisp package with symbolic stream primitives added for communication between nodes and remote evaluation. Remote evaluation allows a Lisp expression to be evaluated on a chosen node returning the answer to the initiator. Also optionally available is version of Virdex Ada.

All system ranges are to a large extent source compatible. Some modifications are needed when porting from the iPSC/1 to the iPSC/2 and upwards due to the small differences between NX and NX/2. The 80860 nodes in the iPSC/860 do not run CCLisp or Ada and do not need vector preprocessing software when used for Fortran.

Tools

Tools can be split into two sections: debugging tools and code parallelising tools. Cubes come with a full source level debugger named DECON. This allows the user to check the status of C or Fortran programs executing in the cube by inspecting and altering variable values on a given node, and looking at message queues. Users can set break points on user defined objects like subroutine calls and variables; single stepping through executing code is available.

Together, Pacific Sierra and iSC are developing a set of tools to aid the parallelisation of dusty-deck Fortran code. The first tool offered is FORGE, used to evaluate and manipulate sequential Fortran programs. FORGE is an interactive tool using the X Windows interface. The user divides the Fortran program into packages, which are then parsed to generate a database. Holding information on variable usage and control flow locally for each package and globally for the entire program. A set of database viewing tools let the user access and analyse information stored in the database. An editor is provided for arranging programs into packages and simple program manipulation. FORGE also allows some program instrumentation that gives information such as to how long the program spends in various DO loops and values of selected variables.

A set of tools built on FORGE, called MIMDizer, are scheduled for release in 1990. MIMDizer will provide interactive tools for manipulating a sequential Fortran program into a parallel program suitable for hypercube execution. It will rely heavily on user involvement since automatic parallelisers, except for simple vectorisers, are still a long way off. It is also likely to offer profiling tools for the analysis of programs executing over multiple nodes.

4.1.5 Sales

Table 4.1 gives approximate sales for each machine range to the end of 1989, together with expected sales for 1990. Most of the systems sold in 1990 are expected to be iPSC/860's with a reasonable number of I/O nodes.

Table 4.1: Sales of Intel Computers by Model

System Range	1989	1990 (expected)
iPSC/1	80	N/A
iPSC/2	130	Combined
iPSC/860	2	60–80

iSC are beginning to sell to commercial companies and have opened an office on Wall Street. They expect to sell $\frac{1}{3}$ of new machines to commercial companies accounting for $\frac{1}{2}$ of total revenue, since these companies tend to go for large machines. The other $\frac{2}{3}$ of machines sold to research divisions of companies, universities, and research institutions. About 15%–20% of machines are sold outside the US accounting for approximately 25% of total revenue. iSC does make a small profit, but more importantly Intel see iSC as an early foothold in the parallel processing markets which will surely dominate computing in the future.

4.1.6   The Market Niche

iSC see their machines as inexpensive high performance computers that would be purchased by a company department or research facility to execute interactively a small number of mainly CPU intensive tasks. This is in contrast with the traditional supercomputer that because of their expense are general company resources executing a large number of batched tasks.

From the beginning, iSC have made a careful study of potential markets for hypercube machines and have followed a development plan based on their findings. The traditional market for high performance machines has been number crunching applications used by company and university research departments. This market has been traditional been filled by vector supercomputers executing vectorised Fortran code. To compete in that market iSC quickly added vector processing capabilities in the form of vector extension options to their machines, together with Fortran vectorising compilers and vector function libraries.

Also perceived early on was the potential of breaking into the embryonic Artificial Intelligence (AI) market. ISC and Thinking Machines (cf. Section 2.3) are the only high performance computer suppliers to take symbol processing support seriously. Although initially sceptical the AI community would be a significant market for their machines, iSC's support has paid off with AI orders accounting for around 20% of total machine sales.

Extended scalar floating point options and supply of C and Ada are intended to attract non-vector customers such as those interested in computer science research. The introduction of the Concurrent I/O facility is intended to support the real-time number crunching and commercial data processing markets which require large amounts of memory bandwidth and disc storage capacity.

The largest problem that all companies marketing MIMD machines face is that of porting existing software, mainly Fortran code, from traditional architectures onto their pet architecture. The current thinking at iSC is that automatic parallelising tools are a long way off but that intermediate high level tools that help the applications programmer organise sequential code into parallel code are possible. iSC's own efforts in this area are embodied in MIMDizer a set of tools developed in conjunction with Pacific Sierra.

By approximately the year 2000, Intel see the possibility of integrating hundreds of 80860-like nodes on a single chip. How the nodes on these chips will be organised is not known. Possibilities include: shared memory MIMD architectures as used in current Sequent (cf. Section 3.7) and Alliant machines (cf. 3.1); and Very Large Instruction Word (VLIW) architectures pioneered by Multiflow (cf. 10.3).

What is known is that crucial to the efficient use of new chips is good compilers, an area in which, traditionally, Intel is weak. As a result of this thinking, in October 1989 Intel bought a 4% stake in Alliant at a cost of $3 M. Alliant will give access to advanced compiler technology and input into the design of new processor chips developed by Intel. Intel already has adopted the Alliant PAX standard architecture, which provides for concurrency in hardware. New versions of the 80860 chip will conform to PAX. In early 1990, Intel also invested $5 M in Multiflow for similar reasons. It is unclear how that investment will pay off, if at all, because of the surprise demise of Multiflow in April 1990.

On the whole, iSC are covering most of the current, and some of the future, trends in the parallel processing industry. However, they are likely to have to answer increasingly to pressure from competitors due to the cautious approach typical of a large corporation.

iSC's approach has been to develop the conservative machine with technology completely tried-and-tested by a third party, such as CalTech, drawing on an existing substantial user base. The result is what one would expect: good machines at average prices but banking on a firm customer base and customer loyalty for future sales. Interest from government bodies will also substantially boost sales.

Some competitors have a more radical approach, however. A prime example are NCUBE who have gone for custom VLSI processors with routing and communications all in one chip and can deliver hypercubes with thousands of nodes now, already rivaling Intel's Touchstone project. Arguably, NCUBE are at least a generation ahead of iSC in terms of hardware and nothing currently proposed by Intel is likely to change that lead in the future.

4.1.7   The Future

Intel announced the Touchstone project in April 1989. The aim if the project is
to produce a 2000 node machine based around the 80860 microprocessor to give a
machine with a peak performance of 120 GFLOPS. The project is to cost in the
region of $27.5 M with DARPA putting up $7.6 M. The project was expected to
deliver prototypes by 1991, but is more likely to do so by early 1992.

The Concurrent I/O facility and the iPSC/860 are stepping stones in the project.
The final configuration is to be from 20 to 2000 processing nodes connected in a
mesh architecture. Recent research at CalTech [MESH] argues that for machines
with large numbers of nodes and wormhole routing, the message times between
nodes are almost independent of node distance — that is, the message time between
any two nodes is constant. Meshes are naturally scalable to thousands of processors
whereas building a similar hypercube is an engineering nightmare. Each Touchstone
node will consist of an 80860 and an improved communications chip to provide
automatic wormhole routing. A substantial part of the project is to develop software
tools to enable users to make efficient use of such a machine. (It is interesting to
note that NCUBE (cf. 4.2) are already marketing a 8196 node hypercube with
custom 64 bit scalar floating point processors and on-chip wormhole routing.)

4.2 NCUBE Corporation

Relevant Activities Design, build, and market massively parallel computers, ranging from 32 to 8192 processor hypercube systems.

Location Headquarters: 1825 NW 167th Place, Beaverton, Oregon, 97006, USA. Telephone: (503) 629 5088. Fax: (503) 654 1737.

Relevant Officers Stephen Colley, President and CEO; William S. Richardson, Executive Vice President; Richard Bassin, Vice President of Sales and Service; Dr. Michael Meirer, Vice President of International Operations; William Woo, Vice President of Marketing; Dr. Steve Johnson, Vice President of Software Technology; Doyle Briggs, Vice President of Finance

Employees Over 100 employees worldwide.

Financial details Privately held company; ownership not divulged.

4.2.1 The Company

NCUBE was one of the first companies to manufacture hypercubes in the early 1980s. Today, if a fully configured version of their second-generation NCUBE-2 product were constructed, it would arguably be the fastest computer in the world, with a peak performance of 27 GFLOPS.

NCUBE was founded in 1983 by John Palmer, Stephen Colley, and William Richardson, who met while working on the 432 Project at Intel (cf. Sections 4.1 and 10.1).

In around the middle of 1982, as the 432 Project was being wound down, Palmer was sent to CalTech to liaise with the CalTech Cosmic Cube project, to which Intel had been donating microprocessors. Under the direction of Geoffrey Fox and Charles Seitz, the project had already built several high performance multicomputers using a hypercube architecture and cheap off-the-shelf microprocessor chips as compute nodes, and had written significant operating and applications software for them. Palmer was impressed by the Cosmic Cube and thought that a commercial version should be built. When he discussed this possibility with Colley and Richardson, Colley was initially sceptical, believing that the wiring and packaging complexity of the Cosmic Cube would be prohibitively difficult, and that even if they could mass-produce such a machine, larger companies like Intel could easily copy their design and produce a cheaper version.

Around that time, however, the concept of the "silicon foundry" was becoming a reality. One could send a circuit design to a silicon foundry, and, as long as it conformed to a particular set of design rules, the foundry would produce the corresponding chips relatively quickly. Such a facility made it possible for small start-up companies to contemplate producing and using custom chips.

By cramming almost an entire Cosmic Cube processing node onto a single chip and implementing the wiring on printed circuit boards, Colley believed that a system could be produced which would have a very low chip count, and consequently very high reliability (since hardware reliability is inversely proportional to the number of components in a system). This approach, made possible by the silicon foundry, could make the computer a viable proposition.

In 1983 the three left Intel and set up NCUBE to design and market a commercial version of the Cosmic Cube. Their charter was to produce "the highest performance machines, to build families of different size machines, but...at the best performance for cost".

By this time, Intel had already chosen off-the-shelf microprocessors with their iPSC machines (cf. 4.1.2). It took NCUBE $2\frac{1}{2}$ years and $3 M to design their processor; by comparison, it has been estimated that designing a Cray-type supercomputer from scratch would take six years and $150 M.

In December 1985 the first generation of NCUBE products was launched. The largest member was the NCUBE/ten, a 10-D hypercube (1024 nodes) in a cuboid cabinet measuring 3' on a side. In 1989 the second generation machine, the NCUBE-2, was launched; the largest member in this series is a 13-D hypercube (8192 nodes) fitting into a cabinet $8' \times 8' \times 6'$.

4.2.2   Hardware

The NCUBE/ten

The design philosophy behind NCUBE's products is to get as much functionality out of each chip as possible. The compute node of the NCUBE/ten computer therefore contained only seven chips: one was the processor, and the other six were 256 kbit DRAM memory chips (two of which were used to implement single-error-correct, double-error-detect memory protection). The processor chip consisted of:

- a 32 bit CPU and IEEE-754 compliant 64 bit floating-point unit

- 128 kbyte of memory

- a dynamic memory controller including memory protection.

- 11 in/out pairs of serial Direct Memory Access lines

The CPU had a VAX-like architecture and supported the full set of VAX addressing modes. It used 32 bit addressing, but due to constraints on the number of pins per chip only 17 bits of address space were available for use.

Special instructions and registers were provided to control the DMA lines used for internode communication, which were bit serial and operate at 1 Mbit/s. Different messages could be sent over separate DMA lines, or a single message broadcast over an arbitrary set of DMA lines by setting bits in a mask register. Once a message had been initiated the CPU could process other instructions; the DMA channels would carry on concurrently. Receipt of a message was signaled and serviced via interrupts. Of the 11 pairs of DMA links, ten pairs were used to form the network for a maximum 10-D hypercube, and the remaining pair used to connect to the I/O subsystem.

The CPU had a clock speed of 10 MHz and a peak performance rating for register-to-register operations of 2 MIPS, 500 kFLOPS (32 bit), and 300 kFLOPS (64 bit). Memory-memory performance was significantly lower than this since — although the chip had 32 bit internal data paths, it could only access 16 bits of external memory per clock cycle.

Each $16'' \times 22''$ processor board held 64 processor nodes. The tracks on each board implemented wiring for a 6-D hypercube. The motherboard held a maximum of 16 processor boards and eight I/O boards; the tracks on this motherboard implemented the other four dimensions of the 10-D hypercube, and the wiring between processor boards and I/O boards. This required 640 connections in all.

At least one I/O board had to be a host board; a maximum of eight I/O boards could be replaced by host boards. A host board consisted of an Intel 80286 CPU, an Intel 80287 floating point co-processor, and 4 Mbyte of memory, which was used as shared memory by the I/O processors. A host board executed the Axis operating system, and supported up to eight terminals, four SMD disc drives, and three Intel iSBX interfaces. These last could accept daughter boards for such functions as graphics or networking.

Axis was a blend of AT&T System V and Berkley 4.3BSD UNIX. It provided the the usual UNIX utilities for editing, debugging, and file management. One extra facility Axis provides was the ability to allocate a 2^n-sized subcube of the hypercube to a user as if it were a UNIX device. Such a "device" was handled like any other file and could be written to, read from, opened and closed. Partioning the hypercube into smaller subcubes allowed many users to share the cube simultaneously. This is usually called spacesharing, and contrasts with the timesharing used to share a single processor's power between many users simultaneously. It was also Axis' job to coordinate the file systems managed by each I/O board into one uniform file system, which could also be merged with external file systems connected via the iLBX network links.

Each NCUBE/ten I/O board had 16 NCUBE processor chips which it used as processing nodes. Each processing CPU had 11 pairs of links. ten of these made up the hypercube; the other one went to an I/O processor. Each I/O processor also had 11 links (since it used the same chip as the processing CPU). Only eight of these were connected to processing CPUs (one link per CPU). Each I/O processor also had one link to the outside world. Since there were 16 I/O CPUs per I/O board, there were $16 \times 8 = 128$ links from the I/O board to 128 processing CPUs in the cube, and $16 \times 1 = 16$ links to the outside world out of it An I/O processor performed an input operation by first reading the data into the shared memory and then transmitting it to the appropriate processor nodes. Output operations were performed in a similar fashion.

Other I/O boards available were the NCUBE NChannel, Graphics Board, Intersystem Board, and Open System Board, each of which carried 16 I/O processors. The NCUBE NChannel was used to interface to mass storage devices. A typical "disc farm" application could support four disc drives per node, i.e. is 64 disc drives per NChannel board. The Graphics Board had a frame buffer and could accept data from the hypercube and display it at 30 frame/s. The Intersystem Board allowed two NCUBE systems to be connected together, while the Open System Board contained only the 16 processors leaving the rest of the board free for user-designed circuits.

The processor boards and I/O boards of a maximum configuration system, together with power supply and cooling fans, fit into a cuboid cabinet of about $3'$ on a side, and produced 8 kW. An additional $3' \times 2' \times 3'$ peripheral cabinet had a 65 Mbyte tape drive and up to four disc drives. A minimum configuration machine had one processor board and one host board, and implemented a 6-D hypercube. A maximum configuration system of 16 processor boards and eight host boards implemented a 10-D hypercube, had 128 Mbyte of memory and an average I/O bandwidth of 90 Mbyte/s, and had a peak performance of around 300 MFLOPS (64 bit).

The NCUBE/four and NCUBE/seven

NCUBE also manufactured smaller systems based on the NCUBE/ten's technology. The NCUBE/four was a single board containing four NCUBE processors and a PC-AT bus interface. Four of these boards could be used in a single PC-AT system. This board was intended for high-volume OEM markets.

The NCUBE/seven was a cut down version of the NCUBE/ten. It contained two regular processors boards, at least one host board, and another host board or another type of I/O board. The system also included one disc drive and a tape drive for system backups. A fully configured NCUBE/seven system had 128 processor nodes, could support up to 16 users, and fit into a desk-height cabinet $15''$ wide.

NCUBE-2

The second generation NCUBE-2 was introduced in June 1989, with production shipments becoming available in July 1989. An NCUBE-2 node processor contains a new VAX-like 64 bit CPU, with an IEEE-compliant floating point unit, 14 DMA channel pairs, and memory management and routing hardware. The performance of the new processors is 7.5 MIPS or 3.3 MFLOPS. NCUBE-2 machines can be expanded from 32 nodes in the NCUBE-2 6401 (64 bit and 2^{10} processors) to 8192 nodes in the NCUBE-2 6480 (8×2^{10} processors).

The number of memory chips has been increased from six to ten, ameliorating problems with the earlier machine's small memory. Minimum memory capacity is 1 Mbyte/node, while maximum capacity is 64 Mbyte/node. Up to 13 of the 14 DMA channel pairs can be used to form a 13-D hypercube of 8192 nodes. The other DMA link pair is reserved for I/O.

The 11 chips making up a node are mounted on a double-sided module slightly larger than a credit card: the processor and six DRAMs on one side, and the remaining four DRAMs on the other. 64 of these modules are then mounted onto a processor board which is wired in the form of a 6-D hypercube.

The NCUBE-2 uses the same packaging technology as the NCUBE/ten. The motherboard has enough slots for 16 processor boards, and its tracks implement the interprocessor wiring for a 10-D hypercube. The motherboard can also carry up to eight I/O cards. Like those of the NCUBE/ten, the I/O cards have 16 processors, each of which connects to eight processors in the hypercube via a total of 128 DMA link pairs.

What is new in the NCUBE-2 is that eight of these mother boards can be connected together to give the other three dimensions needed to implement a 13-D hypercube. As one would expect, the volume of the largest possible configuration has increased by a factor of eight; its dimensions are now approximately $8' \times 8' \times 6'$.

A host I/O board is no longer needed to run the operating system, provide support for terminals, or control part of the I/O system since a front-end workstation controls the hypercube and each node has enough memory to execute an operating system. Other I/O boards which are available include a Real-Time Graphics Subsystem Board, a Parallel I/O Subsystem Board, and an Open System Board. Each I/O board contains 16 NCUBE processors, which it connects to a subcube of 128 processors in the hypercube. Each board can transfer data at a maximum rate of 568 Mbyte/s per I/O slot.

The Real-Time Graphics Subsystem is an enhanced version of the NCUBE/ten's Graphics Board. It has 2 Mbyte of frame buffer memory, a colour lookup table for 16 Mcolours, supports a $768 \times 1024 \times 8$ pixel display, provides hardware pan and zoom, and has an RS343 RGB output. The Parallel I/O Subsystem is similar to the NCUBE NChannel board. It provides 16 serial channels for connecting to peripherals such as discs, networks, frame grabbers, and tape systems. As before, the Open System Board has only the 16 processors, and leaves the rest of the board free for user-defined interfaces.

A maximum configuration NCUBE-2 would have 8192 processors and 512 Gbyte of memory, and in theory produce a peak performance of 27 GFLOPS. Configured with a full complement of 64 I/O boards, such a system would have a peak I/O bandwidth of 36 Gbyte/s, and could support 4096 disc drives. The largest NCUBE-

2 built to date is a 1024 processor machine, which, according to some benchmarks, ran more than 1000 times faster than a single processor, lending some support to NCUBE's claim that performance on their machines scales almost linearly.

4.2.3   The Software

In both the NCUBE/ten and NCUBE-2 systems, each processor node runs a small operating system called Vertex which loads programs and provides three basic calls for passing messages: whoami, nwrite, and nread. whoami allows a program to determine the logical address of the node within the subcube on which it is executing, the size of the subcube, the ID of the host node, and its process number. This allows users to write programs capable of executing on hypercubes of arbitrary size.

nwrite and nread write and read blocks of bytes from and to other nodes. On the NCUBE/ten, store-and-forward packet routing is used for such messages; managing this is Vertex's main function. Messages are stored in a 20 kbyte heap. Individual messages can be up to 64 kbyte long, although Vertex breaks these down into 512 byte parcels for transmission and reassembles the message at the destination node. Vertex also translates virtual node addresses into physical node addresses allowing object code to be portable between subcubes.

On the NCUBE-2, wormhole routing is provided in hardware. Vertex translates the source and destination addresses to physical addresses and passes this information to the hardware module, which then routes the message automatically.

There is a fundamental difference in the way the two generations of machines are managed from the operating system point of view. In the NCUBE/ten at least one I/O board must be a host board running Axis. However, Axis is no longer needed on the NCUBE-2. Instead, each node in the system has enough memory to execute an operating system such as UNIX or VMS. Parasoft have also ported their machine-independent operating system Express to NCUBE products. The hypercube as a whole is now controlled by a front-end host computer, which is either a Sun Workstation or a DEC Vaxstation. This host manages the cube and allocates subcubes to users.

With the NCUBE-2 it is possible to allocate a single node to a user. This makes it possible to use an NCUBE-2 system in much the same way as a collection of networked workstations. In particular, each node can execute its own copy of the user's favourite operating system.

The two languages offered by NCUBE are Fortran 77 and C. These are extended with calls to Vertex subroutines which implement message passing between nodes. All NCUBE computers are source software compatible.

4.2.4 The Market Niche

NCUBE's products are aimed squarely at the scientific number crunching market. In the NCUBE-2, NCUBE claim to have the fastest general purpose supercomputer in the world, with a theoretical peak performance rating of 27 GFLOPS. NCUBE are quick to point out that their machines have scalar nodes, not vector nodes, which means that reasonable performance does not depend on keeping a reasonable number of vector pipelines busy. Multi-processor scalar computers should, therefore, not be limited by Amdahl's Law, and should be able to sustain their peak performance much more easily than their vector computer cousins [3].

Why then have NCUBE computers not taken the supercomputing world by storm? The main reason is that NCUBE's machines have the same problems as other massively parallel distributed memory computers — the tools do not exist to automatically parallelise programs. Without these tools, many users with a significant investment in existing software will not buy an NCUBE computer. The growth of NCUBE, therefore, is limited by the availability of such tools. Until this problem has been overcome they will only sell to researchers with numerically intensive problems who are willing to write programs from scratch if the machine is fast enough.

There is the potential, however, to sell the NCUBE-2 as a general computing resource. Since each processing node can be allocated to a single user, and can run that user's favourite operating system environment at 7.5 MIPS (and provide substantial I/O capabilities as well), NCUBE should be able to attack the market niche currently occupied by shared memory computer vendors such as Sequent (Section 3.7.5), Alliant (3.1.5), and Encore (3.5.5).

One area that NCUBE has been actively chasing is the data processing market. In June 1989, the NCUBE-2 was launched with a joint announcement by Oracle that they intended to port their database system to NCUBE machines. Data processing is the most lucrative section of the computing market, and Oracle accounts for approximately 80% of world database systems. With Oracle ported to their machines, NCUBE might attract attention from large Wall Street firms. However, that announcement was made over a year ago and there is still no sign of an Oracle/NCUBE-2 symbiosis. (BBN's experiences with Oracle (cf. 3.2.6) are a cautionary tale in this respect.)

4.2.5 The Opposition

Strangely, NCUBE's biggest opponents are not other computer manufacturers but DARPA. Most government laboratories depend on money from DARPA to finance

---

[3]Of course, this argument ignores the issues of load balancing and communications overheads...

the procurement of new equipment such as supercomputers. For reason known only to itself, DARPA will not subsidise NCUBE computers, but will contribute up to 50% of the cost of other manufacturers' systems, such as the Connection Machine from Thinking Machines (cf. Section 2.3). NCUBE believe that this is unfair competition. Even when their machine is superior in performance/cost comparisons a DARPA grant will bias the purchaser be buy the rival machine.

DARPA also directly fund research in parallel computer systems, an example being the award of $7.6 M to Intel to help fund their Touchstone Project. Why, ask NCUBE, do Intel, a billion dollar company, need $7.6 M from DARPA? The NCUBE-2 already has more nodes than, and a performance comparable to, the machine the Touchstone Project is supposed to produce, so why is DARPA funding it? Without this biased funding from DARPA, NCUBE believe that several companies (Thinking Machines included) would disappear and leave them with little serious competition.

4.2.6   The Future

NCUBE do have plans for future products, but are not currently willing to discuss them. Like all supercomputer manufacturers they are chasing the teraFLOPS grail, and hope to be the first company to provide a teraFLOPS machine. Future machines will be similar to the NCUBE-2 but bigger and better. The most interesting developments this decade will not be in hardware, however, but in languages and software tools. If and when automatically parallelising compilers become available, NCUBE could become the Cray of the 1990s.

Company Summary 11: Features of the iPSC/860

Source	Intel Scientific Computers.
Type	Medium grained MIMD hypercube system.
Availability	Announced in January 1990. First systems actually sold in December 1989.
Price	Ranges from $265 k for a basic eight node machine to $3.4 M for a full 128 node system.
Processing nodes	Come in two types. Number crunching nodes based on the Intel 80680 microprocessor with 64 bit FPU built in. General purpose nodes are based on the Intel 80386/7 combination.
Memory	Minimum of 8 Mbyte per node; maximum of 16 Mbyte per node.
Communications	Each processing node has a Direct-Connect message routing chip that implements eight bidirectional asynchronous channels at 2.8 Mbyte/s. Nodes are networked into a 7-D hypercube with the 8th link for I/O.
I/O connections	The 8th Direct-Connect channel of compute nodes can be connected to optional I/O nodes using Intel 80386/7 chips giving a maximum of 127 I/O nodes. The SCSI interface supports seven disc drives with 4 Mbyte/s data transfer rate. VMEbus and Multibus options available.
Performance	Peak performance 60 MFLOPS per compute node. Peak performance of 7.6 GFLOPS for maximum system.
Host system	Intel 80386 based PC-type computer with Ethernet link to Suns or Vaxes.
Operating system	Nodes run the NX/2 operating system kernel. Host computer runs UNIX V 3.2 and provides facilities for allocating subcubes to different users.
Programming languages	Compute nodes run Fortran 77 or C extended with calls to the NX/2 node operating system for message passing. General purpose nodes run Fortran, C, Ada, or CCLisp, a full implementation of Common Lisp with added symbolic stream primitives for communication.

Sources   Publicly available information and interviews with key
                     US and UK personnel.

Company Summary 12: Features of the NCUBE-2 range

Source	NCUBE Corporation,
Type	Medium grained MIMD hypercube system.
Availability	Announced in July 1989.
Price	According to January 1990 Parallelogram Jan 90, a 64 node NCUBE-2 costs $495 k, while an 8192 node NCUBE-2 costs $30 M.
Processing nodes	Custom chip containing 64 bit CPU, IEEE floating point unit, memory management unit, 14 DMA serial link pairs. Minimum configuration of 32 nodes; maximum configuration of 8192 nodes.
Memory	Minimum of 1 Mbyte per node; maximum of 64 Mbyte per node.
Communications	Each node processor has 14 DMA serial link pairs. 13 link pairs are used to construct a 13-D hypercube. The remaining link is connected to the I/O subsystem.
I/O connections	14 DMA link pair connected to a I/O node processor. Each I/O node processor connects to eight processor nodes and has one bi-directional serial port for connecting to peripherals. There can be up to 1024 I/O nodes in the maximum system.
Performance	Peak performance of 7.5 MIPS, 3.33 MFLOPS per node. Peak performance of maximum configuration 60 GIPS, 27 GFLOPS.
Host system	Sun workstations executing UNIX or DEC Vaxstations executing VMS/VME.
Operating system	Nodes run a small Vertex operating system to handle message passing. Each node can run either UNIX, VMS/VME, or EXPRESS.
Programming languages	Fortran 77 or C, extended with message passing calls.
Sources	Sales literature and interviews of personnel.

Chapter 5

The Transputer and Its Offspring

The Inmos transputer was the first microprocessor specifically designed with parallel computing in mind, and as a result products based on it have almost completely dominated the European market for parallel computers. While this reliance on a common component has led to manufacturers producing similar machines, there are important differences between these machines as well. Inmos's release of its new H1 chip in 1991 may allow it, and the companies reliant on it, to take a large share of the American market in the next decade.

5.1   Inmos Limited

Relevant Activities Manufacturers of transputers, transputer boards and development tools for transputer systems.

Location Headquarters: Inmos Limited, 1000 Aztec West, Almondsbury, Bristol, Avon BS12 4SQ, UK. Telephone: 0454 616616; Fax: 0454 617910. Inmos Business Centre, SGS-Thomson Microelectronics, PO Box 16000, Colorado Springs, Colorado 80935-6000, USA. Telephone: (719) 630 4000; Fax: (719) 630 4325.

Relevant Officers Michael Wright, Managing Director; Paul Strzelecki, Marketing Director; Jaqui Porter, Director (Human Resources); Tony Gallagher, Financial Director; Harry De Buriatte, Director (Quality); Richard Campbell, Director (New Products); Ian Pearson, Technical Director; Pasquale Pistario, Director (SGS-Thomson); Phillipe Geyres, Director (SGS-Thomson); Maurizio Ghirga, Director (SGS-Thomson).

Employees 1200 in the UK

Financial details A subsidiary of SGS-Thomson Microelectronics, bought from Thorn-EMI in 1989.

5.1.1   The Company

Inmos have one of the most tortuous histories of any of the companies involved in parallel computing. Having started life in the late 1970s as a desperate attempt to bring Britain into the micro-electronics industry, they are now the largest British-based manufacturers of standard microelectronic components. As a manufacturer of silicon chips Inmos would not have been included in this report, however one of these chips, the transputer, has become so important for the development of parallel programming that no survey of the industry would be complete without a section devoted to it.

By the mid-1970s the semiconductor industry in the USA and Japan had advanced well beyond that in Britain. At the time it was thought that it would be impossible for the private sector to finance a British revival. However, there had been a previous example of successful government funding to promote the micro-electronics industry when the West German government gave Siemens £25 M in 1977 as an initial investment. This money laid the foundation for one of Europe's largest semiconductor manufacturers. The Labour government was therefore persuaded to provide the necessary investment from public sources. The money would come from the National Enterprise Board, an agency for restructuring and modernising important sectors of industry. The NEB had an uphill struggle to convince the cabinet to back the Inmos program; they had even greater problems with the subsequent Conservative government, for whom the NEB was the epitome of the interventionist approach to managing industry.

A central point in the plan that convinced the government was that the venture should be started with a heavy dependence on American personnel and manufacturing techniques. The American connection consisted of Richard Petritz and Paul Schroeder, who collaborated with Iann Barron to produce the proposal that lead to the creation of Inmos. Barron had an established position in the British computing world, and therefore the necessary contacts with the NEB. Petritz had been involved in the US semiconductor business from its start, and worked with companies such as Texas Instruments and Mostek, while Schroeder was well known as a leading semiconductor engineer. Between them, they could provide a means of importing American technology. Following a chance meeting between Petritz and Barron they produced the first proposal for the company in November 1977. The proposal was finally passed by cabinet in July 1978, and funding of £50 M agreed.

In November 1978 Inmos set up its headquarters and a research centre in Bristol. This was followed by the construction of a production plant in Newport, South Wales. The American side of the company centred their research and design headquarters in Colorado Springs late in 1978, and had their Cheyenne Mountain production plant underway before the Newport site was even chosen. After Inmos survived a change of government in 1979, both production plants began to manufacture chips late in the year. These first products were mainly 64 kbyte DRAMs and 16 kbyte SRAMs. However Barron and Petritz had always intended to produce a single chip containing a complete microprocessor; the manufacture of memory chips had always been planned to fund and provide a technology base for this device. The final design of the chip was not decided upon until the spring of 1981, and this delay did nothing to help Inmos survive the political storms surrounding it.

The delay in designing the microprocessor was mostly due to the time it took to decide what the chip should contain. Together with David May, Barron intended the device to combine memory and processing ability on a single piece of silicon. The design also included the ability to communicate through on-chip links, which would allow chips to be joined directly together to allow the easy construction of multiprocessor computers. The chip was named the transputer, and turned out to be the key to Inmos's success later in the 1980s.

However, the transputer did not reach the commercial market until October 1985, and much happened to Inmos in the meantime. In 1983 Inmos achieved sales of £83 M, equating to a loss of £14 M. Following the boom in the market in 1984 the company made actual profits totalling £14.4 M. The Conservative government of the time seized its opportunity and sold its 76% stake to Thorn-EMI for £95 M in September 1984. Unfortunately the silicon market promptly slumped. In July

1986 Thorn reported trading losses of $50 M on sales of $94 M. These were difficult times for the company; if it were not for the potential success of the transputer, Inmos might have gone bankrupt.

Although the launch of the first transputer, the T414, was delayed, it was well planned and well received. The chip was launched along with four boards that provided immediate working systems, such as the B004, a plug-in board for the IBM PC. While some provision was made for the use of C, Fortran and Pascal, most effort was put into marketing a new language called Occam, which was based on Hoare's Communicating Sequential Processes (CSP). Occam turned out to be unattractive to industrial users with large investments in the established programming languages, and Inmos's insistence that Occam was the only suitable language for the transputer severly damaged the company's success in its early years.

A massive early sales drive to promote the transputer in the United States made few inroads into the market, and 1987 saw the dismissal of a large number of the American sales team. The effect of this early American antipathy towards Inmos is still apparent today ; all the major manufacturers of transputer based machines are still based in Europe, with few of them selling many machines to the USA.

Despite these difficulties, within six months of its launch over 1000 groups were using the transputer around the world. While the majority of these were small research groups eager to investigate the possibilities of the new device, some were more significant. A few months before the transputer's official launch, a new company called Meiko (Section 5.3) set up headquarters next door to Inmos in Bristol. Meiko was formed by Inmos employees who wanted to concentrate on the production of a parallel supercomputer based on the transputer. Meiko displayed their first machine, a computing engine containing 128 prototype T414s, in August 1985. This computer ran image processing software and achieved a performance of over 100 MIPS. There was also early uptake of the transputer by established manufacturers such as Floating Point Systems (Section 3.6), who announced in April 1986 that their T series hypercube machines would be based on the T414.

The successor to the T414 was the T800, which had a similar design but included an on-chip 64 bit floating point unit and a further 2 kbyte of on-chip RAM. The design for the T800 emerged from the Esprit Supernode program (cf. Section 5.4), as did the funding for its development. The T800 was released in 1987 and has virtually supplanted its predecessor. Parallel computers based on the T800 are now produced by companies including Parsys, Parsytec, Caplin, Meiko, and Telmat. September 1989 saw the release of another addition to the transputer series. The T400 is a 32 bit microprocessor with two communications links and 2 kbyte of on-chip RAM. This is a simple device aimed at bulk producers of simple electronic equipment, and is priced to be the cheapest 32 bit microprocessor available on the world market.

In April 1989 Thorn-EMI's share of Inmos was bought by SGS-Thomson Microelectronics, and Inmos is now part of the SGS-Thomson group. SGS-Thomson have received substantial financial backing from the French and Italian governments in a bid to improve those countries' standing in the microelectronics world. They in turn are providing Inmos with the financial security needed to undertake new research and development projects without the constant worry of immediate profit-making. While it is unfortunate that this support never materialised within the UK, the changes brought about by the takeover seem to have done the company no harm and their product range continues to expand. At the moment new products are biased heavily towards modular boards that provide an interface between existing systems and transputers. However Inmos plans to release a new transputer, the H1, in the first half of 1991. If this chip lives up to its expectations it could mean another major step forward for the parallel computer industry.

5.1.2   The Transputer

The transputer is a 32 bit VLSI microprocessors that has been specifically designed for use in concurrent message-passing systems. The general philosophy behind the transputer is to provide a family of compatible components which are able to communicate with one another using a minimum of external logic. Transputers communicate via point-to-point links, of which each transputer has four. In transputer-based multiprocessors these serial communications links and their interconnection topology constitute the message transfer system. The most important members of the transputer family are the T414 and the T800. These have many common features, but differ enough to warrant separate discussion.

T414

The T414 is a 32 bit microprocessor implementation of the general transputer structure outlined in Figure 5.1. It has 2 kbyte of on-chip SRAM and four standard Inmos full duplex serial links. The fixed-point processor can execute one 8 bit transputer instruction every 100 ns, i.e. at 10 MIPS, when instructions are held in the on-chip RAM. The external 32 bit memory interface, with a peak data transfer rate of 25 Mbyte/s, is capable of addressing up to four Gbyte. External memory interfacing logic is contained on the T414 in the form of a programmable set of memory control signals, which enables the T414 to provide refresh signals for a variety of dynamic memory devices.

Each of the four links provides two Occam channels, one in each direction, operating at 10 Mbit/s. A Direct Memory Access (DMA) controller is associated with each transputer link. Once a processor has initiated a communication on a link, it is immediately free to execute another task while the DMA engine continues message passing.

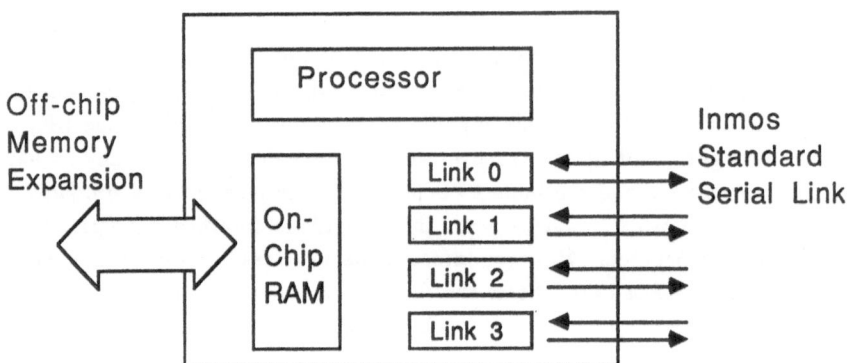

Figure 5.1: Conceptual Structure of the Transputer

The data transfer protocol is independent of word length, enabling the T414 to interface to other devices in the transputer family with differing word lengths. Links operate autonomously, so that transmission and reception of messages can be overlapped with instruction processing. This important feature of the transputer reduces the performance-degrading effects of message-passing, although this can only be achieved when there are sufficient parallel programs. When executing code stored in the on-chip RAM, four instructions can be fetched from memory every 50 ns; if the code is in external memory additional clock cycles will be incurred during fetching.

Communication between two processes on the same transputer occurs via single words of memory. Since the communications primitives and the process scheduler are implemented in microcode they incur very little overhead. For inter-processor communications the 10 MHz links transmit messages as a sequence of packets, each of which must be acknowledged, both to signal packet reception and to maintain flow control. The transmission protocol is asynchronous, and is implemented as a single wire for each channel. Data packets in one direction are multiplexed with acknowledge packets in the other direction on the same wire.

An important feature of the transputer is the speed with which it can swap between processes, something which happens automatically whenever a process is blocked waiting for a communication event. When a high priority process is suspended, and no other high priority processes can run, a low priority process can be scheduled in just 17 clock cycles.

T800

The T800 is the second generation of the transputer. The design is essentially the same as that of the T414, but has extra on-chip memory and an on-chip floating point unit (Figure 5.2). Extra instructions are provided to support floating-point data types and to give direct support to graphics operations. The fixed and floating-point units operate independently, so that a limited amount of implicit overlap of instructions can occur. Synchronisation between the two units occurs when data are moved into or out of the floating-point unit. This permits integer address calculations to proceed in parallel with floating-point calculations.

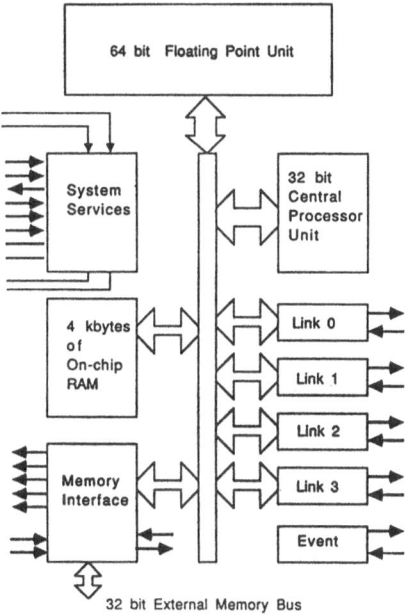

Figure 5.2: The Inmos T800 Transputer Architecture

The 64 bit floating-point unit provides single and double length operation, and produces a peak benchmarked performance of 1.9 MFLOPS for single length arithmetic on 20 MHz devices, with 1.2 MFLOPS achievable on a wide range of real applications. The link interfaces use a block data transfer mechanism to transfer messages between memory and another transputer product. These interfaces and the processor all operate concurrently, allowing processing to continue while data are being transferred.

T400

Released in September 1989 this new addition to the transputer "family" was aimed specifically at the producers of low-cost, mass-production electronic devices, from remote control toys to automatic dishwashers. The chip was a 32 bit microprocessor, with two Inmos links per chip and 2 kbyte of on-chip RAM. The T400 is priced at $20 per chip for large orders and is thus the lowest cost per MIPS (10 MIPS = $2 per MIPS) 32 bit microprocessor available. Inmos hopes that the T400 will keep alive the market for transputers, as well as the Inmos brand name, until the arrival at the marketplace of the H1.

Transputer Modules (TRAMs)

Inmos provides a range of modular hardware products for integration into end-user systems and for use as development platforms for general transputer projects. These TRAMs are small sub-assemblies of transputers and other circuitry, mostly RAM, with a standard interface comprising four serial Inmos links. These links provide communication channels, an input power supply and a route for system signals. The standard interface allows TRAMs to be mounted onto a selection of mother-boards to provide a second-level interface to host systems. Each motherboard can hold a number of TRAMs and thus support configuring facilities for networks of transputers. The use of motherboards and TRAMs allows transputer systems to be hosted by Sun workstations, DEC VAX, IBM PC and NEC machines.

5.1.3   The Software

Inmos provides a range of development tools for use on such transputer systems. These include compilers for C, Fortran and Pascal and a development package containing the Occam Transputer Development System (TDS), the Occam compiler, and a network debugger. A range of software is available from third parties, most importantly an Ada compiler from Alsys that runs on an IBM PC mothercard under MS-DOS.

5.1.4   The Market Niche

From the outset the transputer had been sold as a high-performance 32 bit microprocessor in its own right, as well as a potential component for parallel architectures. Because of its lack of installed base, the transputer was always at a disadvantage compared to other microprocessors on the market, such as the Motorola 68000 and Intel 80x86 chips.

Inmos's largest challenge has been to get the market to accept Occam. The company has been actively marketing the language since the T414 release, and claimed 5000 users by late 1986. However the commercial world has never been so keen, and this is clearly shown by the current move towards the provision of better compilers for the more common sequential languages. This move has come somewhat too late for the company; the loss of initial transputer sales in the United

States has left Inmos with a low profile in the USA. This is a situation from which Inmos may never recover, since American parallel computer manufacturers are now accustomed to buying chips from other sources.

Inmos is successfully selling its products for use in a wide range of applications, from the provision of simple desk-top computers to use in sophisticated telecommunications systems, not forgetting their inclusion in large number-crunching machines. The Inmos sales and marketing group have offices throughout the USA, in Bristol, Marlow, Munich, Paris and Milan to cover Europe, and in Tokyo and Singapore for the Far East. Each office also has an applications support team for liaison with local users. Sales are also made through SGS-Thomson's sales force and distributors.

5.1.5   The Future

Inmos plans to release the next generation of transputer, the H1, in the first half of 1991. Like the T800 the H1 will have a floating point unit, four communications links and memory caching, all integrated into the chip. The processing power and inter-processor bandwidth will scale-up from those achieved by the T800 to 20 MFLOPS and 80 Mbyte/s respectively. However there is more to the H1 than just being a faster version of the transputer.

One of the major restrictions on providing Hoare's Communicating Sequential Processes on transputers has been the restriction of only four communication links, since many topologies require more for direct implementation. Inmos does not intend to solve this problem by adding more hardware links to the transputer. There are VLSI limits in this area, as well as potential future desires for even more communication channels. Instead Inmos aims to implement packet switching communications using multiplexing hardware and a high-speed routing chip. Links will therefore have many *virtual channels* mapped onto them, and each program will have access to as many such channels as it needs. The routing chip will delivers messages to a named destination, freeing the processes from any concern about routing.

The H1 will divide message into 32 byte packets, and then interleave these packets down individual links. Each packet will start with a one or two byte header containing the intended destination of the message, and it receipt will be acknowledged by an empty packet. Each virtual link will contain two virtual channels, one to send and the other to receive. A sending process will wait until its last sent packet is acknowledged, which occurs at reception of the first byte, thus allowing unbroken transmissions should the receiver be ready. If not ready, a one packet long buffer is stored in memory, allowing any number of virtual channels to be set up on each processor up to the limits of processor memory.

Inmos claims that the H1 will be instruction set compatible with the T800. When coupled with the new Inmos switching chip, the C104, the H1 will solve many present-day connectivity problems. The C104 will contain 32 transputer links with a 32×32 crossbar switch, thus allowing any of 32 links to be connected to any other. It could therefore support a maximum of 32 H1s, although it may be more beneficial to use fewer processors (say 8) and allow all four links from each H1 to be connected to increase the available bandwidth. Alternatively, the C104's links could be used to connect several switch chips together to produce a larger and more complex switching network.

The C104 will use wormhole routing in which the switch chip only reads the header of each packet and thus decodes the destination. If the required link to the destination is free the rest of the packet is sent straight through from input to output without any storage in memory. If the destination is not free, the competing message will be stalled. Wormhole routing is totally invisible to the senders and receivers of messages, since it exists at a hardware level beneath the send/acknowledge synchronisation mechanism.

A good routing strategy is therefore necessary to provide low message passing latency. Inmos has chosen to use interval routing (Section A.2) with the H1 and C104. In this scheme each node has a number that is used as an address. Every link in the routing switch knows the addresses of a group (or interval) of destinations that it needs to recognise. These intervals can be arranged to be non-overlapping, so that every destination falls into just one interval for a wide range of generally-used topologies. The interval scheme allows routing to be achieved using a single comparison; moreover, the scheme can be guaranteed to be free of deadlock if cyclic paths are avoided. To avoid the build-up of hot spots when too many message pass through a particular node, random routing will also be used. While this will degrade performance for most regular topologies, it is theoretically proven to be near optimum in the worst-case limit.

Although neither the H1 nor C104 exist in silicon form at present, Inmos has simulations of both chips running now. These simulations suggest that H1/C104 networks will have a capacity under heavy loading that is very close to the theoretical maximum. The results also imply that the average message passing delay remains under control, rising from 12 to $27\mu s$ between a 64 node and 16384 node hypercube. If these results turn out to be valid, the H1 may represent a big step towards producing truly general purpose parallel computers. It is certainly being eagerly awaited by the manufacturers of the present generation of transputer based computers, almost without exception they intend to base their next machines on the H1.

5.2   Caplin Cybernetics

Relevant Activities Manufacture of transputer-based Vax-compatible hardware
and software.

Location Caplin Cybernetics, Poplar Business Park, 10, Prestons Road, London
E14 9RL. Telephone: 071 538 1716.

Relevant Officers Paul Caplin, Managing Director; Steve Guy, Sales & Marketing Manager; Clive Tuckwell, Technical Manager.

Employees 27

Financial details Private company, total capitalisation undisclosed.

5.2.1   The Company

Caplin Cybernetics was founded by Paul Caplin in 1985 in order to exploit a number
of development opportunities in the field of robotics. Caplin's background was as
an electronics engineer, however he had spent several years in the music business,
both as a musician and as a manager. The initial motivation behind his move back
to the electronics industry, and the establishment of Caplin Cybernetics, lay in the
desire to produce robots to perform stage lighting manoeuvres during concerts. This
required the development of machine vision, a branch of artificial intelligence that
involves decision making on the basis of visual information. It was also intended
that this same technology be marketed to industry in general to be used for factory
automation projects.

Very soon after entering the field, it became apparent to Caplin that the processing requirements for machine vision were huge. The hardware available on the
market either lacked the necessary performance, or had physical attributes that
made installation within a robot unfeasible. The company decided that the only
solution was to look toward parallel processing. Caplin had already standardised
on Vax-based hardware, and therefore required a method of retaining the existing
investment in Vax software and experience, whilst greatly increasing processing
speed. The chosen solution was to make use of Inmos transputers.

The first transputer-based products to come out of Caplin Cybernetics were the
QT series of MicroVax hardware modules and software tools. In June 1989 this
series was awarded the British Electronics Week "Product of the Year" TOBIE
award, a choice made through a readers ballot. The QT series did however have its
limitations – it consisted of a hard-wired configuration which reduced the flexibility
of the product as well as the potential performance when used for multiple applications requiring variable processor topologies. In 1990 Caplin Cybernetics released
HEX, the successor to the QT series. HEX is an applications oriented development

of the QT concept. Where the latter is a building block range of products, HEX is
an integrated system of hardware and software. Designed as a multi-user applications accelerator for the MicroVax, it consists of a software configurable transputer
network together with a fully VMS integrated operating system.

5.2.2 Caplin's Product Range

The QT Series

The QT series provides a MicroVax with an arbitrary number of busless, distributed
memory parallel processing subsystems, each containing an unlimited number of
processing nodes. Each node consists of an Inmos transputer, with up to 4 Mbyte
of DRAM memory. The nodes are interconnected via 20 Mbit/s asynchronous
serial links. The subsystems are user configurable, and subsystem control spurs on
selected nodes can be used to produce hierarchical, multi-level systems.

Table 5.1 below gives a summary of the specifications for the various boards
that make up the QT series. All the hardware modules are standard dual height
Q-bus boards. These fit inside a MicroVax cabinet and require no additional power
or external hardware, thus providing transputer arrays as DEC standard devices,
allowing access to VMS file and I/O services.

Table 5.1: The QT range of Caplin products

Board Name	Processor Type	Number of Processors	Function
QT0	T212	1	Vax/transputer interface, provides four transputer links with subsystem control
QT1	T414/T800	1	Transputer module for use with QT0 interface. Up to 4 Mbyte of DRAM
QT2	T414/T800	2	Transputer module for use with QT0 interface. Up to 2 Mbyte of DRAM
QT4	T414/T800	4	Transputer module for use with QT0 interface. 1 Mbyte of DRAM
QTV10	T800	1	Transputer based image processing video I/O board with twin frame stores.

All software supplied with the QT series is fully integrated with the Vax/VMS
multi-user environment, allowing concurrent multi-user compilation and execution
of parallel code. The software can be used in conjunction with standard editors
as well as software management tools. Applications resident on the Vax may call
QT-based routines through applications and communicating sequential processes

(CSP) libraries, and in this mode the Vax/transputer interface is transparent to the user. Parallel program modules can be written in one of the following supported languages; Fortran 77, C, Pascal, Occam, Prolog and Ada, as well as the 3L versions of parallel Fortran and parallel C. Modules written in different languages can be linked together and distributed across the network as required.

HEX

HEX is a transputer based parallel processing system embedded within Vax/VMS or ULTRIX operating systems. It is a multi-user system with dynamically configurable topology and partitioning. The user-created domains are completely independent – there is full signal isolation between different networks. The system guarantees uninterruptable communications paths between each processor and the host, thus easing the use of debugging and system monitoring tools. HEX is designed to be used in three distinct areas:

- An accelerator for existing Vax-based applications – Caplin have achieved speed-ups of 14 times over an existing Vax-3600 application by simple parallelisation and the addition of eight T800 transputers. The speed-ups measured are very much problem dependent, for example for another client company Caplin have achieved speed-ups of over 25 times by adding 12 T800 transputers to a MicroVax-2.

- A development environment for parallel software – HEX is accompanied by a range of compilers and programming tools.

- A supercomputer-class vehicle for single specialised applications.

A HEX system is built from a number of boards linked together by a HEX "data highway" (see Figure 5.3). Normal installation of a small number of boards would take place within the MicroVax. Each HEX processor board contains from one to eight T800 series floating-point transputers, each with from 1 to 32 Mbyte of DRAM. The boards may also feature special purpose graphics, image processing or I/O circuitry. In addition each board contains a monitor and a topology controller, which act with the HEXsys system software to control the HEX functionality. The interface to the Vax is via Q-bus or SCSI links, supporting multiple users. Connection to boards from the QT series, or other transputer boards, is possible through the HXIT board.

HEX is therefore very similar in design to the QT series, but with the added flexibility of user reconfigurability. The configuration resource in HEX is finite, but substantial. The maximum system size would involve 256 processing nodes, giving a quoted processing performance of 2.8 gigaFLOPS.

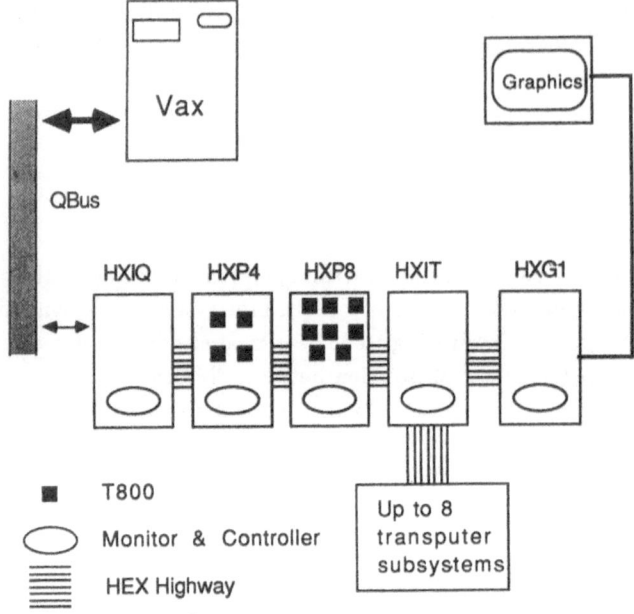

Figure 5.3: Typical HEX System Architecture

HEXsys

HEXsys is a suite of system software which provides a multiuser and multitasking environment for the control and use of HEX hardware. HEXsys manages the dynamic repartitioning of resources into independent subsystems. Each HEX board has a controlling monitor running as part of HEXsys. At the lowest level, a programmer communicates with the controller through HEXlib, a set of routines called from the user code. HEXlib routines can be called directly from the host system, or from nodes within a subsystem.

A higher level interface to the controller is provided via the HEX toolkit library. This offers users more sophisticated facilities and higher level constructs on top of HEXlib. HEX Toolkit functions give programs the flexibility to use whatever processor resource is available at run-time, and can also be used to fine-tune programs by allowing the programmer to specify that certain processors and certain processor links be used for specific tasks.

Caplin offer an entry-level HEX development system for £16,000. This includes HEXsys software, and support for parallel programming in Fortran 77, C, Pascal, Occam or Ada. There is also a library of application support features including GKS, X Windows, Helios (Section 9.2), Express (9.1), complete NAG libraries, Parallel Maths libraries (FFTs, Matrix algebra, linear solvers, etc), image processing libraries and graphics libraries.

5.2.3 The Market Niche

Caplin Cybernetics see no direct competition in the Vax-transputer boards market. In a wider sense they have competition from companies like Meiko and Parsys as regards the production of transputer systems in general. Their marketing is therefore directed towards users of Vax/VMS systems and their product line seems tailored for easy integration into such environments. However there are at present no parallelisation tools available to ease the adaptation of existing code, or the production of new parallel code.

Caplin Cybernetics have installed parallel systems in over 100 sites worldwide. These include BBC Television, GCHQ, The Royal Greenwich Observatory, the Rutherford Appleton Laboratory and British Aerospace in the United Kingdom, Shell (Netherlands), Euratom (Belgium) and Lawrence Livermore Laboratories (USA).

At present Caplin sells around 60% of its hardware within the UK, with the majority of the remainder being sold within the rest of Europe. However there are also HEX systems installed and running in the USA, India, Israel, Japan and New Zealand. The continental European market is their fastest growing sector and they see the balance of sales soon shifting away from the UK. Within the UK sales are split fairly evenly between three major buyers; academia, the defence industry and industry in general. The export market is also evenly divided, however in this case the division is 50/50 between academia and industry. They have a close working relationship with DEC and Inmos, being an Inmos strategic partner and a DEC OEM and CSO [1]. This allows Caplin Cybernetics to make joint tender bids with DEC, and provides customers with the security of DEC maintenance agreements.

Caplin see their immediate future as complementing their present products, maintaining the connections with Vax systems and Inmos processor technology. They intend to maintain the HEX style of hardware, allowing integration of new products with old ones (as was the case with the HEX and QT series boards).

5.2.4 Present Applications

Computational Chemistry

COMMET is a molecular mechanics package developed at the University of Glasgow. It was originally developed for parallel processors, and has been successfully ported across to run on Caplin hardware. It provides tools for modelling all classes of chemical structure and offers a graphics interface to aid visualisation. The package is available for HEX systems, as is MOPAC, one of the most widely used "semi-empirical" molecular modelling suites.

---

[1] complementary software organisation

Finite Element Analysis and Computational Fluid Dynamics

Three popular packages in this field are all available or about to become available on
HEX systems. Phoenics, a CFD code from CHAM, was launched in 1981 and soon
obtained worldwide use. It models 3D laminar or turbulent flows through several
phases. FLOW-3D from AEA Technology is another popular 3D Fluid Dynamics
code, while Paradyne from Rockfield Software is a dynamic analysis tool for use
on two and three-dimensional structures. It differs from the previous software
in that it was designed from the start for concurrent execution. The other two
of these packages represent the successful porting of Vax/VMS based code to the
HEX environment, rather than the development of original programs for transputer
systems.

Relational Database Applications

White Cross Systems have produced a parallel relational database capable of "unlimited" expansion. It offers ANSI standard SQL together with a range of interactive tools. A preliminary version of IPE is now available on HEX systems.

5.2.5   The Future

Caplin have no immediate plans to make major changes to their hardware range.
They are happy with the performance that can be achieved from their present system, and any changes that do occur in the future will reflect changes in transputer
technology. It is therefore likely that when the H1 is released by Inmos early in
1991 this new chip will be incorporated into Caplin systems, thus retaining some
level of compatibility throughout their product range.

However, Caplin do expect significant advances in the near future in the realm of
software. It is certainly in this area that most of their research effort is placed, with
both new software and ports of existing software constantly becoming available for
HEX systems. The development of parallel software standards is considered by the
company as a high priority, and they feel that their close relationship with DEC
may allow them to take on a significant role in the definition of standards.

5.3   Meiko Scientific Limited

Relevant Activities Manufacturers of distributed memory MIMD computers.

Location Meiko Scientific, 680 Aztec West, Bristol BS12 4SD. Telephone: 0454 616171. Fax: 0464 618188. US Office: Meiko Scientific, Reservoir Place, 1601 Trapelo Road, Waltham, Massachusetts 02154. Telephone: (617) 890 7676. Fax: (617) 890 5142.

Relevant Officers H. Miles Chesney, Chairman (World); Richard M. Bloch, President (World) and CEO (US Operations).

Employees Over 125 employees in Bristol R&D Centre. Offices and distributors throughout Europe, Asia and the United States.

Financial details Startup financed by founders. Privately held by employees.

5.3.1   The Company

In 1979 Miles Chesney moved from the Robotics group at Warwick University to join newly-formed Inmos to work on the development of the transputer (cf. Section 5.1). In November 1979 he filed Inmos's first patent for the design of the transputer communications system. That same year Chesney was joined by Eric Barton, who was to develop Inmos's VLSI chip design system; Gerry Talbot, who eventually became Design Manager for hardware products; Principal Software Engineer James Cownie and Roy Bottomley, Project Leader for transputer development. The team that would later found Meiko was completed by David Alden, Business Manager for Inmos's Microcomputer Division, following successful assignments at Unilever and the National Enterprise Board.

Late in 1985, Inmos management recommended a delay in the introduction of the transputer as an economy measure. As a result, the Meiko founding team decided to resign from Inmos to form a company in order to exploit the opportunities which were opening up for parallel processing systems. The new company's name meant "well-engineered" in Japanese.

Meiko was founded using the combined cash flow from three engineering contracts, each with advance funding. One of these projects was to produce a demonstration system for Inmos which would package the transputer and illustrate its capabilities. This was completed less than nine weeks after Meiko was formed, and the demonstration system was first shown at the SIGGRAPH graphics trade show in San Francisco in July 1985. The Computing Surface which developed from it became commercially available in 1986.

By 1987 Meiko had 30 employees, sales had been made in the US and several European countries, and a $2 M system was installed at Toyota Motor Corporation,

Japan. In 1988 world-wide sales exceeded $10 M and the installed machine base exceeded 200 systems. Meiko absorbed Niche Data Systems in 1989, consolidating the US operation established the previous year, and acquired a very experienced President in Richard M. Bloch, formerly a founder of Honeywell Data Systems and later a Vice-President and Divisional General Manager for General Electric.

5.3.2   The Hardware

Meiko's main product is the Computing Surface, a modular and expandable distributed memory MIMD machine. Early versions of the Computing Surface were hosted by Vax, PC or Sun machines. Current versions are self-hosted stand-alone or networkable multi-user systems. From a hardware viewpoint, the Computing Surface consist of:

- An arbitrary number of individual microprocessors (which may be Inmos transputers, Sun CPUs, SPARCs and Intel i860s), each with its own dedicated memory.

- An arbitrary number of special purpose boards or elements to provide I/O, graphics, digital and signal processing functions, etc.

- An interconnection network which provides a communication resource for passing messages within the system.

- A supervisor bus which provides some control functions for the system as a whole.

- An enclosure consisting of one or more electronically linked cabinets.

In a configurable processor array such as the Computing Surface, there should ideally be complete connectivity between all the processors. In practice, this is very expensive to implement and is not scalable, since the number of possible paths grows very quickly with the number of processors and soon requires an interconnection network which is beyond current (or envisaged) packaging technology. The interconnection network in the Computing Surface is therefore a limited resource, designed initially with the transputer's four links in mind. It has two elements: a backplane routing resource and link network interface chips. The link network interface chips are custom VLSI crossbar switches which connect processor links to the backplane routing resource. A manually configured system does not require the link network interface chips and is adequate for systems with a fixed or infrequently changing topology.

Processors mounted on the same board may be connected without drawing on the backplane routing resource, but links between processors on different boards must be routed through the backplane. The backplane routing resource capacity therefore places an upper bound on the number of off-board links that can be routed. By statically allocating the user's virtual processors to the physical processors, it is possible to place them so as to maximise the number of connected processors which are on the same board, thus minimising the backplane routing resource requirements. The precise details of the capabilities of the backplane routing resource have not been released by Meiko. While experience shows that a small number of topologies cannot be wired in large, multi-module systems, Meiko claim that all useful topologies can be created, although it may be necessary to generate this mapping manually for particularly large or complex topologies.

The backplane also supports a supervisor bus, which provides low bandwidth connectivity between all processors in the system. The bus can reset and examine the state of all processors, report errors, and configure link connectivity. Application software can also use the supervisor bus as a communications pathway. This is particularly useful as a means of transmitting debugging information.

The supervisor bus can also be used to partition a Computing Surface into a number of domains, each of which can be used independently of the others. This sort of space-sharing, which is also used on hypercube machines, is a way of providing multi-user service without the overheads of task-swapping on individual processors. Most importantly, it lets users develop code using a small number of a machine's processors, while other users perform production runs using the majority of the processors.

Each Computing Surface module must have a local host board to perform housekeeping functions. The original local host board is the MK014, which has a single processor with 3 Mbyte RAM and occupies a single board slot. It is responsible for managing the supervisor bus and for configuring the link network within the module. In addition, the local host provides IEEE-488 and dual RS232 connections. File access may be provided through these connections, or through an inter-processor link to the hosting system. Further local hosts can be added to provide additional I/O facilities.

Multi-module systems can be built by connecting modules to provide a communications network for the whole machine. The link network is homogeneous within a single module, but links across cabinet boundaries must be routed through special intercabinet links. Supervisor buses in adjacent modules can also be configured to enable a single master host board to configure a multi-module system, although separate host boards are still required in every module. There is no theoretical limit on the number of modules (and therefore processors) in a Computing Surface, but an upper bound on the length of the intermodule link wire imposes a practical limit. The largest system currently in operation, the Edinburgh Concurrent Supercomputer, has five modules and contains over 400 compute processors.

The basic compute boards in the Computing Surface is the MK060, which carries four transputers, each with up to 8 Mbyte DRAM[2]. Each processor's links can run at 5, 10 or 20 Mbit/s.

In addition to the this basic compute board, an unusually wide range of other boards are available, which allow the Computing Surface to be tailored to the purchasers requirements. All boards contain at least one computing element, a supervisor bus interface, and an optional link network interface. Some idea of the range of facilities offered may be gained from the list below:

- The MK041 Octal UART board occupies a single slot and allows eight user terminals to be connected to the Computing Surface. The ports may also be used to provide a high-bandwidth I/O system for a single user. Multiple UART boards can be configured in a single machine.

- The MK015 Display Element has a single transputer with 128 kbyte SRAM. Its 1.5 Mbyte dual-ported frame buffer can be configured as a single high-resolution frame of 500 kpixel at 24 bit/pixel; a single frame of 1.5 Mpixel at 8 bit/pixel; or three frames of 500 kpixel at 8 bit/pixel for animation. Three 256-entry colour lookup tables drive the 8 bit per gun digital-to-analogue converters. Multiple MK015s can be ganged together using a private data highway to give a larger frame store for a single image or to increase bandwidth.

- The MK052 is a more powerful graphics board than the MK015, with 4 Mbyte DRAM for the processor and a 2 Mbyte frame store. Like the MK015, multiple MK052s can be ganged together. Amongst its other features is support for X Windows.

- Video I/O is supported by a number of boards. Pictures are edited or generated on the graphics boards and the video data are then sent out along the pixel bus, together with timing and synchronisation information. Synchronisation may be provided by the graphics boards, or from an external source via an MK038 genlock board, which allows graphical output to be synchronised with an external video signal.

- The MK040 Data Port Element board provides a facility for high bandwidth I/O. Each board carries two data port elements, each of which contains a single processor with 500 kbyte of 20 Mbyte/s dual-ported RAM and a programmable address sequencer. The sequencer uses a clock to control transfers between the data port and sequential locations in memory at rates of up to 80 Mbyte/s. The start location and length of a buffer are specified by the

---

[2]The advent of 4 Mbit DRAM has increased this limit to 32 Mbyte per processor.

Table 5.2: Overview of Meiko In-Sun Computing Surfaces

Board	Processors	Memory per processor	MFLOPS (peak)
MK200	4	up to 12 Mbyte	6
MK201	8	up to 8 Mbyte	12
MK203	16	up to 2 Mbyte	24
MK204	up to 16	up to 2 Mbyte	up to 24

processor when it initiates a transfer, after which it is free for use while the data are transferred.

The data port element attaches to an I/O highway which occupies the customisable portion of the Computing Surface backplane. Multiple MK040s can thus sample a single data stream, allowing data to be distributed for concurrent processing. Applications include real-time image capture, processing and graphics output, multi-head disc farms and interfacing to high-speed channels of third-party systems.

- The MK027 Frame Grabber is based on a single data port element with 1 Mbyte of dual ported memory. It may act alone or as part of the data port data highway, allowing digitised video images to be distributed to many other processors. The frame grabber can capture a monochrome or single colour video frame in a single frame time, while multiple frame grabbers can be used to capture RGB data simultaneously. The MK027 includes an image preprocessing port which allows special-purpose image processing hardware (such as edge detectors) to process the video image before it reaches the data highway.

The In-Sun Computing Surface

Late in 1988 Meiko released a series of add-in boards for Sun-3 and Sun-4 workstations. Meiko provides these in turnkey systems, configured for use, and as separate boards for installation in existing workstations. These products have become popular for low cost prototyping and development of parallel applications under CS Tools.

Each board has between one and four T800 processors dedicated to managing the interface between individual T800 applications processors and the host. These interface processors have a shared memory subsystem with up to 4 Mbyte of multiported RAM. One Mbyte of this memory is dual-ported to the VME bus in the Sun. The interface is entirely transparent to users and programmers, supporting data rates of 2.2 Mbyte/s to the Sun filing system and Sun-hosted front ends.

In-Sun boards have the same software controlled routing network chips as the Computing Surface. A link highway lets the routing networks of several boards be combined, allowing for seamless addition of boards within the Sun chassis. The message links from the interface processors can be routed via the link switches to processors on the same board, on other boards within the Sun chassis, or in an attached Computing Surface module. Interprocessor communication on the boards runs at 1.4 Mbyte/s.

Sun Virtual Computing Surface (SVCS) manages the available processors as a dynamic resource. To users, these applications processors appear as a pool, from which applications automatically claim processors. SVCS transparently re-configures the hardware into the required topology as the application is loaded for execution.

The maximum configuration in a single workstation contains 96 processors, and can yield 150 MFLOPS peak. An external Computing Surface may be attached to the In-Sun Computing Surface to increase the pool of processors available to applications through SVCS. The In-Sun boards support the CS Tools programming environment.

SPARC-based Computing Surface

A technology deal with Sun in late 1989 has led to the licensing of SunOS for the Computing Surface and the production of SPARC-based boards to host it, as well as for use as alternative processing boards. These SPARC boards will allow Meiko to capitalise on the growth of networked workstation products and permit the SPARC-based nodes within the machine to execute standard, shrink-wrapped programs from the SPARCware catalogue. In addition, Meiko and Sun are attempting to use the SPARC-based Computing Surface to penetrate the multi-user UNIX market. In return for the advantages offered by the link with Sun, Meiko have designed a Floating-Point Unit for the SPARC. Meiko is a member of SPARC International, an organisation established to promote the SPARC architecture and set Applications Binary Interface (ABI) standards.

The first SPARC board, the MK083, occupies two board slots and carries a 25 MHz SPARC processor with 8 to 64 Mbyte RAM, delivering 15 MIPS and 1.4 MFLOPS. Two communications processors are configured on the node, giving a peak I/O bandwidth over the CSN of 16 Mbyte/s. These co-processors operate concurrently with the SPARC processor and are dedicated to handling the internal traffic between Computing Surface nodes. The board also has SCSI and Ethernet interfaces and dual RS232 ports, which are controlled by the SPARC processor itself. The MK083 provides access to the system via SunOS 4.1, and has binary compatibility with SPARCware applications written for SunOS 4.1 and higher.

Designed to supply high performance UNIX application serving, the MK085 is based on the higher performance 33 MHz SPARC chip, which delivers 24 MIPS

and over 3 MFLOPS. The SPARC processor's 64 kbyte cache is supported by the
SPARC Reference Cached Memory Management Unit (CMMU) and has between
8 and 128 Mbyte of memory. The MMU has 4096 hardware contexts, and supports
very fast context switching between large numbers of processes. Four communications co-processors provide 32 Mbyte/s peak I/O bandwidth over the CSN. Like
the MK083, the MK085 runs SunOS 4, but occupies only a single board slot. The
MK083 is available now, and the MK085 will be available late in 1990.

i860-based Computing Surface

Meiko's MK086 board consists of two i860-based processing elements. Each 40 MHz
i860 has 80 MFLOPS peak performance, with up to 32 Mbyte of memory. Two
T800 transputers act as communications co-processors for the i860, with a peak
bandwidth of 16 Mbyte/s over the Computing Surface Network (CSN). The interface between the i860 and the transputers is invisible to the user — from a software
perspective the i860 node behaves like an i860 processor with eight communication
links. However, it is unlikely that all applications will be able to use the full power
of the i860 (rated at 80 MFLOPS peak) because of bandwidth limitations imposed
by the transputer links (a maximum of 20 Mbyte/s). Therefore, programs which
require frequent use of inter-processor communication may be bandwidth limited.

The i860 node is fully supported by CS Tools, allowing heterogeneous applications to be built for i860, SPARC and transputer nodes. Meiko's Fortran/860
toolset is scheduled for release by the end of 1990. This cross development toolset
is intended to be hosted on a Sun 3, SPARCstation or Meiko MK083 SPARC node.
It will provide an ANSI Fortran 77 compiler which employs global optimisation,
instruction scheduling, software pipelining and vectorisation to produce high performance code for the i860. However, given the general problems in developing an
efficient compiler suffered by all manufacturers using the i860 chip it is possible that
this timescale might slip. Meiko plan to release a C++ toolset for the i860 early in
1991. Compiled code and the i860 runtime environment will comply to Intel's ABI
and APX standards, supporting cross-language calls and user calls to third party
libraries. APX is an example of an ABI, in fact the first in a series which Intel
are promoting. The toolset will include a full source-level debugger with support
for debugging programs running on several heterogeneous processors. A library of
hand-coded vector routines will be provided. The i860-based Computing Surface
will strengthen Meiko's presence in the high-performance scientific and engineering
computing market. Specifically, they see this machine as competing against the
hypercubes and large shared memory computers.

5.3.3   Programming Environments

The Computing Surface came onto the market in late 1986. At that time, Meiko offered the Occam Programming System (OPS) environment, a modified version of the Inmos TDS (cf. 5.1). This was later developed into Multi-OPS, which allowed several users to work simultaneously on different partitions of the Computing Surface. By mid-1988, a more powerful resource manager called Meiko Multiple Virtual Computing Surfaces (M²VCS) was available.

Meiko were never as enthusiastic about Occam as Inmos were, and compilers for C and Fortran were developed as early as 1987. These compilers provided functional extensions to C and Fortran which allowed sequential processes to communicate through Occam-like channels. An Occam harness "plumbed" the channels in different processes together.

Meiko were also not enthusiastic about the Transputer Development System TDS. It was clear that in order to attract a significant user base it would be necessary to provide a UNIX-like operating system. Rather than port one which was already available, as other manufacturers such as Parsys and Parsytec had done, Meiko chose to develop MeikOS, their own implementation of UNIX, which was released in 1989. Based on AT&T System V and Berkeley 4.3BSD, MeikOS was intended to provide a familiar environment for programming the Computing Surface. SunOS became available for Computing Surfaces with SPARC-based local host boards in 1990.

It is understood that MeikOS 4.x will be derived from SunOS 4.x. This will allow MK085s to provide an industry standard development environment on large, multi-user Computing Surfaces. It will also result in uniform development environments for In-Sun and stand-alone Computing Surfaces, enhancing portability between the two machines. This merger of the two development environments currently supported on their systems will relieve Meiko of a considerable maintenance burden, and free resources for development efforts on a single platform.

5.3.4   CS Tools

CS (Communicating Sequential) Tools is Meiko's development suite for parallel applications. Its purpose is to provide developers working in standard languages access to the full functionality of the underlying hardware. It is supported on all Meiko hardware, except for Computing Surfaces hosted by a Vax, and allows applications to be ported easily from one machine to another. CS Tools is a toolset rather than a parallel operating system; programs are coded in a sequential language, compiled and debugged largely within a familiar host environment, while CS Tools provides message passing extensions to allow concurrent sequential processes to communicate.

The model of communication in CS Tools centres on transports (cf. A.2). Sequential processes create ports and register names for them with the CSN. Other processes can then look up these named ports and send messages to them. The CSN transfers messages between processors, giving the user an impression of homogeneous hardware, and abstracting from the details of low-level message passing. CS Tools supports synchronous and asynchronous messages, and blocking and non-blocking variants of communications operations.

The CS Tools suite includes a Run-Time Executive (RTE) which provides applications processors with access to standard system services to applications. Both local services (such as memory allocation) and remote services (such as file access) are supported, the latter by messaging remote servers through the CSN. Separate configuration tools define the structure and distribution of parallel programs across the available processor resource. These are provided in the form of a PAR file loader (a text-driven facility) and the CS Build library of configuration and system-loading calls. A dbx-like debugger, tdb, allows step-by-step debugging symbolic debugging of parallel programs, is now available on all machines.

Meiko's C and Fortran cross-compilers comply to ANSI standards, run under MeikOS, SunOS and Vax/VMS operating systems, and can generate both sequential and (using CS Tools) parallel code. A validated cross-compilation system for Ada is available from Alsys. This runs on a Vax and generates code suitable for all transputer-based Computing Surfaces. An interface to CS Tools is provided. An implementation of Kyoto Common Lisp (KCL) also runs under CS Tools. Sequential Lisp processes are compiled for execution on the Computing Surface, and then communicate through a streams interface to CS Tools. The Common Lisp Object System (CLOS) is supported. Finally, Meiko are now shipping a C++ compiler.

5.3.5 Sales and Marketing

In its early days, Meiko's customers were drawn almost exclusively from the parallel processing research community. By contrast, the current customer base of several hundred installations is spread throughout the computer-using community. Most of the sales are in the UK and Europe, though a recent survey of the US market by the San Francisco Chronicle showed that Meiko are now the fifth largest parallel computer supplier.

Research institutes with Meiko equipment include CalTech, the Edinburgh Parallel Computing Centre, the Universities of Mainz, Amsterdam, Twente, Oxford, and Syracuse, the Institute of Cancer Research, Rutherford Appleton Labs, the National Physical Laboratory and Daresbury Laboratory in the UK, and the Heinrich Hertz Institute. Meiko's list of commercial customers is equally impressive, including IBM, Intel, Xerox, British Aerospace, Plessey, Rolls Royce, British Telecom, Hewlett Packard, Shell, General Electric, Thorn EMI, Philips, Glaxo and BP. The

Table 5.3: Meiko Sales by Market Sector

Market	% of total sales
Academia	27
Research	20
Military	23
Finance	11
Industry	19

BBC and Independent Television News both use Computing Surfaces to generate graphics and caption sequences. In the defence sector, Meiko have made sales to RSRE, RARDE, RAE, ARA, and ARE in the UK, and to the US Department of Defense, as well as to secret establishments in Europe and North America.

Meiko now have between 300 and 400 installations using their equipment. They are not the only transputer-based manufacturer, for example Parsytec (cf. Section 5.5) and Parsys (5.4) make similar machines. However, it is Meiko's view that these companies are not competing in the same marketplace, due to Meiko's diversification of their product line and their bias towards large installations. Rather, they see Intel (cf. Section 4.1), BBN (3.2), Alliant (3.1), Convex (3.4), FPS (3.6) and to a lesser extent NCUBE (4.2) as competitors for the Computing Surface. In this list one can see that Meiko are targetting the Computing Surface at the mid-price market, rather than at the low-end typified by the transputer add-in manufacturers. Nevertheless, it is clear that Cogent's XTM machines (6.1) are one of a number of competitors for the same market as the Meiko's In-Sun products, although Cogent's poor market penetration in Europe has not yet led to serious competition. Similarly, the various manufacturers of add-in boards, such as Caplin (5.2), are also competitors at this end of the market.

Computing Surfaces are used for a wide range of compute-intensive tasks including simulations, computer-aided design and engineering, graphic rendering, ray tracing and animation, video graphics, image and signal processing, compression and encryption, and oil reservoir modelling. A number of third party packages are available for the Computing Surface: ethosPSC is a seismic data processing and analysis package; ASTEC and Masterflow are Computational Fluid Dynamics packages from the UK Atomic Energy Authority and Flomerics Ltd respectively; and Dyna 3D, a nonlinear finite element analysis package originating from LLL, is also available. In non-numeric fields, Jade's Sim++ is a discrete event simulation environment built on C++, while there is an implementation of TEX for the Computing Surface. Meiko provide consultancy and applications development for customers in order to sell tailored systems.

Meiko is making inroads into the data processing market with its Relational DataCache. This is essentially a dedicated resource for the Oracle Relational DataBase Management System (RDBMS). Front-ended by a Vax, the Relational DataCache takes over all the Oracle processing, boosting performance and freeing the Vax for those front-end applications which it handles more effectively. Relational DataCache systems start at over £120 k, excluding an Oracle licence.

Chemical Design Ltd., Ensign Geophysical and Applied Geophysical Services are amongst a number of companies marketing products based on Meiko equipment. Meiko see the OEM market to be a rapidly growing sector, in which their presence is strengthened by their low-end In-Sun systems.

The more recent introduction of the SPARC- and i860-based Computing Surfaces shows that Meiko are trying to broaden their purchaser base and to compete more strongly in the American market where there has, traditionally, been a reluctance to buy European computers.

5.3.6   The Future

In its first five years Meiko has grown from six founders to an organisation which employing 125 people. In the next five years the company plans to extend its territory world-wide and grow to an organisation of about 3,500 people. Expansion in the US seems likely to build on the absorbed Niche Data Systems. Bloch, with extensive experience of the computer industry in senior management and CEO roles, is likely to play a pivotal role in this ambitious expansion.

5.4 Parsys Limited

Relevant Activities Manufacturers and suppliers of the SuperNode 1000 series
of transputer-based supercomputers and supporting software.

Location Parsys Limited, Boundary House, Boston Road, London W7 2QE. Telephone: 081 579 8683. Fax: 081 579 8365

Relevant Officers Douglas Stevenson, Chairman; David Watson, Managing and
Technical Director; Ian Coburn, Commercial Director; Peter Dzwig, Marketing Manager;

Employees 22 full-time, four part-time, all in the UK.

Financial details Independent limited company

5.4.1 The Company

Parsys Limited provides a typical example of the extent and speed of change within
the parallel computing industry in the past five years. The initial research effort
began in 1985, choosing the transputer as the device on which to centre a new
machine.

From that beginning have come two growing and competing companies manufacturing parallel computers. Parsys is now one of Britain's leading manufacturers of
high-performance parallel computers, and is actively marketing its products within
the usual academic and industrial fields, as well as in the more unusual markets of
financial institutions and government departments.

The Esprit Supernode Projects

Parsys was established to exploit commercially the products of the EC-funded Esprit Supernode project. Esprit was a joint research program set up by the European
Community in order to strengthen Europe's international position in information
technology, particularly in the areas of advanced computer technology and applications. Several of the projects selected for funding by the Esprit committee were
concerned with parallel processing. The majority of these concentrated on the
more theoretical "fifth-generation" role of parallel processing; only the Supernode
project was aimed at traditional number-crunching applications and therefore had
commercial significance.

Supernode received financial backing from both the UK and France. £7 M
was put forward by the European research programme Esprit, the universities of
Southampton and Grenoble, the UK companies Inmos (Section 5.1 and Thorn EMI,
the French companies Telmat SA and Apsis, and the Royal Signals and Research
Establishment (RSRE), part of the UK defence research community. The main

aim of this project, initiated in 1985, was to develop a machine to use transputers in reconfigurable networks, thus producing a low-cost high-performance parallel computer. The base for the development lay in work by Chris Jesshope at the University of Southampton. Following parallel processing experience on the Illiac IV, the Cray (7.1) and the ICL DAP (2.1), Jesshope initiated Supernode as an attempt to meet the computing needs of the University's physics department. In particular, the physicists were running out of computing power to tackle their quantum chromodynamics (QCD) calculations. (This same requirement has inspired other projects such as the Meiko i860-based machine now sited at Edinburgh University.)

At the start of the project the various contributors took on specific tasks. RSRE was the prime contractor and worked on the link switch as well as signal and image processing applications. Thorn EMI had responsibility for real-time I/O, systems software, debugging aids and AI applications. Inmos was charged with the development of a floating-point version of the transputer, which later emerged as the T800. Southampton University continued to develop the architecture, and built the first prototype Supernode, while Telmat was responsible for the manufacture of boards in quantity and the construction of complete machines. Apsis, based in Grenoble, investigated applications in computer-aided design and factory automation, and the University of Grenoble took responsibility for the theoretical aspects of the project and the implementation of Occam on the system.

After two years the project had successfully developed a prototype machine. At that point Thorn EMI decided to commit further funds in order to turn the prototype into a marketable product backed by a strong corporate infrastructure. By this time the aims of Jesshope's original project had shifted somewhat, away from the production of a specialised machine for QCD calculations, towards a general purpose, powerful, yet relatively inexpensive machine. However, the essential philosophy of his architecture remained intact.

By September 1988 Parsys was looking towards the provision of software for their machines. A second Franco-British joint venture was initiated with the aim of producing an automatic parallelising Fortran compiler. This project involved Parsys and System Software Factors (SSF) from the UK, and Telmat from France. This venture gained some funding from the Esprit backed Supernode-2 project, which got underway in June 1989. The project has a target length of four years; its main aims are to produce a distributed Operating System and automatic parallelising compiler for transputers to be used on the Parsys SuperNode machines, as well as the Telmat T-Node series. In addition parallel maths libraries are to be developed by Liverpool University under EC grants.

In March 1990 SSF ceased trading, only a month short of the deadline for delivery of a parallel Fortran compiler for the SuperNode 1000 (SN1000) series. The company was at that time also involved in an i860 project as well as the other elements of Supernode-2. The project is however still underway with Parsys and

Telmat as major funders, along with Thorn EMI Central research laboratories, RSRE, Numerical Algorithms Group (NAG), Syseca (another French company), Grupo APD (Spain), Parsim (Denmark) and the Maths Institute at the University of Grenoble.

Parsys Goes It Alone

Parsys Limited was established in April 1988 under the auspices of the Thorn EMI New Business Ventures organisation. With the establishment of the company came the launch of the first of their products, the SN1000, which utilised T800 transputers in a back-end modular unit based on a minimum configuration of 17 transputers. The system could be hosted by IBM, Sun or DEC systems. Connections between the transputers could be specified through software control to form any independent four-link network. These networks were software reconfigurable, thus achieving the original Esprit project aim.

During their first year of operation the company sold 35 machines, and passed the £1 M sales mark in May 1989. Parsys distributors were appointed for the United Kingdom, Benelux, the Middle East and the Pacific Basin as part of a planned expansion programme to be funded by raising venture capital. Early in 1990 there was a partial buy-out of the company from Thorn EMI. With the financial backing of Electra Innvotec, the directors and staff acquired a significant stake in the company, although Thorn EMI did retain a minority stake. Parsys Limited is now completely owned by Parsys Holdings Ltd., which is in turn owned by Electra Innvotec Limited Partnership, Thorn EMI, and the company's directors and staff.

Telmat Informatique

From the moment of their formation, Parsys has had direct competition from the French company Telmat Informatique. Their partners from the Supernode project also set themselves the aim of producing a transputer-based supercomputer based on the prototype of the Esprit project. Telmat had previously been involved in the manufacture of multi-processor computers based around Motorola 68000s. They therefore took responsibility for the mass production of Supernode boards and the construction of complete machines from the start of the project.

Telmat's T-Node series machines are reconfigurable transputer networks similar to the SN1000 series. With building blocks of eight T800 transputers, programmable switches allow network reconfiguration to produce various domain sizes. These 80 Mbit/s crossbar switches were designed by RSRE as part of the Supernode project, and are used by both Parsys and Telmat. The T-Node series machines contained up to 256 transputers (the TN380), and are advertised as peaking at 1.5 GFLOPS. Telmat supply their TN series machines with a range of software tools, including the Helios operating system (cf. 9.2), and the TDS development environment. Additionally, they supply compilers for Occam, C, Fortran and Pascal.

Early 1990 saw the release of the new MegaNode machines from Telmat. These are similar in design to the T-Node machines, but are larger and provide the user with more software development tools. The MegaNode machines contain from 128 to 1024 T800 transputers, giving an advertised peak power of 2 GFLOPS. Users have access to the Helios operating system and the use of X Windows, and compilers are available for Fortran, Pascal, C, Occam, Ada and STRAND[88] (Section 9.4).

There is a good working relationship between Telmat and Parsys, and they have a collaboration history that goes back to the start of the Supernode project. The basic architectures of the two companies' machines are very similar, using the same processors and switch chips. The basic products, SuperNode and T-Node, are therefore backplane compatible, and all boards are plug compatible. Since the original project both companies have developed additional custom cards, which are compatible to some degree as a result of the mutual exchange of information through the Supernode-2 project.

5.4.2 The Hardware

A Parsys entry-level system contains one compute node of 16 T800 transputers, which can be expanded by adding further nodes up to a maximum of 1024 processors. The advertised performance of the SuperNode series ranges from 200 MIPS to 13 GIPS. The unit cost of a 16 processor SuperNode is around £40 k, with a 64 transputer machine priced at £150 k. Such a machine has performed finite element analysis benchmarking tests at a speed-up of 290 times a Vax 11/750 (i.e. around 150 VAX MIPS). The increased performance is claimed to be virtually linear with the increased cost of the machines, at a rate of £250 per MIPS. This assumes that a linear increase in the number of transputers produces a linear increase in performance. While this is true for the benchmarking results achieved for systems of up to 64 transputers, on larger systems this linearity will obviously not continue. At present the only method of using a SN1000 series machine is via a host computer, such as an IBM PC or Sun workstation, which provides communications, storage, keyboard and display facilities. It is expected that the SuperNode will be available as a stand-alone machine in the very near future.

The basic architecture of the SuperNode is shown in Figure 5.4. The group of 16 worker transputers provide the computational resource for the machine. Support transputers are responsible for I/O and control functions, eg. reconfiguration, disc access and display functions. These each have a local memory of 256 kbyte (SRAM), and 4 or 16 Mbyte (DRAM), the SRAM being used for applications requiring fast access to small amounts of memory. There is a further 16-96 Mbyte DRAM server board which provides access to discs, tape drives and other SCSI-based peripherals.

The main control transputer has 512 kbyte of local RAM and provides access to the software programmable link switch and other external communications ports such as RS232. The SuperNode also contains the Control Bus which is accessible to all transputers. This can be used for link-independent debugging, synchronisation and system control functions.

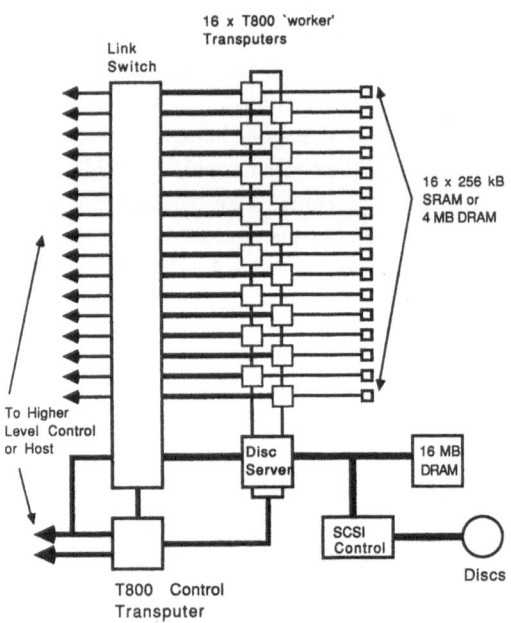

Figure 5.4: A Complete Compute Node for the SuperNode 1000

The SuperNode switch architecture is the key to the operation of the machine. Formally designed and proved during the Esprit project, a single level switch, constructed from eight 72 way crossbar switch chips, can directly support up to 72 transputers and realise any desired connectivity of the available transputers.

A single switch can take on responsibility for the configuration of several networks. The switch is non-blocking which means that subnetwork configurations can be changed without affecting the other processor groups using the switch.

The most common size of SuperNode sold contains four compute nodes (64 transputers). This size of machine can reputedly produce 100 MFLOPS, and takes up 25″ of height in a single standard 19″ rack mount. This configuration, which is known as "tandem mode" since it consists of two nodes, fully populated with processors. It uses a full single level SuperNode switch to achieve full reconfigurability and yet remain compact.

For systems with more than 72 processors SuperNode machines use a second "outer" level of switching. This hierarchical approach provides a machine that, at any architectural level, can be viewed as nodes interconnected by switches. Where

at one level a node is a transputer, at the next level a SuperNode, and at the next
a group of SuperNodes and so on. Normally, by half populating each SuperNode
with 16 computational transputers, full connectivity is maintained within the node
and the other 16 transputer's worth of links are left available for the second level
of switching. Using this type of building block Parsys can construct machines
that are fully reconfigurable (i.e. can configure any single network) for up to 1024
processors, using only two levels of switching. Network topology changes become
more complex at this level. Changes to subnetworks spread across nodes may
require the reconfiguration of some links forming part of another subnetwork. The
Control Bus provides the necessary logic to make these alterations transparently.

Link buffer cards are supplied for running transputer links over moderate distances when building large multi-node machines. These could in theory be used to
construct networks of over 1024 transputers, but at the expense of reconfigurability. The other alternative method would involve the introduction of a third level of
switching, Beñes network style. These issues are however not at the top of Parsys'
list of priorities. They intend to solve the problem should any customer ever require
more than 1024 processors.

Associated with the hierarchical link switching is a corresponding hierarchical
control bus. This provides a global control facility similar to that within a single
SuperNode. An important effect of the link architecture in the SuperNode is that
communication time between neighbouring processors is the same as that between
the most distant transputer in the largest of systems. This is an advantage for large
applications running on complex topologies since all communications involve only
a single link retiming when passing through the outer level of switching.

Parsys offer various modular subsystems to go alongside the basic SuperNode.
A specialised Memory Server consists of a single T800 transputer with up to 96
Mbyte of local DRAM, 128 kbyte of EPROM and an interface to the Control
Bus. The maximum memory bandwidth currently available between the Memory
Server and a SuperNode is 25 Mbyte per second, using a T800-25 transputer and
four cycle DRAM. For larger memory store access Parsys produce a Disc Server
with interfaces to SCSI and optional floppy disc drives. This server can sustain 5
Mbyte/s transfers with SCSI devices in synchronous mode, and can reach a burst
rate of 20 Mbyte/s.

There are six different graphics display subsystems available from Parsys, incorporating one to four transputers. The top-of-the-range configuration gives a
displayable resolution of 1280 × 1024 pixels arranged as a window onto a virtual
resolution of 2048 × 1024 pixels, with two frame buffers each 32 bits deep. This configuration is driven by four transputers allowing all 16 links to be used for display
command transfer.

5.4.3   The Software

The IDRIS Operating System

IDRIS is a UNIX compatible operating system which was developed for DEC and first delivered in 1979 as a development system for the DEC PDP-11. It has subsequently been installed on systems as diverse as Intel 8080-based machines, IBM PC, DEC Vax and Motorola MC68000-based machines. During this time IDRIS has developed to include System V UNIX features and to meet the IEEE POSIX standard.

There were four reasons behind Parsys's choice of IDRIS for the SN1000 series. Firstly, there was the attraction of its established track record of operation on diverse systems. Secondly, the IDRIS kernel is well matched to transputer technology as it is compact, has no requirement for memory management hardware, and has simple device configuration. Thirdly, its adherence to international software standards gives users access to the growing pool of UNIX-based software and allows the development of portable applications. Finally, a number of program development tools are provided as standard features of the IDRIS system.

The IDRIS implementation for the SN1000 is a modular design which may be adapted to suit users' requirements. The centre of the system is the IDRIS kernel, which provides a multi-tasking executive with a scheduler that allows simultaneous execution of real-time processes, interactive time-sharing, and round robin servicing of compute bound processes. A hierarchical file system is supported to provide flexible access to both SuperNode and host workstation disc resources. In addition to the kernel, IDRIS contains the SN1000 Series Switch Setter and IDRIS support packages for the worker, the host and for Ethernet connection. The switch setter provides support for processor resource management on a per task basis. A standard interface permits the allocation of dedicated networks and other resources as required. The worker support package has been designed to allow the user to configure the system to support a uniform UNIX-compatible programming interface, so that POSIX may be supported on every processor in the system. This permits IDRIS utilities and applications to be portable between network sizes and topologies. The IDRIS kernel is the default server for system calls made by user processes running on a worker processor, but there are embedded network servers for the support of high bandwidth system facilities such as interprocessor communication and image display.

The IDRIS TCP/IP Ethernet support package allows integration of SuperNode facilities into Local Area Networks (LAN). The Ethernet connectivity allows file transfer and remote terminal access to a wide variety of machines. Standard UNIX features are made available through TCP/IP protocols, these include Telnet remote login facility, FTP file transfers and utilities such as *rcp* and *rlogin*.

The IDRIS host support package provides for the integration of the SN1000 series into existing computing facilities on a host system. At present these support packages are available for Sun-3 and Sun-4 Workstations, IBM PS/2 and PCs or compatibles. The primary function of these packages is to provide host device access including local and remote terminals and disc access. The package also provides a mechanism for direct communication between user processes running under IDRIS and under the host operating system. Program development under IDRIS is enhanced by the availability of a C interactive source level debugger, profiler, librarian and tools for managing reusable object modules.

IDRIS supports parallelism at the task level in a way similar to Helios (9.2). A collection of autonomous tasks can execute concurrently to solve the particular problem. Each transputer executes sequential programs under IDRIS, at present these programs may be written in C, Fortran or Pascal. The processes are then allowed to communicate via UNIX-like system calls such as *pipe*, and new processes can be spawned using the *fork* system call. Thus the parallel programming paradigm of Communication Sequential Processes (CSP), developed by Hoare [HOAR], can be implemented.

A more trivial parallel programming paradigm is that of batch processing, where a number of independent jobs are assigned across a network of processors. Since there is no requirement for interprocessor communication this type of parallelism is available directly from the shell which permits each task to be executed on any available worker in background mode.

X Support

Parsys is a member of the X/Open collaboration, and SuperNode systems hosted by a Sun Workstation have X Windows and X Lib support. The Sun Workstation interface package consists of a VME to transputer link interface card and associated Sun device drivers. At present the X Windows system (X11 Release 4) is supported, and X Lib procedures are available across the processor array, served by the host or by external X servers.

Transputer Development System (TDS)

The SuperNode series may be used for the development of embedded applications using a version of Inmos TDS adapted by Parsys. This is based on the current (D700D) version of TDS and provides standard Occam support. Adaptations made by Parsys include an automatic SuperNode configuration facility using TDS "wiring diagram" files. A full run time breakpoint and continue debugger has been implemented for Occam using the facilities of the SuperNode Control Bus.

Compilers and Libraries

In addition to the compilers for ANSI C, ISO Pascal and ANSI Fortran that Parsys supply under IDRIS, the SuperNode series also supports the 3L series of parallel compilers for C, Pascal and Fortran. These compilers are designed to allow implementation of CSP on the transputer network, with all communications being handled by the Tiny message passing harness (cf. A.2). Specialist configuration tools are available to allow automated generation of the standard 3L/Tiny configuration languages and integration with the SuperNode architecture. All the latest Inmos compilers and toolsets are supported.

Parsys also offer vector and serial numeric procedure libraries callable from Occam and the IDRIS supported languages. The libraries are coded in transputer assembler, where necessary, and make use of the processors' internal RAM to increase performance over standard compiled code.

5.4.4   The Market Niche

The traditional early users of high-performance computers, the scientific and academic markets, are represented in Parsys' customer list by the Universities of Southampton and Liverpool, University College London and Ministry of Defence research establishments including RSRE. However the company have decided that their potential user base reaches beyond these sectors. They are actively marketing their products to financial institutions, non-military government departments, industry and commerce. It has proved difficult to obtain accurate information about the SuperNode users in the defence and finance industries, since in both cases the customers want their advantage gained through improved hardware kept secret. In the two and a half years of their existence Parsys have an installed base of over 50 SuperNode machines. The majority of sales are within the UK, with the balance being solely within Europe. The European sales are exclusively to academia and industry, with Universities in Spain, Switzerland having bought SuperNode machines.

The largest SuperNode in use contains 256 transputers, and this is also the largest machine tested. Parsys intend to investigate the logistics of larger machines, including those with over 1024 transputers, once they are approached by a customer that needs that much power. The potential configurability problems with the very large SuperNodes will be tackled once the potential application is known, i.e. such machines are likely to be provided without the option of complete reconfigurability.

5.4.5   The Competition

The obvious competitor to Parsys in Europe is Telmat Informatique since they produce almost identical hardware. Within the UK and France there is little interference between the companies as each stick to their home ground. However in the rest of Europe they see the strongest competition as coming from other manufacturers. In particular, Parsys regard Parsytec (Section 5.5) as their largest threat within Europe.

The largest difference between Parsys and Telmat is in their software product range, and it is often on the basis of this that European customers choose between the SuperNode and T-Node machines. Parsys market their machines with a software base of their enhanced TDS, the IDRIS operating system and the 3L products with the Tiny router. Alternatively Telmat offer their own TDS and, more recently, the Helios operating system. However one aim of the Supernode-2 project is the development of a common operating system, so in the future the companies may have less to distinguish their products but in doing so, will offer the user a higher level of product compatibility.

5.4.6   Current Applications

Commercial

Parsys is in partnership with Oracle, working to accelerate the performance of Oracle's database software. Oracle's distributed software architecture is well suited to a parallel implementation, and the IDRIS Operating System features a standard UNIX environment with parallel disc support to provide the necessary platform. The broad range of machines that already support the Oracle database suite should provide a large pool of existing software that could be ported across to the Parsys implementation.

Engineering

SuperNode machines are currently in use for applications involving computational fluid dynamics (CFD) and finite element analysis (FEA). Parsys are working in collaboration with FEGS Ltd., experts in the field of graphics systems for FEA, in order to produce a highly efficient FEA machine. Field Analysis Modeller, a suite of modelling programs for loaded structures produced by FEGS, has been ported to Parsys systems and performs faster than on conventional systems. A particular FEGS benchmark (the half-piston example) uses 21 hours of CPU time on a Vax 11/750. This same example executes in 10 minutes on a 32 T800-20 SuperNode, and in 4 minutes 20 seconds on a 64 T800-25 SuperNode. This latter time corresponds to a speed-up by a factor of 290. Other software available for the SuperNode include fully parallel versions of PAFEC, CRISP and PARADYNE, all established FEA packages.

Finance

Parsys have ported two packages from Risk Decisions Ltd. to run on their SuperNode machines. These programs, RAS (Real-Time Analytics Server) and PREDICT!, are used for calculating the risk factors involved in financial dealings. Parsys seem further interested in this market sector and are investigating the support of other complex financial modelling programs.

5.4.7   The Future

Parsys are happy with the present state of their hardware products. They have no plans at present to introduce new machines, but will continue to develop their present hardware. The only major change likely in the next few years would be the incorporation of the promised new Inmos H1 transputer (cf. 5.1.5) into the existing SuperNode architecture. The main thrust of Parsys's development effort is therefore in the software field. They place great importance on the provision of a stable, standard and portable operating system for their machines. IDRIS is seen as fulfilling this role, and Parsys see the further development of IDRIS and applications as their main concern for the near future.

5.5   Parsytec GmbH

Relevant Activities Manufacturer of transputer-based parallel systems

Location Julicher Strasse 338, D-5100, Aachen, West Germany
Telephone: 0241 166000, Fax: 0241 1660050. Paracom Inc., Barrington
Pointe, 2300 N. Barrington Road, Hoffman Estates, Illinois 60195, USA. Tele-
phone: (312) 490 5386, Fax. (312) 884 9423.

Relevant Officers Falk-Dietrich Kübler, Chairman; G. H. Peise, Director.

Employees 75 in Germany; six in the USA.

Financial details Private Company

5.5.1   The Company

Parsytec (PARallel SYstems TEChnology) make transputer-based parallel systems
ranging in size from single processor plug-in boards for IBM PCs through to stand-
alone systems with several hundred processors. The company was founded by Falk-
D. Kübler, Dr. Gerhard H. Peise, and Bernd Wolff [3] in Aachen, West Germany
in 1985. Kübler first realised the power of micro-processors in 1979 when working
on a project using the Motorola 68000. In 1984 he read about the transputer
concept, which inspired him to form a company to provide parallel hardware using
transputers. During the year between discovering the potential of transputers for
parallel processing and starting the company Kübler and his co-founders, all of
whom were graduates from Aachen Technical University, carried out an analysis of
the market to find out how producing parallel processing equipment could be made
commercially viable.

Originally Parsytec was based in the Aachen Technology Centre, which was set
up by the Technical University, the local savings bank, and AGIT (a local consor-
tium including the city authority, and local industry) in a refurbished factory with
the aim of promoting high technology industry. The Technology Centre provides
an environment which allows the companies involved time to develop their products and get to the market without the initial financial pressures which often stifle
young enterprises. Aachen Technical University provides the technical expertise by
encouraging its academics to use their ideas to develop commercial products using
special risk-tailored finance from the savings bank. The loans made to the startup
companies were at the regular intest rates with the safety net that if the company
failed the owners were not personally liable for the debt. To start with the company was financed by Dm300 k in loans, but were additionally helped by a Dm800 k

---

[3]Bernd Wolff has since left Parsytec

grant from the West German government through an innovation scheme run by the Research Ministry. Kübler avoided using venture capital to fund Parsytec because of the risk of having the rug pulled out from under his feet at a crucial moment; instead, he convinced the banks that Parsytec was worth the risk of investing in.

Having established a sound product base and a network of customers, and with turnover increasing, Parsytec moved from the Technology Centre to their own premises. The company had a turnover on sales of zero in their first year but this has risen to Dm1.5 M in 1986, Dm5.2 M in 1988, Dm9 M in 1989, and Dm15 M in 1990. They have targeted their systems at industry and have a large export market, which in 1988 accounted for one third of their turnover.

The company ParaCom was formed to take care of sales and marketing while Parsytec continued with research and development, which consumes most of the revenues generated. The headquarters of Parsytec/ParaCom (henceforth simply Parsytec) are in Aachen and the American subsidiary is based in the Chicago area. Parsytec employ 75 people in Germany and six in the Chicago office. Most of Parsytec's employees are graduates from Aachen University.

Parsytec have developed parallel systems which can be connected to a wide variety of industry standard systems. This decision was made because it allowed industrial users to expand the processing power of systems with which they were comfortable, without having to throw away existing hardware. Parsytec have close links with Perihelion, makers of Helios (Section 9.2), a UNIX-like distributed operating system for transputer systems. Helios provides an interface to transputer systems which is familiar to many users and so is seen by Parsytec as being an important part of their system. Parsytec are involved with Helios development; for example they have designed the Helios file system.

5.5.2   System Overview

Parsytec produce three levels of transputer system, from plug-in boards with a few processors for popular desk-top machines, through a mid-range system containing a few tens of processors, to stand-alone systems with hundreds of processors.

Plug-in Boards

The first systems produced by Parsytec were boards which plugged into spare expansion slots on the host system's bus; these boards are called "bus-boards", and were built for the IBM PC and its clones. Since then, the range has expanded to include bus-boards for: VMEbus based systems; IBM PS/2 machines; the Apple Mac-II; DEC Q-bus systems; Siemens SMP systems; and Kontron ECB systems. The advantage of these boards is that as well increasing the power of the system they allow the host to be used as normal when the transputer boards are not being used.

The number of transputers on a board and the amount of memory per transputer is constrained by the physical dimensions of the board, as well as power and cooling requirements. Ranging over all bus-boards, the number of transputers per board is between zero and four while memory per transputer is between 256 kbyte and 32 Mbyte.

The bus-boards serve a dual purpose: they provide extra computing power in the machine through the on-board transputers and they provide a mechanism to link with other transputer systems (the bus-boards without transputers serve purely as links to other systems). Some of the bus-boards can be used a motherboards for Parsytec busless boards which provide a wide range of functionality. Boards are linked together through Parsytec's UniLink connector, which joins Parsytec's transputer systems together to expand the computing resource available to the user. The UniLink connection does not permit direct connection to other manufacturer's equipment, although an interface is available which will convert the UniLink to the Inmos standard TTL link. The Parsytec bus-boards can drive either the UniLink connector, or the standard Inmos TTL link. The choice of connection type is determined by the setting of a switch on the board. The physical connection between Parsytec equipment is made through an RS422 cable.

Mid-range Systems

The mid-range system produced by Parsytec is the MultiCluster series, which consists of transputer boards inserted into a stand-alone system unit. The transputers in this system can be accessed from bus-boards in external machines using the UniLink connector, or directly through the terminal connection in the system. The MultiCluster series consists of the MultiCluster-1 and the MultiCluster-2. The first system has a static topology fixed by jumper leads between boards, while the second has a dynamically re-configurable interconnection topology.

The MultiCluster-1 system unit contains its own power supply and cooling facilities, capacity for ten bus-less boards, and a mass-storage controller together with a 3.5″ floppy drive and a 66 Mbyte SCSI disk, as well as a VT100/220 terminal controller. The MultiCluster-1 system can be expanded by cascading together expansion units, which contain slots for 15 bus-less boards. The topology of the transputers in the MultiCluster-1 system is set manually using jumper cables to connect the boards. This introduces an effective upper limit to the expansion of the system, since manually connecting a large array of transputers is not easy.

The MultiCluster-2 has the facilities of the MultiCluster-1 together with the enhancement of Network Configuration Units (NCU) to provide the dynamic reconfigurability of the network. This facility allows the transputers in the MultiCluster-2 to be partitioned amongst several users at run-time. Each system unit has 16 slots for bus-less boards which provide up to 32 transputers. The communications subsystem consists of boards which provide an inter-connection topology between the processors. These boards can contain fixed links, or NCUs which provide a reconfigurable topology.

The MultiCluster-2 system features increased I/O and terminal access over the MultiCluster-1. In addition to the 16 slots for processing modules, the MultiCluster-2 contains space for up to four I/O boards. Because the MultiCluster-2 does not rely on manual wiring between the transputers system units can be cascaded to produce a machine with up to 128 transputers.

The MultiCluster system unit can be decoupled from the host machine by a distance of up to 30 m so that when it is used on an industrial site the host can be situated in an office while the MultiCluster is situated on the shop floor. As an example, consider controlling an industrial robot in a noisy and dirty factory environment. The robot can be attached to a control board in the MultiCluster transputer system which is built to withstand the rigors of an industrial environment, while the host (and operator) can be situated in a clean office environment some distance away. The standard Parsytec MultiCluster system unit is designed to withstand some rough treatment but is not built to military specification.

The processing power of the MultiCluster system is provided by the Eurocard bus-less boards which slot into the system unit. The bus-less boards provide a range of functionality which allows the MultiCluster user a wide choice in configuring the system. The Busless Processing Modules contain between one and four transputers with memory options from 64 kbyte SRAM through to 32 Mbyte DRAM per processor. The Mass Storage Controller board interfaces to all standard SCSI devices, and can control a floppy drive. This board also contains 4 Mbyte of memory which is used as a cache. Several boards can be used together to build a powerful storage sub-system.

The Versatile Transputer Front-end I/O Module contains two T212 transputers with either a T800 or a T414, and is used to provide computing power directly to user circuitry. The T800 or T414 has 256 kbyte of 100 ns SRAM while the T212s have 32 kbyte of 35 ns SRAM each. This board is designed for time-critical applications such as real-time control or high speed data analysis. The board can be programmed by replacing 128 kbyte of the memory with the programmed EPROMs.

The Ethernet Interface Module contains a T800 running the TCP/IP Helios server. This board supports the full TCP/IP protocol. Up to six Ethernet addresses can be controlled by this module.

The EPROM Module has sockets for 16 EPROMs which can be programmed to boot up to four autonomous transputer networks.

The Graphics Display Subsystem board provides a colour display with 1024 × 1024 pixels using 256 colours from a palette of 2^{18} colours. Software support is provided through the GKS package and X Windows.

The Graphics Display Subsystem II board consists of a T800 used as a graphics processor which interfaces with a G300 video controller. The board supports three graphic modes. In mode one the resolution is 1280×1024 with an 8 bit colour map providing a 256 colour palette. The second mode has a resolution of 800×600 with a palette of 2^{12} colours, and the third mode provides a screen resolution of 800×600 with 2^{24} colours.

The Frame Grabber Subsystem board provides a 1024×512 pixel frame grabbing facility. The Digital to Analogue and Analogue to Digital converter boards provide an interface to analog systems. The I/O motherboard can take up to three I/O daughterboards which provide custom I/O capabilities for the bus-less system.

The Stand-alone Systems

The top range machines are the SuperCluster series, which are stand-alone machines with up to hundreds of transputers. The SuperCluster, which was introduced at the Hanover Trade Fair in April 1988, has a software configurable topology, so its computing resources can be shared amongst many users. The basic unit, the Model 64, contains 64 transputers, some topology configuration hardware, an I/O subsystem, and 16 workstation entry points. Larger SuperCluster models with more transputers can be built by connecting several Model 64s together. The architecture of the Model 64 is shown in Figure 5.5.

The basic building block of the Model 64 SuperCluster is a 16-transputer computing cluster which contains a Network Control Unit (NCU) to interconnect the transputers. The interconnection topology of the transputers in a SuperCluster is software reconfigurable and so the resource can be dynamically divided between a number of users at run-time. The topology specified is implemented by NCUs, which are transputer controlled and capable of configuring 96 communication links to any topology. The NCU consists of two 96×96 communications matrices, one for the data links and the other for the reset control links. The communications matrices are implemented using Inmos C004 link switches. A T414 is the master control processor and provides partitioning and configurability control. A T212 monitors the activities of the incoming communication links especially the reset links.

The computing cluster has 16 transputers and one NCU so after providing full connectivity within the computing cluster 32 links remain to interconnect the computing clusters within the SuperCluster. The two NCUs within a Model 64 provide the interconnectivity between the four constituent computing clusters and also provide 64 external links which are used to connect Model 64s together. The SuperCluster's system services cluster provides mass storage capabilities for the system and is also the interface for custom I/O devices. Up to 16 external machines can connect to the SuperCluster through the workstation entry points using the Parsytec UniLink connection.

In the SuperCluster the NCUs are fixed in communications slots on the system backplane and so are separate from the processing boards. This allows the NCUs

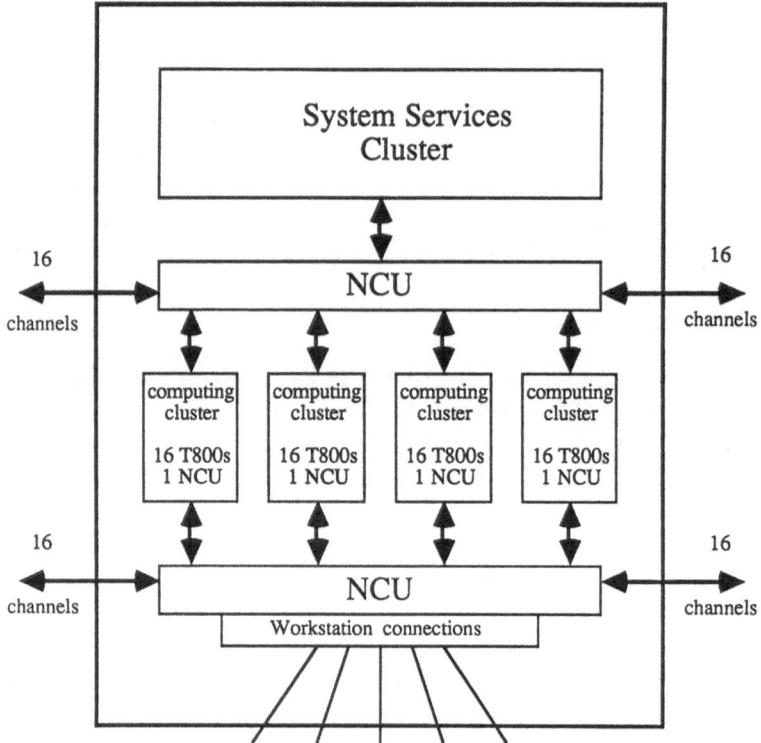

Figure 5.5: The Architecture of the Model 64 SuperCluster

to be replaced by fixed topology boards. For certain applications the ability to reconfigure the system is not needed so a fixed topology can be used. This ability allows the user to control the amount and degree of reconfigurability in the system.

5.5.3   Applications and Performance

Recently a 400 transputer SuperCluster was installed at Shell's KSLA facility in Amsterdam to solve cellular automata problems. The ability to expand the system by adding further processing cubes was important in Shell's decision to choose the Parsytec system, since they hope to be expand the system to 1000 transputers in the future. The system installed has a fixed mesh topology with a theoretical peak performance of 4 GIPS. The cost of this installation was around £500 k.

Dean Microsystems, the UK distributors for Parsytec, have won an order for a system for use by British Aerospace in simulating the effect of lightning striking modern fighter aircraft such as the European EFA fighter. The system comprises three Model 64 SuperClusters and cost £300 k. The package which models the effect of lightning strikes on aircraft is being supplied by KCC Ltd. of Nottingham and is in the process of being ported onto the Parsytec equipment.

The Institute of Thermodynamics at the University of Duisberg have performed a comparison between the Cyber 205 and a Model 64 SuperCluster using code which simulates the molecular dynamics of carbon dioxide. The results are shown in Table 5.4. The Model 64 has a better performance for scalar code but is out performed by the Cyber 205's vector unit.

Table 5.4: Comparison between a Cyber 205 and a Parsytec Model 64 SuperCluster

Number of Molecules	Cyber 205 vectorised	Cyber 205 scalar	SuperCluster Model 64
500	6.04	132.9	24.4
864	9.59	222.6	33.5
1000	10.80	264.2	36.2
2048	21.20	536.5	57.6

5.5.4 The Software

Software for Parsytec machines can be divided into operating systems/development environments, programming languages, and development tools.

In the first category, the Helios system (cf. Section 9.2) is available on all Parsytec machines. Helios is a distributed UNIX-like operating system which provides full multi-tasking, X Windows, standard POSIX libraries, and parallel task management. In addition to Helios, Parsytec provide MultiTool, which is an Occam development system based on Inmos' TDS (cf. 5.1.3).

A wide range of programming languages are available on Parsytec machines. Most are from third party vendors and so are standard to most transputer systems. However some are specific to the Helios operating system. The languages available include: Occam, Parsec's ParC, 3L C, Logical Systems' C, Norcroft C, 3L Pascal, Meiko/Topexpress Fortran 77, 3L Fortran 77, Alsys's validated Ada, STRAND[88] (9.4), and Rowley's Modula-2.

Parsytec have been active in developing tools which help users of their systems develop applications. They provide a standard GKS graphics interface and, through Helios, there is access to X Windows. On systems which have a reconfigurable communications network a Network Configuration Manager (NCM) is used to control the NCUs so that they implement the users choice for the topology. Under Helios the NCM reads the resource map and automatically configures the network described their. While when running the MultiTool system the NCM will configure the topology specified by the configuration file. The VISION system allows users to debug parallel programs written in Occam in a windowing environment. In collaboration with Topexpress, Parsytec have produced some efficient vector and math libraries.

5.5.5   The Market

Parsytec have developed their products for the industrial marketplace, as shown by their product line which contains plug-in boards for common systems, and board-based system units capable of withstanding an industrial environment. The industrial bias is a result of German companies being much more responsive to parallel processing than the academics. In the early days, Parsytec's industrial customers were willing to suffer products which were still in their infancy while paying full prices for the systems. This was due to some extent that the companies involved had no alternative to parallel processing to provide a large amount of compute power at a reasonable cost. The preliminary market research carried out by Kübler and his co-founders prior to founding Parsytec indicated that their main market was going to be in the area of industrial distributed data processing, and this view was confirmed by the fact that most of Parsytec's early customers were buying systems to solve problems of this type.

The type of system which Parsytec are developing has changed through time, originally they produced small systems which were slotted into desk-top machines while recently they have developed machines with hundreds of transputers in them. These larger machines have a much larger potential performance than the smaller systems and so will notionally compete with mini- and mainframe computer manufacturers. The end result of Parsytec's development is a family of compatible products — the boards used in one system can be used in another, and the software is consistent across all of their machines.

The international market is very important to Parsytec since in order to sustain rapid growth a large potential market is needed. This is shown in the export sales figures which have provided half of the annual sales in the past. Also an international market provides a broad user base which provides feedback to direct future development.

Parsytec have a large number of foreign distributors including ones in most West European countries, Japan, Israel, India and Australia. In 1987 Parsytec, with Matsushita, developed a sales network in Japan with some success. The cooperation with Matsushita is important to Parsytec since Matsushita are a very prestigious company and it has enabled them to sell European systems to the Japanese. There is also a possibility of Matsushita producing Parsytec systems in Japan. The subsidiary company ParaCom has sold about 50 systems in the US, which indicates that the American distrust of foreign systems has been overcome to some extent.

5.5.6   The Future

Parsytec are committed to Inmos and the transputer, while other traditionally transputer-based companies such as Meiko are diversifying by developing systems which are based on micro-processors such as the Intel i860 and Sun SPARC. The Inmos H1 microprocessor, the successor to the transputer, will be the basis of the next generation of Parsytec systems. This is consistent with the family approach to system development that the company has adopted. Also Kübler is suspicious of products developed as side-line by a large company, and so he considers the Intel i860 to be an unstable product which was certainly not designed for parallel processing.

At some point in the future the major international computer manufacturers will enter the parallel processing market in a serious way. Parsytec are building larger and potentially more powerful systems which they hope will give them the expertise to compete with the these manufacturers when these companies enter the market.

According to Kübler, Parsytec will stay in private hands until its turnover reaches Dm100 M at which point the company will be floated on the stock exchange. Turnover has been rising at a rate of 70% for the last two years and it is hoped by Parsytec that a similar rise will be achieved this year as well.

Company Summary 13: Features of the Caplin HEX

Source	Caplin Cybernetics
Type	Transputer based MicroVax add-on boards
Availability	Since early 1990, over 100 Caplin systems presently in use across the world.
Price	£16 k for entry level development system with software.
Processing nodes	Standard board has eight nodes. Boards can be linked to give domains of any size.
Processor technology	Inmos transputers
Memory	Up to 64 Mbyte per board.
Communications	Inter-board communications (via Q-bus) at 3 Mbit/s peak, 1 Mbit/s sustained.
I/O connections	Via Q-bus to MicroVax
Performance	Up to 200 MIPS from a 16 node system.
Host system	Vax/MicroVax
Operating system	Vax/VMS or ULTRIX based.
Programming languages	Fortran 77, C, Pascal, Ada and Occam.
Physical configuration	Plug-in boards, extendable to HEX extender cabinets.
Power requirements	8 W (5 Volt DC at 1.6 amp max.)
Sources	Caplin advertising literature, discussions with Paul Caplin and sales staff.

Company Summary 14: Features of the Meiko Computing Surface

Source	Meiko Scientific Limited.
Type	Distributed Memory Reconfigurable Multiprocessor.
Availability	First commercial delivery in 1986. 300 – 400 installations by 1990.
Price	A Computing Surface with four transputer nodes, 8 Mbyte DRAM, 300 Mbyte SCSI disc and quarter inch tape drives: £40 k. As above with twin i860 processors replacing four transputer nodes: £65 k.
Processing nodes	One to hundreds.
Processors	Inmos T800, Intel i860, SPARC.
Memory	0.5 Mbyte to 32 Mbyte per T800; 8 to 128 Mbyte per SPARC; up to 32 Mbyte per i860.
Communications	20 MHz inter-processor bandwidth.
I/O connections	VME, various SCSI interfaces.
Performance	Approximately 1 MFLOPS per processor (T800) on real applications.
Host system	Self-hosting, or hosted by Sun or VAX.
Operating system	SunOS derivative.
Programming languages	Occam, Fortran, C, Lisp, Ada.
Physical configuration	Variable, from single-processor boards to several large multi-board cabinets.
Power dissipation	For a 40 board cabinet containing 160 T800 processors, upwards of 1.5 kW.
Sources	Meiko publicity material and conversations with Meiko staff.

Company Summary 15: Features of the Parsys SuperNode 1000

Source	Parsys Limited
Type	Reconfigurable transputer network.
Availability	Available from April 1988, 50 sold with 40 installed so far.
Price	£40 k per 16 processor SuperNode, £150 k for a 64 transputer machine.
Processing nodes	Each SuperNode contains 16 processors, can have up to 64 such nodes which would provide a 1024 processor system. The largest SuperNode yet sold, or in fact tested, contains 256 transputers.
Processor technology	Inmos T800 transputers
Memory	16 Mbyte DRAM or 256 kbyte SRAM per transputer. Additional memory of up to 96 Mbyte is available via a control transputer, as are links to discs through SCSI devices.
Communications	Special switch chip allows full connectivity for 32 transputers, with a link speed of 80 Mbit/s. In practice there are normally 16 processors per switch chip, leaving links free for secondary level switching.
I/O connections	RS232 external communications port. Ethernet support under the IDRIS operating system.
Performance	100 MFLOPS from a 64 processor system.
Host system	IBM PC or Sun workstation.
Operating system	IDRIS a distributed UNIX-like operating system.
Programming languages	C, Fortran 77 and Pascal under IDRIS. Support for 3L parallel toolkits for C, Fortran and Pascal.
Physical configuration	64 processor machine is 25″ high and fits into a single standard 19″ inch rack mount.
Power requirements	2 kW for a 64 transputer machine.
Sources	Parsys publications and technical personnel.

Company Summary 16: Features of the Parsytec SuperCluster

Source	Parsytec GmbH
Type	The SuperCluster is a transputer based MIMD machine.
Availability	The SuperCluster was introduced in 1988.
Price	A basic Model 64 SuperCluster costs about £100 k, while a system with extra memory and error correction options costs £200 k.
Processing nodes	The SuperCluster is based on 64 node building blocks which can be interconnected to make machines with a large number of nodes.
Processor technology	Inmos T800 transputers.
Memory	1 to 4 Mbyte of memory per processor giving 64 to 256 Mbyte total memory.
Communications	The topology is software reconfigurable; the total communication bandwidth is 230 Mbyte/s.
I/O connections	Each SuperCluster unit can link to 16 host machines. The SuperCluster has a mass storage facility which consists of a 2.2 Gbyte mass storage subsystem containing four 550 Mbyte SCSI compatible 5.25″ Winchester disks thus giving an effective disk I/O of 6 Mbyte/s.
Performance	640 MIPS/ 96 MFLOPS per SuperCluster unit.
Host system	The SuperCluster is accessed from IBM-PCs (and compatibles), Apple Macintoshs, DEC Vaxs, and various workstations (Sun, Siemens etc).
Operating system	The SuperCluster can run the Helios operating system and Inmos TDS system.
Programming languages	Occam, Fortran, Ada, STRAND[88] , C, Pascal, and Modula-2.
Physical configuration	Each 64 node building block comes in its own box. Weight 190 kg, height 1.286 m, width 0.553 m
Power requirements	1.8 kW

Sources   Company literature and conversations with Parsytec
                           personnel, and from the UK Distributors for Parsytec:
                           Dean Micro Systems, 11 Horseshoe Park, Pangbourne,
                           RG8 7JW.

Chapter 6

New Machines For New Niches

This chapter describes those machines which do not fit easily into any of our other chapters. One manufacturer, Teradata, has concentrated its efforts on producing a super-database machine, while the others have created niches for themselves in the workstation market. Together, they show that parallelism offers more than just a faster solution to the same old problems.

6.1   Cogent Research Incorporated

Location Cogent Research Inc., 1100 NW Compton Drive, Beaverton, Oregon,
97006 USA. Telephone: (503) 690 1450.

Relevant Officers Charles Vollum, Founder, Chairman, Chief Technology Offi-
cer; Alan J. Higginson, President and CEO; TC Vollum, Co-founder, Corp.
Secretary-Treasurer, VP; Tom Nora, VP (Sales and Marketing); Tom Mer-
row, Director of S/W Engineering; Ken Smith, Director of Manufacturing;
Rod Strange, Director of H/W Engineering; Nita Fouts-Davison, Director of
Administration and Finance.

Employees 31 staff in the US. Of these four are in R&D, four in Manufacturing,
nine in Sales, Marketing and Customer Service, ten in Software and four in
Administration.

Financial details Privately held by a small number of investors and key employees.

6.1.1   The Company

Cogent was formed in 1986 by Charles Vollum and TC Vollum "to research the
needs in computing in the 1990s". Although the company began as a group of software engineers looking at a number of projects, Cogent soon perceived an unfilled
niche in the high performance computer market. Cogent saw established companies
such as IBM and Cray Research Inc. (Section 7.1) producing systems which cost
in excess of $1 M, with a growing number of companies such as Sequent (3.7), Intel
(4.1), Alliant (3.1), BBN (3.2) and NCUBE (4.2) producing machines in the $500 k
range. The niche Cogent identified lies between these machines and low-end PCs
and workstations, believing that there was a large discrepancy between these two
areas in price/performance and ease of use.

Cogent identified parallel processing as a vehicle for achieving improved performance in a small space at low cost. The XTM series of desktop parallel computers
was to be Cogent's product for this market. After three years of development
the first prototypes were shipped in late 1988, with production units following in
mid-1989.

6.1.2   The Hardware

The XTM is a distributed memory MIMD machine. Such machines require some
sort of interconnection network to support communication between processors. In
systems with very small numbers of processors it is feasible to provide total connectivity – a network which allows every processor to be directly connected to

every other. For larger numbers of processors, this becomes infeasible, due to the bandwidth required.

Distributed memory MIMD machines with a fixed network structure therefore involve messages "hopping" between processors in order to reach distant nodes. On current generation processors, each hop will typically involve interrupts on the intermediate processor, requiring CPU time to forward the message. Bus-based machines avoid this problem by effectively allowing end-to-end communication be-tween processors. A bus offers the additional advantage of multicast and broadcast communications which must be implemented by multiple messages on most mes-sage passing architectures. Unfortunately, only one communication can occur on the bus at any time and contention for the bus increases as more processors are added to the system, leading to problems with scalability.

In the XTM, Cogent use a hybrid system. A bus provides facilities for broadcast and multicast, while a crossbar switch is used for point-to-point communication. Requests for connections through the switch are sent to the switch controller on the bus. The switch is then electronically reconfigured to provide the connection.

The basic compute board in the XTM series mounts two Inmos T800-20 trans-puters, each with 4 Mbyte of RAM. Each processor has a 64 bit IEEE-758 floating-point unit delivering 1.5 MFLOPS sustained, and a 32 bit integer unit giving 5 MIPS sustained. The XTM workstation provides a single compute board in a box which also contains one 190 Mbyte Winchester and a 800 kbyte floppy disc with an Ethernet interface, two NuBus expansion slots and a PC/AT compatible serial port. A 19″ colour monitor and keyboard with mouse are provided as separate units. The XTM Resource Server contains up to 15 compute boards, with 30 processors (Figure 6.1).

A 32 bit, 12 Mbyte/s bus connects all the processors and a special "operator" processor. The operator controls a 128 way, 100 Mbyte/s dynamic crossbar switch which can provide dedicated connections between processors, handling large num-bers of simultaneous messages. Disc servers are available, providing 1.9 GByte of disc and an 810 kbyte optical drive for backups.

Systems comprising multiple workstations and Resource Servers can be config-ured using XTM System Interconnections. Wired links are used for distances of up to 2 m, with fibre-optic connections for up to 2 km. Both types of connection provide data rates of up to 10 Mbyte/s.

The modular nature of the XTM system makes it possible to extend a system from a basic two processor workstation in small increments, potentially to a very large system. A 1900 processor machine has been designed by Cogent for Sandia Labs. Costing \$15 M, this machine will provide computing power roughly equivalent to a Cray X-MP.

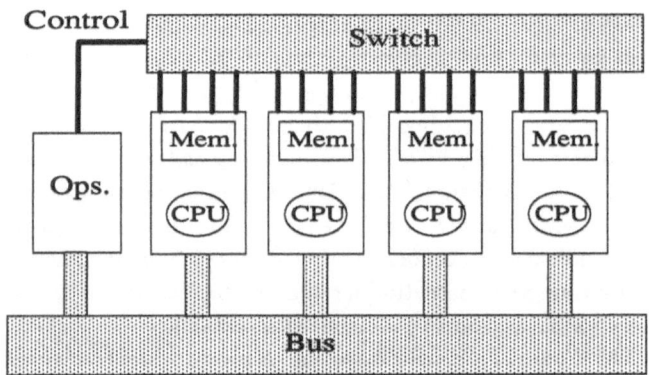

Figure 6.1: The XTM Resource Server

6.1.3   The Software

Cogent realised early in development that incompatibility between parallel machines was a major hurdle to their widespread acceptance. Users do not want to discard or re-engineer existing code, when they move to other platforms or add processors. They were also aware that the difficulties of programming in a distributed memory environment complicated software development on MIMD machines.

To address these issues, Cogent adopted Linda (cf. 9.3) as a central part of their approach. Kernel Linda, a modified Linda, is implemented at a very low level on the XTM series, and the QIX operating system is implemented entirely on top of it. Programs written for UNIX can be recompiled and run under QIX with little or no modification. UNIX-like facilities for file and system management are provided, and standard shells are available. Compilers are provided for C, C++ and Fortran 77. Parallel programs can be written in all of these languages using the Linda primitives. Such programs are independent of the underlying architecture or topology, and can be easily moved to other machines supporting Linda. Similarly, an XTM machine can have processors added or removed and software will continue to run unmodified.

Cogent has been conscious of the need to conform to industry standards. The XTM series supports PIX (Postscript with Linda extensions), NeWS, X.11, Telnet, FTP, TCP/IP, Ethernet, Postscript printers and video I/O. Debugging and monitoring tools are provided. Linda programs can be visualised during execution as set of tuples in tuple space. On the XTM series, a "tuple-space browser" provides a graphical representation of tuple space allowing users to investigate the behaviour of programs and the operating system.

6.1.4   The Market Niche

Cogent believe that "the high performance computer market will exceed $300 G by 1992[1], a market too large for major computer manufacturers to ignore". The XTM is marketed as providing supercomputer performance for high-end workstation cost. Cogent are focusing on market segments where the XTM has a price/performance advantage, and where small size is most needed. The system is felt to be best suited to floating-point intensive applications involving graphical feedback, with a small number of users. Sales efforts are in the aerospace, geophysical, R&D and university markets. Targeted applications within these markets include signal processing, image processing, simulation, database management, CAE, CAD and CIM.

Cogent's customer list includes many large industrial customers, for example: Sharp Electronics, Sony, Nissan Motors, General Dynamics, Hitachi Chemical, Nippon Telephone and Telegraph, Toshiba and Fujitsu R&D. The large contingent of Japanese customers cited in this list represents an achievement which has eluded many other American computer manufacturers. Cogent's success in Japan can be attributed to the company's relationship with the Marubeni Corporation, a $10 G Tokyo-based trading company which has represented Cogent in Japan, South Korea and Taiwan since 1988. Cogent's foresight in having this distribution channel in place before production units were shipping has been rewarded by significant sales (50% of the company's total sales in 1989).

Academic and research establishments with Cogent equipment include: Oregon Advanced Computing Institute, Oregon Graduate Institute, University of South West Louisiana, University of Vienna, Oak Ridge National Labs.

The domestic sales operation in North America includes a direct sales force in major areas, as well as indirect channels such as VARs, OEMs and software developers.

Scientific Computers became Cogent Research's Western European distributor in the 4th quarter of 1989. This UK-based distributor with subsidiaries in Germany and France has thirty years of experience in high-performance scientific computing, especially modelling, simulation and design applications. They saw the XTM as a natural successor to various hardware offerings over the years, which have included the Symbolics workstation and various array processors. Perceiving a parallel processing platform as complementary to their software products, Scientific Computers were impressed by the XTM's software design and the completeness of its implementation. In their opinion the cost performance and ease of programming of the XTM made it an excellent computational server.

Scientific Computers are targeting R&D users in industry and defence, as well as the Higher Education market. Cogent's set of focus applications is extended by

---

[1]An estimate very much larger than that from other companies.

Scientific Computers' background in neural network software. At the entry-level, high-end workstation vendors such as Solbourne, MIPS and Silicon Graphics (Section 6.2) are seen as competitors, while at the computational resource providers such as Convex (3.4), Alliant (3.1), Meiko (5.3), Parsys (5.4), Parsytec (5.5), Telmat, Sequent (3.7) and Encore (3.5) are numbered amongst the opposition for larger systems.

Both Cogent and Scientific Computers are unwilling to reveal sales volumes. They stress that Scientific Computers have been distributing the XTM for less than a year. It seems likely that few, if any, sales have been made in Europe to date. No information on other geographical areas is forthcoming from the company.

6.1.5   The Future

The XTM is a well engineered system supporting a much more integrated environment than is typically found on parallel machines. However, it seems that marketing this product as a low-cost high-performance platform is insufficient to support Cogent, and substantial changes to the company's structure and market direction were initiated in October 1990. Cogent's new strategy is centred on the "integrated computing" market, harnessing non-heterogeneous computing elements, connected by many communications media, to work in unison. Cogent claim that every major computer centre is presently struggling with this integration problem and they are targeting the XTM as the engine which will use Kernel Linda to provide a high-speed interface between machines. Kernel Linda, and the integrated software environment which it supports, is a major attraction of the XTM series. By concentrating on integrated computing, Cogent are extending the domain of their Kernel Linda environment beyond their own hardware.

Cogent refer to a new resource server which will be available in 1991. This will support Kernel Linda and the QIX operating system, and therefore all software on existing XTM machines will run unmodified on the new hardware. This development path will allow Cogent to employ state of the art processors in their products as processor technology advances, whilst retaining their user base.

This is a period of transition for Cogent, and the realignment of the company has involved some staff cuts. Higginson and Nora are no longer with the company, and the engineering staff are also involved in the restructuring and streamlining process. Charles Vollum, now CEO, stresses Cogent's intention to honour their commitment to existing customers, while acknowledging the company's intention to condense as it moves into new, more focused markets in the long term. Cogent have succeeded where others have failed in that they have recognised the limitations of their market niche before it was too late. Whether their new market direction will prove to be more lucrative, and whether they will come through the current reorganisation to exploit it, remains to be seen.

6.2 Silicon Graphics Incorporated

Relevant Activities Supplier of high-end graphics workstations and multiple-processor departmental supercomputers.

Location Corporate Office: Silicon Graphics Inc., 2011 North Shoreline Boulevard, Mountain View, California 94043, USA. Telephone: (415) 960 1980.

Relevant Officers James H. Clark, Chairman; Robert R. Bishop, President (Silicon Graphics International); Edward R. McCreacken, President and CEO (Silicon Graphics Inc); Debby Miller, Marketing VP.

Employees Approximately 1800, mostly in the US.

Financial details Revenue for last financial year (up to 30th June 1989) - $263 M. Revenue up to 30th March 1990 - $299 M, projected to be around $400 M for the full year.

6.2.1 The Company

Silicon Graphics Incorporated (SGI) was founded by Prof. James Clark in 1981. Clark had been head of a research team at Stanford University that had been sponsored by DARPA to investigate and develop integrated circuit based tools to calculate missile trajectories. This work lead directly to the design of the CMOS VLSI implementation of the Silicon Graphics Geometry Engine, a hardware implementation of the transformations needed for 3-D graphics (cf. Section A.3) which forms the basis of the graphics capabilities of all SGI hardware. The complete six person research team which worked on this project left with Clark to form SGI, and are all still with the company in senior R&D posts.

The company developed and marketed their first systems with finance raised solely from private venture capitalists. Their first product was the Iris Graphics Workstation, which was initially little more than an intelligent terminal. The machine contained no local processing for applications programs, but did provide a powerful 3-D graphics environment along with communications over Ethernet and RS232. The current range of SGI machines, the 4D series, was introduced in 1987. All these machines use RISC processors produced by MIPS Computer Systems. This move to mass-produced processors has recently been seen in the products of Stardent Computer (6.3.2), SGI's leading competitor, who also chose the MIPS chips as the computation base for their machines.

The new range of SGI machines includes the Personal Iris graphics workstations (the 4D/20) as well as the Power Series "super-workstations" (the 4D/110). These latter machines reveal a slight shift in emphasis in the SGI product range, away from solely providing graphics oriented hardware towards the provision of machines capable of high-levels of performance, i.e. around 30 MFLOPS. These increased levels of performance have been achieved through the introduction of parallel processing. The move towards parallelisation began in 1988 and SGI machines are now available with up to eight MIPS processors. A recent poll of users of high-powered computers showed SGI in fourth place in the list of favoured suppliers, behind Cray (cf. Section 7.1), IBM (8.3) and Convex (3.4), therefore this slight change in direction seems to have been successful in terms of SGIs standing in the supercomputing market. The change in emphasis is typified by the most recent addition to the SGI Power Series range of machines, the 4D/380. SGI claim that this machine, with its eight MIPS R3000 processors, achieves CPU throughput equivalent to that of $1 M-plus supercomputers, whilst only costing a small fraction of the price. In fact the machine costs $200 k and can deliver up to 33 double precision MFLOPS.

In 1989, SGI sold their Geometry Engine to IBM (8.3) for use in their RS/6000 computers. This was followed by forging a similar link with Multiflow (10.3), although technology transfer between the two companies was limited to SGI porting its graphics front-end facilities onto Trace systems. SGI had no interest in becoming more involved with Multiflow's VLIW architectures (A.4.2) and did not feel that their trading position was significantly undermined by Multiflow's collapse.

These inter-company links do not point towards SGI wishing to open up the graphics market to other manufacturers, on the contrary they believe that maximum dissemination of their technology will only lead to more customers coming directly to SGI for their hardware. They have concluded that high-performance graphics is only one part of their potential market, and the provision of a range of compatible compute resource machines, file servers and graphics workstations are necessary to put SGI into a strong position within the market.

6.2.2   The Hardware

SGI's high-end graphics workstations range from the small, essentially single-user Personal Iris 4D/20 up to the recently announced Power Series 4D/380, which is aimed more at departmental computing and file serving. Each machine contains between one and eight MIPS R3000 processors implementing shared-memory parallelism through a bus-based architecture. The MIPS processors are RISC chips rated at 20 MIPS performance and are supplemented with a MIPS R3010 floating-point co-processor. Work is currently underway to incorporate MIPS' new R4000 chip into a new range of SGI machines.

When compared to competing hardware, for example that produced by Stardent Computer (cf. Section 6.3.2), SGI's machines are noticeably short of floating-point performance, even with the use of the MIPS floating-point co-processors.

The Personal Iris

The Personal Iris is SGI's smallest (but most widely used) product and is intended for use as a desk-side standalone workstation similar to those produced by Sun or DEC. Unlike machines from other manufacturers the machine is completely compatible with the rest of the SGI range and uses the same graphics library and graphics subsystems as their most powerful machines. The Iris uses accepted communications standards such as TCP/IP, NFS and Ethernet, and so can be integrated into existing computing networks.

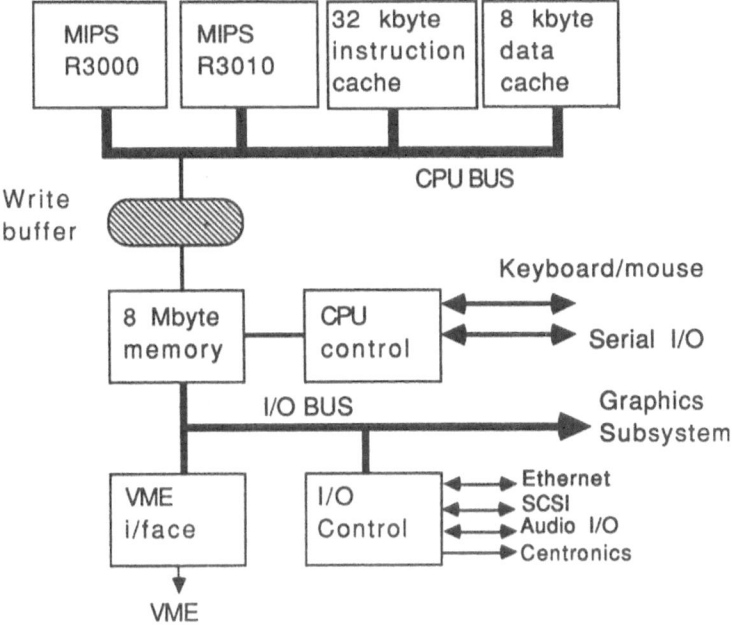

Figure 6.2: CPU Architecture of the SGI Personal Iris

The basic architecture of the Personal Iris CPU is shown in Figure 6.2. The standard system contains 8 Mbyte of memory with a 32 kbyte cache, delivering up to 0.9 MFLOPS, and 1.6 MFLOPS when coupled with the MIPS high-performance floating-point accelerator. The Personal Iris seems to have been designed specifically for integration in a network of machines. There are a large number of standard interfaces built into a single board, including two serial ports, a parallel port, a VME slot, an Ethernet connector, a SCSI bus connector, audio I/O jacks and a single connection for both keyboard and three-button mouse. The Personal Iris allows flexible configuration of the system to meet specific I/O or storage requirements. There exists a range of discs from 190 Mbyte to 3.5 Gbyte, as well as various tape drives. Third-party products available include a VME interface for the genlock video option, an IEEE-488 interface and several high-resolution colour printers.

The SGI POWER Range

The POWER range of SGI machines is aimed at satisfying mid-range applications and high-performance departmental computing needs. All machines are based on MIPS RISC processors and co-processors implemented in a bus-based parallel architecture. The machines contain from one to eight CPUs in an expandable rack-based configuration, allowing relatively easy upgrades within the range.

The POWER Station machines are intended for use as compute servers, file servers or general-purpose technical computer systems. Containing up to four processors these machines can provide up to 80 MIPS (16 MFLOPS) of sustained performance, and support up to 128 Mbyte of memory with more than 20 Gbyte of disc storage available in expansion racks.

The POWER Center systems are SGI's top-of-the-range machines which they claim are the most powerful RISC-based computer systems currently available. The machines include between one and eight CPUs that can collectively deliver up to 160 MIPS (28 MFLOPS) of sustained performance. The package includes memory and disc storage similar to the POWER Station systems, but with an additional option of up to 4.8 Gbyte of high-speed SMD disc storage.

Through the consistent use of standard MIPS processors there is binary compatibilty between all machines in SGI's current range. This allows systems to be upgraded without the need for new releases of software, or the recompilation of the customers own software.

Graphics Facilities and Add-on Hardware

SGI's graphics facilities range from those of a basic colour workstation (8 bit planes) to the top-of-the-range PowerVision VGX with 268 bit planes, 48 of which are used to provide 24 bit, double-buffered colour. All SGI products can be supplied with attached monitors and can include a graphics subsystem containing a number of Geometry Engines. The graphics hardware is based upon custom 1μm CMOS technology and contains four pipelined graphics subsystems. A host-interface takes graphics commands from the CPU, geometry and raster subsystems then perform the relevant operations on the data, and finally a display subsystem deals with the interface to a monitor. This system can deliver very high levels of graphics performance, measures advertised by SGI include 1 Mpolygons/s, 1 M anti-aliased RGB vectors per second, 1.5 M anti-aliased RGB points per second and a polygon fill rate of up to 200 Mpixel/s. The PowerVision system can perform many graphics operations within the hardware, these include real-time texture mapping and fog effects, as well as standard graphics facilities available all SGI machines such as sub-pixel positioning, lighting effects, anti-aliasing and a stereo vision system.

In April 1990 SGI released a new graphics system called IrisVision. This added image processing capabilities to the geometry architecture. IrisVision uses an SIMD approach to processing image manipulation algorithms, with a gate-array of 40 computation nodes performing dataflow transformations from algorithms loaded from a supplied library into a control store. The system is included as standard for the PowerVision machines, and is available to existing users through a site-installed upgrade.

More than 50 companies currently supply additional hardware for SGI computers. These products fall into four main catagories :

- Supplementary peripherals for Graphical data I/O e.g. digitizers, 3-D data input devices, video frame capture: 25 products.

- Communications hardware e.g. Ultranet: 12 products.

- Computation accelerators to improve performance e.g. floating point accelerators, digital signal processing boards: 4 products.

- Storage devices e.g. optical discs, Exabyte tapes: 11 products.

The wide range of third-party products, and the number of companies manufacturing them, points towards the way SGI machines are becoming accepted as something of an industry standard. As this trend continues, SGI's grip on the graphics workstation market becomes ever more difficult for other manufacturers, such as Stardent Computer, to break.

6.2.3   The Software

The Development Machine

SGI provides a range of system software for its machines, these include IRIX, a UNIX-compatible operating system, X Windows and some SGI-specific programs such as the Workspace Manager. This is a visual interface to the UNIX directory structure which allows users to access files and utilities using the windowing interface.

The IRIX operating system is based on AT&T System V.3 UNIX, with most Berkeley 4.3BSD additions included. The system is also compatible with the POSIX and FIPS standards for UNIX. It offers fully symmetric parallel processing such that each of the CPUs in the machine has equal access to system resources via the system bus. When multiple processes are being executed IRIX allocates the tasks across the available processors without the need for user intervention. The operating system is itself distributed across the available processors and is thus similar to Dynix that runs on Sequent machines (cf. Section 3.7), or the UNIX-like operating system available on the Cogent workstations (6.1). The Berkeley 4.3BSD TCP/IP extensions within IRIX provide connectivity in a networked environment, and an Ethernet controller provides an industry-standard communications interface for all SGI machines. Besides the extensions to support parallelism the operating system also provides other facilities outwith basic UNIX. For example, there is a version of the dbx debugger that can handle multiple processes and is able to attach itself to a running process. IRIX also supports memory-mapping of files and shared libraries.

SGI provide software libraries (based on those used to create the IRIX operating system) to allow the use of explicit parallelism through extensions to the Fortran and C languages. The company also market parallelising compilers for Fortran and C. The Power Fortran Accelerator (PFA) automatically parallelises Fortran code in terms of identifying data independent loops and passing their execution through different processors streams. The Power C pre-compiler analyses data dependencies in serial programs and then rewrites the source code, producing a listing with embedded parallel compiler directives. This can then be altered by the programmer to introduce specific parallelism that the analyser may have missed, before being finally compiled into the multi-processing code.

Graphics and Third-party Software

The graphics language used to access the graphics facilities of SGI systems is GL (Graphics Language). This provides triangle primitives and lighting models as well as hooks into SGI's 4sight windowing system. GL calls are issued from C or Fortran programs by including a library at link time. GL routines are available to support object interaction, manipulation, drawing and rendering, multiple lighting, dithering and pan and zoom functions. The Distributed Graphics Library (DGL) is also supplied as system software, this enables GL commands to be issued from a remote machine over an Ethernet connection.

SGI's main competitors, Stardent have had much success with their Application Visualisation System (AVS), an object-oriented graphics software package (cf. Section 6.3.3). SGI are now developing tools similar to AVS for use in future systems. Craig Upson, a member of the AVS design team, has recently left Stardent and started work for SGI in this area.

The third-party software base for SGI's range of machines is provided by the company's *Geometry Partners*, a variety of software companies which have formed links with SGI. There are currently 216 of these companies, providing a wide range of software. Table 6.1 shows the number of software products that exist within a certain groupings. The figures show a clear bias towards scientific and engineering production and research work. However this may not exactly represent the true usage of SGI machines since certain customers may use their machines for specific applications, for which they may use specialised software.

Table 6.1: Analysis of SGI software

Product Type	Number of Products
CAD/CAM/CAE	127
Science (geology, chemistry, general, CFD)	101
Tools and Utilities	55
Visual Simulation	41
Animation, Graphic Arts & Publishing	40
Architectural and Engineering	16
Image Processing	11
Electronic Design Automation	9
Medicine	5

6.2.4 The Market Niche

At the time of their formation, SGI's main competitors were Stellar, Ardent and Evans & Sutherland. After the merger of the first two of these, and Evans & Sutherland's concentration on the high-end of the market, SGI now have a strong lead in this area, and by far the largest share of the market.

The company has sold approximately 10,000 machines to date, installed in over 1000 sites. Engineering companies represent 45% of SGI's sales, while scientific sales form approximately 25%. There is growing interest in using SGI workstations to display data from powerful compute servers. For example, at the Edinburgh Parallel Computing Centre, a Power Series 4D/220 GTXB is being connected to a Meiko Computing Surface (cf. Section 5.3) and an AMT DAP 610 (cf. Section 2.1). This sort of arrangement has worked successfully at NASA/Ames where a Cray was connected via a high-speed link to a SGI machine for visualisation of flow simulations.

SGI consider themselves to be prominent in a variety of markets, and to have different competitors in each. In the R&D market, Stardent provide the main competition, whereas in engineering it comes from DEC and Sun. In the provision of compute power SGI see Convex (cf. Section 3.4) are their main competitors (though Stardent also have a section of this market). SGI feel they have no competition at the moment in the field of visual modelling, although Stardent would presumably take task with this point.

The company cite the obscure processors used by Stellar as the reason for their lack of commercial success. SGI have worked closely with MIPS to ensure that all of their systems can make use of parallel processing and will be binary compatible. Similarly, they feel that Ardent failed to provide the compatibility and standards that SGI provided with their MIPS systems. The superior AVS visualisation software provided with the Stellar was not enough to offset the advantages of the SGI machines (see Table 6.2) and SGI's more capable marketing methods. However since the merger of Stellar and Ardent and their move over to MIPS processors (cf. Section 6.3) SGI may now have more to fear in the marketplace.

Table 6.2: Comparison of SGI and Stardent for a £75,000 system

Aspect	SGI	Stardent
Performance	30 MIPS	30 MIPS
	5 MFLOPS	32 MFLOPS
Rendering	100,000 poly/s	50,000 poly/s
Graphics System	GL (basic)	AVS (advanced)
Software	IRIX, X	UNIX, X, Vectorising compilers
Other factors	Large user base	Incompatibility with other Stardent systems

Recently SGI have been taking a very aggressive sales position, and offering substantial discounts on the Personal Iris 3-D workstations. This followed the sale of $35 M of convertible stock to the NKK Corporation of Tokyo. This sale has funded the price cuts in an attempt to provide a larger user base in both the Japanese and European markets.

6.2.5   The Future

In general, SGI plan to increase the computational power of their computers by improving the power of each processor rather then raising the number of nodes beyond the present maximum of eight. They see the the problem of increased bus contention and the difficulty of developing software for highly parallel machines as problems they wish to avoid. How long they can retain this point of view and still be competitive remains to be seen. The company does however seem committed to small-scale parallelism. Although there is a faster ECL implementation of the R3000 processor, SGI do not use the chip in their systems as it lacks some of the bus-control facilities needed for use as part of a multiprocessor computer. The constant improvement of processor performance requires the regular upgrading of hardware to keep in touch with the best available technology. SGI are currently working on introducing the new R4000 MIPS chips into their machines, and they hope to announce new GaAs versions of their graphics hardware in late 1990; these faster machines should be available in mid-1991.

6.3   Stardent Computer Incorporated

Relevant Activities Manufacturer of multiprocessor graphics workstations.

Location Stardent Computer Incorporated, 880 West Maude Avenue, Sunnyvale, California, 94086, USA; Telephone: (408) 732 0400; Fax: (408) 732 2806. Stardent Computer Limited, 7 Huxley Road, The Surrey Research Park, Guildford, Surrey, GU2 5RE, UK; Telephone: 0483 505388; Fax: 0483 505352.

Relevant Officers Former Stellar employees: John William Poduska Sr., President and Chief Executive Officer; Ian R.G. Edmonds, Executive VP and Chief Operating Officer; Christopher Andrews, Corporate VP, Administration and General Counsel; Lester M. Crudele, Corporate VP, R&D; Wallace E. Smith, Sr. Corporate VP, Sales, Marketing and Service
Former Ardent employees: Gordon Bell, Corporate VP and Chief Scientist; Joseph R. Bronson, Corporate VP, Finance and Chief Financial Officer;

Employees Approximately 350 worldwide, plus 340 Kubota personnel involved in Stardent production and sales.

Financial details Financed by partnership with Kubota Corporation and by various venture capital firms. $160M investment capital raised between 1986-90.

6.3.1   The Company

Stardent Computer Limited was formed in October 1989 through a merger of Stellar Computer Incorporated and Ardent Computer Corporation. Both Stellar and Ardent had been major performers in the high-powered graphics workstations market. They had developed in a remarkably similar fashion, consistently producing similar machines at identical times. By 1989, both companies were losing market share to Silicon Graphics Inc. (SGI, cf. Section 6.2) and the financial problems this produced led to their collaboration and eventual merger. The resulting company now has over 350 employees worldwide, most of whom are in the USA. In addition the Kubota Corporation, Stardent's Japanese partners, have over 300 personnel dedicated to the manufacture and distribution of Stardent products.

Stellar Computer Incorporated

Formed in 1985 and based in Newton Massachussetts, Stellar aimed themselves at both the high-performance graphics and the standard minisupercomputer market. Their first machines were released in 1988, the GS1000 (Graphics Supercomputer) in March and the DS1000 (Departmental Supercomputer) in September. Both these machines were based on custom VSLI technology and could produce a peak performance of 40 MFLOPS from a four processor deskside system. The GS1000 differed

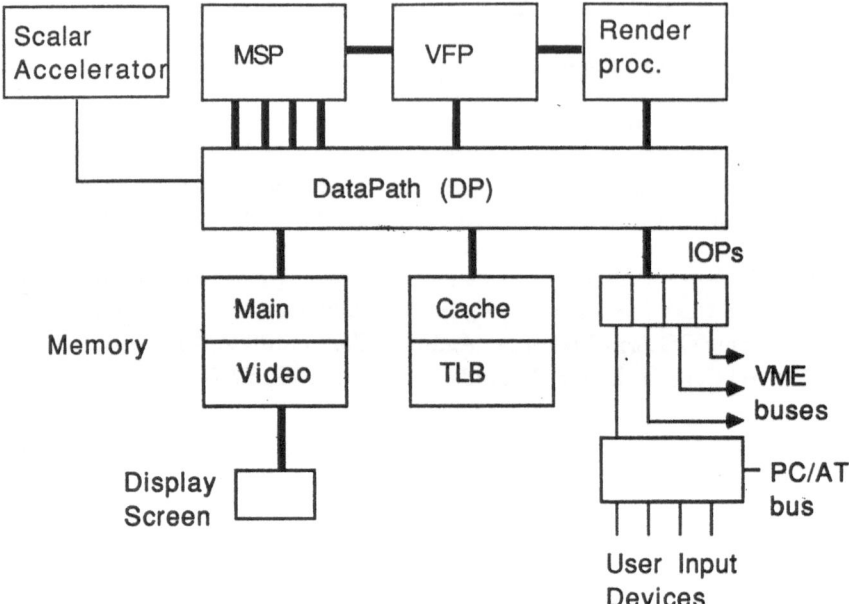

Figure 6.3: Stellar Hardware Architecture

from the DS1000 only in the extra provision of specialised graphics hardware. This processor added a 3-D graphics capability and an interactive user visualisation environment that could achieve 150 kpolygon/s for graphics rendering (cf. Section A.3). The machines ran a version of UNIX (V.3) called the Stellix Operation System and boasted compilers for automatic vectorisation and parallelisation of Fortran and C code. These compilers would do a first pass analysis of code and identify data-independent sections that could be run concurrently. Stellar systems were sold in the price range $98 k and upwards, depending on the options added.

The basic architecture of the Stellar machines can be seen in Figure 6.3. The *DataPath* architecture maintained a high data bandwidth (more than 3 Gbit/s) among a tightly-integrated array of functional units. Each of these units time-share for use of the system bus, and therefore this high-level of architecture contains no true parallelism. However, parallelism is used within the multiple-stream processor (MSP). This combined four essentially independent purpose-built CPUs in a single functional unit. Each processor could execute instruction streams concurrently, and included specialised *concurrency registers* to enable stream-to-stream synchronisation. The four streams shared a single main memory, cache and translation buffer. The Stellar compilers and operating system automatically restructured code to allow concurrent execution on several processors.

There was also shared-data parallelism within the vector/floating-point processor (VFP) which contained four floating-point processing units configured to work separately or in tandem. Following the release of the 2000 series machines in May 1989, the VFP unit was increased to contain eight CPUs. These new machines also included improved versions of the specialised processors in the MSP, and offered an optional scalar accelerator. This gave an additional instruction stream for non-vector processing, which could boost performance by 10 – 15 MIPS.

In April 1989 Stellar released the first version of their Application Visualisation System (AVS), which provided users with advanced visualisation techniques without the need for in-depth knowledge of graphics programming techniques. Three-dimensional interactive graphics, combined with the computing power of the machine, provided a real-time environment for analysing and manipulating data that became a major selling point of the Stellar and later Stardent computers.

The background to the Stellar operation looks like that of a successful company, yet within four years of their formation they had to merge with Ardent to survive. The reason for the company's lack of success in the specialist graphics field has to come down to their choice of custom-built hardware. The incompatibility between binaries for Stellar systems and those of any other, led to problems porting code. Without a strong base of applications software the company was destined to obscurity. The merger with Ardent helped to overcome this problem since their choice of the widely-used MIPS RISC chips produced far more potential for the porting of code.

Ardent Computer Corporation

Ardent were also formed in 1985 and were based in Sunnyvale, California, the present site of Stardent headquarters. Like Stellar they intended to exploit the rapidly growing market for high-performance graphics workstations, which they aimed to achieve through the use of custom made hardware for polygon rendering, with multiple processors for computation. The processors chosen to make-up the CPU of the Ardent Titan series of computers was the MIPS RISC chip — the same chip chosen by SGI (cf. Section 6.2.2) for their workstations. These MIPS processors have a benchmarked performance of 6.1 Linpack MFLOPS, and an advertised peak performance of 16 MFLOPS when used with a co-processor and floating-point unit. The Titan machines contained from one to four such processors thus producing a theoretical maximum peak performance of 64 MFLOPS, from a machine priced in the range $80 k to $150 k.

Following a trend of development similar to Stellar, Ardent released their first production graphics workstation, Titan 1, in March 1988, and the non-graphics version, the Titan Departmental Supercomputer, in September of that year. These machines used their multiple MIPS processors in a shared-memory arrangement, with identical but independent memory caches. Together with the custom floating-point vector co-processors, enough compute power was available to make real-time visualisation a possibility. The next version of the Titan workstation (the Titan

2) was never released by Ardent, but was introduced by Stardent after the merger. Some aspects of the Titan 2 design, including the use of MIPS processors and co-processors, were enhanced and introduced by Stardent for their first production machine, the Stardent 3000.

Ardent also developed a high-level graphics interface to allow complex objects to be constructed, manipulated and rendered in an object-oriented manner. This software was called Doré (Dynamic Object Rendering Environment) and was first released in February 1988. This early release (before the first Ardent machine) was in the hope that Doré would become the *de facto* 3-D graphics standard. As well as this imaging software library, Ardent also ported other software packages to the Titan machines, for example the MATLAB graphical numerical computation system, and an Ada compiler from Meridian Software. Such porting of software was made relatively simple since Ardent had chosen to use the widely available MIPS hardware as the computation base for their machine.

By July 1989, three months before the merger with Stellar, Ardent had installed over 200 Titan graphics workstations in less than a year. These machines had gone to a wide variety of customers, ranging from the MIT Graphics and Animation group to the Radioactive Therapy Unit at St. Thomas' Hospital, London. However, these sales still accounted for a small proportion of the total graphics market, and most of which was being taken by SGI. Consequently, Ardent and Stellar joined forces to produce a single company capable of competing with SGI in the world marketplace.

The Partnership with Kubota

Stardent Computer is currently financed through its strategic partnership with the Kubota Corporation, a $6 G worldwide industrial equipment manufacturer. The solid financial backing available from Kubota, along with the $160 M of investment capital raised between 1985 and 1990 by both Stellar and Ardent, has allowed Stardent to move out of the development phase and towards a potentially profitable business enterprise. The company estimates the graphics workstation market to be worth $1 G worldwide in 1990, with a compounded annual growth rate of 30%. By providing fully integrated manufacture of Stardent products, Kubota assures high-volume manufacturing capacity, giving Stardent very competitive production costs. When this is tied to the extensive sales and distribution network of the Japanese firm, it places Stardent in an excellent position to exploit the growing market.

Stardent's revenues have increased steadily from $32 M in 1989 (sum of revenues from Stellar and Ardent), through $45 M (estimated) in 1990 to a projected $68 M in 1991. This shows percentage growth similar to that seen in the relevant market sectors.

6.3.2   The Hardware

Following the merger of Stellar and Ardent, Stardent continued to market machines from both the Titan and the Stellar GS/DS ranges. Much effort was put into porting the major software products onto both machines to make them compatible. A product renaming scheme began with the Stellar GS1000 and the Titan 1 both becoming known as the Stardent 1000, the Stellar GS/DS 2000 as the Stardent 2000, and the Titan 2 as the Stardent 1500. Further the design of the new Titan machine was merged with the planned Stellar 3000 to become the Stardent 3000. This new machine was released in November 1989, one month after the merger of the two companies, and is obviously intended to keep the market alive while final decisions are made about the direction of future products. However much can be surmised from the format chosen for the initial release of the Stardent 3000, basically the hardware design comes from Stellar but using Ardent's choice of processor, and the major software is an amalgam of both the companies major visualisation packages. Stardent has announced that it intends to merge all product lines by 1991.

Stardent 3000

Following in the tradition of all its predecessors the Stardent 3000 was released in GS and DS varieties. In hardware design the machine is a direct descendent of the Ardent Titan, with the R2000 MIPS chip upgraded to the R3000. For the graphics the Stardent 3000 uses a processor with very little specialised hardware, unlike the SGI graphics engines for example. Instead it relies on a vector processor with some help from the R3000.

The Stardent 3000 is a shared-memory multiprocessor system which can contain from one to four CPUs (see Figure 6.4). Each CPU contains the R3000 integer scalar processor along with an R3010 scalar floating-point co-processor, two independent 64 kbyte direct-mapped caches (one for instructions the other for data), four-deep write buffers, and a specialised vector processor. This Stardent designed chip handles all vector operations and during graphics processing it serves as the geometry engine for the system. Some versions of the machine also contain a Weitek co-processor within the CPU unit, and it is these versions that can reach the peak performance figures detailed below. One draw-back of having this extra co-processor is that there is binary incompatibility between the different machines in the Stardent range, since earlier machines were not supplied with the Weitek chip.

The memory system of the Stardent 3000 is closely coupled with the bus-based architecture of the machine. There can be from one to four memory boards, each with 8, 16 or 32 Mbyte of memory. Depending on configuration the memory system can provide either 8-way or 16-way interleaving. The two buses used by the Stardent 3000 for memory access are also used for communication with I/O and graphics

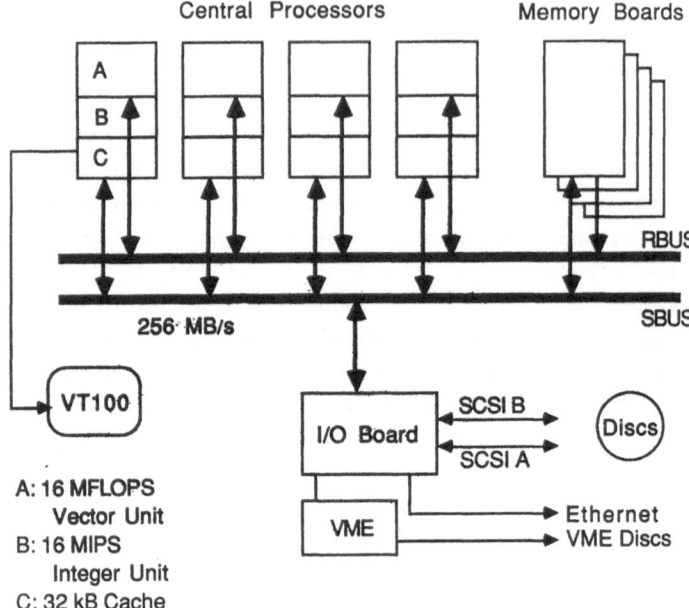

Figure 6.4: Architecture of the Stardent 3000

subsystems, both have 32 bit address and 64 bit data paths and operate at 16 MHz. All I/O, other than for graphics, is handled by a single board that can accommodate seven SCSI devices and a VME interface.

When configured with the maximum four processing units the Stardent 3000 is advertised as delivering a peak power of 192 MFLOPS. In actual benchmarking tests (Linpack 100 × 100) the machine produced 11 MFLOPS, and on the Dhrystone benchmark provided almost 30 Vax MIPS of sustained performance. The shortfall in performance is almost certainly due to the fact that the benchmark binaries would take no account of the specialised architecture of the Stardent CPU. However the same would be true of the majority of third-party software produced for the Stardent machines.

The Stardent 3000 falls into the minisupercomputer class. A minimum entry level system containing a single CPU, 32 Mbyte of memory and a single 380 Mbyte SCSI disc drive (but without graphics facilities) is competitively priced midway between, for example, a Sun SPARCstation and a typical MIMD machine. The full Stardent 3000 system with four CPUs, 256 Mbyte of memory and three disc drives falls in the same price bracket as the SGI top-of-the-range machine.

6.3.3 The Software

Operating System and Compilers

The Stardent 3000 runs a UNIX-like operating system compatible with release 3 of AT&T's System V UNIX, and incorporating extensions from Berkeley 4.3BSD. The system is a multiprocessing and multitasking version of UNIX offering asynchronous multiprocessing with the operating system running in parallel on all processors. Stardent's UNIX is unusual in one respect: it supports single-process, multithread micro-tasking, where a single process can be divided into several threads to be executed concurrently. This parallelisation is provided through the compiler by code being preprocessed so that data independent sections are flagged for concurrent execution. This preprocessed code can then be analysed and amended by the user. The operating system also supports TCP/IP and NFS network protocols, which are becoming standard with most UNIX-based systems, and the company also offers optional DECnet emulation. There is growing collaboration between Stardent and DEC as the range of DEC compatibility features on Stardent machines grows. There is now strong support for Vax Fortran, an EDT-like text editor, a DCL command interface emulator as well as a varied collection of LIB$ and SYS$ run-time library routines.

Within their UNIX environment Stardent provides compilers for C and Fortran, with an Ada compiler available for the Stardent 1500 but as yet unvalidated for the Stardent 3000. These compilers only differ in their front-ends which compile code into an intermediate language, all vectorisation, parallelisation and optimisation is then carried out by a standard second stage. The C compiler is based on AT&T System V release 3 C with ANSI C extensions and libraries from both System V and Berkeley 4.3BSD. The Fortran compiler is based on ANSI standard Fortran 77, with extensions from Vax Fortran version 3.0 as well as a number of Cray Fortran directives.

Visualisation Systems

The user interface to Stardent's visualisation system is via their own implementation of the X Windows system, called X+. This use of a growing standard system allows simpler porting of applications to Stardent machines as well as attracting users to a known system. Applications that use the X Windows X lib library calls will run under X+, since the extensions made by Stardent to the system are mainly for the X server and include support for double-buffering windows and true- or pseudo-colour windows.

Stardent had the choice of two major graphics software libraries to offer with its graphics workstations. These were Doré, the object-oriented package from Ardent, and the Phigs-based AVS from Stellar. The first Stardent computers were supplied only with Doré, however the company has chosen a new version of AVS as the system for its latest machines. This software uses the X Windows facilities as well as the graphics library from Doré (the previous AVS was based on Phigs+) and is therefore to some extent a merger of the two systems. AVS provides a real-time environment for data analysis and manipulation. It is not intended for graphics programmers, but rather it builds on the graphics library resources to provide an object-oriented environment that allows very high level input and transformation of data. The basis of the AVS user interface is an interactive, mouse-driven Network Editor which allows users to connect various modules together. These modules each perform a graphical function on input data, which can be provided from other modules, taken from files, or generated within the module. The concept is similar to that of a UNIX pipe, but more versatile. This is a very significant move away from the experienced programmers use of data files and simpler graphics packages, and whilst undoubtedly easy to use and innovative, may require some user re-education before it becomes generally acceptable.

AVS was first released in 1989 and has been growing in reputation ever since. In March 1990 AVS was licenced by DEC for provision on their machines, and Convex (cf. Section 3.4) followed suit in May 1990. As the use of AVS becomes more widespread and the number of applications ported to the system increases, it is possibly the acceptability of AVS that decides the success of Stardent as a whole. The move from Phigs+ to Doré as the lower-level graphics library may prove to be something of a risk. It is the low-level library which often determines the ease of porting, and Doré was less successful in the marketplace than its direct competitors Phigs and GKS, which seem to be the main contenders for a "graphics standard". However the union of AVS and Doré may prove to be a combination which could swing the market in Stardent's favour.

Third Party Software

Stardent run an application alliance programme to encourage the porting of third party software onto their machines. The Stardent 3000 currently supports more than 60 such packages in a variety of disciplines including computational fluid dynamics, mechanical computer-aided design, computational chemistry, medical and military imaging, seismic exploration and animation.

6.3.4   The Market

Over 1000 Stardent systems have been installed at over 500 sites. Like other graphics workstations, they are primarily sold to in areas such as imaging (25%), chemical visualisation (21%), mechanical computer-aided design (9%), computational fluid dynamics (14%) and general scientific (16%). BNR, Boeing, Eastman Kodak, General Electric, the Scripps Clinic, SERC, and a large number of American and European universities are members of their Technical Cooperation Program.

There is no doubt that the high-performance graphics workstation market is dominated by Stardent and SGI (cf. Section 6.2.4). Since the market is ever expanding, there is no reason why one should fail and the other survive, as long as they both continue to meet the end-users needs. Both companies have such a solid base in the market that is seems unlikely that another specialist producer could break their domination. There is however strong competition between the two companies, and small differences in their respective products that may allow users to choose between the available machines. The Stardent 3000 gives better compute performance than SGI Iris workstations, benchmark tests have shown that a two processor Stardent gives 30% more MFLOPS than a four processor SGI Power Iris (4D/420). However this advantage is balanced by the fact that SGI machines can render polygons at twice the rate of similarly priced Stardent workstations. The user therefore has to choose between the required mix of raw processing power and rendering performance that is required, as well as the range of software available on the systems.

It is unlikely that the current, or expected, machine-specific graphics facilities offered by the parallel supercomputer manufacturers pose much of a problem for Stardent or SGI. Stardent may, in fact, have a potential market in supplying graphics systems to owners of such machines if work were undertaken to improve the inter-machine communications facilities, for example using HiPPI. However, the specialist graphics workstation manufacturers may be threatened if companies such as Sun were to upgrade the graphics performance of their machines, either by using multiprocessor add-in boards or by providing special-purpose hardware such as SGI's Geometry Engine. The potential of such companies lies in their massive installed base and the correspondingly large amounts of software already available on their systems. Stardent will need to match this threat by ensuring that its graphics capabilities remain at the leading-edge of the technology. The desire to do this is evident from the fact that over a third of Stardent staff are employed in research positions.

6.3.5   The Future

Graphics support is definitely Stardent's speciality, and the provision of graphics systems for all types of high performance computers may well be the best route for the company to maintain its present rate of growth. The competition with SGI is healthy for the graphics workstation market, and users can only hope this will continue. The software provided on Stardent systems will undoubted continue to grow and their contribution to the competition for a visualisation standard (AVS) is strong. Further development of visualisation tools is the largest sector of Stardent's current R&D efforts.

There is no doubt that over the next few years there will have been further advances in processor technology and these will undoubtedly be incorporated into future Stardent machines. However it seems likely that the Titan-like hardware design will survive at least to the middle of this decade, and customers are being assured of source-code compatibility with both previous ranges of machines.

6.4 Teradata Corporation

Relevant Activities Manufacturers of parallel database computers.

Location Corporate Headquarters: Teradata Corp., 100 North Sepulveda Blvd., El Segundo, California 90245, USA. European Headquarters: Teradata Europe Ltd., The Albany Works, Queens Road, Thames Ditton, Surrey KT7 0QX, UK.

Relevant Officers K.W. Simonds, President, Chairman and CEO; J.E. Shemer, Vice Chairman; D. Cantor, Chief Operating Officer; R.C. Reed, Senior VP and Chief Technical Officer; M.F.G. Ashby, VP Finance; J. Brandeau, VP Human Resources.

Employees Approximately 1500 worldwide

Financial details Private company

6.4.1 The Company

There is more to parallel computing than MFLOPS. While scientists and engineers have traditionally measured computer performance in arithmetic operations per second, business, which makes up the other 90% of the computing market, has been more interested accessing and manipulating large data sets. Some of this work must be done in real-time to support on-line systems, such as banking machines, but a significant portion is *ad hoc* database analysis. Companies usually have the data they need to ascertain how they are performing — the problem is sifting and correlating it.

Teradata was founded in 1980 by two former employees of Transaction Processing Limited, a wholly-owned subsidiary of the American financial conglomerate Citibank which was, in effect, Citibank's data processing department. Teradata's aim was to produce a computer capable of handling queries on hundreds of Gbyte of data. In order to achieve this, they decided to process each query using several processors simultaneously. This in turn required the database to be partitioned between many storage devices, so that the processor/storage interface would not be a bottleneck.

Teradata's first sale was in 1985. Since then they have grown by roughly 70% per annum, turning over approximately $224 M worldwide in 1989/90. The largest system they have sold to date has a capacity of 300 Gbyte; few of their machines have a capacity of less than 40 Gbyte.

Their habit of talking about machine sizes in terms of Gbyte, rather than MFLOPS, reveals a great deal about the company's aims, as does their emphasis on the reliability of their machines. Teradata did not set out to build parallel computers. Rather, their machines are parallel because no other design is capable of delivering the performance they need to offer in order to be commercially successful.

6.4.2   The Hardware

The machine Teradata produces is called the DBC/1012[2]. The DBC/1012 is not a standalone machine. It is intended for use as a database engine coupled either to mainframes (e.g. IBM, DEC) or to workstations and personal computers through a local area network (LAN) such as Ethernet.

The heart of the DBC/1012 is a proprietary switching network called the Ynet. Teradata calls the Ynet a bus, but in fact it is a binary tree whose nodes contain logic for routing and transferring messages, and for selecting and sorting database records. The Ynet operates at 6 MHz.

Each leaf node of this tree is either an Interface Processor (for communicating directly to a host mainframe), or Communications Processor (for communicating through a LAN), or an Access Module Processor (AMP), which performs data manipulations and returns results through the Ynet. These different processor types can be mixed in a variety of ways to tailor a particular machine to its users' needs. A typical entry-level configuration would contain two Communications Processors or six Interface Processors, and 20 AMPs, each managing two discs. However, particular configurations are strongly influenced by the size of the data base and the application's requirements; according to Teradata, there is not really a "typical" configuration.

Processors are grouped in cabinets; each cabinet may hold up to eight processors of any kind. There are interconnected within the cabinet through the backplane to a Ynet node board. Up to four Ynet node boards can be connected via cables to a Nodex board. For timing reasons, all Ynet cables are the same length (30′). This means that two interconnected processor cabinets cannot be more than 22′ apart.

The Ynet is hardware only — the logic gates in the nodes control routing, collisions and merges by propagating state conditions back down the tree to processors, which can then take appropriate actions.

All nodes in the Ynet are synchronized to a single clock. Messages are sent in blocks, each of which contains control fields carrying type and destination information. Contention logic sorts and merges messages as they travel from the originating processors toward the root of the tree; messages travelling from the root are simply forwarded.

Interface and Communications Processors translate user requests into indivisible database actions, sequence those actions, and transmit action requests through

---

[2]DBC stands for DataBase Computer, while 1012 refers to the maximum data storage which can be configured: 1 Terabyte (10^{12} byte).

the Ynet to the appropriate AMPs. The Ynet supports both point-to-point, broadcast, and multicast (i.e. broadcast to a specified subset of targets) communications. When results return from the DBC/1012's AMPs, the Interface and Communications Processors collate them and return the result to the user.

Connected to each AMP are up to four Disc Storage Units, or DSUs. Each of these is a single high-capacity Sabre disc. As requests reach an AMP, it orders its DSUs to perform the required operations and sends an appropriate response to the IFP or COP which initiated the action.

The processors used in the DBC/1012 were originally Intel 8086s. The present generation of machine uses the 80286 and 80386 chipsets, with 80486's being incorporated in the near future. Teradata has not invested in processor technology, trusting that semiconductor manufacturers would be able to continuing speeding up conventional microprocessors. Instead, Teradata's hardware development effort has been concentrated on its proprietary Ynet.

The mix of processors in a particular machine is determined by the user's requirements. Each Communications Processor provides a single Ethernet connection. If the DBC/1012 is configured on a LAN, the number of Communications Processors required is clearly determined by the peak network traffic.

The situation is more complicated if Interface Processors (IFPs) are being used to provide direct mainframe/DBC connections. The number of IFPs required is dependent on the nature, as well as the number, of SQL requests directed to the DBC. The IFP parses each SQL into primitive steps. For simple index directed requests, this can take a significant portion of the total time, while for complex queries requiring long AMP processing times, parsing becomes insignificant. This means that OLTP applications, or other applications which generate a large number of small SQL requests, tend to require a large number of IFPs, while so-called "decision support" applications require fewer. The performance of bulk operations, such as database dumping and restoring, is obviously limited by the number of IFPs available.

Under normal conditions, the speed of the DBC/host link does not limit performance, since the DBC/1012 returns (small) absolute answers to the host. Link speed is important when large volumes of data are being moved to and from the DBC, for example during database dump and restore. In a mainframe environment it is not unusual for an IFP to share a channel with another device, such as a disc controller. In such configurations high-traffic operations are usually carried out overnight or on weekends.

The number of AMPs needed in a configuration is determined by four factors:

- Since each AMP can manage at most four Disc Storage Units, enough AMPs are needed to meet the total data storage requirements.

- The throughput of the DBC is directly proportional to the number of AMPs.

- The response time is (in general) inversely proportional to the number of AMPs, since each services $1/N$ of the database.

- If the connections to the outside world are not a limiting factor, the time required to load a database is directly proportional to the number of AMPs available.

Finally, the number of disc storage units required depends on the size of the database (for obvious reasons), and on the volatility of the data. If a small amount of data is accessed regularly, each AMP should be responsible for only one or two DSUs, in order to avoid overloading. If, on the other hand, a large amount of data is accessed infrequently, each AMP can be configured with a larger number of DSUs.

Teradata has a sizing tool which they use to help design configurations.

6.4.3   Interface Software

From a user's point of view, a DBC/1012 processes SQL (Standard Query Language), an ANSI standard for interrogating relational databases. The wide use of this standard greatly simplified the task of designing the DBC/1012, since the machine's designers could work to optimise the performance of programs written in a single language.

DBC/1012 users can compose queries in several ways. The most direct are interactively, using Interactive Teradata Query (ITEQ), or in batch mode using BTEQ (ITEQ's batch equivalent) on either a mainframe or a workstation. Both of these interfaces are fairly conventional — ITEQ, for example, provides such things as screen editing of queries.

Users can also write programs on their host computers in Cobol, PL/I, or C which include SQL commands. These commands are translated into Call-Level Interface routines by a pre-processor before the code is compiled. After compilation the program may be linked with Call-Level Interface routines to create an executable module, or the routines may be dynamically loaded at run-time.

The call-level interface routines build an SQL request, which is passed to a director program running on the host computer. This same director program then passes the request to the DBC/1012, and returns the response to the user program. (It is interesting to note that at some points in their documentation Teradata only mentions the availability of pre-processors for Cobol and PL/I, indicating that C was a late addition, probably prompted by the growing popularity of UNIX.)

The DBC/1012 can also be used in conjunction with some of the more popular database software, including:

- Aion/ADS Interface (Aion): an expert system

- Intellect (Artificial Intelligence Corp.): a natural language query facility

- Ingres/Teradata Gateway: allows access to DBC/1012 using Ingres tools

- Metaphor/Teradata Gateway (Metaphor): allows access to DBC/1012 using Metaphor tools

- Nomad2 (Must Software), Focus (Information Builders), and DYL-280 (Sterling Software): fourth-generation query languages

There are clearly advantages to both parties in such arrangements. Every alternative interface Teradata can support opens up more potential customers who already have an investment in that interface. From a software manufacturer's point of view, the 'advantage' is more the absence of a disadvantage — being unable to communicate with Teradata machines could be a costly mistake if Teradata's already large share of the high-end database market continues to grow.

In addition to these interfaces, Teradata provides system administration software to reconfigure the DBC/1012, log database accesses, etc. Such facilities, while expected on conventional multi-user computers, are something of a novelty on parallel computers. For example, there is no provision in the Meiko Computing Surface (cf. 5.3) for controlling user access to particular processor partitions. However, the DBC/1012's market expects (and would claim it requires) such system management and protection facilities, which Teradata has therefore provided, by implementing the SQL Grant and Revoke operations, since its inception.

6.4.4 Internal Software

Actions inside the DBC/1012 itself are controlled by the Teradata Operating System (TOS). This virtual-memory, multi-user operating system runs on each interface, communications, or access module processor, and contains:

- a task scheduler (for managing tasks, interrupts, and timeouts)

- a Ynet driver (for message traffic to and from the Ynet)

- a host driver (to control input and output)

- a disc driver

- a segment subsystem (for memory management)

TOS is completely non-standard, but in Teradata's case that is not a liability: since users don't work with the machine itself, its operation can be allowed to be idiosyncratic. Teradata is currently exploring the possibility of incorporating the UNIX produced by Charles River Data Corporation into their machines.

The DBC/1012 automatically partitions the rows of each database table between its AMPs using a hashing algorithm, so that queries can be processed in parallel. As new AMPs are brought into a configuration, or as AMPs are removed, the DBC/1012 can re-partition database entries to maintain an even distribution.

6.4.5   Support for Critical Environments

One of the most striking features of the DBC/1012 is the provision it contains for use in critical environments, where a length loss of machine access could be extremely costly. While an academic's papers may be delayed if his or her supercomputer is off-line for a day or two, a large financial institution or corporation could suffer painful financial losses.

The DBC/1012's two biggest safety features are its inclusion of two Ynets in each machine, and (optionally) the use of a fallback copy area for each database. In normal operation, a machine's two Ynets operate concurrently to share the communications and sort/merge loads. If a component of one should fail, however, the machine will continue to function. This is "all-or-nothing" redundancy — because the Ynet is a binary tree, the loss of any non-terminal (i.e. non-processor) node renders some part of the machine inaccessible. If any of a Ynet's nodes fails the whole of that Ynet must be taken out of service. However, since one Ynet can be repaired while the other is operating, the system as a whole is extremely robust.

Fallback copy areas can be set up so that if an AMP is disabled the data on its Disc Storage Units can still be accessed. To increase reliability, the system administrator can create clusters of two to 16 AMPs, so that the system is robust in the face of loss of two or more AMPs. The fallback copy area on a particular AMP contains duplicates of some of the database rows stored on other AMPs in the same cluster. The fallback copies of rows contained on one AMP are distributed equally amongst all the other AMPs in its cluster. If the primary AMP should fail, messages for its records are re-routed to a backup AMP.

Users cannot, however, control where particular fields of particular databases are put. The hashing algorithm used is fixed and unmodifiable. According to Teradata, this algorithm is optimised to ensure an even spread of rows across all available AMPs.

6.4.6   The Marketplace

Teradata's market is almost exclusively large corporations and financial institutions, such as retail department stores (K Mart and Mervyn's), banks and insurance companies (Citicorp, Transamerica Insurance Group), and cosmetics manufacturers (Helene Curtis). Sixteen machines have been installed to date in the UK. Only three machines have been installed in US universities; one of these, at the University of California at Irvine, is used for research into Alzheimer's Disease.

Teradata's customers typically have very large databases of information gathered by point-of-sale systems. Their problem is interpreting this information. For example, after a new life insurance policy is marketed, a company may want to know what market segment is taking it up. To discover this, its data processing department needs to correlate information from hundreds or thousands of regional sales offices. The turnaround time for such queries on conventional uniprocessor mainframes is typically measured in days, weeks, or months. A heavily-configured DBC/1012, on the other hand, can provide the answer in a much shorter time, possibly even interactively. Teradata claims that this can dramatically improve effectiveness.

Another common application of Teradata machines is stock control. The high capacity of the DBC/1012 allows users to examine information collected from electronic point-of-sale systems on the same day, and to take corrective action if a shortage or falling demand is noticed.

6.4.7 The Future

One sign of Teradata's ambitions is their acquisition of Sharebase, which manufactured powerful uniprocessor database machines suitable for managing up to 50 Gbyte of data. There are approximately 800 Sharebase machines installed, as opposed to 100 of Teradata's DBC/1012s. This not only gives Teradata a product to offer low-end customers, it may also be a sign of the manner in which Teradata will develop their flagship product — the Sharebase machine's performance depends on its ability to cache large amounts of data in RAM, a technology which could obviously be used in a multiprocessor machine. At present, Teradata has no plans to move to custom processors, believing that progress by the established manufacturers such as Intel will continue to give them a doubling in speed every two years.

Company Summary 17: Features of Cogent XTM

Source	Cogent Research, Incorporated.
Type	Distributed memory MIMD, desktop.
Availability	Prototypes from late 1988. Production from mid-1989.

Price

Basic workstation	$19,800
Two CPU Resource Server	$35,000
Compute Boards (two CPUs)	$12,000
Workstation + 32 CPU Resource Server	$200,000
Disc Server	$60,000

Processing nodes	Two upwards, a 1900 processor machine has been designed.
Processor technology	Inmos T800-20 giving 5 MIPS (32 bit integer operations) or 1.5 MFLOPS (64 bit floating point).
Memory	4 Mbyte RAM.
Communications	128 way dynamic crossbar switch with 100 Mbyte/s bandwidth for point to point communication. 32 bit, 12 Mbyte/s bus for broadcast/multicast and configuring the switch.
I/O connections	Each workstation has: one to two NuBus expansion slots; one PC/AT compatible serial port and two RS422 serial ports.
	Support for I/O standards: Digital audio tape, Optical disc, 9 Track tape, SCSI.
	Workstations and Resource Servers networked via 10 Mbyte/s: wired links (up to 2 m) and fibre-optic links (up to 2 km).
Performance	Theoretically, a 32 processor machine offers 320 MIPS peak with 160 MIPS sustained, and 96 MFLOPS peak with 48 MFLOPS sustained.
Host system	None
Operating system	QIX — UNIX-like parallel operating system based on Kernel Linda.

Programming languages C, C++, Fortran 77, PostScript. Linda extensions.

Physical configuration	Workstation 14″ × 14″ × 6″
	Resource Server 14″ × 18″ × 6″
Sources	Cogent Research, Incorporated.
	Scientific Computers, Limited.
	BYTE, November 1988, pp278 – 279

Company Summary 18: Features of the SGI 4D Series

Source	Silicon Graphics
Type	Coarse grain shared memory bus-based multiprocessor
Availability	Widely available from 1985, over 10,000 machines installed in over 1000 sites
Price	Personal Iris 4D/20 Base system - £11 k (£8.5 k discless) Power Series 4D/380 with VGX graphics - £200 k
Processing nodes	Up to eight processors.
Processors	MIPS R3000 RISC processors.
Memory	8 Mbyte standard, larger systems can accommodate up to 160 Mbyte.
Communications	CPU bus connecting processors and caches runs at 100 Mbyte/s. VME bus connecting CPU bus and I/O bus Main Memory. I/O bus (also 100 Mbyte/s) connecting VME bus with I/O control gate array (Ethernet etc.) and Graphics subsystem.
I/O connections	Supported connections include: Ethernet, RS 232(2), Centronics, VME slot, audio, Ultranet and SCSI.
Performance	The Power Series 4D/380 has a claimed peak performance of 234 MIPS, 33 MFLOPS (64 bit). Graphics performance is up to one million 3D lighted, Gouraud-shaded, Z-buffered polygons per second.
Host system	None
Operating system	IRIX - A UNIX hybrid, based on AT&T System V and Berkeley BSD.
Programming languages	Fortran, C and Ada.
Physical configuration	SGI hardware comes as a single unit, containing all boards, discs, graphics hardware etc. The 4D/380 VGX is contained within a cabinet $0.65 \times 0.65 \times 0.68$ m, weighing 84 kg.
Power dissipation	Power Series 4D380 requires 1425W supply.

Sources   Publicly available material plus discussions with UK Marketing staff.

Company Summary 19: Features of the Stardent 3000

Source	Stardent Computer Inc.
Type	Coarse grain shared-memory bus-based multiprocessor.
Availability	Available from end of 1989.
Price	£75 k for an entry-level system, and up to £156 k for the largest (four processor) system with the fastest graphics hardware.
Processing nodes	Up to four.
Processors	MIPS R3000 RISC processors with R3010 floating point co-processors, both running at 32 MHz. Optional custom floating-point accelerators.
Memory	Standard 32 Mbyte, upgradable to 512 Mbyte.
Communications	There are three main buses in the CPU, the processor bus (200 Mbyte/s) linking the MIPS processors, their caches, and the S and R buses. The S and R buses (both 128 Mbyte/s) connect the vector processor, the MIPS processors and the rest of the machine (graphics subsystem, I/O devices etc.)
I/O connections	Four RS232C ports, a parallel interface, Ethernet, and audio output.
Performance	Four processor system rated at 128 MIPS, 192 MFLOPS peak.
Host system	The Stardent 3000 is a stand-alone machine.
Operating system	An enhanced implementation of UNIX V.3.
Programming languages	Fortran, C and Ada (not yet validated).
Physical configuration	Single cabinet 22″ × 23″ × 50″. Air cooled.
Sources	Stardent literature and marketing staff.

Company Summary 20: Features of the Teradata DBC/1012

Type	Massively parallel database engines.
Availability	100 machines installed to date at commercial, government, and military sites.
Price	$1 M and up.
Processing nodes	A mix of Communications and Interface Processors, Access Module Processors, and Disc Storage Units.
Processor technology	Intel 80286 (now 80386).
Memory	The largest configuration to date holds 400 Gbyte of data.
Communications	Proprietary Ynet (2 per machine) running at 6 MHz (12 MHz total).
I/O connections	Ethernet and other LAN, direct mainframe links.
Performance	300 transactions/s and up for debit/credit applications.
Host system	Mainframes (DEC, IBM), workstations (Sun, IBM-PC).
Operating system	None (O/S resident in DBC/1012 is invisible to user.)
Programming languages	SQL, possibly embedded in a program written in another language running on a host computer.
Physical configuration	A two cabinet group (10 cabinets in total) requires 56.5 sq. ft.
Power requirements	16.5 kW for the configuration on page 226.
Sources	Teradata publicity information, discussions with Teradata staff.

Chapter 7

Vector Supercomputers: It's Never too Late to Parallelise

While most new manufacturers have built parallel computers by combining a large number of microprocessors in a single machine, the vector supercomputer manufacturers have been increasing the performance of their products by combining small numbers of vector processors. This approach, like that of the multiprocessor manufacturers described in Chapter 3, allows users to re-use much of their code, and much of their knowledge. While the age of the vector machine may now be past, multiprocessor vector computers will play an important role in the struggle for the high-end supercomputer market in the 1990s.

7.1   Cray Research Inc.

Relevant Activities Design, market, and manufacture multiprocessor pipelined
vector supercomputers.

Location Headquarters: 608 Second Ave. South, Minneapolis, Minnesota 55402,
USA.

Relevant Officers John A. Rollwagon, Chairman and CEO; Marcelo A. Gummu-
cio, President and Chief Operating Officer.

Employees Over 4700 worldwide.

Financial details Public company. For end of year 1989: revenue $784 M; net
earnings $89 M; earnings per share $3.02.

7.1.1   The Company

Cray Research Inc. (CRI) was founded in April 1972 by Seymour Cray, the man
who most deserves the title "the father of the supercomputer". It has always been
Cray's aim, and hence that of CRI, to build the fastest computers in the world.

From 1957 to 1972 Cray worked for Control Data Corporation (CDC), where he
was the chief architect of the CDC 6600 and CDC 7600 computer systems. In 1972,
he worked on the CDC 8600 project, which was intended to be the replacement for
the CDC 7600, but when this project was cancelled due to financial cutbacks at
CDC, Cray left to form his own company.

The first Cray-1 was produced in 1976 and delivered to Los Alamos. Architecturally, this machine was similar to the CDC 7600, but contained some major new
features. It was the first commercial computer to offer pipelined vector processing
hardware, vector chaining, and a large interleaved memory. It had 1 Mword of
64 bit ECL memory arranged in 16 banks, and, with its 12.5 ns clock cycle, could
reach peak speeds of 130 MFLOPS. The Cray-1, however, was severely I/O limited,
since the CPU handled I/O interrupts as well as executing applications code. In
1979, this prompted the production of the Cray-1S, an enhanced Cray-1 that could
be configured with two to four I/O processors. Main memory was increased to a
maximum of 4 Mword, which significantly increasing throughput since less time
was spent swapping data to and from memory.

Since the Cray-1S, CRI have followed two parallel development paths, both of
which have used denser, faster chip technology and parallel processing techniques:

- Cray X-MP $\rightarrow$ Cray Y-MP $\rightarrow$ C90.

- Cray-2 $\rightarrow$ Cray-3.

These two directions are discussed in more detail below.

7.1.2   Cray X-MP → Cray Y-MP → C90

After the release of the Cray-1 in 1972, CRI intended to design and market the Cray-2. This would be a multiprocessor version of the Cray-1 with architectural enhancements, and would be implemented using gallium arsenide (GaAs). After much work it was found that GaAs technology had not reached the point where such a machine would feasible and the project retreated to silicon technologies. This meant that chips had to be redesigned and the development was servely delayed. Consequently, CRI needed a new product which could be brought to market quickly and cheaply: the Cray X-MP.

Much of the development of the Cray X-MP (Multiple Processor), had been done before Steve Chen joined CRI, and took over the management of the project but he is given much of the credit for its success. Chen had been a computer designer with the Burroughs Corporation before joining CRI in 1979. Subsequently, he made a considerable contribution to the design of the Cray Y-MP, and later to a project called MP, which had the goal of designing a machine with approximately 64 processors. However, the MP project was closed down in 1987 because it was thought to be too ambitious and risky, so Chen left to found his own company, Supercomputer Systems Inc. (cf. Section 7.3).

Cray X-MP

The Cray X-MP project was started in 1978, the X-MP was a shared memory multiprocessor. Each CPU had the Cray-1 architecture, with an instruction set compatible with the Cray-1, but extended to support multiprocessing. The X-MP was introduced in 1982 and was originally designed as a two processor machine with an expected performance 1.5 to 2 times that of the Cray-1. It was followed by an enhanced four CPU version and also an entry-level single processor version in 1985.

X-MP processors shared a large central memory of up to 8 Mword built from fast ECL technology. The memory was divided into 64 interleaved banks, and was accessed via four ports: two for memory loads, one for memory store, and the fourth for I/O. This design allowed for eight simultaneous memory accesses per clock cycle.

Each machine had one, two, or four CPUs constructed from 16 gate ECL gate arrays (in contrast with the gate arrays used in the Cray-1 which had only two gates), which allowed a clock cycle of 9.5 ns. The CPU organisation was much the same as the Cray-1. New gather/scatter hardware was introduced to support the sparse matrix computations and conditional loops common in many Fortran programs. The size of the instruction buffers was doubled to 32 words to allow for larger vector subroutines. Each CPU was connected to shared memory via three ports: two for vector load, one for vector store. Another port, shared between all the processors and the central memory, was for I/O transfer, which allowed each processor to service interrupts. Single CPU performance reached a maximum of approximately 200 MFLOPS.

Processors in a P processor machine shared P+1 register clusters for interprocessor communication. Each cluster consisted of eight 24 bit shared address registers, eight 64 bit shared scalar registers, and a 32 bit semaphore register. Semaphores operated using a busy-wait algorithm, in which a processor had to wait for a particular semaphore bit to clear before it could re-set it. The operating system could allocate a cluster to zero, one or more processors. Processors also shared a system clock.

The interprocessor communications of the X-MP were designed to allow processors to cooperate in a tightly coupled way. Small, vectorisable loops within a larger outer loop could be passed to a separate processor for vector execution. CRI called this *multitasking*.

An integral part of the X-MP system was its Solid State Storage Device (SSD), a large fast memory used either as a solid state disc for storing intermediate files manipulated by user programs, or as swap space for the operating system. The SSD, which initially contained 32 Mword, was connected to the I/O subsystem via a 1 Gbyte/s communications channel.

The I/O subsystem (IOS) of the X-MP consisted of: four 100 Mbyte/s channel pairs for connection to the I/O port of each of the CPUs, two 1 Gbyte/s channels for connection to one or two SSDs, and four 6 Mbyte/s channels for connection to slower I/O devices such as discs and tapes. It also had 8 Mbyte of buffer memory.

The X-MP used the same packaging technology as the Cray-1, with freon circulating though coldbars as a coolant. Parts for the X-MP were deliberately made to resemble those of the Cray-1 so that retraining of construction teams and retooling of manufacturing plants would be minimal. This tactic was so successful that the first Cray X-MP produced even bore a Cray-1 serial number and helped to make the X-MP the cheapest project, next to the Cray-1, that CRI have undertaken. It was also the most successful supercomputer ever, with over 160 machines still in operation by the end of 1989. Its popularity was largely due to its software compatibility with the Cray-1.

Cray Y-MP

As soon as the first X-MP was shipped, work began on its successor, the Y-MP. This was to be a cheap development of the Cray X-MP, preserving software compatibilty.

The Cray Y-MP was announced in 1988. Initially, only the eight processor version was available, machines with two and four processors arrived a year later in 1989. The CPU of the Y-MP had a similar architecturally to that of the X-MP, but with minor changes. The address registers have been extended from 24 bits in the X-MP to 32 bits in the Y-MP, and a system clock has been added. The Y-MP uses 2500 gate ECL technology, which allows an entire CPU to reside on one board. The clock cycle time is 6 ns, giving a peak performance of 333 MFLOPS for a two processor system, and 2.67 GFLOPS for a system with eight CPUs.

The central memory has 16 to 128 Mword of directly addressable ECL memory arranged in 64, 128, or 256 banks. The Y-MP comes with at least one IOS, with a second IOS optional. Each IOS has four I/O processors sharing 4 Mword of buffer memory. An IOS has eight 6 Mbyte/s channels, eight 100 Mbyte/s channels, and two 1000 Mbyte/s channels. Optional SSDs are available with 32 to 512 Mword of solid state memory.

The Cray Y-MP uses liquid cooling like the Cray-2. The standard 'C' shape has been abandoned for a 'Y' shape. The processors form the centre of the 'Y', an IOS one arm, and a SSD another arm; a second IOS can be positioned up to 3 m away from the main configuration. The whole machine occupies 1.5 m² of floor space. The Y-MP is set to be as popular as the X-MP, with over 30 machines having been installed by the end of December 1989.

The C90

The C90 is the future successor to the Cray Y-MP. This will have 16 processors and a larger shared memory. The processors will have two vector pipes to maintain the scalar-to-vector speed ratio of the Y-MP, and will be built using 10,000 gate ECL technology. It will be software compatible with the Y-MP and is likely to be available by 1992 – 93.

7.1.3   Cray-2 → Cray-3

While the machines above were developed under the leadership of Steve Chen, the Cray-2 and Cray-3 were and are designed and developed by Seymour Cray himself. Cray is well known for his aggressive approach to machine design, especially in packaging, and this is reflected in these machines.

Cray-2

The Cray-2 was introduced in 1985, three years after the first X-MP was installed. Its architecture consists of four background processors, which are connected to a large common memory and controlled by a single foreground processor.

The architecture of a background processor is similar to that of the Cray-1, except that some intermediate registers have been replaced by 16 kword of local memory. A schematic diagram of a background processor for the Cray-2 is shown in Figure 7.1.

The local memory is intended to be used to hold intermediate scalar and vector results and has a similar access time to the main memory of the X-MP. The number of functional units in these processors have been reduced from 13 to nine, although

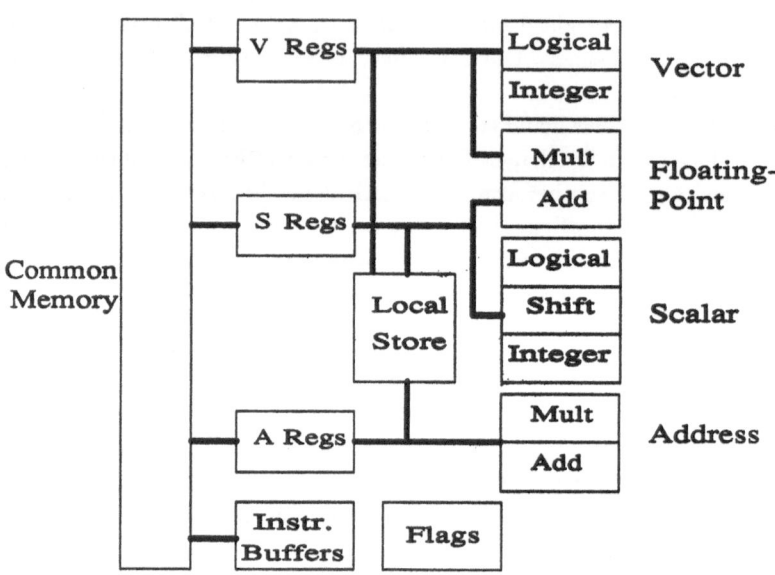

Figure 7.1: The Background Processor on the Cray-2

some of these units now perform several functions — the floating-point reciprocal unit has gone, but the floating-point multiply unit now has hardware square root capability.

The processor's address registers have been extended to 32 bit. A bank of eight single bit semaphores and a status register are provided for interprocessor synchronisation; a task can have one semaphore bit assigned to it when the machine is running in multitasking mode. There are eight instruction buffers holding 64 16 bit instruction packages. The Cray-1's popular vector chaining facility was not retained.

The design of the Cray-2 is centred around its large central memory, which consists of 256 Mword of directly addressable MOS memory. Customers wanted to be able to execute programs with very large datasets without having to swap to secondary storage. The memory, which is arranged in four quadrants of 32 banks, is relatively slow and is best compared to a SSD. Processors have phased access to the memory, which means that a processor can access a particular quadrant only every fourth clock cycle, and must wait for its allocated phase slot for that quadrant.

This approach trades less memory conflict problems for potentially longer memory access times.

Each background processor is connected to the main memory via a single port, as in the Cray-1. Although the CPU has a clock cycle of 4.1 ns, instructions are issued from the instruction buffer every other clock cycle, giving an effective cycle time of 8.2 ns.

The foreground processor supervises the background processors, shared memory, and peripherals via four 4 Gbyte/s communications rings. Each ring has a background processor, up to seven disc drives, and a port to shared memory. The data rings transfer 16 bit packets every clock cycle.

The entire Cray-2 machine is contained in a 4' high by $4\frac{1}{2}'$ diameter 'C' shaped cabinet. The machine consists of 320 modules each measuring $1'' \times 4'' \times 8''$. The entire machine, including power supplies, is cooled by immersion in 200 gallons of an inert liquid fluorocarbon.

The strength of the Cray-2 is its extremely large memory. Its weaknesses are that the main memory is slow, multiprocessing is not as simple as with the X-MP, and it is not software compatible with the Cray-1. The Cray-2 has therefore gained only limited popularity in comparison with the X-MP series. Cray-2s are purchased primarily by organisations willing to trade software compatibility for the ability to run programs with very large data arrays in main memory. About 30 Cray-2 machines have been installed.

Cray-3 and Cray-4

In 1985, as soon as the Cray-2 had reached production, Seymour Cray and team started work on the Cray-3, which was to be a GaAs implementation of the Cray-2. It was thought that GaAs technology would be viable by 1988/89, which was the original production target date for the new machine. However, the Cray-3 is still not available and is not expected until 1991 at the earliest.

Some of this delay is due to problems with using advanced technology, especially in the area of packaging, and some is due to the physical moves the project has made. In the spring of 1988, the Cray-3 project moved from Chippewa Falls to Colorado Springs. This was done to focus the project on the Cray-3, since Chippewa Falls was mainly geared to producing the Y-MP. In November 1989, the CRI management decided that it could no longer support both the C90 and Cray-3 projects. The most promising project was the C90, so to avoid closing down Seymour Cray's own project, the development of the Cray-3 was spun off into a new company called Cray Computer Corporation (CCC). CRI transferred a facility and other equipment to CCC, along with an $85 million promissory note to fund future development of the Cray-3. CRI hold 10% of the stock of CCC, the other 90% of stock being distributed among CRI stockholders. This has prompted another change in location for the Cray-3 project and caused more delays.

CRI dealt with Rockwell for the GaAs chips for the original design of the Cray-2. By the time the Cray-3 was being designed a small spin-off company from Rockwell called Gigabit had started up; they now supply the Cray-3 project with chips.

In November 1988, at a supercomputing conference in Florida, Seymour Cray described the architecture, technology and packaging of the Cray-3, and some design targets for the Cray-4. The Cray-3 will be 12 times faster than the Cray-2. A factor of three speedup will come from the use of GaAs technology, which will give the Cray-3 a 2 ns clock cycle. The remainder will come from using four times as many processors as in the Cray-2. Seymour Cray noted that one problem with the Cray-2 was its primitive interprocessor communication mechanism. As a result, the Cray-3 will use the communication architecture of the Y-MP series.

The expected performance of the Cray-3 will be 8000 MIPS or 16 GFLOPS. It will have 512 Mword of main memory. The entire machine will fit inside a cuboid cabinet measuring 1' on each side. The reason for the small size is that reducing the machine's linear dimensions by a factor of three gives a corresponding improvement in speed, but a reduction in volume of 27. The maximum allowable wire length throughout the machine is one foot.

Producing a machine of such tiny proportions requires radical packaging technology, an area in which Seymour Cray excels. Each processor will be constructed from four modules. The whole machine, including the central memory, will be built from 200 modules, each of which will measure $4'' \times 4'' \times \frac{1}{4}''$, contain 1024 VLSI circuits, and be built from circuit wafers stacked and bonded together. The machine will be liquid cooled using technology developed for the Cray-2.

The largest problem faced on the Cray-3 project is how to automate machine production. There are 12000 connections to be made in every 4 in^2 using a complex interconnection scheme. To do this, laser welding and cutting equipment is required, as is robot assembly technology.

Seymour Cray is already thinking about the Cray-4. This is likely to have a 1 ns clock and will test the limits of GaAs technology. After the Cray-4, he expects that a new material will be needed, possibly indium phosphate layers on a silicon substrate.

7.1.4 The Software

The Cray-1 was shipped with the least amount of software that would make it usable. It had a simple batch operating system called Cray Operating System (COS) and a vectorising Fortran compiler. In those early days of supercomputing the national laboratories in the US produced most of their own operating systems, compilers, and programs, and were happy to receive a machine with little software.

COS, however, soon became outdated with the advent of the Cray X-MP, since it could not handle multiprocessing and was difficult to maintain. A new operating system was implemented called the Cray Time Sharing System (CTSS). This was Cray's version of an OS written by Lawrence Livermore Laboratories. The Cray-2, however, was not software compatible with the X-MP and would not support either COS or CTSS without major rewrites. CRI decided to search for a machine-independent OS that they could support on all their machines.

In the early 1980s, when the Cray-2 was being developed, UNIX was fast becoming an industry standard OS for workstations. Cray decided to create a version of UNIX called UNICOS, an implementation of AT&T UNIX. This was shipped with the Cray-2, and appears on all subsequent machines.

The advantages of UNICOS to the user are many. Users already have workstations with UNIX operating systems and large libraries of user UNIX commands. These libraries can be easily ported to UNICOS, giving an identical working environment on all their machines. It takes very little effort to interface machines executing UNIX communication protocols to a Cray running UNICOS, which was not true with COS and CTSS. UNICOS offers a uniform file structure, file mounting facilities, and file security. But probably the most important feature of a UNIX-based OS is that interactive use of the computer becomes possible. A workstation executing a windowing package can access a Cray and interactively use editors, compilers, and graphics display tools. This increases programmer productivity over the older operating systems. UNICOS is now the standard operating system for all new Cray machines, and has been ported to all Cray machine systems. It is expected that users using older operating systems will eventually move to UNICOS. COS will still be offered as an OS running under UNICOS for those customers that have programs that rely on COS calls.

UNICOS has several standard tools for the development and management of user programs, such as editors, debuggers, job recovery processes, and accounting utilities. Standard program debugging and information tools include utilities that print the dynamic call graph of a program, dump statistics about its use of subroutines, offer single-step execution simulation, and give dynamic memory use information.

Another area in which CRI excel, apart from hardware design, is in the implementation of vectorising Fortran compilers. They realised very early on with the Cray-1 that customers would need compilers that could automatically vectorise standard Fortran codes to take advantage of the vector hardware intrinsic to the design of Cray machines. Before the advent of vectorising compilers, programmers had to write critical subroutines in assembler language to take advantage of vector pipelines.

A crude vectorising compiler was supplied with the Cray-1. This has steadily been improved to vectorise more types of Fortran code. With the production of the Cray X-MP and Cray-2 multiprocessor machines CRI recognised two types of parallelism: *macrotasking*, which is the parallel execution of large code sections, and *microtasking*, which is the parallel execution of vectorisable loops that operate over independent data sets. Macrotasking was never popular at the compiler level and is handled by the operating system. Microtasking, however, can give significant improvement in program speed.

To take advantage of microtasking, users add special comments to their program which indicate to the compiler independent DO loops that can be executed in parallel. The compiler then replaces the comments with calls to the Fortran microtasking library. In 1988, CRI introduced an *autotasking* compiler called CTF77 that performs this task automatically. This compiler has three phases. First , it analyses a program and computes dependencies between vectorisable DO loops. Second, it generates code with added compiler directives indicating independent loops. Third, it performs the compilation, replacing directives with library calls and performing scalar optimisations. The compiler does not always identify potential microtaskable program blocks, so user compiler directives can still be incorporated into programs to tell the compiler to ignore certain blocks or consider others that it would usually overlook. Autotasking helps to make Fortran programs portable between differing computer architectures and processors numbers while maintaining efficient execution. At runtime, independent loops that have been identified for microtasking are executed on different processors. Process scheduling and memory management are performed automatically.

Autotasking is really an extension of the idea of vectorising compilation. The scheme is particularly easy to implement on shared memory architectures, such as those used by CRI, where communication of routine calls and data sets can be done by the communication of a few pointers into shared memory. Since the loops are guaranteed not to operate of the same data, memory consistency conflicts need not be considered.

In addition to Fortran 77, CRI also offer a vector parallel C which applies the Fortran vectorising technology to C. Compilers are also available for Pascal, Lisp and Ada, and for CAL, an assembly language for writing programs requiring hand optimisation.

CRI do not produce any applications software, they do, however, give considerable assistance to users wishing to port codes to the Cray. One reason for this is that many of their customers, in such areas as weapons research, and the petroleum and automotive industries, have developed their own software which is highly confidential. CRI accordingly offer training courses in vector programming and the use of their compilers, and offer advice on how to make the best of hardware.

7.1.5   The Market Niche

Cray computers are used in compute-intensive scientific fields such as high energy physics, weapons research, crash simulation in the automotive industry, aerospace

Table 7.1: Sales of Cray Computers by Model

Machine Type	numbers installed
Cray X-MP	160
Cray Y-MP8	26
Cray-2	24
Cray-1	17
Cray Y-MP4/2	12

engineering, biomedical research, and petroleum exploration. By geography, 67% of CRI's sales are in the US, and 33% in the rest of the world. 58% of machines are sold to government laboratories, 25% to commercial companies, and 17% to universities. Information about the segmentation of the installed customer base by machine type is given in Table 7.1. (This information is taken from the 1990 company report; its statistics are correct as of that financial year.)

The revenue of CRI was $784 M, its operating income $117 M, and its net earnings $89 M. CRI target to spend 15% of their revenue on R&D compared, with the computer industry average median of 8.2%.

The cheapest computer system CRI currently sell is the Cray Y-MP2/116, which has two CPUs and 16 Mword of main memory and costs $5 M. The maximum specification machine is the Cray Y-MP8/8128, which has eight CPUs and 128 Mword of main memory, and costs $22.9 M. The cost of a Solid State Storage Device ranges from $600 k for 32 Mword to $5 M for 512 Mword.

7.1.6 The Competition

From their own statistics, CRI have a 79% slice of the current world supercomputer market. They have achieved this, not only by continually supplying the fastest computers in the world, but also by working closely with customers when incorporating new features into products. CRI have had little competition in the scientific supercomputer market in the past; however, opposition is growing in several areas in the US and abroad.

Three Japanese companies — Fujitsu, NEC (cf. Section 7.2), and Hitachi — have been making supercomputers for several years, and are fast approaching CRI's level of hardware technology. Fujitsu is aggressively attacking European markets and currently supplies 25% of supercomputers sold to Europe, although they account for only 8% worldwide. In compiler technology, CRI has already been overtaken by its Japanese rivals; Fujitsu's vectorising Fortran compiler vectorises more types of DO loops than CRI's equivalent compiler.

Nearer to home, IBM is trying to move into supercomputing. If IBM succeed in producing a Cray-class supercomputer, either via one of their own projects or via an IBM/SSI (cf. 7.3) collaboration, then CRI will have a formidable rival with which to contend.

CRI may also face competition from Seymour Cray himself and his new company, CCC. This problem, however, is unlikely to be significant, since CRI will be able to take advantage of any research advances made by CCC, and may eventually market the machine themselves.

CRI is also facing mounting opposition from the vendors of massive parallelism, such as Thinking Machines (cf. 2.3) and Intel (cf. 4.1). Intel supply the iPSC/860, a 128 processor computer whose nodes contain vector microprocessors, the aggregate performance of which is 7.6 GFLOPS. The power of this machine rivals that of the eight processor Cray Y-MP, but the iPSC/860 costs one tenth as much. The 65,536 processor Connection Machine from Thinking Machines has a peak speed of 28 GFLOPS, and has been able to sustain ∼20% of this speed in real applications (cf. Section 2.3.6). Currently, automatic parallelising compilers do not exist for the massively parallel machines, which makes the porting of dusty-deck Fortran programs prohibitively expensive. When such compilers do become available, as these companies hope they will in the next five years, it is hard to see why customers would continue to choose Cray.

7.1.7   The Future

What are CRI doing to answer the opposition? First, they are developing their Y-MP architecture to contain 16 processors in the C90 project. It is difficult to see how the architecture could be extended beyond this limit. As more access ports are added to a shared memory system, address conflict resolution hardware becomes more complex, and access time ultimately suffers. Very few coarse grained shared memory systems support more than 20-30 processors, a limit which the C90 is rapidly approaching. From the C90, two paths are currently visible. The first is to implement its architecture in a faster semiconductor material, such as GaAs (which Seymour Cray is currently attempting). Whether CRI do that or not rests largely on whether the Cray-3 ever reaches production. The second path is for CRI to produce their own massively parallel machine, something which they are now researching.

CRI's second answer to its opposition is to broaden its customer base downwards into the minisupercomputer market. In March 1990 CRI bought Supertek Computers, who supply Cray-compatible minisupercomputers. For CRI this is a significant development; since its inception, the company has only been interested in developing the world's fastest supercomputers. The Supertek S-1 machine costs approximately $300 k and is compatible with the Cray X-MP. Prior to acquisition,

Supertek were working on a Y-MP-compatible machine, the S-2; CRI will now market and develop this. Customers on sub-million dollar budgets will soon be able to buy a "baby" Cray with an option to upgrade to a more powerful one later.

It is probably still true that Cray is synonymous with the ultimate in supercomputing. However, the warning signs are appearing that this reign might be coming to an end. In 1989, a 65,536 processor Connection Machine achieved a sustained performance which beat the peak power of an eight pipe Cray Y-MP by a factor of two (cf. Section 2.3.6). The response from CRI is awaited.

7.2   NEC

Relevant Activities Manufacture multi-processor vector supercomputers.

Location 7-1, Shiba 5-chome, Minato-ku, Tokyo 108-01, Japan. Telephone: (3) 454-1111. UK Head Office: NEC House, 1 Victoria Road, London W3 6UL. Telephone: 081 993 8111.

Relevant Officers Tadahiro Sekimoto, President; Kenzo Nakamura, Chairman of the Board.

Employees Several hundred in management and development of supercomputer systems.

Financial details NEC's Computers and Industrial Electronic Systems division did $9.535 billion of business in 1989/90; what proportion of this was made up by supercomputer sales is unknown.

7.2.1   The Company

Founded in 1899, NEC is one of the largest suppliers of electronic equipment in the world. NEC is represented in Japan by 56 consolidated subsidiaries, 62 plants, and more than 300 sales offices; the company has an additional 68 subsidiaries and affiliates in 28 countries, and operates 27 production plants. Its net sales in 1990 were $21.8 G, an increase of 12% over the previous year. Computers and industrial electronic systems were the single largest component in this.

Of the three Japanese firms which currently build supercomputers [1] only NEC currently markets a family of multi-processor machines. Its SX-3 supercomputers are descended from its SX-2 series of single-processor vector supercomputers, which were developed and marketed during the 1980s. The SX-3 machines combine fine-grained vectorisation with coarse-grained parallelism through multi-tasking in a manner similar to that used by Cray Reseach Inc. in the Cray Y-MP (cf. Section 7.1). Marketing in the United States is through HNSX Supercomputers Inc., a joint venture of NEC and Honeywell.

7.2.2   The Hardware

The SX-3 series of computers use high-speed Current Mode Logic (CML), a silicon VLSI technology, in order to achieve high performance, reliability, and dense packaging. NEC's bipolar process technology has reduced the gate delays in these chips to 70 ps, allowing SX-3 systems to have a clock cycle of 2.9 ns (345 MHz). NEC's choice to continue development of its silicon technology, rather than use GaAs or

---

[1] The other two are Fujitsu (the VP-200 and VP-400) and Hitachi (the S-810 and S-820).

some other exotic material, may be read either as an indication that the company believes that silicon will remain competitive long enough for them to recoup their investment in the SX-3 series, or that they are confident that most of the architectural ideas of the SX-3 series will be usable when new process technologies have developed further.

The computers in the SX-3 family are divided by the numbers of processors they contain (one, two or four) and by the number of sets of arithmetic pipelines in each processor (again one, two or four). For example, the entry-level SX-3/11 contains a single processor with one sets of pipes, while the mid-range SX-3/24 has two processors with four pipes each (see Figure 7.2) and the top-of-the-line SX-3/44, which has a theoretical peak performance of 20 GFLOPS (680 MIPS), contains four processors with four pipes each. Prices for these machines range from a low of $6 M to approximately $24 M.

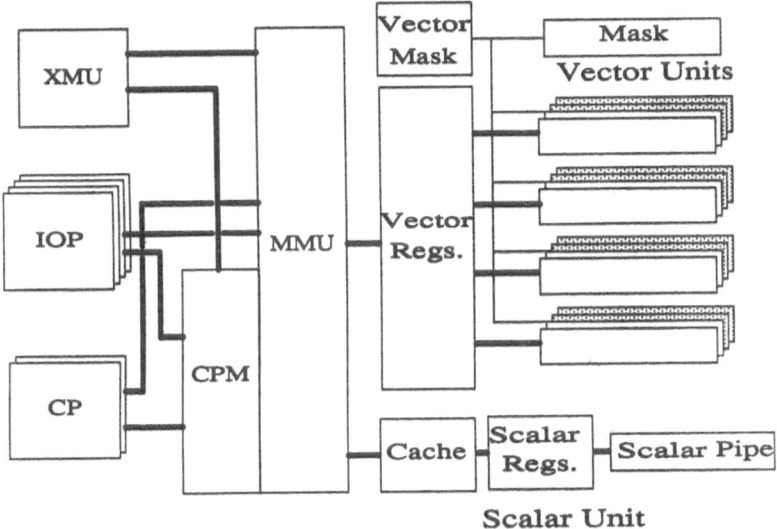

Figure 7.2: NEC's SX-3 Series Vector Supercomputer

Each vector pipeline set contains two add/logical pipelines and two multiply/shift pipelines, all of which can operate simultaneously. In addition to its sets of pipelines, each processor also contains one or more scalar-processing pipelines rated at 170 MIPS, which can also operate concurrently. The reliability of the system is enhanced by the inclusion of built-in diagnostic circuitry consisting of real-time integrity checkers within each functional unit.

All processors access a shared main memory of between 64 Mbyte and 2 Gbyte, with 1024-way interleaving. Segments of this memory can be protected by individual processors as necessary.

I/O is done through special input/output processors which can be configured with channels running at speeds from 3 to 100 Mbyte/s; each SX-3 machine may operate up to four of these concurrently. Processors communicate with each other through main memory, using a shared communications register containing 256 words of 64 bits each for control. The bandwidth between processors and extended memory is 2.75 Gbyte/s.

7.2.3   The Software

The SX-3 family's operating system is SUPER-UX, an outgrowth of the SXOS operating system developed for the earlier SX-2 computers which is compatible with System V UNIX. Standard protocols such as NFS and TCP/IP are supported.

Fortran 77, C, and Pascal are all supported with automatic vectorisation and parallelisation tools. According to a report prepared by Hideo Yoshihara for the US Office of Naval Research (Far East), and distributed to USENET by David Kahaner (of the same organisation), "The performance of the autovectorizer of Japanese computers was outstanding, vectorizing 99 percent of the benchmark code without directives." NEC complement such automatic tools with interactive vectorisers which can display the proportion of CPU time the program is expected to spend in each program loop while the program is being edited. While NEC's tools for distributing work between the CPUs in the SX-3 series will obviously not initially be as well developed as their vectorising tools, it is reasonable to expect that they will not be allowed to lag behind for long.

NEC also supply a tool called CONVERTER/SX to help users convert Fortran programs written for other supercomputers to SX-3 Fortran. Cray data formats and compiler conventions are used. Visualisation is catered for by SXview, a graphics package that allows users to display data as two- or three-dimensional graphs, and to record animated displays on videotape. Applications packages currently being ported include the fluid dynamics packages FLUENT and PHOENICS and Dyna 2D/3D, a structural analysis program.

7.2.4   The Market

The SX-3 is targetted at the same market as other high-performance vector supercomputers: those applications (such as structural engineering, fluid dynamics, and nuclear physics) which will always need more power than they have, and which have the financial backing to buy machines based on performance, rather than price/performance, criteria. What makes the SX-3 special is that the most powerful machine in the series, the SX-3/44, is among the most powerful computers announced to date by any company. Yoshihara's report, quoted above, predicts that the SX-3/44 will achieve a sustained performance of 7 GFLOPS on real codes like the alternating direction implicit Navier-Stokes program used as a benchmark. By covering the whole of the top-end numerical computing market with a range of compatible machines, NEC will not only be able to amortise their development costs quickly, they will also put the field's acknowledged leader, Cray Research Inc., under even more pressure.

To date, NEC have sold more than 35 of their SX-2 machines to a wide variety of Japanese customers. They have already sold one SX-3 in Japan, and will soon be delivering machines or upgrading SX-2s to SX-3s at the National Aerospace Laboratory in the Netherlands, the University of Cologne in Germany, and the University of Singapore. They see their main competition coming from the Cray Y-MP and from Fujitsu's VP2000 computers; competition from the latter will become more important when Fujitsu bring out their own multi-processor machine in 1991.

7.3   Supercomputer Systems Inc.

Relevant Activities Design and manufacture a multiprocessor vector supercomputer.

Location Headquarters: Supercomputer Systems Inc., 1414 W. Hamilton Avenue, Eau Claire, Wisconsin 54701, USA. Telephone: (715) 839 8484.

Relevant Officers Steve S. Chen, President, CEO, Head of Product Development Group, and Chief Architect and Designer; Douglas Paffel, VP Technology and Engineering; James Kelly, VP Marketing and Sales; Dean W. Nordahl, VP Finance and Administration.

Employees Approximately 45.

Financial details Private company, total capitalisation undisclosed. Some investment from IBM.

7.3.1   The Company

SSI was founded in October 1987 by Dr. Steve Chen, formerly a vice president at Cray Research Inc. (CRI) (cf. Section 7.1). The company has one central idea: to produce the next generation of parallel supercomputers with overall system performance 100 times faster than any current machine. Apart from that statement, which occurs repeatedly in connection with SSI, the company talks only in the sketchiest terms about the proposed specification of their machine, except to say that they wish to develop their own technology, rather than utilise that of CRI.

SSI also make the political statement: "These systems will set the new standard in high performance computing and help sustain the US lead in science, engineering and applied technologies." This is probably calculated to attract attention from DARPA, and large computing laboratories, such as the Lawrence Livermore Laboratory and Los Alamos National Laboratory. A common tactic by US supercomputer manufacturers is to involve a national laboratory in the design of their computer in the hope that the laboratory will buy one when it reaches production[2]. It is likely that SSI is using the same approach; if they can convince a laboratory to install a prototype, a lot of interest and confidence would be generated which would ultimately sell machines.

In April 1988, IBM and SSI signed a formal partnership agreement for the development of advanced computer systems. SSI will receive financial help from IBM, and both will exchange technical information. However, this may not be as significant as it first appears. Since 1961, IBM has put scientific supercomputing on

---

[2]The first Cray-1 was lent to Los Alamos rent free for six months. The first ETA[10]was 'sold' to Florida State University although it had no operating system.

a back burner due to the commercial failure of STRETCH, marketed as the IBM 7030. Only seven of the IBM 7030s were sold, and IBM lost out to Control Data's faster CDC 6600. Meanwhile, IBM have concentrated on the more lucrative data processing market. Since the introduction of the IBM 3090 Vector Facility in 1985, IBM has been looking seriously again at scientific supercomputing.

This is where Steve Chen comes in. For IBM, Chen is a good bet to produce a Cray-class supercomputer by the early 1990s, and SSI will cost IBM relatively little capital investment. Even if SSI fails to produce a working computer, IBM will absorb technical knowledge from SSI and if SSI does succeed then IBM may have the most powerful computer in the world.

7.3.2 Who is Steve Chen?

In 1975, Chen received his PhD from the University of Illinois. He studied under Dr. David Kuck, head of the Center for Supercomputer Research and Development. From 1975 to 1978, Chen worked as a project engineer for the Burroughs Corporation where he was involved in the hardware and software development of the Burroughs Scientific Processor, a pipelined vector array processor. From Burroughs, he spent a short time in 1978/79 at Floating Point Systems before joining CRI in 1979 to coordinate the X-MP project.

Chen made his name with the Cray X-MP, although this machine was largely designed before he joined the company. However, according to some it was his skills as a project leader and designer that made the X-MP project a success. From 1982, Chen was chief architect on the Cray Y-MP. Before this was complete, he was given his own MP project to develop a multiprocessor machine like the Y-MP, but with 32–64 processors and a more aggressive approach architecturally and technologically. The design of the machine required significant research in several areas, such as optical interconnects, packaging, cooling, and software. However, it did not meet its deadlines or budgets.

At the same time, CRI was funding two other rival projects: the Cray 3, headed by Seymour Cray, and the C90, a conservative follow-on from the Y-MP. CRI could not support three system designs and eventually closed down Chen's MP project in 1987. This prompted him to leave CRI, taking some of the MP team with him, to set up SSI.

7.3.3 SSI's Options

SSI's first machine will be constrained by several factors. They wish to be 100 times faster than the fastest machines available in 1987, but still ship in "the early 1990s". There are also price constraints; it will be extremely difficult to sell a machine for more than $30 M. Whatever is built, SSI will be competing directly with both CRI and Seymour Cray's new company, Cray Computer Corporation.

In previous designs, Chen developed machines that incorporated a significant amount of multiprocessing; SSI's first product, therefore, is likely to have up to 64 processors. Assuming a 2-3 ns clock cycle, such a machine would be approximately ten times faster than the Cray Y-MP. The machine will almost certainly be implemented in silicon technology, probably using ECL chips, although BiCMOS is also a possibility.

The machine will also need a massive memory to provide enough workspace for 64 processors, probably about 2 Gword. Whether this will be multiported shared memory, as in current CRI machines, is not clear. The expense of providing a 64 port memory may be prohibitive, and may force the machine to have a distributed memory organisation with secondary solid state storage, similar to the architecture of the ETA[10] (cf. 10.2). The machine will definitely have an IBM front-end computer, and will probably execute an IBM operating system.

Software is the biggest problem for SSI. Current compiler technology is not sufficiently advanced to automatically partition programs between large numbers of processors. The software tools that SSI provide will have a large influence on how well their machine will sell. SSI have a lot of technological problems to overcome in developing their first computer. Even so, producing the machine is the easy part. By the time the SS-1 arrives CRI will have a new computer of their own coupled with the advantage of a large customer base. Competing for customers with CRI and the Japanese vector supercomputer manufacturers is going to be the hard part.

Company Summary 21: Features of the Cray Y-MP

Source	Cray Research Inc.
Type	The Cray Y-MP: a multiprocessor pipelined vector supercomputer.
Availability	From spring 1988.
Price	Cray Y-MP2/166 consisting of two processors and 16 Mword of main memory: $5 M.
	Cray Y-MP8/8128 consisting of eight processors and 128 Mword of main memory: $22.95 M.
Processing nodes	Based on the Cray-1 with an extended instruction set to handle interprocessor communication.
Memory	A large shared memory containing 16 to 128 Mword implemented in ECL technology. Memory arranged in 64, 128, or 256 banks.
Communications	Interprocessor communications via shared semaphore registers and shared memory block transfers.
I/O connections	Each CPU and the central memory are connected to an I/O subsystem via 100 Mbyte/s channel pairs. The I/O subsystem has two 1 Gbyte/s communication channels for connection to solid state storage, and four 6 Mbyte/s channels for connection to external peripherals such as disc drives.
Performance	The processor clock cycle is 6 ns, giving a performance of 333 MFLOPS per CPU. An eight processor system has a peak performance of 2.67 GFLOPS.
Host system	Front-end communication with IBM, CDC, DEC, and Honeywell computer systems.
Operating system	UNICOS, Cray's own UNIX based on AT&T UNIX.
Programming languages	Vectorising, autotasking Fortran 77 compiler, vector parallel C, Pascal, Lisp and Ada.
Sources	Books, newspapers, Cray Research publications, scientific papers, and interviews with Cray personnel.

Company Summary 22: Features of the NEC SX-3 System

Source	NEC (UK) Systems Division
Type	Multi-processor vector supercomputers.
Availability	Available September 1990.
Price	$6 M – $24 M.
Processing nodes	Up to four, with up to four sets of pipelines per processor.
Processor technology	CML with 70 ps switching time per gate.
Memory	64 Mbyte – 2 Gbyte.
Communications	Processor to memory bandwidth not public.
I/O connections	The external bandwidth is up to 2.6 Gbyte/s (1 Gbyte/s through I/O processors plus 16×100 Mbyte/s through HiPPI link.).
Performance	1.3 GFLOPS per pipeline set (up to 22 GFLOPS total).
Host system	None.
Operating system	UNIX-compatible SUPER-UX.
Programming languages	Fortran, C, Pascal.
Physical configuration	Several cabinets spread over $7.2 \times 5.5 \times 1.5$ m.
Power requirements	Not public.
Sources	Dataquest report (May 1989), USENET articles, NEC brochures.

Chapter 8

The Giants: Biding Their Time

Of the companies described in this chapter, only DEC currently produces a truly parallel computer, and even that is marketed as an extension to their existing VAX product line. However, as IBM's entry into the personal computer market showed in the 1980s, as soon as any of these giants decide to move, their choices will become the framework within which all other companies must operate.

8.1   Digital Equipment Corporation

Relevant Activities Manufactures a wide range of networked computer systems, including several multiprocessors.

Location Digital Equipment Corporation, 143 Main Street, Maynard, Mass. 01754, USA, Telephone (508) 493 5111, Fax (508) 493 8780.
UK office: Digital Equipment Corporation, Digital Park, Imperial Way, Reading, Berkshire, RG2 0TE, United Kingdom, Telephone 0734 441333, Fax 0734 867969

Relevant Officers Kenneth H. Olsen, President; John F. Smith, Senior VP of Operations; John L. Sims, VP of Strategic Resources; William R. Demmer, VP of Vax VMS Systems and Servers; Domenic J. LaCava, VP of UNIX-based Software and Systems;

Employees Approximately 123 500 worldwide.

Financial details For the quarter ending September 29, 1990, total operating revenues were approximately $3.1 G, net income $26 M, and total assets $11.5 G.

8.1.1   The Company

Digital Equipment Corporation (DEC) manufactures mainframe, mini and workstation computers. Several of the more recent machines are shared memory multiprocessors, and the company also has current research programs into other areas of parallel processing.

DEC was founded in 1957 by Ken Olsen, and is now one of the major forces in computing. The company has development laboratories worldwide in addition to its worldwide sales network. Of the $3 G revenue in the quarter ending September 29, 1990, $400 M was spent on research and engineering.

The mainstay of DEC's business over the past decade has been the Vax range of mini-computers, starting from the earliest Vax 11/780 to the most recent Vax 9000 series machines. With a common instruction set and operating system these machines have provided a stable development environment for many applications.

DEC's earliest experiences with parallel processing came with their involvement in Carnegie-Mellon University's Cm* project, starting in 1975. Since then they have developed various multiprocessors and have research groups working in other areas of parallel computing (cf. 8.1.5). DEC's current parallel processing products owe much to the company's early networking experience. As the size of the problems users wanted to tackle increased, computers were linked together to cooperate on large problems. DEC's Vaxcluster and DECnet products allowed Vax users to connect their computers together, though the amount of cooperation possible between processors was limited because of the large overheads of interprocessor communication.

8.1.2 The Hardware

The Cm*

The Cm* project at Carnegie-Mellon was based on the LSI-11 processor, a Large Scale Integration version of DEC's popular PDP-11. While this machine never progressed beyond the research laboratory it gave DEC, as well as the researchers at CMU, an insight into the problems and issues that needed to be addressed in developing a parallel computer. Each processor had its own memory and optional I/O devices, which together formed a Computer Module. Groups of up to 14 Computer Modules were connected together in a cluster using a bus. Clusters, in turn, were linked together by a further series of buses, which allowed machines to have many hundreds of processors. Each processor was able to address directly all of the main memory in the machine. If a reference was not local, the request was first put onto the cluster bus and then, if still not satisfied, onto the intercluster bus to the processor whose memory contained the required data. This mechanism allowed the developers scope to experiment with a variety of interprocess communication mechanisms, based on both message passing and shared memory.

ASMP and SMP

As users demanded more processing power, DEC introduced shared memory dual processors. The first of these, the Vax 11/782, was introduced at the beginning of the 1980's. The software environment provided to support this development was called ASMP (Asymmetric Multi-Processing), and was incorporated into Vax/VMS from Version 2.0. Under ASMP one CPU is the primary processor and handles all operating system calls. Any other processors only handle user jobs. This introduced a performance bottleneck which resulted in very poor CPU utilisation, and led DEC to introduce the SMP (Symmetric Multi-Processing) model.

SMP is a bus-based shared memory model of parallel computation to which all Vax systems running Vax/VMS Version 5.0 or later conform. Each processor can independently and equally access all operating system code and system resources. However, the model constrains processors to reside physically close together, so that they can communicate through shared memory. On Vax systems this has usually been implemented by having all processors and memory attached to the XMI bus, though the Vax 9000 does not follow this pattern.

Programs written in the SMP model on one Vax system will run on any other Vax system, regardless of the number of processors. Sequential applications will run on multiprocessors and parallel applications will run without modification on uniprocessors. Transparent utilisation of the available parallelism has been a major goal for DEC (cf. 8.1.3). DEC machines conforming to the SMP model include those mentioned in Table 8.1.

Table 8.1: DEC SMP Machines

Machine	Processors	Performance Per Processor (MIPS)
6000-240	4	2.8
6000-360	6	3.8
6000-460	6	7.0
8840	4	6.0
9000-440	4	40.0

Vax 9000

The 9000 series is DEC's recently announced mainframe class machine. The Vax 9000 is a shared memory multiprocessor based around a 2 Gbyte/s crossbar switch. This switch the major architectural difference between the 9000 and its predecessors in the Vax range, which were all bus based.

The largest 9000 series configuration supports four processors; with the current crossbar switch design this figure is a hard upper limit on the number of processors in a system. Earlier SMP machines, such as the Vax 6000, could contain more processors, though each processor had a significantly lower performance.

In another move to improve the performance of their high end Vax systems DEC recently extended the Vax architecture to include vector processing facilities. The vector architecture adopts a vector-register design, in which all vector operations are performed on operands held in vector registers. This contrasts with the Vax scalar architecture, in which memory to memory operations are supported. Each vector register contains 64 elements, each of which is 64 bits long. The architecture allows the vector processor to function as an asynchronous coprocessor beside the scalar processor. Each system may have multiple scalar-vector processor pairs, and asymmetric configurations can exist, in which only some of the Vax processors in a multiprocessor system support a vector processor.

The vector architecture has been implemented for both the 6000 and 9000 series Vax machines. The 6000 series version can achieve a peak single precision performance of 90 MFLOPS; some figures for the vector performance of the 9000 series are given in Table 8.2.

Table 8.2: Vax 9000 Vector Performance

Vax 9000-210 or -410	Performance (MFLOPS)
Peak Vector Performance	125.0
1000 × 1000 LINPACK	80.0
Perfect Club[A]	5.8 to 23.8

Vax 9000-440	
Peak Vector Performance	500.0
1000 × 1000 LINPACK	312.0

A: These tests are apparently baseline,
and optimized results will be released later.

Firefly

At DEC's Systems Research Centre (DEC SRC) in Palo Alto a great deal of work has been done on the Firefly shared memory multiprocessors. Built from microVax[1] processors these workstations were, until 1990, used both to investigate different aspects of building multiprocessors and as a major computing resource for other work at DEC SRC, thus providing a real life load for the machines under development.

The main features of the Firefly design are the use of a dedicated I/O processor, and the use of caches to reduce the average load on the memory bus. This contrasts with the usual use of a cache system to reduce the average time required to access memory. In addition to responding to processor requests, the caches also watch the memory bus for updates to data they hold. Also, when a processor first references data held by another processors cache, the data is supplied from the cache rather than from primary memory if the cache data is more recent than that in memory.

Support for the Firefly has recently ceased, as researchers at DEC SRC have moved on to other areas of research, particularly software. For example, DEC SRC was a major force in the design of the Modula-3 language, which takes several ideas from their own version of Modula-2 (see 8.1.3).

8.1.3   The Software

Vax Software

Recent releases of the Vax/VMS operating system provide support for the SMP model of parallel processing on top of the multiprocessor hardware of many Vax

---

[1]The microVax processor is a single chip implementation of the Vax architecture.

systems. This support is embodied in a Parallel Processing Run Time Library, which contains routines allowing process creation, synchronisation and destruction. DEC's C and Fortran compilers allow programmers to create multiple processes to deal with different sections of a problem through calls to the library. Processes created through the library may run on any processor, and their actual placement is transparent to the user. The synchronisation primitives are implemented using spin locks.

In addition, the Fortran compiler performs some automatic parallelisation when its High Performance option is used. As well as providing a selection of powerful vectorisation facilities, the compiler is able to automatically decompose iterations of DO loops to execute on different processors. Presented with a triply nested DO loop, for example, the compiler might simultaneously vectorise the innermost loop and create separate processes to execute successive iterations of the outermost loop, enabling as much of the work as possible to be done concurrently. The compiler uses dependency analysis to decide whether loops may be vectorised or parallelised, but it can also prompt the user for hints that may aid program decomposition. These hints are stored by the compiler and used in subsequent compilations unless the user explicitly forces the compiler to discard them. The dependency analysis is often not powerful enough to allow the compiler to perform all possible optimisations, and assertions — for example that a variable is always greater than zero — may allow the compiler to be more aggressive.

Firefly Software

The Firefly multiprocessor software supported parallelism both through a traditional multi-tasking operating system, and at a lower level through a lightweight process mechanism. Both of these were supplied by Taos , the Firefly operating system. "Threads", as lightweight processes were known, shared a common address space, although each thread had its own stack. Threads could synchronise with one another through the use of semaphores.

On top of this the Firefly user saw a software environment, known as Topaz, which provided the Modula-2+ programming language, various utility programs and the library interfaces. Modula-2+ was a DEC SRC extension to Modula-2 that provided facilities for thread creation, destruction and synchronisation. All parallelism was explicit and under user control. Some of the features now incorporated in Modula-3 have been taken from DEC's Modula-2+ extensions, including the support for multi-threaded programs.

Taos emulated the Ultrix system call interface, allowing Topaz applications to run on Ultrix and Ultrix applications on Taos. Ultrix was been provided with a threads support library that emulated the parallelism using co-routines.

8.1.4 The Market

In the company's own words, "Digital is focusing on mainframe-style computing, client/server computing and systems integration." In the mainframe arena DEC are aiming their multi-vector processors at a general scientific and engineering market, such as universities and engineering companies, as well as the large-scale transaction processing market. The high end SMP machines, such as the Vax 9000 series, provide the company's main product in this marketplace, in which they will be competing against the likes of IBM (8.3) at the bottom end of the ES/9000 range (cf. 8.3.2), and Sequent with their Symmentry machines (cf. 3.7.2).

8.1.5 The Future

In the short term DEC will continue to expand its SMP range, and increase the power of each processor in these machines. Improvements in bus bandwidth and crossbar switch technology will enable DEC to continue to utilise the SMP model over the next five years. The software technology already exists to allow efficient utilisation of these architectures, and this will continue to provide the backbone of DEC parallel processing.

In the client/server and workstation marketplace DEC are providing high performance workstations and servers. Applying multiprocessing to such systems to increase performance is clearly a natural approach, particularly for a company with many years experience building multiprocessors. Given DEC's investment in SMP any new machines in this category are likely to adhere to that particular model of parallel computation. Here they will be competing against companies such as Sun Microsystems, who are likewise likely to see multiprocessing as a useful tool for delivering performance to the desktop.

DEC also has a research group working on a Massively Parallel Processor (MPP). Started in the mid-1980's, this project is developing a high performance SIMD parallel machine similar to the MasPar MP-1 (2.2). The MPP is intended to function as an attached processor subsystem, perhaps to a Vax 9000 series machine. In building such a machine DEC are aiming at a similar market to that targetted by Thinking Machines Corporation for the CM-2 (2.3). There are close links between this project and MasPar — Jeff Kalb, who founded MasPar in 1988, previously had some responsibilities for the development of the MPP. That split appears to have been amicable, and DEC seem to be using MasPar to test the SIMD market and keep abreast of market driven developments.

The prototype MPP, completed in 1989, contains 16384 processing elements, as many as the largest available MP-1. There is hardware support for floating point, and the machine supports both grid and router connectivity. The whole machine is hosted by a microVAX. According to DEC a second prototype is under development at present, though the long term future of the project and its place within DEC's

overall strategy is unclear. DEC are addressing the compiler and other software
issues to make use of the MPP transparent to the casual user.

8.2 Fujitsu

Relevant Activities Manufacture vector supercomputers and MIMD processor arrays.

Location Fujitsu Europe Ltd., 2 Longwalk Road, Stockley Park, Uxbridge UB11 1AB, Tel (081) 573 4444 FAX (081) 573 2643
6-1, Marunouchi 1-chome, Chiyoda-ku, Tokyo 100, Japan.

Relevant Officers Tadashi Sekizawa, President; Takuma Yamamoto, Chairman of the Board.

Employees Several hundred thousand in Japan and abroad.

8.2.1 The Company

Fujitsu Limited was founded in Japan in 1935. Its original interest was in telephone switching equipment — in 1938 it delivered Japan's first automatic switching system — but in the 1950s the company turned its attention to computer systems. Fujitsu built Japan's first commercial computer, the FACOM 100, in 1954, and in 1961 produced an early transistor-based computer, the FACOM 222. The company entered the mainframe data processing market with the FACOM 230 series of mainframes in the mid-1960s, and one of these machines, the 230-60, was the first commercial computer in the world to use integrated circuits. By 1973, Fujitsu had started producing LSI chips in commercial quantities, chips which it quickly put to use in computers like the FACOM M-190. The production of one of the first 64-kbit RAM chips in 1978, and the move to producing vector supercomputers in the early 1980s, were natural parts of Fujitsu's growing presence in the world's computing and telecommunications markets.

8.2.2 Vector Computers

Fujitsu began manufacturing vector supercomputers in the early 1980s. Their first machines, the VP100 and VP200, were introduced in 1983, and were the first Japanese-built supercomputers. Several further models were added to their product line in succeeding years: the VP50 and VP400 in 1985, and the VP30 in 1986.

By October 1988 Fujitsu held approximately 55% of the supercomputer market in Japan. However, by that time their VP machines were using technology which was almost a full generation behind that of their major competitors. Accordingly, the company developed their current machines, the VP2000 series, which are among the most advanced vector supercomputers in the world, capable of producing a peak performance of 5 GFLOPS on some calculations. While all of Fujitsu's vector

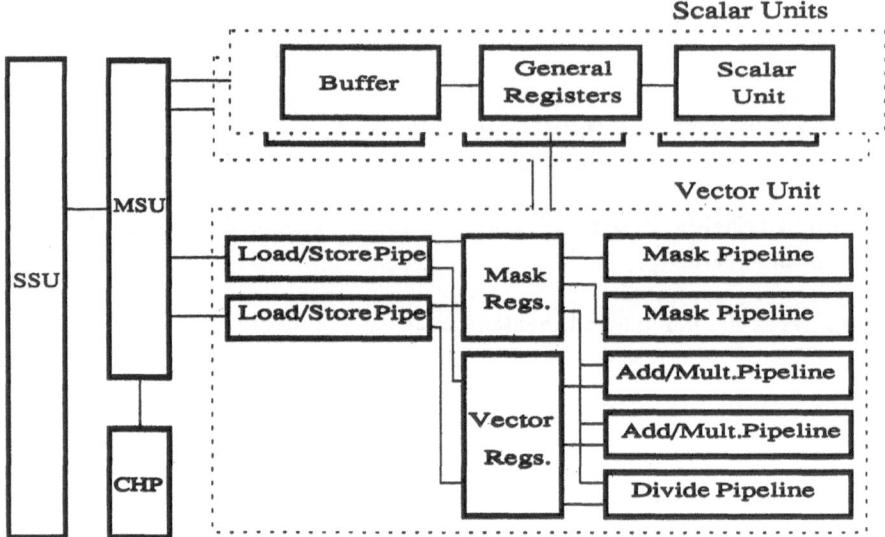

Figure 8.1: Fujitsu's VP2000 Series Vector Supercomputers

supercomputers to date have been uniprocessor machines, NEC's introduction of
the SX-3 (cf. 7.2) obviously requires some sort of response in the near future.

Each VP2000 series machine contains one or two vector processing units, from
one to four scalar processing units, a main storage unit, a system storage unit, and
a channel processor (see Figure 8.1). The vector processing unit contains both a
large vector register (up to 64 kbyte) to hold operands and a mask register (up to 1
kbyte) to control vector operations, enabling conditional branches within loops to
be vectorised. Each vector processing unit can also contain up to seven pipelines;
a fully-configured processor has two load/store pipelines, two mask pipelines, one
divide pipeline, and two pipelines for doing multiplication, addition, and logical
operations. Processors are built using ECL VLSI chips containing 15,000 gates
each, with a 70 picosecond propagation delay per gate. Fujitsu were the first
company to introduce glass ceramic as a board material to mount these chips, and
use liquid cooling to disperse the 4.6 kW generated by each circuit board.

The processor's vector processing unit is supported by one or two scalar processing units, each of which contains a 128 kbyte storage buffer 16 general-purpose
registers which are 32 bits wide, 8 floating-point registers which are 64 bits wide,
and 16 control registers (also 32 bit). If two scalar processing units are configured
together, they can both be allowed to use the vector unit (which improves throughput if both scalar jobs and vector jobs with a low vectorisation rate exist), or one
scalar unit can be dedicated to scalar jobs and the other given exclusive control of

the vector unit (which improves throughput if vector jobs with a high vectorisation rate exist).

Since August 1990, Fujitsu have been making multiprocessor versions of the VP2000 machines. A fully-configured VP2400/40 contains two vector processing units and four scalar processing units, and has a peak performance of 5 GFLOPS. An enhanced Fortran compiler for these machines, Fortran 77 EX/PP, now includes support for multitasking.

The storage system contains two layers. The first, the main storage unit, has up to 2 Gbyte of CMOS RAM, built using 1 Mbit static RAM chips with a 35 nanosecond access time. The secondary system storage unit, which can contain up to 32 Gbyte, uses 4 Mbit dynamic RAM chips with a 100 nanosecond access time; some of this unit's logical elements are built using GaAs LSI chips. The system storage unit can be used as a vector job swapping area (if the machine is operating in multi-user mode), for implementing a Fortran virtual I/O system under Fujitsu's MSP-EX operating system, or to provide a memory-mapped file store for Fujitsu's UXP/M Unix-like operating system.

Finally, the VP2000 series' channel processor can accommodate up to 256 optical or block multiplexer channels, allowing a total maximum throughput of 2 Gbyte/s. Each optical channel operates at either 9 Mbyte/s or 36 Mbyte/s, while the block multiplexer channel has a maximum throughput of 4.5 Mbyte/s. Both HIPPI and UltraNet connections are supported.

As mentioned above, Fujitsu provide two operating systems for their VP2000 machines. The first, MSP-EX, is a non-standard operating system originally developed for Fujitsu's M Series general-purpose mainframes. MSP-EX includes a Vector Processor Control Facility, which allows VP2000 machines to be used as a stand-alone machine or as a networked computing resource through TCP/IP, Fujitsu's DSLINK, and UltraNet. MSP-EX also allows a VP2000 to be used as a back-end numerical processor for machines running either MSP-EX or IBM's MVS operating system, in which case the VP2000 can share the front-end computer's disk drives and datasets.

UXP/M, Fujitsu's Unix-like operating system for the VP2000 machines, contains a Vector Processor Support Option which allows program to store data and programs in the system storage unit, and to make use of the swapping function supported by the machine's hardware to transfer these quickly to and from the main storage unit. Batch processing is provided under UXP/M by the Network Queueing System, originally developed by Sterling Software for NASA.

Vectorising compilers for the VP2000 are available for both Fortran and C, along with performance monitoring and tuning tools, while scalar support is given to Cobol85, Pascal, Prolog, and Lisp. Interestingly, Fujitsu also advertise that their vector machines can be used in AI applications. An object-oriented Fortran tool called FORTRAN/KR allows AI programs to make use of the VP2000's vector

Table 8.3: VP2000 Applications

Application Area	Number of Programs	Example
structural analysis	43	ABAQUS
chemistry	33	MACCS
fluid dynamics	27	FLUENT
pre/post processors	25	PIGS
software development	23	HISTORIAN PLUS
electronics	19	FSPICE/VP
graphics	14	CGMS
CAD	10	CADAM
mathematics libraries	9	CPC
image processing	6	IPEX
EM analysis	2	MAGNA/FIM
acoustic analysis	2	BOOM

processing facilities, while ESHELL/X is an AI system development tool based on the Lisp programming language.

Fujitsu's VP2000 machines are primarily used in the traditional vector supercomputing arenas. Table 8.3 lists the number of programs already mounted on the VP2000 in different application areas, and gives examplars of each.

According to Fujitsu's own figures, they currently have a 51% share of the Japanese supercomputer market, having built 63 of the 123 supercomputers installed in Japan by March 1990. (The other companies mentioned are Cray (19%), NEC (15%), Hitachi(14%), and CDC (1%).) Of these machines, 48% have gone to manufacturing industry, 34% to universities and other research institutions, and the remaining 18% to government and private laboratories. Only 18% of these machines are in the VP2000 class, but that number will obviously increase in the coming years.

8.2.3   The CAP-C5 Array Processor

While Fujitsu have not yet produced a massively parallel computer commercially, they have been experimenting with prototypes since the Cellular Array Processor (CAP) project began in 1983. The first generation of machine produced by this project, the CAP-C3, had 64 processing nodes, each containing an Intel 80186 microprocessor with an 8087 floating point co-processor, and discrete hardware implementing a variety of management and communications functions. The more recent machines, the CAP-C5 and the AP-1000, which could quickly become products if Fujitsu were to decide to enter the highly parallel market, are described below.

The CAP-C5 is an MIMD computer with 256 nodes, each containing an Intel 80186 microprocessor, an Intel 8087 floating point co-processor, 2 Mbyte of RAM, 64 kbyte of ROM, and 96 kbyte of video RAM. Each of these nodes runs a light-weight operating system called the Cell OS, which provides a multi-tasking environment and handles some aspects of inter-task communication. In addition, each node contains a custom CAP-VLSI chip, fabricated using a 1.8 μ CMOS gate array, which:

1. manages the six internode communication ports

2. manages the two common bus interfaces for global communication

3. handles hardware synchronisation

4. acts as a window controller for fast image-data transfer

These functions are described in more detail below.

The machine as a whole is controlled by a host computer, which is connected to every processor through a shared command bus running at 2 Mbyte/s. This bus is used to load programs and, in some applications, to send data to all processing nodes. Each CAP-VLSI chip has two command bus interfaces, one used for communication with the host and the other for communication with other cells, each of which is buffered by a 16-bit 8-word FIFO memory. Any node can use this bus to broadcast messages to other nodes, or send messages to the host computer; normally, however, the bus is used for host-node communication.

In the event of bus conflicts, arbitration is managed by hardware polling on the CAP-VLSI chip. This polling is executed in two stages: the first selects a column containing a node which is trying to access the bus, while the second selects the row containing the node. This two-phase technique reduces the polling time from $\mathcal{O}(N)$ to $\mathcal{O}(\sqrt{N})$ for an N-node machine.

Each node contains six full-duplex communications ports, each of which can transmit 15 Mbit/s in both directions. While the CAP-C5 is usually configured as a two-dimensional torus, in which each processing node is connected to four neighbours in a wrap-around NEWS grid, this only uses four of each node's six links. More complicated topologies such as cubes, pyramids, and low-dimensional hypercubes can be constructed by utilising the "extra" two links.

The CAP-VLSI chip uses a bypass technique for intercell communication. Any two of the six ports on the chip can be bound together by commands from the node's processor, establishing a through route between distant cells. Such paths are set and released dynamically.

Since global synchronisation is often needed by parallel algorithms, each node in the AP-1000 has special status registers for this purpose. Outputs of the status register of each node are wire-ORed on one of 6 status lines which can be read by the host or any cell. Cells can explicitly set or clear their status registers to indicate such things as completion of a particular task. The host, or any cell, can then read the logical AND or OR of the statuses in all cells. Each status line handles an independent synchronisation request. Two control lines are used to automatically time-multiplex up to 16 different synchronisation requests simultaneously.

Local inter-node communication is handled through directly-connected ports. Data is transferred in packets containing 16 data bits and 3 header bits which identify the packet type (data, interrupt, non-maskable interrupt, or acknowledge). Connected cells communicate using a handshaking protocol in which each packet is acknowledged. Cells can also interrupt one another by sending interrupt packets whenever the target node has not been bypassed; nonmaskable interrupt packets are used to interrupt nodes which have been bypassed.

All nodes in the CAP-C5 are connected by a second bus, which is used to transfer video data. The window controller in each node's CAP-VLSI chip maps its portion of the image onto a part of the screen, allowing nodes to co-operate in constructing images. This mapping pattern can be changed as needed to improve the load-balancing aspects of graphics programs (see below). Image data is read via the video bus every 33 ms refresh cycle; data can be input and output at this rate simultaneously by using two video buses.

As mentioned above, each node in the CAP-C5 runs a lightweight operating system called the Cell OS. This provides multitasking on each node, which gives programmers more freedom to create and map tasks, and handles some aspects of message transfer. Each task is identified by its node and task number; messages in which the destination node and task ID are both specified are sent only to that task, while messages in which only the task ID is specified are broadcast to the task with that ID on each node. (If the destination task specified does not exist, a run-time error is generated.)

Messages are automatically queued as they arrive at their destination, and read in the sequence in which they arrived. Messages sent to distant nodes (i.e. non-locally) are dynamically routed to avoid contention; the CAP-C5's routing algorithm runs on all of the topologies in which it can be configured. If a message could travel toward its destination in one of several directions from a node, the output port through which the message is routed is chosen by selecting the one for which the fewest messages are currently queued. Since this might change the order in which messages arrive, each message is automatically tagged with a sequence number and a source node ID, and re-ordered upon arrival. Intermediate and final buffering is done using part of the cell's memory; in all cases, the sender trusts the receiver to have enough buffering space.

Each node also runs a display manager, which is the basic software package for image generation and display. This not only handles the mapping of each node's sub-image onto the global display, but also provides routines for distributed drawing of two-dimensional geometric primitives such as lines, spheres, and characters for any of the standard CAP-C5 topologies. Additional graphics facilities provided by the display manager include zooming, panning, clipping, and animation of frame buffers.

As well as writing a program for the nodes in the CAP-C5, users must write a program to run on the host computer. The interface between this host program and the CAP-C5 is called the *cell driver*. It is responsible for setting up the execution environment for the tasks which are to run on the CAP-C5, which is done using a library of functions which initialise the CAP-C5, load application tasks, set the priorities of those tasks, etc., and to handle broadcast and receive operations by the host program. 255 different priority levels are provided; a task's priority is set statically, and high-priority tasks always run before low priority tasks.

The CAP-C5 was designed with graphics applications in mind, as shown by the special hardware and software provision for such applications. In particular, the CAP-C5 is an excellent vehicle for doing ray tracing. By statically dividing the image into many small blocks, and scattering these blocks among the available processing nodes, a ray-tracing program on the CAP-C5 can ensure a reasonable degree of load balancing, which in turn leads to very high performance. Experiments carried out by Fujitsu have shown that with a fine-grained distribution of the image, overall processing times differed by less than 10% between different processing nodes. The overall performance of the CAP-C5 in this application is approximately three times that of a mainframe computer such as the IBM 3081.

But Fujitsu have not stopped there. Because ray-tracing is a point-based method, aliases (such as the jagged edges of angled lines) can easily occur. By communicating pixel values between nearest neighbours and next-nearest neighbours, the CAP-C5 ray-tracing software can perform anti-aliasing with little reduction in total processing time. The large memory of the CAP-C5 even allows a program to store the whole of the ray-tracing traversal tree in memory, so that if lighting, shading, or surface model parameters are changed the image can quickly be re-generated.

8.2.4   The AP-1000 Array Processor

The AP-1000 is similar to the CAP-C5 in many ways, but there are also some significant differences. The most obvious of these are:

Topology: The AP-1000 is configured only as a torus, with at most 1024 (32×32) processors. Accordingly, each processor has only four links to other processors. To improve performance, this configuration is supported by a separate broadcast network and by a synchronisation network, both of which are described below.

Processor: The AP-1000 uses a 25 MHz SPARC chip supported by a custom 12.5 MFLOPS FPU.

Memory: 16 Mbyte of RAM and a 128 kbyte cache are provided for each processor; the ROM and video RAM of the CAP-C5 have disappeared. The RAM is quadruple-interleaved, with a 160 ns access time for word write operations.

External interface: Each cell has an LBUS interface to which fast I/O devices, disks, vector co-processors, or extra memory can be attached; the two video buses have disappeared.

Support hardware: The single CAP-VLSI chip has been replaced by a suite of four chips, described below.

The most important change is in topology. Rather than allowing users to configure the machine in one of several standard topologies to reduce inter-processor messaging latency, Fujitsu have produced fast special-purpose hardware for message routing, which relies on the topology being fixed as a square grid. The routing network which implements this torus is called the T-net, and consists of point-to-point 16-bit-wide connections between adjacent processors running at 25 Mbyte/s.

Beside the T-net is a broadcast network, or B-net, which provides efficient 1-to-N communication. The B-net is a hierarchical 32-bit bus running at 50 Mbyte/s, which can be used either by the AP-1000's host computer, or by any of the AP-1000's processors. Both the T-net and the B-net use pipelined handshaking controls to improve throughput.

Finally, a separate signalling and synchronisation network called the S-net, which consists of two globally-accessible sets of signal lines, connects the AP-1000's processors as a tree. One set of signal lines is time-sliced to provide eight different event signals, while the other set is time-sliced to provide 32 event signals. These signals are used to synchronise processors, effectively providing a hardware implementation of barrier synchronisation.

Inside each node, four chips have replaced the single CAP-VLSI chip used in the CAP-C5. These are a routing controller (RTC), a B-net interface (BIF), a message controller (MSC), which is also a cache controller, and a dynamic memory controller (DRAMC). There is no memory management unit as such, but a Memory Protection Table can be used to segment memory between different processes.

The RTC chip contains one controller for routing in the X direction, and another for routing in the Y direction; messages are always routed X-wards, then Y-wards. Wormhole routing is used in conjunction with a structured buffer pool to prevent deadlocking. The maximum network size the RTC can accommodate is 32×32, but within that network it can route data at a rate of 160 ns/word. Localised broadcasts across a rectangular region of the torus is provided in hardware by the

RTC; this is often useful in matrix calculations. Finally, the RTC chip also acts as the LBUS interface, and contains several read/write FIFO buffers for this purpose.

The MSC message controller chip, which operates asynchronously, handles interaction between the processor and the T-net. The MSC contains two read and write pointer registers, which together implement a ring buffer in hardware. Messages to be transmitted are automatically added to and taken from the outgoing buffer, while messages received are added to and taken from the incoming buffer. If buffer overflow occurs a processor interrupt is generated. The MSC then waits for the processor allocate more buffer space.

The MSC doubles as the cache controller in order to make transmission and reception more efficient. Quite often, the data to be sent or received will be in the cache, so the MSC sends it directly to the RTC or to the broadcast network interface as if it were flushing the cache. Otherwise, direct memory access (DMA) is invoked automatically. The MSC not only allows for strides in DMA, so that data at regular offsets in memory (i.e. elements in a particular column or row of an array) can be selected, it also provides hardware support for list vectors, in which the values in one array point to the values in another array which are actually to be sent. List vectors are quite often used in FORTRAN programs to manage irregular data structures, so direct hardware support for them can make parallelisation of such programs much more effective. Finally, the MSC also implements indexed message reception — rather than placing incoming data at a specified location in memory, it can generate an address for the data using 10 bits of information supplied in the message header. In this way, data being sent to a single point by many different processors can be stored in an array automatically.

The last of the AP-1000's processor support chips is the broadcast network interface (BIF). This puts several 8-stage FIFO buffers between the processor and the B-net. During a normal broadcast, all of the data being broadcast is read into a FIFO by each node, then taken by the memory controller. During a gather or scatter operation data is always read or written by the BIF, but may or may not be passed on to the network or the processor depending on the value of a status flag.

8.2.5   The Future

While Fujitsu is heavily committed to vector supercomputing at the present time, the development of the AP-1000 shows that they are looking to a more parallel future. It is clearly a second-generation machine — the inclusion of hardware support for broadcast and synchronisation, as well as the sophisticated through-routing mechanism it implements, show that its designers have learned from the experiences of those who built the first generation of hypercube and SIMD computers. Its mixture of SIMD and MIMD features is also an indication of the way in which current debates about the shape of parallel computers may be resolved by producing hybrid machines. Finally, the way in which the CAP-C5 has been aimed directly at the high-performance graphics and image processing markets, and with the CAP-C5's graphics software being ported to the AP-1000, indicates the way in which current major computer manufacturers, such as Fujitsu, may choose to enter the parallel computing marketplace. By competing in one niche market at a time, rather than producing a general-purpose parallel computer, Fujitsu will not only avoid competing with their own existing product lines, but will also establish a foothold from which to move into other areas of high-performance computing one by one.

8.3   IBM Corporation

Relevant Activities Manufacture of a large range of computer hardware and software.

Location Corporate Headquarters: IBM Corporation, Old Orchard Road, Armonk, New York 10504; Telephone: (800) 426 3333.
UK Headquarters: IBM UK Ltd., P.O. Box 41, North Harbour, Portsmouth, Hampshire, England. Telephone: 0705 321212; Fax: 0705 388914.

Relevant Officers John F. Akers, Chairman of the Board; Jack D. Kuehler, President; Sir Edwin Nixon, Chairman (UK); A.B. Cleaver, Cheif Executive (UK); D.M. Campbell, Secretary (UK).

Employees Approximately 383 000 worldwide.

Financial details A publicly listed company on all of the major stock exchanges. Assets at the end of the 1989 financial year: $77.7 G, revenue: $62.7 G and net earnings: $3.8 G.

8.3.1   The Company

IBM is one of the largest companies in the world, and certainly the biggest computer manufacturer. Within such a enormous and diversified organisation it is not surprising that parallel programming is still regarded as something of a niche market which does not yet merit a large investment of effort. There are signs, however, that this situation may be set to change.

The company took a leading role in the early days of scientific computing with with the development of STRETCH. However, when this machine was marketed in 1961 as the IBM 7030, it was not a commercial success. Users preferred the faster CDC 6600, and only seven 7030's were ever sold. IBM therefore opted to concentrate on the more lucrative data processing market, a decision which has resulted in them growing much more strongly than any of their contemporaries.

Recently, however, IBM has reconsidered its decision. The company re-entered the scientific computing scene in 1985 with the introduction of the IBM 3090 Vector Facility (VF). By 1988, there were as many 3090's installed as Cray's, and the number of 3090's has grown faster since. IBM now claim that the shared-memory supercomputing marketplace is dominated by themselves and Cray Research Inc.

IBM has been involved in several research projects in high-performance parallel computers during the past two decades. One of these was the RP/3, a shared memory MIMD machine developed in cooperation with New York University whose 512 CPUs had an aggregate peak performance of about 800 MFLOPS. SIMD computing was also investigated through the GF/11, an 11 GFLOPS system based

on 556 processors delivering 20 MFLOPS. These compute nodes were linked by a
nonblocking Beneš network and implemented a modified form of true SIMD parallelism. The machine was designed primarily for QCD calculations, though iwas
was later extended to support a number of other major scientific problems.

In April 1988, IBM signed a partnership agreement with Supercomputer Systems Inc. (cf. 7.3) for the development of new high-performance computers. As
part of this arrangement IBM will fund part of the development of SSI's new vector supercomputer and exchange technical information, although the final design
adopted by SSI will not necessarily be incorporated into future IBM machines. IBM
has over ten thousand such relationships in marketing and systems integration, and
aims to continue increasing this figure, so its support for SSI does not necessarily
signify a major commitment by the company.

In September 1990, IBM announced the ES/9000, a range of machines designed
to replace its existing 9370, 4381 and 3090 machines. The company now manufactures and markets a wide range of computer hardware and software from the
PS/2 and PS/1 personal computers, through mid-range business machines, the new
RISC System/6000 UNIX workstations, to the top-end ES/9000. Of these, only the
ES/9000 currently uses parallelism. Nevertheless, the introduction of the RS/6000
may have significant effects upon the low-end of the parallel computing industry
(cf. 11) and this same technology also forms the basis of a new parallel computer
being developed by IBM (cf. 8.3.6).

8.3.2   The ES/9000

The new ES/9000 machines are available in a variety of configurations, and are
intended to replace the IBM 9370, 4381 and 3090 series machines. All the ES/9000
range machines are built with the same basic architecture, and support the same
operating systems and other software, but there are three distinct species within
the series:

- Rack-mounted (successors to the 9370 range)

- Air-cooled (successors to the 4381)

- Water-cooled (successors to the 3090)

While all of the rack-mounted models are uniprocessors, the other models can
be configured with up to six processors, and implement the shared-memory MIMD
model of parallelism. The processor used in the ES/9000 range is based on bipolar
CMOS technology with up to 2600 ECL and DCS circuits per chip, and up to 549
connections per chip. Multiple chips sit in oil-filled thermal conduction modules
constructed using an aluminium heat-sink with copper pistons.

Every machine in the air and water-cooled ranges can have an optional Vector Facility (VF) added to it. This raises the peak instantaneous execution rate for 64 bit floating point calculations to 138 MFLOPS (manufacturer's figures). This VF is a fully integrated extension of the scalar processor and does not operate independently. It can boost the overall throughput of each processor by three times, with higher speed-ups (up to eight) obtainable on vectorisable kernals. For the top-end Model 820 and Model 900 machines (which are due to be released in 1991), the processor technology will remain based on bipolar CMOS but with up to 5620 ECL and DCS circuits per chip. The thermal conduction modules will be made from glass-ceramic substrates providing 63 layers and 2772 pins per module. The new chips will have an advertised peak performance of over 400 MFLOPS, this is significantly more than the 333 MFLOPS of a single-pipe Cray Y-MP (cf. 7.1.2). In a multiprocessor configuration, any or all of the processors may have a Vector Facility installed; the operating system automatically handles asymmetric situations in which only some scalar processors have a VF.

The Model 820 and Model 900 ES/9000's with VF have four and six processors respectively. The peak instantaneous execution rate of the six CPU ES/9000 Model 900 VF is described by IBM as "likely to be about 2.5 GFLOPS." A further increase in performance can be achieved by coupling two Model 900VF's via a HiPPI connection. This link can run at rates of up to 100 Mbyte/s and gives the capability to produce a machine with 12 parallel streams. However when the HiPPI link is in operation one processor at each end of the link must be dedicated to its supervision, thus reducung the number of processors available for calculation. Such a coupled configuration is advertised as having a peak instantaneous performance of about 5 GFLOPS. While a 12 processor system is currently in operation at Cornell University there are no benchmark figures available to support these performance figures; however, the company claim that for suitable applications (i.e. ones in which communication time is negligible) the machine has produced speedup of nearly twelve times over a single-processor configuration.

A sample multiprocessor ES/9000 models is shown in Table 8.4, while Figure 8.2 shows the basic architecture of these machines. The water-cooled models are constructed using one or two "sides". Each side can have up to three tightly coupled processors under the control of a System Control Element. Machines with two or three processors in a single side are described as "dyadic" and "triadic". Two sides may then be coupled together to form the four or six processor configurations. Communication between processors in the same side of the machine runs at a different speeed from that between the two sides, as can be seen from Figure 8.2. (For exact figures see Company Summary 25.)

The memory on both sides of the machines is shared by all processors, allowing the system to appear as a seamless multiprocessor. Other processor combinations are logically possible but not currently available in the ES/9000 range. (For ex-

Table 8.4: IBM ES/9000 Models

Model	No. CPUs	Cooling	Max. Memory (Mbyte)	Peak Rate (MFLOPS)
440 VF	2	Air	1024	~ 250
480 VF	2	Air	1024	266
500 VF	2	Water	2304	276
580 VF	3	Water	2304	414
620 VF	4	Water	4608	552
720 VF	6	Water	4608	828
820 VF	4	Water	9216	~ 1600
900 VF	6	Water	9216	~ 2400

ample, in the old IBM 3090 series there were two distinct two processor models. One, the 3090 Model 200, had a single dyadic side, while the 3090 Model 280 had two sides with a single processor each. The significant difference between the two models was that a two sided machine could be physically partitioned and the sides operated independently.) I/O for the ES/9000 is controlled by a specialised Channel Processor. This device can support up to 256 multiple independant ES-COM channels. These are based on fibre-optic technology and can achieve up to 10 Mbyte/s over distances up to 9 km.

There are at the moment few figures available to reveal the efficiency of the parallelism available from the IBM ES/9000 machines. However the 3090 series was rigourously analysed using the LINPACK benchmarks by Jack Dongarra at Argonne National Laboratory. The results showed a good increase in performance as the number of CPUs was increased (Table 8.5). It is clear that with the small number of processors in this machine communication delays do not appear to be a significant problem, at least for some classes of computation. IBM obviously hope that this will remain true for the ES/9000.

Table 8.5: LINPACK Benchmarks on Multiprocessor IBM 3090

Model	No. CPUs	Speedup	Efficiency
200S VF	2	1.99	0.99
300S VF	3	2.96	0.99
400S VF	4	3.85	0.96
500S VF	5	4.78	0.96
600S VF	6	5.64	0.94

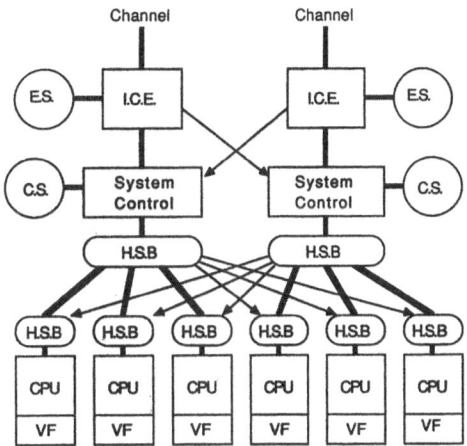

I.C.E.: Interconnect Communication Element
H.S.B.: High Speed Buffer
C.S.:   Central Storage
E.S.:   Expanded Storage
VF: Vector Facility
━━━ : Data/Control
──▶ : Data Flow

Figure 8.2: A Schematic Diagram of the IBM ES/9000

8.3.3   Operating Systems

IBM supports three operating systems on the ES/9000: MVS, VM/CMS and
AIX/370. AIX/370 (AIX stands for Advanced Interactive eXecutive) is a mainframe UNIX-like operating system for IBM mainframes. However, it does not
currently support parallel processing on the ES/9000 series.

The other two operating systems do have facilities for parallel processing, and
much software is common to both MVS and VM/CMS; in particular, IBM's VS
Fortran Version 2 compiler (cf. 8.3.4) runs under both systems. While the user
interface is common across MVS and VM/CMS, the way in which the parallel
tasks are created and viewed by the operating system is very different.

MVS

MVS is a virtual storage system which supports a timesharing system called TSO
together with a sophisticated batch capability. Each TSO user and batch job occupies a separate address space of up to 2 Gbyte and must consist of one or more
separately dispatchable tasks. A parallel Fortran application runs in a single address space but generates separate subtasks within that space. MVS maintains a
single priority ordered queue of all ready tasks from all address spaces, and has a
system resources manager which allows priority rules between address spaces to be

defined. There is no association between a task and a physical processor; whenever a processor becomes free (for example because the task current running on it executes an I/O operation and enters a wait state) MVS immediately dispatches the highest priority ready task from its queue to the processor. The only exception to this happens in incomplete Vector Facility configurations. In these cases, a task that uses vector operations will not be dispatched to a processor which does not have a Vector Facility.

VM/CMS

The central component of VM (Virtual Machine) is the Control Program (CP), which simulates a complete virtual hardware processor with memory, I/O devices etc. In principle, any operating system that can run on a real machine (such as MVS) can run on one of CP's virtual machines. VM has a timesharing component called CMS (Conversational Monitor System). Each CMS user runs in a separate Virtual Machine. The older releases of VM did not support parallel processing comfortably because the Fortran application environment ran within a single CMS virtual machine and was single threaded. With the arrival of VM/XA SP Release 1 a single Virtual Machine can be a simulation of a multiprocessor — that is, multiple virtual processors are allowed within a single virtual machine. The parallel Fortran compiler therefore maps the parallel threads onto separate Virtual CPUs within one Virtual Machine. The number of Virtual CPUs within a single Virtual Machine need not bear any relationship to the number of real CPUs available, and the CP manages the dispatching of all the competing tasks (virtual CPUs) under its control to the real processors at its disposal automatically.

8.3.4   Programming Languages

Parallel Fortran

Parallel Fortran is implemented by the IBM VS Fortran Version 2 Release 5 compiler (VSFV2.5). In earlier releases, the parallel functions in the standard compiler were limited to the relatively primitive Multi-Tasking Facility (MTF) which provided only subroutine-level parallelism. Synchronisation was limited to the main task waiting for all subtasks to complete. VSFV2.5, on the other hand, provides a set of parallel functions ranging from the automatic parallelisation of DO-loops to subroutine scheduling. Except for the automatic parallelisation of DO-loops, the parallel functions are implemented by means of language extensions. These generate threads of code which can run in parallel, either by being mapped into individual subtasks (in MVS), or onto a Virtual Processor (in VM/CMS).

As was discussed in Section 8.3.2, it is possible to connect two ES/9000s with either four or six processor each to create an eight or twelve processor machine. Fortran support for such a coupled system is provided by the IBM "Clustered

Fortran" compiler. This is based on the VS Fortran Version 2 Compiler but is currently marketed as a separate product.

Other Software

The IBM Engineering and Scientific Subroutine Library (ESSL) provides a set of Fortran-callable mathematical subroutines. Its original *raison d'etre* was to provide vector performance on the IBM Vector Facility, so the compatible scalar library provided testing purposes was not optimised for high performance. Now, with Release 4, ESSL has been expanded to provide high-performance scalar, vector and parallel libraries. These include support for linear algebra, eigensystem analysis, Fourier transforms, sorting, interpolation, numerical quadrature and random number generation.

The ES/9000 does support programming languages other than Fortran, and standard sequential compilers are available for C, Pascal, Cobol and Ada amongst others. However, Fortran is the only language for which there is a parallelising compiler, although there is a possibility of a parallel C compiler being produced in the future.

8.3.5 The Market

1989 was not a good year for most computer companies. Over the last 25 years the information processing market has grown by approximately 15% per annum. However, in the past three years this has dropped to between 8% and 10%. IBM have not been immune to this recession and in 1989 their profits were only 70% of the 1988 levels. In order to combat this decline, IBM are currently reducing staffing levels and costs. They expect to shed 10,000 jobs in the US during 1990, and to cut the company's overheads by $1 G per year. IBM is also changing its balance of internal investment away from hardware and towards software, reflecting the growing demand for total solutions rather than just a computer. The company's investment in the software side of the market rose by 41% during 1989.

Since their entry into the scientific and technical computing market in 1985, IBM have been aggressively marketing their 3090 Vector Facility. They believe that the shared-memory supercomputing marketplace is dominated by Cray (cf. 7.1) and themselves, with small market shares going to CDC/ETA, Amdahl, Hitachi and NEC. In the lower end of the market IBM regard Convex (cf. 3.4) as the major competition for the smaller ES/9000 machines, as well as their own RS/6000 workstations.

In 1988 the number of IBM VF installations overtook those of Cray and have been growing faster ever since. Although IBM see this as giving them a lead in the market, when one concentrates specifically at the very high-performance scientific installations, Cray still remain the premier supplier. If the predicted performance of the new processors for the ES/9000 series machines becomes a reality, then this situation may well be reversed.

Since the release of the ES/9000 series in September 1990, sales have been steadily rising. There was little gap between the release and the first large sales since many regular IBM customers were waiting for the new machines specifically. The vast majority of these sales have been in the commercial field, in which most users are currently operating IBM machines or the IBM-compatibles produced by Amdahl, Hitachi and NEC. ES/9000 sales are expected to reach the thousand mark before the end of 1990, with technical and scientific sales accounting for no more than 100 installations. These will be going to a wide range of customers including universities, government research establishments and engineering firms such as Rolls Royce and British Aerospace.

8.3.6   The Future

IBM's System/6000 workstation technology is currently being exploited to develop an extension to the GF/11 project. It is anticipated that the new project, ALPS, will produce a machine operating at approximately 50 GFLOPS. The ALPS machine will contain an array of 512 such boards, each carrying two 25 MHz RISC System/6000 processors capable of 40-50 MFLOPS per processor. However, the project is in its initial stages and no information is currently available on the topologiess and communications methods likely to be used.

Company Summary 23: Features of the Vax 9000 Series

Source	Digital Equipment Corporation.
Type	Multiprocessor vector mainframe.
Availability	First available in 1990; 75 machines have been installed.
Price	£2.8 M for a fully configured 4-processor Vax 9000-440.
Processing nodes	From one to four Vax processors.
Processor technology	ECL gate arrays with a 200 ps switch time.
Memory	256 Mbyte and 512 Mbyte; 2 Gbyte in future.
Communications	2 Gbyte/s crossbar switch, with an $N-to-N$ topology.
I/O connections	Four XMI I/O buses included on Vax 9000-430/440. Up to 14 VAXBI channels available. Maximum throughput 320 Mbyte/s.
Performance	Scalar: 40.0 MIPS per processor Vector: Peak 125 MFLOPS per vector processor; up to four vector processors in a Vax 9000-440.
Host system	None
Operating system	Vax/VMS or Ultrix (on Vax 9000-210/410/420 only).
Programming languages	C, Fortran, Pascal, BASIC, Bliss, PL/I, Ada, Cobol and assembly language. The Fortran Compiler can perform automatic parallelisation. Debugging, performance analysis and coverage analysis tools are available.
Physical configuration	(Vax 9000-440) Two CPU cabinets $36'' \times 29'' \times 72''$, System Control Unit and Memory $26'' \times 29'' \times 72''$, two XMI Cabinets $29'' \times 29'' \times 72''$, VAXBI Cabinet $29'' \times 29'' \times 60''$, two Utility Port Conditioner Cabinets $45'' \times 29'' \times 60''$.
Power requirements	On a 208 V 50/60 Hz supply with 100 amp/phase per circuit, a Vax 9000-440 will draw 51 amp/phase on each of two circuits.
Sources	Information supplied by DEC, discussions with DEC staff and users.

Company Summary 24: Features of the Fujitsu AP-1000 Array Processor

Source	Fujitsu Europe Ltd.
Type	Massively parallel MIMD supercomputer.
Availability	Not commercially available.
Price	N.A.
Processing nodes	1024.
Processor technology	SPARC processor (25 MHz), plus 12.5 MFLOPS FPU.
Memory	16 Mbyte RAM, 128 kbyte cache.
Communications	25 Mbyte/s point-to-point torus network, 50 Mbyte/s broadcast network, 40-event signal network.
I/O connections	LBUS interface provided on each processor.
Performance	Approximately 3 GFLOPS (estimated).
Host system	Sun-4 with VME interface and 32 Mbyte RAM.
Operating system	Light-weight Cell OS on each processor.
Programming languages	C and FORTRAN with function libraries.
Physical configuration	Unknown.
Power requirements	Unknown.
Sources	USENET articles, Fujitsu brochures, material provided by Fujitsu staff.

Company Summary 25: Features of the IBM ES/9000

Source	IBM Corporation.
Type	Shared memory MIMD parallel computer.
Availability	Introduced in September 1990; top-of-the-range models not available until 1991.
Price	Single processors 320VF: £1.2 M Six processor 900VF: £5-6 M
Processing nodes	From one to six processors; these may be connected to form single compute resources with more nodes.
Processors	Custom silicon VLSI chips stacked in Thermal Conduction Modules consisting of multiple glass-ceramic substrates.
Memory	Up to 9.2 Gbyte.
Communications	Data and control buses within each side of the machine; additional data buses between processors on different sides. A HiPPI interface is available between complete units.
I/O connections	Up to 256 independent parallel ESCOM channels per Channel Processor. Each channel uses fibre-optic technology to achieve up to 10 Mbyte/s.
Performance	Approximately 2.4 GFLOPS for the six processor machine (predicted).
Host system	None.
Operating system	MVS and VM/CMS (proprietary IBM operating systems) support parallel processing on the ES/9000. AIX, a UNIX-like operating system, is also available, but does not support parallelism yet.
Programming languages	Parallel Fortran and sequential C, Pascal, Cobol and Ada.
Physical configuration	Base frame $32'' \times 65'' \times 80''$ weighing 840 kg, with an expansion frame of $32'' \times 42'' \times 75''$ weighing 650 kg.
Power dissipation	From 40 W for the 340VF model to 170 W for the 900VF.

Sources   Publicly available material plus discussions with IBM
                           staff.

Chapter 9

Software: Efficiency vs. Portability?

Computers by themselves are nothing more than expensive room heaters; what makes them valuable is the software that runs on them. Unfortunately, robust, machine-independent software environments for parallel computers have been notable to date primarily by their absence. While many groups are working toward compilers which will automatically parallelise programs, others have concentrated their efforts on producing systems which will let users write programs which can run on a wide range of parallel platforms. In this chapter we discuss four such systems and try to evaluate their strengths and weaknesses.

9.1 Express

Company Parasoft Corporation

Relevant Activities Supply and support the Express parallel programming environment.

Location 27415 Trabuco Circle, Mission Viejo, California 92692, USA. Telephone: (714) 380 9739. Fax: (714) 458 7557

Relevant Officers Adam Kolawa, President; John Flower, Vice-President; Larry Lesser, Sales and Marketing Manager.

Employees 5.

Financial details Privately held corporation; total capitalisation unknown.

9.1.1 The Express Family of Products

Express is a generic name used to cover a family of products related to distributed memory MIMD computing, one of which is the Express Communication Environment. Together, these products form a consistent programming environment which provides the functionality required in real applications.

Express is very portable and currently runs on NCUBE and Intel iPSC2 or iPSC/860 hypercubes (Section 4.1.2), transputer-based machines, and a variety of i860 systems. There is also a Workstation Express which allows a network of machines to function as a parallel computer. This currently runs on Sun, DEC and IBM RS/6000 workstations.

The product family includes the following[1]:

- The Express Communication Environment

- Cubix – a set of parallel input/output routines

- Plotix – a simple graphics system

- PM – a multiprocessor profiling system

- Ndb – a multiprocessor debugger

- MAPV – a data dependency analyser for sequential programs

- Aspar – a parallelisation tool

---

[1] Aspar and Mapv are due to be released in November 1990

9.1.2 History and Philosophy

As applications were being developed for the various hypercubes at CalTech's Concurrent Computation Program in the 1980s, programmers noticed that large sections of existing applications could be copied wholesale into new applications. These sections contained all the involved code to handle interprocessor communication and I/O through the operating system of the host computer. All that needed to be written in the new application was the program that performed the actual computations.

Express was developed as an environment to free programmers from the messy details of the parallel machine. Express does not claim to be an operating system, merely a set of tools, but it offers a consistent user model, and does the simple things that most programmers want to do easily and relatively efficiently. It accomplishes this by placing one copy of the user's single, sequential program on each of the available computing nodes, and dividing data between these nodes. This quasi-SIMD approach helps give the programmer the impression that he or she is working with a sequential machine.

Programs written on top of Express do not tend to contain a heterogeneous mix of tasks, such as a master, several workers, and a graphics task. Instead, there is usually a single type which accesses the file and graphics systems via generic servers which are part of Express. All tasks tend to be equal; each works on a different part of the application's data, and communicates with other tasks via an interface which handles replication and any necessary synchronisation.

9.1.3 Express

The Express Communications System (cf. Appendix A.2) provides both synchronous and asynchronous message passing services, with both blocking and non-blocking read and write functions (although not with all possible combinations) between an arbitrary number of processors connected in an arbitrary topology. Messages are sent to processors, which are labelled with unique numeric identifiers. It is possible to run more than one task per processor, but they are not addressed separately. Messages are labelled with a type, which can be used to differentiate between them at their destination.

Express provides more than the basic message passing system functionality. It supports broadcast, multicast and combine operations, and provides for global synchronisation between tasks. In addition, it performs a range of functions which are more complex, and also very useful. A simple example of this "added value" is the **exchange** function which simultaneously sends a message to one task and receives another message from it or from some other task. Such exchanges are frequently used in problems involving boundary value exchanges. Another example is the **exvchange** function. This performs the same function as **exchange**, but can build up a message from non-contiguous memory with a constant stride. This means that it can select one row or column of a multidimensional matrix, such as fred[x][5], where x varies between 0 and the array size.

Express provides direct support for grid-based applications programs via its exgrid utilities. These manage the decomposition of a Cartesian grid in N dimensions across the hardware of a multicomputer. The grid is decomposed into subgrids, and each subgrid is mapped to a different task. Express provides functions to translate between task identifier and Cartesian grid coordinates and vice-versa. It also provides functions to swap grid points across block boundaries in a given direction and a given dimension. The use of these functions is illustrated in the following example:

```
#include "express.h"
#define HORIZ 0
#define VERT 1
#define TYPE 33
#define BUFLEN 128
{
    int npr[2];
    char ibuf[BUFLEN], obuf[BUFLEN];
    struct nodenv nodedata;

    exparam(&nodedata);
    if ((nodedata.nprocs % 4) != 0) exit(1);

    npr[HORIZ] = nodedata.nprocs/2;
    npr[VERT]  = 4;

    exgridinit(2,nprocs);
    upnode   = exgridnode(nodedata.procnum, VERT,  1);
    downnode = exgridnode(nodedata.procnum, VERT, -1);
    exchange(ibuf, BUFLEN, upnode, type,
          obuf, BUFLEN, downnode, type);
}
```

Express provides the necessary setup calls to run tasks, replicated one to a processor, in parallel across a number of processors. When the above code runs, the call to exparam() puts the identifier of the task and the number of tasks into nodedata. Assuming this is divisible by four, each task then calls exgridinit to say that it wishes to be considered as part of a $4 \times nprocs/4$ array of tasks, and then exgridnode twice to find out who two of its neighbours are. Each task then exchanges messages across the boundaries of the decomposition, putting its obuf into its neighbour's ibuf.

9.1.4 Cubix and Plotix

Other things that many applications want to do are handle files and communicate with keyboard and screen. These operations are handled by Express's Cubix I/O routines in a way that maintains the illusion of sequential programming. This is done by allowing processors to read and write only those parts of a file which correspond to data which they have been assigned. The Plotix graphics system works in a similar way, allowing processors to build up only the parts of the image corresponding to their data.

Cubix provides three different ways in which the filing system can be referenced. These are best illustrated using the three different write operations:

- fsingle: All the tasks make a call to write, but only one record appears in the file.

- fmulti: All the tasks make a call to write, and a record appears in the file from each of them in a well defined order.

- fasync: Any task can make a call to write, and the output appears in the file in any order. In the case of formatted write the records can be intermingled.

fsingle is useful for parts of programs which are reading and writing file headers, for example. fmulti, on the other hand, is useful for parts of programs which read and write distributed data structures; this is frequently done when a program's state is dumped or restored. fasync is used in programs which consist of completely independent tasks writing to independent files, or for error reporting where an error may not occur on every processor.

Apart from the above extensions Cubix looks and feels like a native operating system. For example, consider the following C fragment:

```c
#include <stdio.h>
main()
{
    struct nodenv nodedata;

    exparam(&nodedata);
    fsingle(stdout);
    printf("Hello Worlds\n")
    fmulti(stdout);
    printf("I am processor %d\n", nodedata.procnum);
}
```

If this is run on four processors it produces the output:

```
Hello Worlds
I am processor 0
I am processor 1
I am processor 2
I am processor 3
```

The above shows the default order in which processors read and write records. This can be reset by **forder**. Note that the requirement that all tasks, rather than a subset, output a record means that dumping multidimensionally decomposed data structures using a certain number of processors, and rereading that data using a different number of processors (i.e. from a different size of hypercube) is not straightforward.

9.1.5   Other Utilities

Ndb and PM are parallel equivalents of traditional tools available on sequential computers. Ndb allows simultaneous debugging of a network of processors. This is not particularly useful in large systems because of the flood of data it generates, but can be used effectively when prototyping code on a small number of processors. PM shows processor utilisation, interprocessor communication bandwidth utilisation, and timings of message transfers. This performance monitor works *post mortem* — it stores up performance statistics and re-plays them at some later date. The reason for this is that many parallel programs suffer significantly from the so-called Heisenberg effect: the very act of monitoring a parallel program can change its qualitative behaviour. By concentrating on *post mortem* monitoring, Parasoft have been able to minimise the disruption caused by their monitoring software.

Aspar and Mapv are tools which help to automate the generation of programs to run under Express. They analyse dependencies in sequential programs and try to insert appropriate calls to Express and Cubix. Naturally this will only work if the program is capable of being subdivided in the way that Cubix and Express require, but for the majority of scientific applications so far parallelised, this appears to be the case.

9.2 Helios

Company Perihelion Software Ltd.

Relevant Activities Producers of the Helios distributed operating system.

Location The Maltings, Charlton Road, Shepton Mallet, Somerset, BA4 5QE. Telephone: 0749 4203.

Relevant Officers Tim King and Jack Lang, Founders and directors; Jessica King, Director.

Employees 22.

Financial details Privately financed.

9.2.1 Perihelion and Helios

Helios is a UNIX-like distributed operating system for transputer systems developed by Perihelion Software Ltd. The Perihelion Group was founded in 1987 by Tim King and Jack Lang, and initially consisted of Perihelion Software and Perihelion Hardware. The hardware company ceased trading after the unsuccessful Atari Transputer Workstation (ATW) project. However, because the software company was an independent entity within the Perihelion Group it was unaffected by the failure of Perihelion Hardware. Perihelion Software have associations with Distributed Systems Ltd (DSL) who are the UK distributers of Helios. Part of the development effort for Helios has been taken on by Parsytec (cf. 5.5) who have produced the Helios file system.

9.2.2 The Helios Model

Helios is system which at the surface looks like UNIX but has extensions to allow users to make use of the parallel resource upon which it is running. The Helios file system uses a similar format to the UNIX file system, and the Helios shell is similar to the UNIX C shell, although a little idiosyncratic (particularly when shell programming is attempted). Helios uses the POSIX standard for UNIX and its libraries, and contains many of the standard UNIX utilities. The Helios system is not tied to any one transputer manufacturer's equipment and at the moment runs on systems supplied by Parsytec, Transtech, Meiko, Telmat Informatique, and Inmos (5.1). When running on Sun-hosted transputer systems Helios makes use of the windowing environment to provide a graphical interface to applications running on the transputers. The Sun can also be used as a gateway onto a local area network.

The purpose of Helios is to run user jobs on the transputer network, control access to system resources (such as disc, screen, keyboard, and mouse), and to provide an interactive environment for the user. Processes created as a result of running user jobs by Helios are real transputer processes. They are said to be sympathetic to the transputer architecture since they incur no extra timeslicing and context switching overheads.

Helios is fault tolerant to a degree since messages have a time-out period attached. If a response is not received within the time-out period the message is resent. After a number of retries, an alternate route to the intended receiver is used in an attempt to avoid a dead link.

Helios is based on the client-server model, in which resources are controlled by servers which respond to requests for resources from clients. The system servers are distributed throughout the transputer network, which allows many requests to be dealt with locally, however these requests may result in message passing at the Helios kernel level. A request to print a string on a screen made on a node without console access will result in the string being sent through the network, at the kernel level, to a node attached to the console. The default action is for client's requests to be delivered to servers on the local transputer. However the client can over-ride this and specify that a request goes to a specific server.

A set of libraries are supplied with Helios to allow users to write their own client and server programs.

9.2.3   The Helios Network

The physical connectivity of the transputers and the resources available to the system is described by a resource map which is used to boot the network with the Helios kernel:

```
subnet NetA {
    subnet Cluster1 {
        terminal 00; ~01, , ,~02;         T414, Helios, SCSI;
        terminal 01;    ,NetA/Cluster2/00, ~00, ;
                                          T414,Helios,bit_display;
        terminal 02;    , ~00, , ;        T800, Helios;
    }
    subnet Cluster2 {
        terminal 00;  , NetA/Cluster1/01, ~01, ;
                                          T800, Helios, console;
        terminal 01; ~00, , , ;           T800, Helios;
    }
}
```

This example defines a Helios network with two clusters of processors. The first contains a T414 with a SCSI disc attached, a T414 with a bit-mapped screen, and a T800, while the other contains two T800s one of which has a console connection. The physical connectivity of the transputers is specified in the map e.g.

```
, NetA/Cluster2/00, ~00,
```

defines that link 0 is unused, link 1 connects to transputer 00 in Cluster2, link 3 connects with transputer 00, and link 4 is unused. A network manager controls and monitors the network of transputers and is responsible for detecting dead transputers and then attempting to re-boot them. It also manages the load balancing of tasks.

Two separate Helios networks can be joined to produce a larger parallel machine simply by telling one Helios network that the other exists and through which transputer link it can communicate with it. This assumes a physical connection between the networks. The join information is specified in another resource map. As an example consider, an ATW with four transputers running Helios and a PC with five transputers also running Helios. The systems can be used independently or can be joined to produce one Helios system with nine transputers and all the resources of both. Performing a network join introduces a higher level in the naming hierarchy which has the joined networks as sub-systems, e.g. if the top-level name is **top** then:

```
prompt> ls /top
ATW PC_Name
prompt> ls /top/ATW
Cluster1 Cluster2
prompt> ls /top/ATW/Cluster1
00 01 02
prompt>
```

The host computer runs the Helios I/O server, which provides an interface between the host's resources and the transputer network. The I/O server provides access to the disk filing system of the host and its terminal display facilities. In theory all that is required to port Helios to a transputer system is to get the I/O server running on the host.

The naming convention in Helios is hierarchical and covers the network resources, processors, running tasks, and filing systems. At the top of the hierarchy is the network name. Below this is the I/O server and the clusters of processors which contain the numbered processors. The disk filing system of the host computer is accessed through the IO subdirectory of the network. If a client program wants to send a message to a particular server on processor 01 in a particular cluster in a particular network, it should address the message to: **/NetworkA/Cluster5/01/server**.

However an address of /server would address the message to the nearest server. The location of the nearest server is determined at run-time by a distributed search in an ink blot fashion.

All resources appear in the naming hierarchy. For example, programs resident in memory on the local transputer appear in the loader directory /loader while running tasks appear in the /tasks directory. In order to kill a task you must 'remove' it from the /tasks directory. Once networks have been joined the file systems attached to each are globally accessible, however a network name must be used to address a remote file, e.g. if the shell is running on NetB then to edit a file on NetA the command ue /top/NetA/IO/usr2/joe/file would be used.

The transputers in the system which are running Helios are each booted with a Helios kernel which provides memory management and message passing. Each transputer also runs two system servers, the loader and the process manager. The loader is responsible for loading and unloading user and system modules on demand, and the process manager is responsible for process creation on its processor. The loader unloads commands once they have terminated in order to make available the memory used, but the cache command can be used to keep programs resident in memory. Part of the transputer memory can be used as a RAM disc to store commonly used files, which reduces the network traffic and access for these files.

Not all of the transputers in the network need to run Helios. Some can be declared as running 'native', and in which case their links are not used for Helios communication. These transputers can still communicate with Helios using a private message protocol to a link managing server. The 'native' transputer runs non-Helios code (generally Occam), which is useful in situations where performance is important or there isn't enough memory to run a Helios kernel.

9.2.4   Helios Programming Environment

Helios comes with various tools to help with program development, and a graphical interface is provided through the X Windows system (assuming that the transputer system has a graphics subsystem attached). The source level debugger can debug programs which are running on separate processors and can individually analyze the multiple threads within these programs. If the Helios/Sun system is being used then the debug information for the processes can be displayed in separate Sunview windows.

The individual programs which make-up a task are separately compiled and can be written in: C, Fortran (supplied by Topexpress and Meiko), Modula 2 (Rowley), and Pascal (Prospero). In addition to these compiled languages the STRAND[88] (9.4) system runs under Helios. Programs communicate through UNIX-like streams. To read a message the program inputs from a stream and to send a message it outputs to a stream. The system takes care of connecting the various streams together so that the messages are delivered to the correct processor. These streams are not quite standard, and must be manipulated by non-ANSI library commands such as fdopen().

The Topexpress maths and vector libraries are available and contain efficient code for commonly used routines for matrix calculations, Fast Fourier Transforms, sorting, curve fitting, and various vector calculations. As an example of the efficiency of their code, Topexpress give figures comparing the performance of Fortran compiled code and their library code for a vector multiply operation. The Fortran compiled code achieves a performance of 180 kFLOPS while the library routine gets 650 kFLOPS from the transputer (This was for a T800-20 with 4 cycle memory and operand and result vectors stored off chip).

Having written the individual programs which make-up the task, the next step is to specify how the component programs are to be distributed. This is done by specifying a task force from either the Helios shell using some basic constructs, or for more complicated examples in a Component Distribution Language (CDL) specification. One of the task force specifiers is the pipe, |, construct, using this a simple pipeline can be specified at the shell level, for example with the command prog1 | prog2 | prog3 which is passed onto a server called the task force manager (TFM) which then assigns the programs to processors and ensures that the correct communication streams are joined together. The system attempts to do some load balancing and so will distribute tasks so as to minimise the multi-tasking on each processor.

A CDL script which contains the definitions of system components and their inter-relationships, is compiled to produce a CDL object file which is used by the TFM to schedule the tasks onto processors. CDL components are abstract entities whose attributes define their behaviour and needs. Some examples of these attributes are code (the name of the separately compiled program that is to be executed); processor (the type of processor which the code must run on); and memory (the minimum memory requirement for the code). Defined below is a component, widget1 which has the code Cprogram attached and must run on a T800 with at least 1Mbyte of memory available.

```
component widget1
{
        code Cprogram;
        processor T800;
        memory 1000000;
}
```

Components can also contain the definition of their communication streams.

```
component widget2[i]
{
        code PipeElement;
        streams <| pipe{i}, >| pipe{i+1};
}
```

This example defines a subscripted component which reads from pipe{i} and writes to pipe{i+1}. Subscripting allows multiple usage of the same component description to replicate the functionality while retaining a 'handle' on the individual components and their attributes.

The relationships between the components in a system are described in terms of four primitives which are based on Hoare's CSP model. The first primitive is the pipe relationship, A|B, which specifies that the input of B is the output of A. The second primitive is the bi-directional pipe, A<>B, which specifies a two way communication link between A and B. The third primitive is the general parallel constructor, A^^B, which specifies that A and B are to run in parallel with no default communication between them. The last primitive is the task farm, A [n] ||| B which specifies that component A's output is interleaved between the n workers B. The use of replicators, as in the task farm example, allows multiple use of components to be specified neatly.

Communication connections between components through streams can be explicitly defined through the stream attribute of components as in the widget2 example declared above.

```
widget2{0} ^^ widget2{1} ^^ widget2{2}
```

or by default through the use of the pipe, bi-directional pipe, and task farm primitives:

```
widget1 | widget1 | widget1
```

A stream must have a reader and a writer and so the widget2 example above is incomplete since there is no writer defined for pipe{0} and no reader for pipe{2}.

Using component definitions and the CDL primitives complicated systems can be defined, such as:

```
master | (||| [4] worker ) | ResultsCollector
```

This defines a task farm where master distributes work amongst the four worker processes who write to a stream read by the program ResultsCollector. A more complicated example in which a 3 × 3 grid of programs which communicate with their neighbours to the right and below is:

```
component mult[i,j]
{
        code gridProg;
        streams <| across{i,j}, >| across{i,j+1},
                <| down{i,j},   >| down{i+1,j};
}


^^ [i<3,j<3] mult{i,j}
```

9.2.5 Helios as an Environment

It is Perihelion's intention that Helios should provide an interface to parallel hard-ware, specifically transputers, that is familiar to users of the UNIX operating system, and yet allow then to write parallel programs to achieve the processing power available to the system. However Helios does have problems caused by its similarity to UNIX since it is not exactly UNIX-like. There are differences in the commands available and facilities supported, which which make it annoying to an experienced UNIX user. Some of these deficiencies are caused by the lack of sophistication of the transputer and so are unavoidable.

9.2.6 The Market for Helios

Perihelion consider the UNIX similarity of Helios to be its most attractive feature. Parsytec (5.5) see the need for such a system and have been heavily involved with the development of Helios. Perihelion consider the export market to be very important, particularly in Western Europe. The sales are split with 80% in Europe and the remaining 20% in the rest of the world. The expected turnover for 1990 is £1 M.

9.3   Linda

Linda is a generative communication paradigm, developed by David Gelernter and colleagues in the Department of Computer Science at Yale University. The fundamental concept in Linda is the *tuple space*, an associative object store, populated by vectors of typed fields — *tuples*. There are two types of tuple in tuple space: *passive* tuples (data) and *active* tuples (processes) which will become passive tuples on completion of execution.

Passive tuples are sequences of one or more typed fields. Each field has either an *actual* value or a *formal* pattern-matching value. Tuples are anonymous — they are neither owned by, nor considered to have originated from, a particular process or processor. Tuple space can contain several identical tuples.

Tuple space is an associative memory; unlike conventional memories, in which objects are accessed through the address at which they are stored, tuples in tuple space are accessed by pattern-matching on the values of their fields. Two tuples match if and only if they have the same name and number of arguments, and each pair of corresponding fields match. Two fields match if they have the same type and either they are both actuals with the same value, or one is an actual and one is a formal. A formal never matches another formal.

Linda is not a new language for parallel processing. Instead, Linda's operations are embedded in a sequential language to provide a dialect for parallel programming. Examples of tuples in C-Linda are ("foo"), (6, ?x, 9), (9, "fred"). Note the use of the ? prefix to denote a formal.

The tuple space abstraction has the following goals:

Simplicity. The operations on tuple space supported by Linda are intended to be sufficiently simple to be added to any existing programming language to produce a hybrid parallel language. Implementations of C-Linda and Fortran Linda are currently commercially available, and other implementations based on other host languages exist, including Ada, C++, Common Lisp, Modula-2, object-oriented languages, PostScript, Prolog and Scheme. Linda frees the programmer from issues of low-level message-passing or representation and manipulation of shared objects.

Portability. Linda aims to overcome the tremendous barrier to portability of parallel software caused by the great diversity of parallel hardware architectures by abstracting away from architectural details to provide a virtual parallel machine. Linda implementations exist for a large number of both shared memory machines, for example the Encore Multimax (Section 3.5.2), Sequent Balance and Symmetry (3.7.2) and the Alliant FX/8 (3.1.2). Distributed memory multicomputers supported include the Intel iPSC (4.1.2), the AT&T S/Net and the Meiko Computing Surface (5.3.2). Linda has also been implemented on clustered Vaxes and local area networks of workstations.

Scalability. Part of the abstraction away from architectural details is that Linda programs should be scalable – that is, programmers should not have to modify their programs in order to have them run on a different number of processors, nor should they have to rewrite parts of the program if they wish to increase the number of processes cooperating to perform the computation. This is achieved by decoupling processes through the tuple space.

9.3.1 Linda operations

Linda provides six operations on the tuple space to support interprocess communication, shared data structures and process creation.

out(*t*)

A process adds a passive tuple *t* to the tuple space using out(*t*). All the fields of the tuple are evaluated prior to the tuple being added to tuple space. Formals (host language variables) may occur in tuple fields.

The anonymity of tuples ensures that any subsequent matches with such a formal will have no effect on the corresponding variable in the process which out()ed the tuple. Hence formals in out()ed tuples are essentially place holders, or "don't care" values. Formals in out()ed tuples can be used to prevent some matches, since only templates[2] with an actual in the corresponding field will match.

in(*s*)

in(*s*) causes precisely one tuple *t* which matches the template *s* to be withdrawn from the tuple space. If there is not matching tuple in tuple space when in(*s*) is executed, the in()ing process is blocked until one becomes available. Any formals in *s* have the corresponding values from *t* assigned to them during the match. By using host language variables as formals in the template, the in()ing process can import data from the tuple space.

Simple message passing between two processes can be implemented by out() and in(). The sender executes out(destination, message) and the receiver executes in(destination, ?message).

rd(*s*)

rd(*s*) is similar to in(*s*), except that instead of removing the matching tuple from the tuple space, a copy is made to instantiate formals in *s*. Like in(*s*), rd(*s*) blocks until a matching tuple is available.

---

[2]Template is the term used for a tuple argument of an in(), rd(), inp() and rdp() operation. This convention is to distinguish between the tuple argument and the tuples in tuple space.

inp(*s*) and rdp(*s*)

inp(*s*) and rdp(*s*) are the predicate forms of in(*s*) and rd(*s*) respectively. They behave similarly to their namesakes, but if no matching tuple is available these predicate operations immediately return failure rather than waiting for a matching tuple to become available.

eval()

eval() allows active tuples to be added to tuple space. eval() is similar to out() except that the tuple's fields are evaluated *after* it is added to the tuple space rather than before. This evaluation implies the creation of a process to evaluate each of the tuple's fields. When all the fields have been evaluated, the eval()ed tuple becomes a passive tuple comprising the evaluated fields.

For example, eval("foo", 3+6, 4*5) will eventually result in a tuple ("foo", 9, 20) in tuple space.

9.3.2   Linda Examples

Two simple examples of how Linda can be used are presented below.

Client-Server

In the client-server model, a server process provides a service to a number of client processes. The server accepts requests for this service from the client processes, and performs the requested service. If the service returns a result (as we assume here) the server then returns the result to the client process Figure 9.1 shows how this might be implemented using Linda.

When a client wishes to use a remote service, it out()s a request tuple labelled with some unique id. The client immediately in()s the corresponding result tuple, blocking until such a tuple becomes available. The server repeatedly in()s request tuples, processes the data contained to derive results, and out()s the results. Result tuples contain the identifier from the request to ensure that clients receive the correct results. Importantly, additional servers could be added without modifying any of the existing processes. This transparency is one benefit of the tuple space abstraction.

Task Farm

The task farm is a popular model for parallel software. A source process generates tasks which are performed by a number of worker processes. The (partial) results produced by the worker processes are combined by a sink process to obtain the final result. In many cases, the source and sink processes are combined in a single master

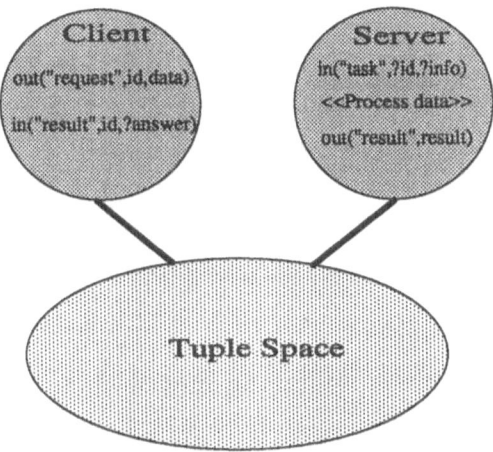

Figure 9.1: The Client-Server model in Linda

process. The task farm is the inverse of the client-server model, with one client process (the master) and many servers (the workers). A Linda implementation of a task farm is shown in Figure 9.2. The source process places a number of task tuples in tuple space. These tuples contain only data to be processed, and are not directed at specific worker processes.

Each worker repeatedly in()s a task tuple, processes the data it contains and out()s a result tuple containing the result. The sink process in()s these result tuples and merges them to obtain the result.

One attraction of the task farm model is its ability to load balance itself. Even if tasks can involve widely differing amounts of computation, the decomposition of the problem into a large enough number of tasks will ensure that all workers will be equally busy. While one worker is struggling with a single large task, its colleagues can deal with a large number of simpler tasks.

9.3.3 The Future

Linda has been used in a wide range of applications by the Yale group and others. These include matrix calculations, parallel database searchers for DNA sequence comparison, and lattice process models, as well as a number of more novel projects, such as intensive-care patient monitoring.

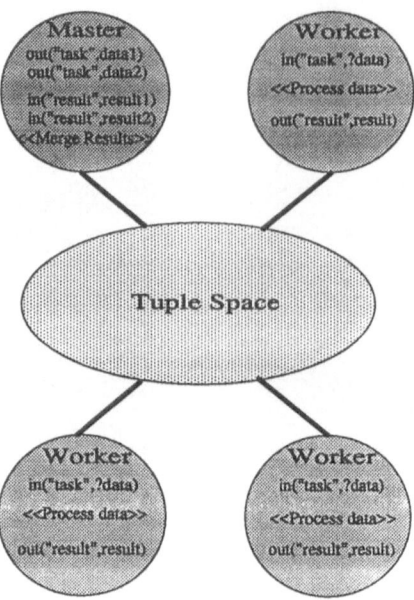

Figure 9.2: The Task Farm in Linda

Debugging and profiling tools are available for Linda programs. These visualise a Linda program in execution through a graphical representation of tuple space, and allow the user to interact with the program by performing Linda operations on the tuple space directly.

Linda, like any high-level abstraction, imposes an overhead compared to parallel programs written with lower-level message passing. Precompiler technology which analyses patterns of tuple space usage and generates message-passing calls to implement the Linda operations results in code of acceptable efficiency for most applications. However, some applications will always require the highest level of performance which can only be achieved by low-level programming. For the remainder and as a prototyping environment, Linda has much to offer.

Linda is attracting significant commercial interest. Scientific Computing Associates of New Haven, Connecticut, are marketing C-Linda implementations for a wide range of machines. Apple are actively researching Linda systems for local area networks. Cogent Research have developed a transputer-based workstation with an operating system built on top of their "Kernel Linda" (cf. 6.1.3). Hewlett-Packard have announced plans to support C-Linda on their workstation ranges.

9.4 STRAND$_-^{88}$

Software Developer Strand Software Technologies Limited

Relevant Activities Supply and support of STRAND$_-^{88}$

Location Strand Software Technologies Ltd., Greycaine Road, Watford, WD2 4JP, UK. Telephone: 0923 247707.

Relevant Officers David Catton, Managing Director; Martin Gittens, Technical Director; Rick Barnes, Technical Director; Will Pickles, Technical Director.

Employees Four

Financial details Private Company. Total capitalisation undisclosed.

9.4.1 History

STRAND$_-^{88}$ is a programming system for multiprocessor computers, produced by Strand Software Technologies Limited (SSTL), who until September 1990 were a division of Artificial Intelligence Limited, a software company based in Watford. SSTL are now an independent company concentrating solely on the development and support of STRAND$_-^{88}$.

Artificial Intelligence Ltd distribute AI based software such as Prolog, Smalltalk and C++, and some knowledge based systems. AI Ltd. first became involved in parallelism around 1985 when they were approached by Intel to produce a parallel version of Lisp, this followed on from the parallel programming research by Dr. Stephen Taylor and Dr. Ian Foster [FOST], STRAND$_-^{88}$ eventually emerged from this work. The STRAND$_-^{88}$ design stresses portability and the re-use of existing sequential code. A rapid expansion of the facilities and aims of the original language lead to the first (Admiralty) release of STRAND$_-^{88}$ in 1989, in which the emphasis on STRAND$_-^{88}$ as a programming system became apparent. Since then STRAND$_-^{88}$ has been successfully implemented on a wide variety of multiple processor architectures with applications portable across all. STRAND$_-^{88}$ is described in detail book by Foster and Taylor [FOTA] which describes both basic and advanced programming methods. SSTL are now becoming involved in the production of software that runs with STRAND$_-^{88}$. For example, they have been working on versions of the NAG numerical routines as well as a seismic signal processing workbench. This seems to be a relatively new side to the company's production, and rapid increases in STRAND$_-^{88}$ based software are promised.

Artificial Intelligence Limited were awarded the 1989 British Computer Society Award for Technical Achievement for the development of STRAND$_-^{88}$, because of its technical innovation, practicality and commercial viability. In June 1990 the

second (Buckingham) release of STRAND⁸⁸ became publically available, and this
will be followed in the future with a third (Cleopatra) release.

9.4.2   Design

STRAND⁸⁸ is designed to allow a program written in the language to run efficiently
on single processor machines such as workstations as well as on a growing list
of both shared and distributed memory parallel machines. The key features of
STRAND⁸⁸ are:

Parallel Semantics

Existing languages can be extended so that they may execute on multiple processor
hardware through the addition of explicit constructs to handle synchronisation and
message-passing. This can often create a version of the language that is complex
and intricate. However STRAND⁸⁸ is based on a parallel model of execution,
just as the Occam language is based on the communicating sequential processes
(CSP) model developed by Hoare [HOAR]. This provides it with parallel semantics
that are founded on a strong theoretical base. Therefore all the concurrency, flow
of control and synchronisation is expressed in the program without the need for
understanding the hardware architecture or particular configuration. This is true
of almost all parallel systems, however STRAND⁸⁸ handles this distribution of work
dynamically, unlike, for example, Occam, which statically distributes the work.

Portability

STRAND⁸⁸ is specifically designed to allow the language itself, and applications
written in it, to migrate easily to the latest generation of hardware. The language
consists of STRAND⁸⁸ kernels, STRAND⁸⁸ system calls and user procedures. Compilation of STRAND⁸⁸ code produces modules which are executed on the Strand
Abstract Machine (SAM). The SAM itself is a C program which can be compiled on
any hardware with a C compiler. This is of obvious advantage to the programmer
since the migration can take place without re-writing or re-compiling the program,
subject to any incompatibilities that may already exist when running sequential C
programs on various machines. STRAND⁸⁸ is guaranteed to execute consistently
across all the supported hardware platforms (provided that the high level language
is consistent between these machines). This is made possible by the data flow synchronisation of processes which is unaffected by timing. SSTL now offer customers
a porting facility for STRAND⁸⁸ which allows users to transfer STRAND⁸⁸ onto
their own local hardware.

STRAND⁸⁸ is currently available on hardware platforms based around the most
popular processor types. It is now fully supported on a wide variety of hardware,
including Sun-3, Sun-4, Sony News workstations, Solbourne, 386 UNIX machines,

Intel iPSC/2 Hypercubes (including the latest i860 versions, cf. Section 4.1.2), Sequent Symmetry and Balance (3.7.2), Encore Multimax (3.5.2), Cogent XTM (6.1.2), MIPS workstations, Atari ATW transputer workstations, Parsytec (5.5.2) and Telmat SuperNode transputer machines and plug-in transputer boards for Sun and PCs from many suppliers. There are also STRAND^{88} prototypes running on the BBN TC2000 (3.2.2), NeXT and Meiko (5.3.2) machines, Apple Macintosh, and versions being developed for Cray (7.1.2 and 7.1.3), Hewlett-Packard, Apollo, NCUBE (4.2.2), DEC (for the 3100 and 5000 range of MIPS based products) and the IBM PS2 range.

At present there are no benchmarking figures comparing the performance of STRAND^{88} between these various machines. However the performance is certainly not uniform, and transputer based machines in particular produce a degraded performance relative to the other platforms. This is mainly caused by the inefficiency of running C on hardware that is not designed to take it.

It also runs under a variety of operating systems such as UNIX, NX, Express (9.1) and Helios (9.2).

Foreign Language Interface

One of the greatest barriers to the conversion of existing applications into parallel versions is the apparent need to re-write the programs to allow them to run on the new parallel architectures. Over the last thirty years millions of lines of sequential code have been written. These applications represent substantial initial and ongoing investment. A key feature of STRAND^{88}'s advertising is its foreign language interface. At present STRAND^{88} has interfaces for Fortran and C, although more are planned for the near future. The interface for both these languages seems fairly straightforward. The user defines new kernels in the foreign language, these are then added to the SAM and thus become extensions to the language itself. The claim is made that existing applications can be re-analysed, through functional and data decomposition, and a STRAND^{88} harness added, to allow the latent parallelism to be exploited. This is not a trivial task, and such re-analysis of existing code can be expensive, particularly in cases where the original code is unstructured. Much code does not lend itself to decomposition in the first place. SSTL provide no tools to help with this decomposition of existing code because such tools are still be too complex to produce.

An example of a simple STRAND$^{88}_-$/Fortran program which averages a list of integers is shown below. The first section of code is the Fortran routine which determines the average value of the list.

```
      REAL*8 FUNCTION f_ave_list (length,list_ar)
      INTEGER*4 list_ar(*),length,i,sum

      sum = 0
      DO 10,i=1,length
      sum = sum + list_ar(i)
10    CONTINUE
      f_ave_list = sum / length
      RETURN
      END
```

Next there is the STRAND[88] interface specifier which tells STRAND[88] to convert the list of integers into an integer array, and to expect a real result.

```
4113 body ave_vec f_ave_list (int[]?):real^ fortran
```

Below is a STRAND[88] module, called *example*, which makes the call to the Fortran code.

```
-compile(free).
-exports([ave/2]).

ave(A,B):-
ave_vec(A,B).
```

And finally an example of the above code running.

```
1> example:ave([1,2,34,56,23,11,9,70],Result)
[started 1]
[exited 1]
2> display_nl(Result)
25.75
```

9.4.3   Markets for STRAND[88]

Looking at the percentage share of program code in the world, we see that around 90% is written in Cobol and 5% in Fortran. The remaining 5% is made up of all the other languages. This is a strong indictment on the potential success of new languages. Why, therefore, should a new language like STRAND[88] become a commercial success when so many other languages have failed to impact the hold of Cobol and Fortran? Even C, which many regard as a new development due to its current surge in popularity, has been available for over fifteen years without making significant inroads into the computing marketplace.

The most important point to be made about STRAND^{88} is that it has been designed from the outset to describe execution on hardware with multiple processors. It therefore does not challenge the established sequential languages directly, since it is aimed at a problem which they were never designed to tackle. It is this distinction that provides the key to STRAND^{88}'s potential success in the marketplace. SSTL have identified five market sectors in which they aim to promote STRAND$^{88}_-$:

Academic Institutions:

The academic sector is one of the largest growth areas for parallel programming. Researchers frequently wish to try out new programming styles and to test new theories. The parallel semantics of STRAND^{88} are advertised as providing a sound base for these types of investigation, and STRAND^{88}'s availability on a wide range of hardware platforms gives most academic establishments immediate access to the language. The precise language specification of STRAND^{88} may attract theoriticians, and the language expressibility, support documentation and text books may also prove attractive towards the potential teaching of parallel programming. SSTL are therefore pushing the formalism of STRAND^{88} on the academic market.

Applied commercial research laboratories:

The commercial research sector is also interested in the potential of parallel programming. However, there is now a greater requirement for profitable research that will produce production code in the future. Therefore for this sector of the market, STRAND^{88} is advertised as being both portable and future-proofed as well as having the parallel semantics to attract the program writers.

Hardware manufacturers:

Assuming that a hardware manufacturer intends to provide its customers with multiple processor machines in order to satisfy their price/performance requirements, they are coming under increasing pressure to also provide the customer with a transitional route for their software. By encouraging the harnessing of sequential language applications now, hardware manufacturers can provide a feasible upgrade strategy for their present customer base, allowing the transfer to parallel implementation to be as painless as possible. SSTL is therefore active in selling STRAND^{88} to a variety of hardware manufacturers, and there is some evidence that once the language became available on one major supplier's hardware it became a requirement on that of any other serious competitor. A list of hardware manufacturers that support STRAND^{88} on their machines is given later. The list contains many leaders in the parallel hardware field, and it seems to be growing monthly.

Software houses:

Software houses face great difficulties as multiple processor hardware becomes increasingly prevalent. They already face problems in maintaining many different versions of their software for the vast array of available hardware. Add to this the complexity of even more hardware, now with multiple processors, upon which existing sequential applications do not run, and the software house's position becomes increasingly complicated and untenable. One answer to their problems would be the development of STRAND[88] harnesses in order to produce "future-proofed" multiple-language versions. These would execute on any hardware platforms on which STRAND[88] and the relevant other languages were available.

STRAND[88]'s portability and parallel semantics, together with the foreign language interface, are crucial factors in STRAND[88]'s potential success in this market sector. To date there is no software company producing programs that use STRAND[88] other than Artificial Intelligence Limited and SSTL, and they themselves are only just beginning to produce STRAND[88] based software packages such a those mentioned in Section 9.4.1.

Application developers:

This section of the market is regarded by SSTL as the long term goal of the Strand Project, since it represents the bulk of main-stream data processing. However it may be a long time before general applications are developed for multiprocessor computers as the norm. By that time, SSTL recognises that language requirements may well have moved on from STRAND[88] in its present form. However they predict that the same underlying design features of parallel semantics, portability and investment protection through multiple language programming, will be just as relevant.

STRAND[88] is an active competitor at the moment in the first three of these market sectors, that is in academic institutions, commercial research and hardware manufacturers. The aim of the producers is to expand in the software house area over the next 1–2 years, and during this time, begin to look into the applications development sector also.

9.4.4   The Competition

STRAND[88] faces competition in two areas of the parallel software market. Firstly, the language itself has certain attributes that make it a logic-type of language. There are a small number of alternatives available in this field, and figures suggest that STRAND[88] outperforms them all. Parlog is much more an academic research tool and it is therefore not surprising that its performance is well behind STRAND[88] . However the Japanese produced logic-type languages KL1 and GHC (which run on specialised hardware) have been produced to perform, yet in tests performed at Argonne STRAND^{88} outperforms the other languages with ease.

However, perhaps the area in which STRAND^{88} will meet the strongest competition will be in portable parallel programming – the provision of harnesses to parallelise sequential code. For small sectors of this market there are products such as CS Tools, however this is a transputer-oriented harness and therefore covers only a restricted part of the hardware market. In fact, work is being carried out at present to port STRAND$_-^{88}$ to run under CSTools on transputer based machines, in order to widen still further the range of portability of STRAND^{88} . Perhaps the largest competitor to STRAND^{88} is therefore Linda (cf. 9.3). Linda tackles the programming of multiple processor computers essentially through explicit extensions to existing sequential languages, hence C-Linda and Fortran-Linda. SSTL hope that as the number of processors in parallel machines grow, and potential applications become more irregular and complex, Linda's capabilities will be exceeded, leaving STRAND$_-^{88}$ as the leader of the market. Whether this view is realistic depends upon the future development of Linda. a subject covered elsewhere in of this report.

9.4.5 The Future

SSTL plans future extensions and strengthening of STRAND^{88} . The next planned release (Cleopatra) promises significant target execution speed improvement, an object oriented system for writing STRAND^{88} programs, a graphical user-interface, improved debugging facilities and many other items. They will be constantly looking for new parallel hardware upon which to mount STRAND^{88} , and so hope to secure a large section of the parallel software market.

Chapter 10

Machines Past

While some parallel computer companies have been extraordinarily successful, there have also been some notable failures. The story of ETA's rise and fall is well known, but other firms have also failed, often despite the high quality of their products. In this chapter we describe some of the most interesting of these, and try to analyse why they didn't make it.

10.1   BiiN

Relevant Activities Manufacturers of fault-tolerant multiprocessors; ceased operations in April 1990.

Location 2111 N.E. 25th Avenue, Hillsboro, Oregon, USA.

Relevant Officers Joseph J. Kroger, President and Chief Executive Officer; Leslie Vadasz, Chairman of the Board (Intel Senior Vice President); Dr. Horst Langer, Siemens Corporation (U.S.) Chairman and CEO.

Employees 270 initially (transferred from Intel and Siemens), 400 peak.

Financial details Joint venture by Intel and Siemens, with $300 M investment.

10.1.1   The Company

BiiN was another outgrowth of Intel's iAPX 432 multiprocessor project, the ancestor of iPSC (cf. 4.1) and NCUBE (cf. 4.2). BiiN began in 1982 as Gemini, a research project equally funded by Intel and Siemens. The project's aim was to design and build a complete system for so-called "mission critical" computing, such as on-line transaction processing, industrial control applications (such as managing nuclear reactors), military applications intolerant of computer down-time, and national television services. The central themes of the R&D effort were to be transparent multiprocessing and file distribution, dynamically switchable fault tolerance, and a high level of security. Siemens provided the funding through its energy division UBE, who had an interest in fault tolerant computers for use in nuclear installations, while Intel provided the technology, and the whole project was organised with alternate layers of Siemens and Intel management and engineers.

In 1985 the project became BiiN Partners, and in July 1988 was launched as a company wholly-owned by Intel and Siemens. Since neither Siemens nor Intel could see how to market this new architecture if it were broken up, BiiN was created. A second company wholly owned by Intel, called BiiN Federal Systems, was also created in order to avoid FOCI (Foreign Ownership and Controlling Interest) problems in selling to the US government. Intel owned all the silicon designs which were licensed to Siemens, while Siemens owned all the software and documentation and licensed them to Intel.

10.1.2   The Hardware

BiiN's aim was to produce a computer which was fault tolerant, secure, and powerful. To do this, they employed a number of innovative design features, of which parallelism was only one.

All BiiN machines were based on a custom processor designed by Intel, fabricated using 2μm CMOS and running at 16 MHz. This processor was a "grown-up" version of Intel's 80960 microcontroller, and its instruction set was a superset of the 80960's. The processor had some RISC features, such as a load/store architecture, a 512 byte instruction cache, and efficient hardware mechanisms for saving and recovering the contents of its 32 registers, but with 240 instructions it could not properly be called a RISC chip. Floating point calculations were supported by an on-chip FPU and four 80 bit floating point registers.

BiiN's entry-level system was the BiiN 20. This contained one or two processors, connected through a Bus Exchange Unit to a single system bus. Each processor board also carried a separately programmed communications processor, which provided access to industry-standard connections such as SCSI and RS232. Boards carrying 8 or 16 Mbyte of memory were also connected to the system bus. Additional battery-backed memory was used as a file system cache; reads and writes would be done from this cache, rather than directly from and to the disc, in order to reduce execution times. Because this cache was battery-backed, its contents could survive an unplanned interruption of processing.

The BiiN 20, and its larger counterpart, the BiiN 60, which could support up to eight processors, were to a large degree self configuring. At boot time the machine would check its contents in order to determine the number of processor and memory modules it contained. These machines could also operate in a geographically distributed environment — dispersed machines could be connected to run as a single multiprocessor machine, with the only degradation in performance being due to the latency of the network. Both of these features were implemented by maintaining a decentralised, redundant "clearinghouse" of information about the system's configuration.

Along with automatic re-try in the event of a parity error being detected, the bus provided two unusual facilities intended to improve the machine's performance. The first of these was burst transfer — any bus operation could transfer between 1 and 16 byte of data, which reduced the setup time required. In addition, transfers were packetised, so that the bus could be used by one processor while another was waiting for a reply from memory to an earlier request.

BiiN's machines were symmetric multiprocessors. The machine as a whole kept a single queue of runnable processes, from which all processors took their workload. This automatically provided a degree of load balancing for multi-tasking applications.

BiiN computers, especially the larger BiiN 60, could use parallelism either for fault tolerance or to increase throughput. BiiN implemented three levels of fault tolerance: standard, fault-checking, and continuous operation. In standard mode, each processor worked independently, but the hardware did error checking and single bit error correction, the bus re-tried in event of parity errors, and so on. In fault-checking mode, processors were paired so that they could check one another's calculations. In event of an error, the processors would stop, and the self-checking circuitry would determine which was faulty. This processor would then be excluded from the system, and the computer would re-start. Finally, in continuous operation mode these fault-checking pairs were duplicated, so that if an error occurred the second (or shadow) pair could immediately take over the calculations.

10.1.3   The Software

From a software point of view, the BiiN 20 and 60 were Ada machines in the way that the transputer was a CSP machine. BiiN/OS, the proprietary operating system developed for the machines, was written entirely in Ada, and based on object-oriented features in the Ada model of parallel processing. For example, every object known to BiiN/OS, such as a file, a directory, or a utility program, carried with it an access control list which specified the operations that could be performed on the object by different individuals, groups of individuals, or programs. These lists were managed and checked directly in hardware.

Another object-oriented feature which was used to increase security was the way that software modules could be grouped into a protected address space, and then made accessible only through a restricted set of interface functions. This was supplemented by the use of 33 bit words. The first 32 bits of each word contained data, while the 33rd was used to indicate whether the value was a pointer or not. If it was, certain operations which could corrupt the pointer were not permitted. BiiN's literature repeatedly emphasizes the need for secure computing and the dangers of viruses; these hardware features were clearly intended to provide some prophylaxis.

BiiN/OS and the BiiN machines were designed to work together intimately. One example of this is the way the hardware supported multi-tasking. For example, a processor could block one process and schedule another to run immediately without O/S intervention, something which can dramatically improve the performance of programs in which many processes co-operate through message passing.

The type of application BiiN intended their machines to support can be inferred from the software they provided with their machines. Along with a fault-tolerant and highly secure operating system (with an industry standard UNIX-like interface), and compilers for the five most popular programming languages in the business and scientific fields (Ada, C, Cobol, Fortran, and Pascal, all conforming to appropriate industry standards), BiiN also supported the Ingres database management system, and had tailored some of their hardware's features to support it. Along with the battery backed filestore cache, the hardware provided mechanisms for grouping transactions, so that either all or none of the transactions would succeed. Security of this sort is obviously valuable in areas such as OLTP, in which transferring funds from one account to another may require several primitive operations. By grouping these operations into a single transaction, BiiN ensured that the transfer as a whole would go through properly or not at all.

10.1.4 The Market

BiiN pursued the fault-tolerant market, rather than trying to compete directly on price/performance, for marketing reasons. When it was formed the only entrenched competition in this market were Stratus and Tandem. Had BiiN gone for the low end parallel processing market, on the other hand, they would have been competing against DEC, Sequent (Section 3.7), Pyramid, and other, smaller firms. One source stated that in retrospect the company should have started selling machines as early as 1987 or 1988, and introduced an enhanced machine meeting their original design goals as soon as it was ready, rather than waiting to produce a "killer" machine. As well as establishing BiiN in the market, this would have ameliorated the company's negative cash flow.

When BiiN was shut down in October 1989, pre-production machines had been sold to US government research labs, "a very significant Wall St. firm", and several aerospace companies. Most of these were returned when BiiN folded, although Hughes Aircraft, which was using the silicon architecture for the Advanced Tactical Fighter, is still using its machines.

10.1.5 BiiN's Demise

BiiN was shut down in October 1989 when the two parent companies could not agree on further financing. At this point, approximately $300 M had been invested in BiiN, and the product was still not complete. While there is no doubt that BiiN was expensive — for example, implementing connections to other machines would have required another substantial investment — much of this cost was simply due to the leading-edge nature of the development being done. Lacking the long view which most Japanese firms have of investment in new technology, BiiN's parent companies were unwilling to wait three or five years for BiiN to prove itself.

Another reason which has been suggested for the company's closure was a major reorganisation within Siemens in mid-1989. Until that time, the computer division UBK had not been involved in the BiiN project, but had formed a relationship with Sequent. After the reorganisation, the leaders of UBK became the managers of the BiiN project. According to one source, they were "less than enthusiastic about the amount of money that was being spent on a 'competing' architecture."

After the company closed, a large number of its employees returned to Siemens and Intel. Sequent hired a significant number as well. The rest found positions in smaller businesses in the growing electronics industry in Oregon. Some of the hardware packaging technology, and a little of the higher level architecture, were sold to Pyramid. Because of its heavy investment in MIPS processors, Pyramid was not interested in any of the silicon or software. Pyramid also hired a large number of the hardware developers and a few architects.

10.2   ETA Systems

Relevant Activities Designed and manufactured pipelined vector supercomputers with between two and eight processors. Produced the first liquid nitrogen cooled supercomputer.

Location ETA: 1450 Energy Park Drive, St Paul, Minnesota 55108, USA. Control Data Corporation: PO Box 0, Minneapolis, Minnesota 55440, USA.

Relevant Officers Lloyd Thorndyke, President and CEO from 1983–1987; Carl Ledbetter, President and CEO from 1987–December 1988 and from February 1989–April 1989; Neil Lincoln, Chief Architect; Tony Vacca, Chief Technologist; Dale Handy, Head of Engineering.

Employees Peaked at around 800.

Financial details Originally a spin-off company from Control Data Corporation. By the time ETA was wound up CDC held 100% of ETA stock.

10.2.1   The Company

The story of ETA is one of the saddest in the history of computing. ETA was started in August 1983 as an independent spin off from the Control Data Corporation (CDC). By early 1987, after only four years, ETA had produced and delivered their first multiprocessor supercomputer, the ETA[10]. In April 1989 ETA was closed down with the loss of over 800 jobs.

The beginnings of ETA can be traced back to the early 1980s. In 1981/2 CDC had decided that surviving in the supercomputing market was becoming a risk and that to start a small dedicated company would focus development and minimise the financial risk to the parent company.

Three CDC employees — Neil Lincoln, Dale Handy and Tony Vacca — had been attempting to start their own supercomputer company since late 1982. They had already identified much of the structure and technology of the machine they wanted to build but were having problems finding financial backers. When, in June 1983, CDC eventually decided to start up a separate supercomputing company, it asked these three to run it. Tony Vacca become Chief Technologist; Dale Handy become Head of Engineering; and Neil Lincoln become Chief Architect.

ETA was formally set up in August 1983 with equipment and $4 M from CDC in exchange for 60% of ETA stock. The idea was that ETA would eventually be an autonomous company. CDC would retain 20% of the stock; ETA employees would share a further 20% of the stock; and the remaining 60% stock would be floated on the stock market. The brief for ETA was to produce the fastest supercomputer in the world by 1986.

10.2.2   The Hardware

The target performance for the ETA[10] was 10 GFLOPS (hence the ten in ETA[10]). The only way to achieve this would be to use multiple processors. A maximum of eight processors was decided on. These constraints fixed the machine clock cycle to around 7 ns.

Traditionally ECL had been used in supercomputers such as those built by Cray Research Inc. to provide clock cycles to about 5 ns. ECL, however, was expensive, power consuming, hard to cool, and not easily upgradable. In addition it was recognised that chip manufacturers were pouring money into developing VLSI MOS circuits. MOS's advantages are its low power consumption, the fact that its speed can be increased by photographically reducing circuit sizes, and the large number of MOS circuits that can be crammed onto a single chip compared with other processes. Its major disadvantage is that it is slow compared to ECL or GaAs technology.

MOS technology was eventually chosen, even though it was realised that something in the region of 10,000 gates per chip would be needed if the chips were to be fast enough to be viable. At the time (1982), 1000 gates per chip was the usual limit. Luckily, Honeywell had been working on chips containing about 20,000 gates, so ETA contracted them to develop and supply MOS chips for their computers.

To reach a 7 ns clock time the ETA[10]'s processors would need to be cooled with liquid nitrogen, since MOS gate speed increases by a factor of two when cooled to 77 K. However, slower and cheaper air cooled versions running at half the speed could be built using the same technology. By using the same design, parts, and manufacturing process, ETA would develop two computers for the cost of one.

The architecture of the ETA[10] was based around a large shared memory of 64 to 256 Mword of SRAM, a word being 64 bit. Attached to the memory were two, four, six or eight CPUs, each of which was essentially a Cyber 205. Simply, it was a shared memory machine with message passing communication between processors. The instruction set of the ETA[10] was compatible with that of the Cyber 205, but extended with instructions for interprocessor communication and synchronisation. Each CPU had 4 Mword of DRAM local memory. (Due to developments in RAM technology the shared memory was eventually expanded to a maximum of 1 Gword, and private memory expanded to 16 Mword.) A CPU was connected to shared memory via a 200 Mword/s (12.8 Gbit/s) communication channel. Since the speed of the CPU/memory port was slow compared with the speed of the arithmetic pipelines it was assumed that CPUs would compute using private memory and then shift the results back into shared memory.

Also connected to the shared memory were up to 18 I/O processors, based on Motorola 68020s, for linking to peripherals. IOPs were connected to shared memory via a 400 Mbit/s ports. Interprocessor communication and synchronisation was made possible via a high speed communications buffer.

An entire two pipe Cyber 205 CPU had been reduced down to 250 CMOS chips tightly packed onto a 42 layer printed circuit board measuring only $16'' \times 22''$. The 42 layers form 2.5 miles of interconnect. For testing purposes each chip has a 1,500 gate (roughly 20% of the silicon) testing system named OCMS — the On-Chip Maintenance System. With OCMS each chip could signal whether it was faulty or not. In addition, chips were connected by test pins in a ring circuit allowing chips to test their nearest neighbours for faults. Using this hardware test facility together with simulation and diagnosis software it was possible pin-point chip/board errors extremely quickly. To attain the desired 7 ns clock cycle the CPU board was lowered into a tank of liquid nitrogen at 77 K. The memory, however, although physically connected directly to the CPU board was air cooled and sat above the cryostat.

The first processors were built and tested in late 1986. These processors were found to run at a maximum clock speed of 10.5 ns when cooled. This fell short of the desired 7 ns target but showed that the technology was feasible. The 10.5 ns components formed the basis of the E-type machine. The first two processor version was shipped on December 30th 1986 to Florida State University only two years after Honeywell given the designs for the first chips.

From there Honeywell managed to reduce the feature size of the chips from 1.8μm to 1.0μm. This yielded 8 ns F-type chips, which were never used in production, and eventually the desired 7 ns G-type chips. The first G-type machine was built and shipped in 1988. Luckily, since the machine design was centred around the 7 ns figure although the chip speeds were becoming faster none of the supporting technology needed redesigning.

In just four years ETA had managed to achieve their 7 ns target. This had been made possible largely through good early design decisions that were adhered to throughout the project and the extensive use of software tools in the design and testing of hardware.

In December 1987 a series of air-cooled machines named Piper, running with 18 to 22 ns clocks, became available. These were made in one and two processor versions. The Pipers were considerably cheaper than their supercooled brothers since they did not need the expensive cryostat mechanics. Accordingly, Piper machines rapidly became popular, filling the gap between mini- and supercomputers. This market niche is now filled by computers from Convex (cf. 3.4) and by the Supertek S-1, now marketed by Cray Research Inc. (cf. 7.1. The hardware and software for the Piper was identical to that of the ETA[10]; only the cooling mechanism was different.

10.2.3   The Software

From the earliest days of the company, it had been decided to provide UNIX as the operating system for the ETA[10]. UNIX was just emerging as a possible industry standard OS for small machines and it looked as though the trend would be carried up to large machines. At that time very few people had used UNIX and established CDC customers were reluctant to learn yet another operating system.

In mid-1984, ETA decided to offer the Cyber 205 operating system VSOS as a UNIX shell executing on a UNIX sub-operating system; this system would be called EOS. Unfortunately, not enough attention was paid to the software development of EOS. Its development quickly moved away from the underlying UNIX subsystem. and grew in scale. It was never fully implemented, and what was implemented was very unreliable. The basic problem was that the engineers in the EOS team had little knowledge of or exposure to UNIX, but a great deal of knowledge of VSOS.

Neither of the operating systems took real advantage of the parallel architecture of the ETA[10]. Processes could be farmed out to processors, where they would execute in local memory with no interprocess communication at the operating system level. Future releases of UNIX were to implement UNIX interprocess communication protocols, which would have greatly increased the functionality of the OS.

A Fortran 77 compiler was developed by ETA in-house, presumably borrowing heavily on Cyber 205 compiler technology. Multitasking capabilities were added to Fortran 77 through the use of special multitasking libraries developed by ETA together with Kuck and Associates and Pacific Sierra. The Fortran compiler was the saving grace of the liquid cooled machines. EOS never ran to the satisfaction of customers, but the machines could run Fortran code in stand-alone mode with no operating system. This setup was used on the machines purchased by the UK and German weather services, who were content to run their huge Fortran programs in this manner.

10.2.4   Costs and Sales

The liquid nitrogen cooled ETA[10] machines cost in the region of $10–$20 M, and as a result competed directly in the Cray market. The air-cooled Piper class machines were about $900,000 for a single processor machine and about $1.5 M for a two processor version. Running at just over half the speed of a comparable full ETA[10], Piper machines were very attractive to company departments on sub-million dollar budgets.

The first four processor E-type machine went to Florida State University in December 1987 at a cost of $12.5 M. A further three went to the UK Meteorological Service, the German Weather Service, and a National Science Foundation consortium at Princeton. All of these four processor E-types have been returned but the only E-type supplied with eight processors is reportedly still in operation at the University of Tokyo.

Of the Piper air-cooled machines, 27 were shipped to various sites in the US, Canada, and Europe. A few days before the close of the company seven Pipers had been ordered from Australia. Very few of the Piper class machines were returned, and they are still sought after in the second hand supercomputer market.

10.2.5   What Went Wrong?

ETA was closed down on April 17th, 1989. Its demise had four main causes:

- the state of the stock market at the time.

- bad management from inside ETA.

- problems with marketing.

- problems in its relationship with CDC.

The Stock Market and Financing

When ETA was started, it had always been CDC's intention that the company should eventually be completely independent. The plan was that CDC would start the company with equipment and money in return for 60% of ETA stock. As soon as was possible, CDC would reduce its stock to a minority holding of 20%, ETA employees would own a further 20%, the remainder would be made public.

From the start of the company in April 1983, ETA were talking to stock brokers about a stock issue of the company. In that year many hi-tech companies were looking for finance on the stock exchange, so ETA were optimistic of being floated as early as January 1984. At the end of 1983, Gene Amdahl's supercomputer company Trilogy went public but was heavily undersubscribed because of rumours that the company was having problems with technology. Also at that time a number of smaller computer companies closed on the stock exchange. Suddenly, by early 1984, the financial environment became unfavourable for hi-tech companies looking to go public. Instead ETA had to look for other investment. In spite of negotiations with various interested companies, by the end of 1986 an investor still had not been found.

At the same time CDC were in grave financial difficulties having sustained over \$500 M in losses over the previous two years. In late 1986, Tom Roberts was made President of CDC to bring the company back to profitability, which he tried to do by removing as many unprofitable divisions within CDC as possible. In addition, their own product line was unpopular. Consequently, it was decided to buy back their loan from ETA in order to increase their range of machines. By early 1987 CDC owned 100% of ETA stock and had full control over the company. This move, apparently, led to resentment from the ETA staff.

ETA Management

ETA had serious management problems from the start. The three principal founders were engineers with little inclination towards management. Lloyd Thorndyke was appointed as President and Chief Executive Officer. His background had been in design of peripheral devices for high-performance computers.

ETA also had problems with the software management of the company. None of the principal founders had a background in software; they were all engineers whose primary interest was in building the fastest computer in the world. When the company was started, ETA desperately needed to recruit an experienced software manager. The appointee, however, was also a hardware man with no background in software and this had a detrimental effect on the morale of the software group.

Nothing was done about this problem until early 1987 when Carl Ledbetter joined the company, by which time software development was in a sorry state. EOS had been repeatedly extended and had moved away from its UNIX roots, and although the EOS development team consisted of about 300 staff, a working version never emerged. In addition, the majority of purchasers of liquid-cooled machines were former CDC customers interested in Cyber 205 compatibility. The problems with the development of EOS, therefore, hampered full acceptance of theETA[10]machines actually delivered. This cost ETA over \$30 M in sales.

By late 1986 and early 1987 ETA was \$380 M in debt, having made only one sale worth \$12.5 M.

Marketing

Originally ETA had their own marketing operation. However, by 1986 this had been merged with CDC's marketing to save resources. This caused confusion with the CDC sales force who had to assimilate the capabilities of the ETA[10]. However, financial pressures caused the machine to be oversold before it became a stable product. Promises were made about the hardware and especially the software that could not be met.

An extreme example of this can be found in the sale of the eight processor machine to the University of Tokyo. The machine never reached the expectations of the Japanese buyers. It had countless hardware problems, and although shipped with UNIX suffered from an unstable software environment. It was costly for ETA/CDC to send engineers to Japan repeatedly just to service one machine, and the loss of confidence by a large and influential Japanese customer must have hurt future sales.

On top of this, the CDC sales force was supposed to be marketing CDC's new machine, the Cyber-990. This seemed very much like the Piper class ETA[10], except that the latter was cheaper and ran faster. The conflict between these product lines did not help project a unified marketing strategy to customers.

CDC Management

A significant factor contributing to ETA's downfall were a number of personal conflicts between members of the CDC and ETA management teams. Unfortunately,
such differences are common when an organisation is in trouble and generally do
not help with employee morale. So it was with ETA. CDC's recall of their loan to
ETA also reduced staff commitment to the new company.

In addition, the conflict between the CDC Cyber-990 and the ETA Piper did
little to reduce the rivalry between the opposing camps. However, it was eventually
agreed that the Piper should be sold. At this time ETA was still losing money and
by April 1988 the ETA management calculated that they would have to shed at
least 300 people to survive. CDC were having their own financial problems and in
March 1989 CDC had decided that it could no longer support ETA. Attempts had
been made to sell the company, but the asking price had been set too high — in
the region of half a billion dollars. It has been said that one reason for this was
to enable CDC to bury some of its financial losses over the years through inter-
company charges. In the end, no purchaser could be found and ETA was officially
closed on 14th April 1989, with the loss of 800 staff and approximately \$400 M.

10.3   Multiflow

Relevant Activities Manufacturer of VLIW machines and compiler technology.

Location Headquarters in New Haven, Connecticut, USA. European Headquarters in Belgium.

Relevant Officers Donald E. Eckdahl, President; Joseph A. Fisher, Exec. Vice-President.

Employees In early 1990: 154 (US) five (UK and Europe) and one (Japan).

Financial details Voluntary liquidation early in the 2nd quarter of 1990.

10.3.1   Going Up

In April 1984, three colleagues from Yale University's Department of Computer Science left the university to found Multiflow. Joseph A. Fisher, an early force in VLIW technology (cf. Appendix A.4.2 and [VLIW]) was then a professor in the department. He was joined in the Multiflow venture by graduate student John Ruttenberg and systems manager John O'Donnell. Their aim was to enter the high-performance scientific computing market with VLIW machines supported by advanced compiler technology.

The company was initially funded by an advance of $500 k from Apollo, while negotiations on a technology agreement progressed. This deal was never closed, and six months into the life of Multiflow, Apollo offered to buy the company out. Instead, the founders set about raising venture capital. By February 1985, $7 M had been raised, to which Apollo added their original loan.

A year later, in February 1986, a further $10 M venture capital package was arranged. In May 1987 Multiflow obtained a further tranche of $16 M as they reached market with their first products, the Trace /200 machines (Table 10.1). Multiflow claimed peak performance of 30 MFLOPS for the bottom model Trace 7/200, with 6 MFLOPS on Linpack.

Table 10.1: The Trace /200 Series

Model	Bits/Instruction	Max. Simultaneous Operations
Trace 7/200	256	7
Trace 14/200	512	14
Trace 28/200	1024	28

By the time Multiflow reached the market their principal competitors in the mini-supercomputer market, Convex (Section 3.4 and Alliant (3.1), were already well established. Multiflow was further disadvantaged by having to convince customers of the validity of what was seen as a radical architecture, while competitors were marketing more conventional vector and parallel designs. For the first 12 months of shipping this was a serious disadvantage for Multiflow. A major marketing effort aimed to convince potential customers that despite the exotic underlying architecture, users could treat the machines as "normal" computers. By mid 1988, the public conception of the machines had been improved.

Multiflow's compiler technology allowed them to pay particular attention to the dusty-deck market from the start. Existing sequential Fortran codes could be mounted on the Trace machines unmodified, without the expensive and time-consuming process of parallelisation required by many other machines. The compiler could either guess how to best assemble traces, or rely on "sample data" provided by the user, which was used to determine the flow of control on the source program. No explicit user guidance of the compiler was necessary. Multiflow's ability to extract parallelism from scalar as well as vector code was an advantage over vector machines which were typically reduced to uniprocessor operation by scalar code.

Early in 1989, Multiflow's introduced its second generation machines, the Trace /300 series.

Although they retained the clock cycle of the /200 series, performance gains of a factor of four were made through a number of software and architectural advances. Hardware improvements included: improved register topology; new floating point instructions; ECL floating point circuitry; I/O processors supporting up to 60 Mbyte/s (burst); and VME bus compatibility. The compiler for the /300 series was a development of the /200 series compiler, capable of packing instructions more densely into VLIW formats, achieving performance improvements of up to a factor of three over its predecessor. The introduction of the new range led to the discontinuation of the Trace 14/200 system. The Trace 7/200 was retained as an entry-level system.

Although a distributor had been established in West Germany in 1987 (GEI, a Daimler subsidiary), Multiflow initially had little presence outside North America. This weakness had been recognised, however, and steps had been taken to extend Multiflow's market. Mid 1989 saw the conclusion of a Japanese distribution deal with C.Itoh. In Europe, distribution channels were set up in France (Metrologie), and Italy (Delphi, a subsidiary of Olivetti). A European headquarters was established in early 1990 in Belgium, complementing the existing European distribution arrangements.

By the end of 1989, some 100 machines had been delivered to 75 purchasers. More than 50% of these installations were commercial sites, with the remainder split roughly equally between universities and government installations. 30% of these sales had been made outside North America, and the company was aiming for 50-55% of its sales overseas in the short term. These sales were seen as an excellent start by the company, and the volume of shipments achieved in just two years compares well with many other parallel computer manufacturers.

When the Trace /300 range was announced, four orders had already been placed, all from Fortune 100 companies. Users of Multiflow systems in North America included NASA, AT&T, Alcoa, AMP Inc., Grumman Data Systems and Carnegie-Mellon University. West Germany was a significant export market for Multiflow with a number of research sites housing machines, including the Society for Biological Research at Braunschweig and the Institute for Technology at the University of Bochum. No sales of Multiflow equipment were made in the United Kingdom.

Intel (4.1) invested $3 M in a technology agreement with Multiflow in January 1990. This gave Intel the rights to Multiflow compiler software, which they hoped to apply to producing good optimising compilers for the i860 and its derivatives.

10.3.2   Going Down

The collapse in Spring 1990 of a larger deal involving DEC, rumored to have been worth around $12 M, precipitated the failure of Multiflow. Unable to raise capital, the company went into voluntary liquidation while there was still enough in the coffers to honour outstanding debts.

When the company folded, their new ECL series was on the point of being announced. The development of the ECL processor for these machines had been funded by a $7 M R&D partnership with Prutech, a division of Prudential Bache. Had the ECL series seen the light of day, it would have been six times faster than the existing Trace /300 series, but is now unlikely to be built by anyone else.

DEC and HP have obtained rights to Multiflow's technology. Multiflow's employees have scattered. Members of the compiler team are to be found at Alliant, Cray Research Inc., Intel, HP Apollo, Silicon Graphics and Thinking Machines. It is interesting to note that DEC, although they bought rights to the technology, did not hire ex-Multiflow people. A number of consultancies and software companies have been started up in Connecticut by former Multiflow employees, but these are unlikely to be involved in VLIW work.

At the time of writing, Multiflow is still winding up its operations, liquidating assets and paying off debts. The North American maintenance business has been sold to Bell Atlantic. Elsewhere, distributors hold sufficient stocks of components to provide maintenance and support to existing installations.

10.3.3   Why Did Multiflow Fail?

Multiflow's collapse can be attributed to a number of technical and business factors. Multiflow's compilers were the most advanced of their genre. However, there was a tendency within Multiflow to rely on compiler technology to provide performance, and to neglect hardware efficiency. The Trace machines had very slow cycle times compared to competitors machines. Until late 1988, the compilers could put the machines back on an even footing, but the arrival of the Convex C2 (3.4.2) with a cycle speed 3.5 times that of the Trace machines tipped the balance for Convex. With better hardware, and lower cycle times, Multiflow's compilers could have been an advantage, rather than just making up for poor hardware performance. Multiflow were also hurt a little by the very long compile times on their machines.

The long term future of Multiflow was less than certain. The recent rise of the high-performance "killer micro" is a serious threat to the traditional mini-supercomputer, and Multiflow's machines were in danger of becoming a new breed of dinosaur.

However, it is generally held that Multiflow's products were well-engineered and not the major reason for failure. Instead, the company's collapse is widely attributed to a typical problem of a startup — the lack of a complete integrated operation. In Multiflow, marketing, distribution and applications were weak. Multiflow always suffered from being late to market behind Convex and Alliant. The lack of foresight which left Multiflow without channels into overseas markets had serious repercussions. The company was deprived of revenue from these markets, and exposed to undercutting in the North American market, since competitors could make up their margins in markets where Multiflow was not competing. Although European and Japanese distribution channels were in place by late 1990, they were 30 months too late to exploit the newly opening markets.

Like many other computer manufacturers, Multiflow was hit by the slump in the market in 1989, but a major factor in their downfall was Convex. Convex fought Multiflow hard for control of the market for high-performance scientific computing. Their marketing expertise and wider geographic markets were a winning combination.

The final nail in Multiflow's coffin was the inability of their sponsors to provide the capital needed to sustain the company until its state of the art research and development bore fruit.

10.3.4   A Future for VLIW technology?

VLIW has failed as a commercial technology to date. In addition to Multiflow, Cydrome, manufacturers of VLIW-ish machines have also folded. However, this may have more to do with business acumen than technical issues. It seems unlikely that DEC, HP and Intel would purchase rights to Multiflow technology if the technology itself was the problem.

Fisher firmly believes that, "In 5–10 years virtually every high performance processor in use will incorporate instruction-level parallelism". The choice of which instructions to execute in parallel can either be made dynamically (as the program executes) or statically (when the program is compiled). The dynamic approach leads to the class of architectures becoming known as "superscalar", while static decisions lead to the VLIW technologies developed by Multiflow. The VLIW approach involves much less hardware, and proponents argue that, in general, more parallelism can be found by static analysis of code. The major disadvantage of VLIW is object code compatibility. The code produced by compilers is so dependent upon hardware latencies that it will not execute on other machines on the same series. The time taken to compile code for VLIW machines is another problem, although this has fallen as the technology has advanced.

Fisher's view seems vindicated by the industry. HP has sold the LIW DN10000 successfully for several years. FPS are producing LIW machines. Intel's i860 has some characteristics of an LIW processor, and has spurred interest in VLIW compiler technology within the company. One of the compiler companies for the i860 is The Portland Group which worked on the original FPS-164 and FPS-264 compilers (cf. 3.6.4). DEC are another potential developer of VLIW technology. Ruttenberg and members of Multiflow's hardware team are at Silicon Graphics (6.2). HP have rights to both Multiflow and Cydrome technology in addition to the DN10000, and employ both Fisher and Bob Rau (co-founder of Cydrome), so they are strategically placed for future developments, although their plans for VLIW work are not clear at this stage.

10.4   Myrias Research Corporation

Relevant Activities Manufacturers of massively-parallel supercomputers; ceased operations on October 26, 1990.

Location 10611-98 Avenue, Suite 900, Edmonton, Alberta, Canada T5K 2P7. Telephone: (403) 428 1616

Relevant Officers Fredrick T. (Ted) White, Chairman and CEO; Monica Beltrametti, Director of Software Development; Paul Senechal, Director of Hardware Development and Manufacturing; Chris Thomson, Director of Systems Architecture; Daniel C. Wilson, Director of Systems Development; Martin A. Walker, Director of Applications.

Employees 107 (89 Canada, 18 US)

Financial details Private company (capitalisation $28.7 M)

10.4.1   The Company

Myrias Research Corporation was founded in Edmonton, Alberta, in 1983, by five members of staff at the University of Alberta in the departments of Computer Science, Biology, Chemistry, and Economics. Their stated aim was to develop a new range of high-performance computers based on massive parallelism which would be appropriate for "large, economically important problems" and which would provide a continuous upgrade path over several generations of technological change. Believing that many existing supercomputers are difficult to program because their designers followed a "hardware-first" approach, and that non-portability of programs between supercomputers compounds these difficulties, Myrias designed a virtual machine (the G machine) and its user-level software environment before developing their hardware.

10.4.2   User-Level Model

Parallelism on Myrias machines is available to users only in the limited form of the PARDO construct. Each "iteration" of a PARDO is in fact a child process whose memory image is identical to that of its parent except for the value of the iteration variable. For example, the Fortran fragment:

```
      PARDO 100 I=1,10
        PROCESS(I)
100   CONTINUE
```

creates ten processes which can be run in an arbitrary order, either in parallel or sequentially, and which are identical except for the value of I.

At a PARDO, the parent is suspended until all of its children have been completed. At that time, any changes made by the children in their memory images are merged to create a new memory image for the parent according to the following[1] rules:

- If no child has modified X, X is not changed.

- If exactly one child has modified X, that modified value is in the final memory image.

- If several children have modified X, and all final values are the same, that value is in the final memory image.

- If several children have modified X, and the final values are not the same, the new parent value is unpredictable.

In practice, memory is not copied and restored every time a PARDO is used. Instead, blocks, or pages, of the parent's memory are copied by the child only when the child accesses a value in that page in order to minimise the number of unnecessary memory operations.

Unlike the parallelism construct PAR in the transputer language Occam, the Myrias PARDO is fully dynamic; any process may create any number of child processes (subject to available memory). PARDO's may be nested, so that children may spawn children of their own:

```
PARDO 100 I=1,10
     LIM = SOMEFUNC(I)
     PARDO 200 J=1,LIM
          ANOTHERFUNC(I,J)
200       CONTINUE
100  CONTINUE
```

Myrias extended standard Fortran by allowing recursion so that functions may invoke themselves (i.e. so that a process of type P may create copies of itself) from within a PARDO.

Myrias provided another way to express parallelism which was simply a shorthand for a commonly-occurring use of the PARDO. In Myrias Parallel Fortran (MPF), PARBEGIN/PARALLEL causes one copy of each child process to be spawned, while in Myrias Parallel C (MPC) the same effect is achieved using parallel/par:

---

[1] According to Myrias, their next software release will include reduction operators for merging, i.e. MAX(), SUM().

```
MPF                MPC                PARDO equivalent
PARBEGIN           parallel {         pardo i = 0, n {
   ...BLOCK-0...      ...block-0...    if (i == 0) then
PARALLEL           par                   ...block-0...
   ...BLOCK-1...      ...block-1...    else if (i == 1) then
PARALLEL           par                   ...block-1...
   ...and so on...    ...and so on...  ...and so on...
END PAR            }                  }
```

10.4.3 Claims About the User-Level Model

Having restricted the user-accessible parallelism of their machines, Myrias made certain claims about program execution. The foremost was that program execution was deterministic — the same program would give the same answer no matter what size of machine it was run on, because process execution order is rendered invisible by the semantics of the PARDO (so long as programs never use variables which may have been given several different values by different PARDO-spawned child processes). (In fact, any parallel program would behave deterministically if restricted in this way; what made Myrias special was the extra support they provided for this model.)

A subsidiary claim was that this determinism makes programs easier to debug on Myrias computers than on most other multiprocessors. So long as variables whose values may be undefined due to memory merging are not used, users could stop any process at any point and examine it without disturbing either other concurrently-executing processes or the calculation's results.

In practice, there were several ways to write non-deterministic programs for Myrias machines, including:

- using variables whose values are left undefined after memory merging, or (in the next software release) using floating-point variables produced by merging operators such as SUM(), whose values may, due to roundoff error, depend on the (undefined) order in which the arithmetic of the merge was carried out;

- relying on pointer values returned by memory allocation routines;

- relying on real-time clock values;

- performing parallel I/O without using the special functions provided (see below).

However, these restrictions were not particularly severe, and should be followed as part of a good programming style in any case.

10.4.4   Compromises in the User-Level Model

Unfortunately, there are several types of application whose parallelism cannot be expressed using PARDO or its variants. For example, one way to parallelise database queries is to give each processor a copy of the complete database, and to optimise each query in as many different ways as possible. One of these optimised queries will normally execute much faster than any of the others; once the processor given this form of the query finds an answer, all other queries can be terminated. However, since processes cannot explicitly signal or terminate other processes from within a PARDO, it would seem that such applications could not be mounted on a Myrias machine.

To eliminate such blind spots, Myrias provided a hack called a "Eureka Jump". If a task branched to code that is outside the PARDO that created the task, the siblings of the jumping task were killed off and the PARDO would complete as though the jumping task was the only one that executed. For example, in the C fragment:

```
    pardo (i = 1:10){
        if (found_answer(i)) goto EUREKA;
    }
    exit(1);
EUREKA:
    exit(0);
```

whichever task found an answer first would terminate its siblings by jumping outside the PARDO that had created it.

10.4.5   The Virtual Machine and Its Implementation

The PARDO model of parallelism was implemented by a virtual machine called the G machine. The G machine has a fetch-store architecture; each instruction is a quad containing an op code and three operands (either constants or addresses). The Myrias Parallel Fortran (MPF) and Parallel C (MPC) compilers produce G instructions, which are then optimised and targetted to the particular Myrias hardware.

Spawning and merging processes are atomic operations in G. The assignment of processes to processors was managed by the Parallel Application Management System (PAMS) — users could not intervene. The PAMS assigned tasks to processors when they are created, and moved them during execution if necessary to balance processor workloads. (There was therefore load balancing only at the task level.) The PAMS also copied and merged fragments of memory images when processes were spawned and merged.

The PAMS implemented paged virtual memory. Instead of storing pages on disc, however, the PAMS allowed one processor to claim part of the memory of another. If a program required a large amount of memory, it could be provided only by allocating processors, some of which would in fact be idle.

Finally, the PAMS was responsible for inter-process communication, which was only allowed between parent and child processes during spawning and merging.

10.4.6 The Product Range

While Myrias was founded in 1983, detailed design of their first prototype hardware only began in 1985, the intervening years having been spent designing the G machine and the user-level software environment. In February 1987, a prototype Scalable Parallel Supercomputer (SPS) became operational. The SPS-1 contained 512 Motorola 68000 processors with 512 kbyte RAM each, sharing 300 Mbyte of disc. The system was hosted by a Vax 11/750. While by 1985 this hardware was no longer state-of-the-art, it showed that the basic design was practical. In addition, it demonstrated the soundness of Myrias' software-first strategy, since there were compilers, most of an operating system, a performance monitor, and many test application programs in both Fortran and C ready for it on its first day of operation.

Myrias began design work on the SPS-2, its first commercial machine, in June 1987; the first of these machines was sold in April 1989. This machine used the M68020 processor running at 16 MHz with an M68882 co-processor for floating point calculations. Each processor had 4 Mbyte of 80 ns RAM with a 256 byte instruction cache. and the machine as a whole had 1-4 Gbyte of disc.

An SPS-2 consisted of a master controller cabinet housing a Sun workstation, which acted as a system console, connected the SPS-2 to the outside world, and provided UNIX system services for application programs, plus one or more cabinets containing up to 64 processors each on four-processor cards. A 64 processor SPS-2 could deliver 10 MFLOPS sustained, 23 MFLOPS peak; the largest SPS-2 built was a 1044 processor test configuration, which achieved a peak speed of 630 MFLOPS. The SPS-2 provided 1 Mbyte/s peak bandwidth to the outside world through the console.

All inter-processor communication in an SPS was managed by the PAMS. Example types of messages include page faults, load balancing information, and domain availability requests. Individual processors in an SPS were identified by the PAMS by:

<type,cabinet,board,processor>

where **type** distinguished control and service processors from user-accessible processing elements. Message passing was handled hierarchically — messages between processors on a single board were handled on that board, and messages between processors in a single cabinet were handled without use of the inter-cabinet communications system. Communication was initiated by the sender, but controlled by the receiver. If the receiver was not ready to accept the message, the communication is aborted and an error message returned to the sender, which could either re-transmit or ignore the failure.

From the user's point of view, the SPS-2 was a decomposable networked supercomputer resource. Using a utility called mrun on his or her Sun, a user could claim a subset (called a domain) of SPS-2 processors, which were his or hers for the duration of the program run. These domains could be of any size, a feature which is similar to Cogent's XTM (cf. 6.1) and the BBN TC2000 (cf. 3.2), but contrasts with the static domain-size determination in the Meiko Computing Surface (cf. 5.3), or the power-of-2 size of domains in the Connection Machine (cf. 2.3.2). Users could not share domains; if there were not enough processors to satisfy a user's request, the request was queued until sufficient processors become available.

The supervisor software in the PAMS which managed domain allocation always tried to allocate an "optimal" domain, i.e. one whose processors were as closely connected as possible. The supervisor software would allocate a non-optimal domain if requested. There were schemes for locking groups of processors and making multiple runs on them, and for allocating specific processors. These facilities were normally used by system management software to build more sophisticated batching and accounting systems.

The operating system on the SPS-2 was developed by Myrias, and was UNIX-like. While it never provided the full functionality of UNIX, most system calls were implemented. Supplementary functionality was added to manage simultaneous I/O by multiple processes, as in Express (cf. 9.1).

Along with their MPF and MPC compilers, Myrias supplied an interactive debugger and a performance monitoring tool. These could be used with both Fortran and C programs because these were compiled down to G machine instructions. The performance monitor provided information only on the performance of a processor as a whole, not on processes running on that processor. The debugger was similar to the standard UNIX dbx debugger, but buffered traps as they occurred so that processes on different processors could be debugged together. The debugger could also detect values which were undefined as a result of memory merging. It did this by keeping a "ghost" copy of the whole of memory, whose words flagged the state of memory in the main copy.

Myrias staff have stated that moving software from the SPS-1 to the SPS-2, and thence to the SPS-3, was "proving to be quite easy" because of the use of an abstract underlying machine.

10.4.7 Sales

Myrias was capitalised by a total of $28.7 M. $16.3 M of this has come from private investors, including the company's founders; CDN$4.4 M came from a joint development contract funded by the Canadian Department of Regional Expansion and the US Department of Defense, while a final CDN$7.5 M came from the Province of Alberta. The list price of a 64 node SPS-2 was $300 k. Myrias placed nine of these machines, four with military customers in the United States and Canada, one with NOVA Corp. in Alberta, a petroleum exploration company which used it for pipeline and reservoir simulation, and four with academic institutions. Two of the military machines contained 128 processors; the others all had 64 processors.

10.4.8 The End

Myrias was explicitly targetting the Fortran number-crunching market. While the limited parallelism they provided was not suitable for some types of applications (programming with Eureka Jumps would be hair-raising), it was well-suited to applications which were intrinsically load balanced, such as oil reservoir simulation and aerodynamic modelling on fixed meshes. In practice, the parallelism Myrias offered was mid-way between rigid SIMD parallelism and full MIMD parallelism.

Having designed their machines with upgrades through different technologies in mind, Myrias hoped to provide a stable long-term environment for the development of scientific codes, in the same way that IBM and DEC provided generations of 370 and Vax machines. This, rather than parallelism, *per se*, would have turned out to be their strongest selling point.

Myrias had expected that their third-generation SPS-3 will be available in the third quarter of 1990. The SPS-3's processors would have been Motorola 68040s with on-board floating point capability and 8-16 Mbyte of RAM each. (Myrias chose the M68040 over the M88000 because their floating point capabilities are similar and the 88000 requires more chips for the floating point complex.) The machine would have had a 10-100 Gbyte disc capacity, and would have used a proprietary SPARC-based console. As with the SPS-2, its operating system would have been UNIX-like. Myrias expected to achieve 8.2 MFLOPS peak per processor on the SPS-3, and expected to deliver 2-3 MFLOPS per processor sustained. The bandwidth to the console was to be increased in the SPS-3 to 32 Mbyte/s.

Unfortunately, immediately after Hewlett-Packet announced that they would not be investing in the company, Myrias went into receivership on October 25, 1990.

10.5   Symult Incorporated

Relevant Activities Suppliers of the Symult 2010 distributed memory MIMD machines.

Location Arcadia, California, USA.

Relevant Officers President: Yin Shih; Technical director: Hal Finney.

Employees 100 employees when the company ceased trading.

Financial details Symult ceased trading in June 1989 and closed down in June 1990.

10.5.1   Ametek and Symult

Ametek was a large conglomerate with over 6000 employees and 26 US divisions. In 1983 it formed a computer research division, which in 1985 produced the Ametek-14 hypercube computer. This first generation machine was superceded in January 1988 by the Ametek Series 2010 system, which contained many advanced features including hardware routing. In 1988 Ametek was dissolved. The computer research division became Symult, a subsidiary of the newly formed company Ketema. In June 1989, Symult stopped production of the S2010 machine, although they continued to provide support for existing machines for another year.

In total about a dozen S2010 machines were sold to academic establishments, industry, and the US DoD. The list of sites includes CalTech, the University of Texas, Michigan Technological University, the University of Southern California, Ohio University, the Weizmann Institute (Israel), MCC, Mitre Corp., and Trading Techniques Inc. The machine was popular with users – only one site was not fully satisfied with the system. The biggest S2010 installation, consisting of 192 nodes with 50 vector processors, is at CalTech. This system is still heavily used, and provides the highest performance available for many applications.

10.5.2   The Symult S2010

The S2010 machine consisted of up to 1024 processors connected by a high performance communications network. The processing element was a 25 MHz Motorola 68020 with a 68881 (420 kFLOPS) co-processor, or an optional 68882 (630 kFLOPS) co-processor. Each processing element had as standard 1 Mbyte of memory, which could be expanded to 8 Mbyte. A VMEbus interface allowed up to three VME devices to be attached to each processing element. One of these slots could be used for a vector floating point unit which provides a peak performance of 20 MFLOPS. This unit consisted of a Weitek chip set and had memory options ranging from 2 Mbyte through 10 Mbyte.

The VME interface on each processing element provided the S2010 with very powerful I/O facilities. Each node in the system could potentially have a SCSI disc attached thus providing a huge mass storage capability.

The S2010 was hosted by a Sun-3 workstation which was used for compilation. The compiled code was then downloaded to the S2010. This arrangement is very similar to that used by Intel with their iPSC computers (Section 4.1.2). The Sun-3 host could optionally contain a graphics processor linked to the S2010 by a 80 Mbyte/s connection.

The S2010 processing element did not run a full operating system, since users could not directly access these processors. They ran a reduced operating system called the Reactive Kernel, the result of work done at CalTech. The Reactive Kernel had a UNIX-like disc filing system which could interface to other filing system's through Sun's NFS. The distributed filing system appeared to the user as if it were any other UNIX file system with each processing element's disc partitions appearing in a special root directory. This file system was accessible through a Local Area Network and could be used by external machines. The file tables were distributed throughout the system allowing an open file to be accessed by any process. The user had to manage parallel access to files by hand although there were library routines to assist in this task.

The Symult S2010 could be programmed in either C or Fortran, and there were vectorising compilers for both of these languages. STRAND[88] (9.4) would run on the Symult, and a concurrent Lisp system was also available.

10.5.3 The Communications Network

The major feature of the S2010 was its advanced communications network, which uses hardware routing. Most of the so-called first generation parallel machines used a store-and-forward communications network in which the processing elements themselves had to route the messages to the correct destinations. This introduced considerable latency into the communications network and reduced the performance of the whole machine dramatically. The router in the Symult S2010 is shown in Figure 10.1.

Most of the second generation machines, such as the S2010, have a separate router attached to each processing element which through-routes messages using special-purpose hardware. This allows each processing element to operate independently of the communications network, while the router provides a high speed communication link between processing elements.

The S2010's communications network was mesh based and was hardware reconfigurable. The system's topology could be altered by physically manipulating inter-node connections. The router attached to each processing element had five 20 Mbyte/s bi-directional links and was implemented using custom CMOS VLSI de-

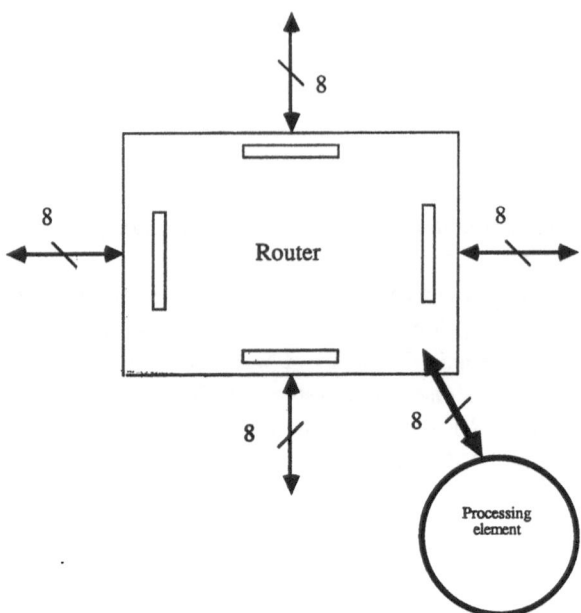

Figure 10.1: The Symult S2010 Router

vices. One of the five router links connected the router with the processing element; the others provided links to the communications mesh.

The S2010 used wormhole routing, in which a continuous link is established between message source and destination, through which the message flows in its entirety. In quiet networks, this routing method reduces the effect on communication time from passing messages through intermediary nodes. In one experiment on the S2010 the effect of path length on communications performance was found to be less than 0.4% for an 8 kbyte message [ENBO].

The routing strategy implemented in hardware by the routers in the S2010 was to pass messages along the rows of the mesh and then down the columns. This algorithm prevents deadlock since network resource requirements can never be cyclic. Once a route to the destination node has been established the entire message must complete transmission before the network resources are released. If a message cannot proceed because its next link is being used then its transmission halts until the link becomes free, with the tail remaining in the originating processing element and in the routers traversed so far. In order to prevent a message from blocking out other messages the network, the Reactive Kernel implemented a packetisation scheme whereby network messages were automatically split into 256 byte chunks.

While the S2010 enjoyed the advantages of wormhole routing described above, it suffered because of contention for network resources and the packetisation scheme. The effective link effective link bandwidth of 17 Mbyte/s for messages of size less than 256 byte was reduced to 6.5 Mbyte/s by the packetisation scheme, in one experiment [ENBO].

10.5.4 Why did the S2010 fail?

Symult failed because its market (universities, and industrial and government research establishments) was relatively saturated with the systems produced by Intel and NCUBE, which led to poor sales for the S2010. Although, the Symult machine had many advanced features, such as the hardware support for wormhole routing, it failed to compete with these other machines, and the poor sales caused Symult's parent company to lose confidence in it and close it down.

The Symult S2010 served a very valuable purpose, since it brought an advanced communications system to the market and provided a goal for others to aim at. It was unfortunate that Symult's parent company could not see the future for the machine and its successors. However, the technology which was introduced in the S2010 is very much alive in the Touchstone Project (4.1.7) and will see the light of day in the next generation of Intel machines.

Company Summary 26: Features of the BiiN 60

Source	BiiN
Type	Fault-tolerant multiprocessors.
Availability	BiiN has ceased operations.
Price	$240 k for a low-end machine; "well over" $1 M at the high end.
Processing nodes	Up to 8.
Processor technology	Custom $2\mu m$ CMOS.
Memory	80 Mbyte, with 16 Mbyte stable-store memory.
Communications	40 Mbyte/s internal bus, with burst transfer and packetising.
I/O connections	32 Mbyte/s per I/O channel.
Performance	4.5 MIPS per processor.
Host system	None.
Operating system	BiiN/OS with POSIX-compatible interface.
Programming languages	Ada, C, Fortran, Cobol, Pascal.
Physical configuration	Unknown.
Power requirements	Unknown.
Sources	Company literature, discussions with former staff.

Company Summary 27: Features of the ETA[10]

Source	ETA Systems.
Type	Liquid nitrogen cooled and air-cooled pipelined vector supercomputers. Liquid cooled systems had from two to eight CPUs. Air cooled systems had one or two CPUs.
Availability	First four processor computer was shipped in December 1986. ETA ceased operations in April 1989.
Price	Air cooled machines: $900 k – $1.5 M. Liquid nitrogen cooled machines: $10 M – $20 M.
Processing nodes	Based on the Cyber 205 pipelined vector CPU, with and extended instruction set for inter-processor communication. CPUs were constructed from VLSI CMOS chips on a 42 layer printed circuit board.
Memory	Each processor had from 4–16 Mword of DRAM. Shared memory was in the form of 1 Gword of SRAM.
Communications	Inter-CPU communication was via a global communications buffer and shared memory by calling message passing instructions.
I/O connections	Up to 18 I/O processors based on Motorola 68020 CPUs were connected to the shared memory via communications links.
Performance	Peak performance per node was 800 MFLOPS. Peak performance for the fastest eight processor machine was 10 GFLOPS.
Host system	CDC equipment.
Operating system	VSOS from the Cyber 205 offered as a UNIX shell, and a full version of UNIX.
Programming languages	Fortran 77 with libraries offering multiprocessing capabilities.
Sources	Publicly available books and papers. Interviews with key ex-ETA personnel.

Company Summary 28: Features of the Multiflow Trace /200 and Trace /300 Series

Source	Multiflow Computer Inc.
Type	VLIW
Availability	Trace /200 series available from mid 1987, Trace /300 series available from February 1989. 100 sales to 75 installations in North America, continental Europe and Japan by end 1989.
Price	Typical configurations: 7/200 (entry-level system) - $299,500; 7/300 - $514,300; 14/300 - $646,300; 28/300 - $1,025,600.
Processing nodes	Seven (7/200 and 7/300), 14 (14/300) or 28 processors (28/300).
Processor technology	Custom VLIW processors.
Memory	Up to 512 Mbyte of memory (Trace /300 series).
I/O connections	VME bus compatible. I/O processors supporting up to 60 Mbyte/s (burst).
Performance	The peak performance of the Trace 28/300 was 120 MFLOPS; LINPAK benchmarks were 70 MFLOPS and 20 MFLOPS on 1000×1000 and 100×100 tests respectively.
Operating system	UNIX
Programming languages	C, Fortran, Pascal and Ada. Powerful parallelising compilers.
Sources	Parallelogram, Supercomputing Review.

Company Summary 29: Features of the Myrias SPS-2

Source	Myrias Research Corporation
Type	Massively-parallel supercomputers
Availability	Since April 1989, nine systems sold in Canada and US.
Price	$300 k for a 64 node SPS-2
Processing nodes	64 to 1024 nodes.
Processor technology	Motorola 68020 (68040 in SPS-3).
Memory	4 Mbyte per processor (8-16 Mbyte/processor in SPS-3).
Communications	SPS-2: 33 Mbyte/s on board and in cabinet ($\times 2$ backplane buses), 11 Mbyte/s between cabinets. The SPS-3 will use four backplane buses in cabinet, and provide 33 Mbyte/s between cabinets.
I/O connections	Unknown.
Performance	Unknown.
Host system	Sun 3/280 (SPARC-based console in SPS-3).
Operating system	Parallel Application Management System (PAMS) for process scheduling and load balancing, UNIX lookalike for system services.
Programming languages	Fortran 77 and C with PARDO extensions
Physical configuration	Cabinet footprint is 76 cm $\times$ 76 cm.
Power requirements	SPS-2: 2.5 kW per 64 processor cage, plus 2 kW for the console. SPS-3: $\sim$ 3.4 kW for each cage, plus 500 W for the console.
Sources	Discussions with Myrias staff, USENET articles.

Company Summary 30: Features of the Symult S2010

Source	Symult
Type	The Symult S2010 was a distributed memory multi-processor with wormhole routing.
Availability	The S2010 was introduced in January 1988 and production was stopped in June 1989, and about a dozen machines were sold.
Price	A 64 node system with 8 Mbyte per node memory and 32 vector processors together with a couple of discs would have had a list price in the region of S1.5 M. However, most systems were sold at 20% to 40% discount depending on circumstances.
Processing nodes	Up to 1024 68020 processing elements could be configured. The largest machine sold had 192 nodes.
Processor technology	The processor was the Motorola 68020 with 68881 co-processor with the option for a 68882 co-processor. A 20 MFLOPS vector unit could be added.
Memory	The standard memory per node was 1 Mbyte but this could be expanded to 8 Mbyte.
Communications	The S2010 had a mesh topology communications network with through routing done by custom hardware routers. Each router had four network links which were individually rated at 20 Mbyte/s.
I/O connections	Each processing element had its own VMEbus which provided I/O capabilities on each node. SCSI devices could be used in these slots to provide mass storage capabilities.
Performance	An S2010 with 1024 nodes could have provided 4000 MIPS, 20 GFLOPS, 10 Gbyte of Vector processor memory, and 8 Gbyte of processing element memory.
Host system	The S2010 was hosted by a Sun-3 system.
Operating system	The Reactive Kernel was used on the processing elements.

Programming languages C and Fortran using vectorising compilers; concurrent Lisp and STRAND[88] .

Physical configuration The machine is boxed in standard 19″ RETMA racks. Up to 32 processing elements can fit in a single cabinet with dimensions 24″ × 48″ × 60″. A larger cabinet capable of holding 128 processing elements is available. The system is air cooled.

Sources The information was gathered from personnel at Epic Systems Group who currently provide support for the S2010.

Chapter 11

Machines Future

This book has described both the machines currently available, and those which played a significant part in the development of parallel computing in the 1980s but which have since disappeared. In this chapter we look forward to the next decade, and try to predict what the machine of the year 2000 will be like.

Today, a decade after parallel architectures began to leave the laboratory, the target is to produce the teraFLOPS computer, or more generally the "3T" machine, i.e. one with over one TFLOPS power, with one Tbyte of main memory and one Tbyte/s of memory bandwidth. Much of the impetus for the development of these machines comes from so-called "Grand Challenge" problems, such as quantum chromodynamics, weather simulation, and molecular biology which involve computational problems many orders of magnitude larger that can currently be tackled.

As discussed in the preceding chapters, many manufacturers are currently designing and developing teraFLOPS supercomputers, for example Thinking Machines (cf. Section 2.3), BBN (3.2), Cray Research Inc. (7.1) and SSI (7.3). While none of these companies is yet prepared to disclose any details about how the goal is to be achieved, it is clear that we are approaching the limits of conventional semiconductor technologies. Although more exotic materials such as GaAs promise speed improvements it is unlikely that these will deliver the required performance unaided. Furthermore, although research and development work is actively being carried out on optical computers, such a machine is still some time away. It may be supposed, therefore, that the next generation machines must utilise large numbers of (vector?) processors operating in parallel, if they are to achieve teraFLOPS performance.

Given the differences in their current architectures and the commercial success of many of these companies with their present machines we may surmise that the solutions adopted by different manufacturers will not be the same. Consequently, we do not anticipate the demise of SIMD or MIMD parallelism. However, the increasing communications rates being offered by HiPPI and Ultranet means that heterogeneous machines will be constructed which combine both SIMD and MIMD elements from existing computers. This may provide a significant enhancement for some users in the ease with which their problems can be mapped on the machine.

While parallelism is secure at the top-end of the performance scale the situation at the low-end is not so clear in the immediate future. The development of very fast, single processor machines, for example the IBM RS/6000 and those based upon the Intel i860, will deprive small parallel machines of their market: why bother parallelising code when similar performance may be achieved from a single chip? It is always dangerous to make predictions about the reactions of the market to different products, but we suspect that the impact of these fast, single processor machines will be felt most strongly by those parallel manufacturers who produce general purpose machines. Purchasers interested in, for example, small SIMD machines are less likely to find the new, fast single processor computers fitting their requirements.

Another trend which has appeared and grown strongly over the last five years is the use, by MIMD manufacturers, of conventional microprocessors and memory chips. This significantly reduces both development times and costs and it is likely that this move will continue for the forseeable future. There are notable exceptions to this pattern: the SIMD manufacturers require a simple, cheap processor at each node and it is probable that this will continue to be developed in-house. Also, the vector supercomputer companies, for example Cray Research Inc. and SSI, show no sign of using more conventional technologies. Indeed it would be remarkable if they did so, since their machines require the highest possible clock speeds which can only be attained from specialised architectures. Moreover, the end of the classical Cray has been predicted by others for some time without any evidence that the company are contemplating this move. For example, "Cray must move into the cube business to maintain its position; we predict therefore that Cray will announce a supercomputer cube product, probably before the end of 1987" (Ovum report pg. 21). We are still waiting.

Although most MIMD computers have distributed memory, there is an increasing tendency for manufacturers to hide the machine parallelism from the user by combining software and routing hardware to make the memory appear shared. In order to make this approach reasonably efficient it requires considerable hardware support in the form of wide interprocessor data-paths and fast switches. However, it does increase the ease of use of such computers and it is probable that this trend will continue. The users' model of these machines will be one of processes which can communicate either through explicit calls to send and receive functions, which will supplement existing serial languages, or through more traditional methods such as semaphores. This machine model represents a convergence of the MIMD shared memory and MIMD distributed memory computers. A good example of this architecture is the BBN TC2000 (cf. Section 3.2.2) in which the memory is distributed amongst the processors but appears to the user to be shared.

The rise of UNIX over the same period does now seem to be complete and its future, or that of some derivative, such as MACH is secure. All major manufacturers, including IBM and DEC have now released versions of UNIX of their machines. There are moves to define a new standard operating system which is well adapted for parallel architectures and MACH, originally developed for DARPA at Carnegie-Mellon University, has been selected by the Open Software Foundation (OSF) as their choice. Since the OSF represents many of the major American manufacturers it is possible that MACH may be generally adopted. In any case, we are entering the realm of a standardised operating system. However, the situation regarding software tools resembles that of operating systems a decade ago, may be see the same sort of unification there? The answer is, probably, no. Nevertheless, the growing tendency to use standard chips should mean that there will be a reduction in the range of such tools available as hardware manufacturers turn to third-party suppliers for basic software. Although for the last thirty years software development costs have exceeded those for the hardware we are still some way from having good standard toolsets, especially on parallel computers.

In 1985 Johnson and Durham said "... we are not forecasting that parallel processing will lead users to spend significantly more money on computer hardware than the industry is already expecting them to spend. On the other hand they will be able to purchase considerably more performance with their money." (Ovum report pg. 22). We believe that the price/performance ratio will improve for machines using standard technologies for the forseeable future.

If we review the manufacturers listed in the preceding chapters it is clear that the majority are from the US, with Europe in second place. It is clear, however, that Japan is rapidly becoming a strong force and a number of companies have plans to release high-performance parallel computers within the next couple of years. Given their virtual monopoly of many electronic and related markets it will be interesting to review the geographical distribution of producers in five years time. We suspect that it may look rather different from that today.

Bibliography

[MACH] M. Acetta, R. Baron, W. Bolosky, D. Golub, R. Rashid, A. Tevanian and M. Young — "Mach: A New Kernel Foundation For UNIX Development", in *USENIX Summer '86 Conference*, pp. 93-113, 1986.

[ALGO] George S. Almasi and Allan J. Gottlieb — *Highly Parallel Computing*, Benjamin Cummings, 1989 (ISBN 0-8053-0177-1).

[MESH] William C. Athas and Charles L. Seitz — "Multicomputers: Message-Passing Concurrent Computers", *IEEE Trans. Computers*, Vol. 21, No. 8, pp. 9-24.

[ENBO] Suresh Chittor and Richard Enbody — "Performance Evaluation of Mesh-Connected Wormhole-Routed Networks for Interprocessor Communication in Multicomputers", in *Supercomputing*, 1990.

[TINY] *Tiny Version 1.0: Discussion and User Guide*, Lyndon J. Clarke, Edinburgh Concurrent Supercomputer Project User Guide 9, May 1989.

[BULL] John Ellis — *Bulldog: A Compiler for VLIW Architectures*, ACM Distinguished Dissertations Series, MIT Press, Cambridge, Massachusetts, 1985.

[FISH] Joseph A. Fisher — *The Optimization of Horizontal Microcode Within and Beyond Basic Blocks*, Ph.D. Thesis, New York University, October 1979.

[VLIW] Joseph A. Fisher — "VLIW Architectures and the Eli-512", *10th Computer Architecture Conference*, 1983, pp. 140-150.

[FOTA] Ian Foster and Stephen Taylor — *Strand: New Concepts in Parallel Programming*, Prentice-Hall, 1989.

[FOST] Ian Foster — *Systems Programming*, Prentice-Hall, 1989.

[SPCP] Geoffrey Fox et al — *Solving Problems on Concurrent Processors: Vol. 1*, Prentice-Hall, 1988 (ISBN 0-138-23469-8).

[HILL] W. Daniel Hillis — *The Connection Machine*, ACM Distinguished Dissertations Series, MIT Press, Cambridge, Massachusetts, 1985 (ISBN 0-262-58097-7).

[HOAR] C. A. R. Hoare — *Communicating Sequential Processes*, Prentice-Hall, 1985 (ISBN 0-131-53271-5).

[MACK] Donald Mackenzie — "Perestroika and Parallelism: Advanced Information Technology and the Soviet Union", in *Technology Analysis and Strategic Management*, Vol. 1, No. 2, pp. 145-56 (1989).

[MOL1] Alfonso Molina — "Information Technology: Anatomy of a Successful European Collaboration", in *Technology Analysis and Strategic Management*, Vol. 1 (1989).

[MOL1] Alfonso Molina — "1992 and European Integration: Opportunities and Difficulties in High Technology Collaboration", in *Futures*, Vol. 22, pp. 496-514 (1990).

[MOL1] Alfonso Molina — "Technology Collaboration — 1992 and Beyond", in *The Single European Market and the Informaiton and Communictaion Technologies*, ed. G. Locksley, Belhaven, 1990.

[OVUM] Tim Johnson and Tony Durham — *Parallel Processing: the challenge of new computer architectures* Ovum Ltd., 1986 (IBSN 0-903969-31-9)

[PELA] Eloína Peláez — "Parallelism: Performance or Programming", in *Computers and Society*, Vol. 19, 4-8 (1989).

[PELA] Eloína Peláez — "Parallelism and the Crisis of Von Neumann Computing", in *Technology in Society*, Vol. 12, 65-77 (1990).

[PONT] "Computer Graphics", in *International Workshop on Algorithms and Parallel VLSI Architectures*, European Association for Signal Processing (EURASIP), p. 549, June 1990.

[COCU] Charles L. Seitz — "The Cosmic Cube", *Comm. ACM*, Vol. 28, No. 1, pp. 22-33.

[WEES] Neil Weste and Kamran Eshraghian — *Principles of CMOS VLSI Design*, Addison Wesley, 1985.

Appendix A

Technology

These appendices are short summaries of some of the concepts encountered in parallel computing. Caching is an important technique which can greatly improve the performance of shared memory multiprocessors; good compilers are as crucial to parallel computers as they are to their serial cousins, but seemingly much harder to produce; message routing is perhaps the key technology on distributed memory multicomputers; and visualisation is now accepted as the only effective mechanism for interpreting large or complex data sets.

A.1   Cache Memory

A cache is a small, fast buffer in which a computer keeps those contents of main memory which are likely to be used soon. The purpose of the cache is to improve system performance by providing the capacity of the large, slow memory with an average access rate close to that of a small, fast cache. This is only possible if most memory references can be serviced by the cache without the intervention of the slower memory.

A.1.1   Performance

There are two important cache performance metrics to be aware of: miss ratio[1] and effective access time. The miss ratio of a cache is the ratio of the number of misses with cache against the number of processor references. The miss ratio is implementation independent, although obviously comparison of miss ratios between the Cray-1 instruction buffers and the MC68040 on-chip instruction cache is meaningless because the technologies and workloads are different.

Effective access time is defined as the average time for which a processor must wait for its memory request to be serviced. The method by which the cache is used can be adjusted by the hardware designer to optimise the effective access time for a given cost and CPU system.

A.1.2   Cache Update Policies

Cache update policies are necessary to ensure that data written to the cache is updated in main memory. Some machines, for example the Motorola's RISC 88000 microprocessor, allow users to select the most suitable policy for a particular application. The chosen policy should keep memory traffic to a minimum. On a single processor architecture, updating is simple because it is not necessary to consider the possibility of neighbouring processors accessing old data in main memory.

Write-through update policy writes a cache block frame (a location in the cache that holds the data, an associated address tag, and state bits) to main memory whenever that cache block frame is modified by the CPU. This ensures that memory data are always valid, so that other system bus devices, for example peripherals or neighbouring CPUs, can access memory and be assured of accessing correct data. If the application running on the CPU requires many updates this policy is safe but puts heavy traffic on the bus. The copy-back update policy reduces bus traffic under these circumstances. Cache writes are copied to memory the first time the cached data are written; then updates are not written to memory until the cache block frame is flushed from the cache. Although this policy reduces memory traffic,

---

[1]References found in the cache are said to hit; those not found are said to miss.

memory data are not always updated and inconsistencies may occur in a shared memory system.

A.1.3 Multicache Consistency

Large modern computer systems often have several independent processors, consisting of several CPUs and zero, one or several caches. Unfortunately, in such a multiprocessor system, a given piece of information may exist in several places at a given time and it is important that all processors have access to the same, unique value. Several solutions exist and have been proposed for this problem; in particular the "write-invalidate" and "write-broadcast" techniques. In the former a processor invalidates all other cached copies of shared data and then updates its own without further bus operations. Under write-broadcast, a processor broadcasts updates to shared data to other caches, so that all copies are the same. Both techniques have been criticised and enhancement protocols have been added to achieve a better bus performance across all cache configurations.

A.2 Message Passing Systems

Distributed memory MIMD computers, or *multicomputers*, such as the various hypercubes and transputer-based machines, consist of processors with local memory, connected by some form of communications network. In order to run on such a machine, a computation must be divided into tasks which do not need to share memory and which communicate with each other by passing messages. It is this division into tasks, and their placement on processors, that constitutes the art of multicomputer programming.

A multicomputer is usually programmed using its message passing system directly, without any higher level abstraction such as that provided by STRAND[88] or Linda. While this has its disadvantages, both because the software interface available is often primitive and non-intuitive and because calls to the interface are not standard across the various manufacturers' machines, it does have the advantage of imposing relatively low software overheads. Since performance is still the critical issue for most users of multicomputers, the pain of dealing with the machine this way is usually considered worthwhile.

An archetypal stripped-down no-frills message passing system for transputers is called Tiny, and was developed at the University of Edinburgh. Similar message passing software is provided with the Intel iPSC and on NCUBE machines. Various software environments for multicomputers make a message passing system directly available. On hypercubes, there is the Express kernel, which contains a message passing system. On Meiko's Computing Surface, there is the Computing Surface Network, which is accessible through CS Tools. You get direct access to a message passing system in Trollius/Genesys, while in Helios and other UNIX-like operating systems there is a message passing system hidden in amongst the OS's pipes and sockets, although the overheads of using it are not small.

Message passing systems for multicomputers can be seen in the context of the Open Systems Interconnect standard for computer networking. The major difference is that in the case of the message passing system the network is inside the computer, and thus the functionality that it needs to provide is smaller. (For example, multicomputer tasks rarely send electronic mail to each other.)

A complete message passing system must have all of the following:

- An addressing scheme for the destinations of messages

- A technique for avoiding deadlock in the message passing system

- A policy for deciding when messages can be sent

- A mechanism for sending messages between tasks

- A mechanism for selecting between messages at destination

- A mechanism for locating tasks on processors

A.2.1   Addressing of Messages

At some level in the message passing system all message destination identifiers must be translated into unique numeric identifiers which are used to select a path on which to route the message. However, there are three common ways in which the destination of a message can be specified by users.

Numeric Task and Type Identifiers

In Express and Tiny, and other similar message passing systems, each task is given an identifier, which is specified when the task is placed on the hardware. Messages are then addressed directly to tasks. Messages are sent with a task identifier and a type identifier. Messages arriving at a task can be selected on the basis of their type (cf. A.2.5).

Depending upon the low-level implementation, tasks are numbered by *(node, task-in-node)* pairs, or by a single integer task identifier. The advantage of referring to tasks directly by a numeric identifier is that it is often useful to perform arithmetic on these identifiers. For example, in applications in which a regular data space is split up into tiles, which are then assigned to tasks, the identifiers of tasks which are processing tiles adjacent to the one held by a given task can be calculated by simple arithmetic on the given task's ID.

Ports

In CS Tools messages are sent to ports. Tasks create named ports whose network identifiers can be found by other tasks by querying a name-server. The network identifiers that are sent back can then be used to send messages to destination tasks. A task may create more than one port for itself, and can select messages from each independently. Since the port identifier is defined by the message passing system, it is not amenable to arithmetic. The ports/name-server scheme is similar to that used in NFS, and has the advantage that operating system services such as keyboard and screen can be identified by name.

Channels

In Hoare's Communicating Sequential Processes (CSP), and in the Occam language which embodies it, messages are sent along named channels between tasks. The language associates identifiers with these channels at compile time. In the case of the current generation of transputers, all channel identifiers, including links between processors, are just locations in memory. In the next generation (the H1) there will be support for communication between non-adjacent processors via a hardware message passing system, in which channels will be given network identifiers similar to those used in other systems.

There are serious problems with programming on top of channels. There are many similarities between channel communication and the old-fashioned Fortran GOTO — programmers spend a lot of time wondering "Where does this channel go to?", tracing it through multiplexers and changes of name. In addition, to allow communication between arbitrary tasks in an Occam program we require a channel from every task to every other. Plumbing together the million channels required for a thousand-task program can be a little tortuous.

Operating System

Tasks often require access to the facilities of the execution environment. This is usually achieved by sending messages to and receiving messages from special tasks in the multicomputer through the same low-level message passing system used for communication between tasks in the application. The simple task enumeration approach to identifying tasks requires that certain task or type identifiers be reserved for system messages. Labelling message destinations as ports, on the other hand, provides a mechanism for identifying operating system tasks. A related issue is that it rarely makes sense for tasks within a multicomputer to have access to an operating system as independent entities. In most cases, the functionality of the operating system must be extended to allow, for example, transparent simultaneous write access to a single file from many tasks.

A.2.2   Deadlock and Related Issues

Deadlock is a well known problem in concurrent systems, and occurs both in message passing programs and in shared memory programs. In its simplest form, deadlock occurs when a task A must wait for a task B to do something, but task B cannot proceed until task A has done something else. It is useful to prove that message passing systems cannot introduce deadlocks into a correct program. In the context of message passing systems this property is usually referred to as deadlock freedom. Deadlock cannot occur if there can never be a cycle of messages inside the message passing system which are waiting on each other's transmission. In the case of parallel programs written on top of message passing systems with flow control properties equivalent to those of CSP, it is possible to prove the non-existence of deadlock even when the application is non-deterministic. Proofs are also possible in the case of other message passing systems, although they are harder, and it usually turns out to be easier to write programs that work most of the time and occasionally deadlock.

There are four approaches used to avoid deadlock. The first, as used in the ECCL message passing system, is to restrict incoming message flow, and never to commit to routing messages in cyclic routes. The second approach, used in CS Tools, is to multiplex an acyclic virtual network across the links of a cyclic network. The third approach, used in the H1, the hypercube machines, and Tiny, is to disallow certain link-to-link message transfers in the processor network so as to avoid cyclic message paths, while still maintaining full connectivity. The final approach, often used in computer networking, is simply to throw away some messages. This is usually avoided in message passing systems, with the exception of the Helios kernel.

A.2.3   Controlling Message Transfer

In the simplest message passing systems (ones without flow control protocols) messages are sent when the programmer wants them to be sent. This is known as *asynchronous* messaging. When messages arrive, they sit in buffers at their destination until they are read by the application. This can lead to a situation in which the buffers at the destination are full and messages start backing up in the network, eventually clogging and deadlocking the application. This can be avoided if the number of outstanding messages at a task can be bounded and a large enough buffer allocated.

An alternative approach, called *synchronous* messaging, is for the receiving task to request messages as and when it wants them (a request transfer protocol). A more elaborate approach is for the sending task to send an indication that it is ready to transmit, which is buffered and replied to only when the destination task is ready to receive. Only then is the actual message sent. This is known as a request acknowledge transfer (RAT) protocol. RAT has several advantages: only requests are stored, rather than whole messages; the destination task can select between requests; and RAT corresponds to the model used in CSP. Its disadvantage is that three message are sent for each message transferred, although this can be reduced to two if the message is small enough to be contained in the request.

An issue related to synchrony is the blocking or non-blocking of communication functions. A process is blocked by a function if it cannot do any further processing until that function call completes. With a blocking read or write, the task performing the communication cannot proceed until the read or write has completed. A call to a non-blocking read, on the other hand, sets up a communication event, but does not wait for it to complete before continuing with other calculations; a non-blocking write behaves similarly. Systems which provide non-blocking operations must obviously also provide a way to check for the termination of non-blocking read/write transfers. Non-blocking read/write pairs can be used to overlap communication and computation, especially in data-parallel applications in which boundary values can be swapped at the same time as the values of interior points are being updated.

A.2.4   Delivering Messages

There are three approaches to message delivery. First, the message may be fragmented into packets and each packet stored and forwarded separately, being placed in a queue at a node if its output link is not ready. The message may then be re-built at its destination. This is known as *packet switching*. Another approach, called *circuit switching*, is for a pre-message to be sent through the network to the destination. This pre-message sets up a path for the message. The message is then sent, and the message's tail frees up the path. The third approach, *wormholing*, is for the head of the message to set up the path itself. Extravagant claims are made for the efficacy of wormholing. While it does improve the speed of message transfer in quiet networks, it causes a head-of-line blocking problem in fully loaded networks, where packet switching systems tend to provide roughly twice as much aggregate bandwidth. In practice, wormhole routing's main advantage is that it can be easily implemented in hardware.

Quite often, applications need to send a single message (such as a signal to start or stop working) to more than one destination at a time. When this is done to every task in the network it is known as a *broadcast*; when it is done to some arbitrary subset of tasks it is called a *multicast*. It is possible to do this by replicating the message inside the message passing system. The technique can result in significant speedup over the alternative approach of repeated message sends, since less bandwidth is consumed. The inverse of broadcast or multicast is a combine operation, which can be used to perform such things as a global sum operation efficiently. The problem with broadcasts or multicasts lies in defining the set of tasks involved without incurring a large overhead. In this context, it helps if the system can partition the address space of the message passing system so that tasks only receive appropriate messages.

A.2.5 Message Selection

Message selection is tightly bound up with the issues of message addressing. In the three approaches to addressing described earlier it was possible for tasks to differentiate between messages on their arrival. In the case of task/type addressing, messages may be selected on the basis of their type, and also on the basis of their source. In the case of ports, a task may create more than one port and select messages by receiving only from one of them. In the case of channels, a task can can select messages from any of the named channels that are its inputs.

There can exist, however, a situation when a task is prepared to receive a message from a subset of the inputs that it may differentiate between. This is referred to as *wildcarding*. Occam provides the ALT construct to allow wildcarding on any subset of the channels that are inputs to a task. The problem with ALT is that this involves searching through a list of channels to see if any of them is ready to communicate, something which is at least linear in the length of the list. While there is some firmware on the transputer to support this, it is still an expensive operation.

The addressing mechanisms which use port or task/type identifiers provide selection on the basis of a user specified property of messages. This often gets rid of the need for wildcarding, and thereby improves efficiency.

A.2.6 Placing Tasks

The final problem, that of placing tasks on processors, is one which is solved in different ways by different message passing systems. Tiny can be configured either inside an Occam harness, or by using the configuration facilities in the 3L compilers. CS Tools provides a low-level mechanism for writing a program to build a network of tasks, or alternatively a higher level file-based interface which provides limited subset of the same functionality. Trollius provides two *schemata* which name processors and associate tasks with them, while Express provides a similar functionality with its config files. The functionality provided by these various systems is broadly similar, but the syntax with which tasks are placed on processors varies dramatically.

A.3 Visualisation

One of the greatest growth areas in computing in the 1980s has been computer graphics. In particular, scientists and engineers have found that in many cases the only way to understand the output from their programs is to turn those results into a picture.

Consider, for example, a simulation of stresses in a concrete arch. The mesh used to describe this structure may contain tens of thousands of points. Displaying the output from the analysis program as a stress vector at each grid point is unlikely to improve the designer's understanding of what is going on. A colour-coded picture, on the other hand, can let the designer see instantly where the strain on the arch is greatest. Graphics is particularly useful for understanding simulation programs in which the evolution of some values over time is a crucial feature.

Such *scientific visualisation* underlies the concern of many manufacturers with developing high-bandwidth connections between their machines and graphics hardware, whether this be workstations or custom-built equipment. It is also one of the driving forces behind efforts to develop standards for high-bandwidth connections, such as HiPPI.

A.3.1 Doing It In Hardware

It is a general rule in computing that general-purpose processors running good software is almost always more cost-effective than special-purpose hardware. The hard times experienced by companies based on specialised processors, such as manufacturers of Lisp workstations, have shown that the much greater resources devoted to developing general-purpose processors, and to training people to program them, quickly negates any temporary superiority in speed which a special-purpose architecture might provide.

Three-dimensional graphics is an exception to this rule. Most high-performance graphics workstations now use special-purpose VLSI chips, rather than the main CPU, to perform the calculations required to display images. The development of such chips is economic because of the specialised nature of the calculations being done. A performance of 100 kpolygon/s requires 10 MFLOPS just for transformations. Since only one algorithm is employed, and this technique is unlikely to change, a custom VLSI implementation turns out to be the most cost-effective way of providing this performance. The use of such hardware is now spreading from special purpose graphics workstations to compute engines, eg. Alliant (3.1) and personal computers, eg. IBM RS/6000.

Most systems, like those built by Silicon Graphics (cf. 6.2) and Stardent (cf. 6.3) use a graphics pipeline (Figure A.1) which splits the graphics transformations into stages which can operate independently. Some vendors add extra stages to the pipeline to provide functionality such as texture mapping.

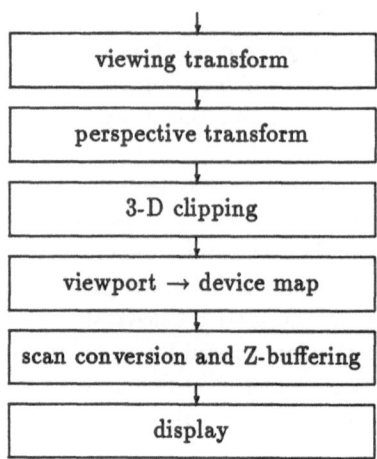

Figure A.1: A Typical Graphics Pipeline

A.4   Parallel Compilers

A compiler for a parallel machine is a compiler whose object code has some explicit notion of simultaneous execution, whether the source code reflects this or not. Many such compilers trace their origins to the vectorising compilers developed for supercomputers in the late 1970s and 1980s. The problems involved in building a full parallelising compiler go far beyond those found in vectorising compilers, since data dependences must not only be analysed within loops but also across procedures.

The advent of parallel computers resulted in a proliferation of new, explicitly parallel, programming languages, and explicitly parallel extensions to sequential languages. These languages have failed to gain widespread acceptance. This is in part due to the massive reengineering effort required to convert the existing software base to the new languages. Another reason for the unpopularity of these languages lies in the portability problems they create. These languages are very rarely machine-independent, and many of them are supported on only a few machines. Differences in architectures and programming models necessitate major re-engineering of applications when moving them to new machines. The scale of this task dwarfs the problems encountered in porting sequential code between sequential machines.

The great dream for parallel machines is a parallelising compiler which can extract the implicit parallelism from sequential programs and produce parallel code toe exploit the capabilities of a particular architecture. This would save the effort of parallelising code by hand, and avoid the portability problems of explicitly parallel programs. Scientific and engineering applications, traditionally the major application area for high-performance computers and therefore parallel machines, typically involve loops with a large number of iterations. There seems to be a lot of potential parallelism to be exploited in this type of loop:

```
for (i = 0; i < 10000; i++)
  data[i] = 0;
```

A.4.1 Vectorising Compilers

With the advent of vector processors such as the Cray-1 there was a need for compilers that would allow existing code (typically Fortran) to take advantage of the vector capabilities of the new machines. Typical programs in scientific and engineering applications involve loops with a large number of iterations. Where successive iterations are independent, the operations may be overlapped and issued as a vector instruction. For a set of loop iterations to be independent, they must not modify a variable which is used by another iteration in the set.

```
int data[10000];
/* First Loop */
for (i = 1; i < 10000; i++)
  data[i] = i;

/* Second Loop */
for (i = 1; i < 10000; i++)
  data[i] = data[i-1];
```

If this condition is violated, we cannot be certain whether another iteration reading the variable will get the old value, or the new one, so the behaviour of the concurrent iterations may become *non-deterministic*: different results may be obtained from different runs from identical starting conditions. Consider the loops above. The first loop has 10000 completely independent iterations, all of which could run in parallel if there were enough processors. The iterations of the second loop, on the other hand, are not independent. If we scheduled the iterations for i=1 and i=2 in parallel, the value of data[2] would depend upon whether or not the i=1 iteration had set data[1] to data[0] (i.e. 0) before the i=2 iteration read its value. If data[1] had been updated, then data[2] would become 0, otherwise data[2] would become 1, the value of data[1] before the second loop. Detecting dependencies of one iteration on another (loop-carried dependencies) can be an expensive and complicated process.

The latest compilers are able to vectorise Fortran DO loops that contain IF statements, provide cost analyses of individual statements, and suggest reason why certain statements could not be vectorised — for example, the cost of adding sufficient run-time checks might offset the gain from using vector instructions in some cases.

A.4.2 Parallelising Compilers

Vectorising compilers have been reasonably successful in the commercial field, and the problems involved in building them are well researched and understood. As multiprocessors became increasingly available, new compiler technology was required to exploit their facilities. Full-blown parallelising compilers, which do not simply look for independent loop iterations but also for program sections — typically procedures — which may be executed in parallel, have not yet become generally available. While detecting dependencies between iterations of a loop can be expensive and complicated, detecting dependencies across a whole program is significantly more costly. This problem is exacerbated by the vast range of different architectures and programming models currently available.

Current research has taken many of the dependency tests found in vectorising compilers and extended these to attempt to deal with the fully parallel case. Most researchers have chosen a single target environment and developed systems to produce parallel code for that environment. Recent efforts in this direction include PTRAN at IBM, PTOOL at Rice, and Parafrase.

Little is yet known about program restructuring and compiling for message-passing multiprocessors. In this case, distributed memory forces the compilers to consider data distribution when deciding whether or not to parallelise a section — for instance, does the cost of moving the data to and from the processor outweight the advantage of performing the operation in parallel? Data structures involving pointers are even more problematic to represent or move in distributed memory.

One final area of current research suggests that, because of the large amount of program information gathered by the compiler, there should be a tighter interaction between the user, the compiler, the run-time system, and the operating system. The well-defined interfaces between these entities for serial computers become more fuzzy in the case of parallel machines. For instance, functions that have traditionally been viewed as the operating system's tasks may be carried out more effectively through the compiler on a parallel machine.

VLIW Technology and Trace Scheduling

Very Long Instruction Word (VLIW) architectures can be thought of in terms of Flynn's classification as either liberated SIMD or orchestrated MIMD machines. Like SIMD, and unlike MIMD, all processors obtain their instructions from the same instruction word. In a SIMD machine the instruction word is a single instruction, and every processor executes this instruction. In VLIW machine, the (very long) instruction word contains more than one instruction. Each processor receives a fragment of the instruction word containing a single instruction, which it then executes. This allows processors in a VLIW machine to execute different instructions simultaneously, unlike those in a SIMD machine.

VLIW machines are very difficult to program at a low level, since the programmer must keep track of what all the processors are doing at any time, and merge these concurrent execution sequences into a single sequence of very long instruction words. Due to these difficulties with hand-coding, advanced compilers are used to generate VLIW code.

Trace Scheduling

An intermediate stage in code generation considers *basic blocks*, sections of target code which can only contain a jump if it is the last instruction in the block.

```
for (i = 1; i < 10000; i++)
    data[i] = (data[i] * 0.9) + (data[i-1] * 0.1);
```

A simplified basic block representation of the program fragment above is shown in below:

```
BLOCK 1:     i = 1

BLOCK 2:     t0 = data[i] * 0.9;
             t1 = i - 1;
             t2 = data[t1] * 0.1;
             data[i] = t0 + t2;
             i = i + 1;
             if (i < 10000) goto BLOCK 2

BLOCK 3:     ...
```

An alternative to vectorisation is to concentrate on extracting the implicit parallelism within basic blocks. In the last example above t0 can clearly be calculated in parallel with t1.

This approach avoids the expensive loop-carried dependency analysis of vectorisers, and can extract parallelism from a wider variety of structures than the highly regular loops required by vectorisers. Unfortunately, the basic blocks produced in compiling many programming languages are often too small to support substantial parallelism. In target code compiled from Fortran programs, jumps typically occur every four to eight instructions, resulting in very small basic blocks.

Such small basic blocks rarely allow for much parallelism, and speedups of more than three are uncommon.

Larger basic blocks are likely to contain more parallelism and therefore to provide greater speedup. Many scientific and engineering programs involve simple control structures such as nested loops with a few conditionals which branch one way most of the time. This makes it possible to predict the outcome of conditional jumps quite well. Basic blocks can be concatenated into larger blocks called *traces* which have a high probability of being executed from beginning to end without interruption. A trace can be treated as a large block, providing greater potential parallelism than the basic blocks which compose it. This technique is called *trace scheduling*. Returning to the example code fragment above, the compiler would "unroll' the loop iterations and concatenate them into a single large block. Independent operations within the large block can then be scheduled concurrently.

In order to help some compilers guess the outcome of branches, sample input data for the program can be provided. Trace scheduling compilers are well suited to VLIW architectures, since they can generate code which exploits VLIW machines' potential for parallel execution, a task which is very difficult to do by hand. Generating code for a VLIW machine is slow, due to the analysis of dependencies within basic blocks, and the cost of optimising the generated code is high, since multiple instruction streams are being manipulated in each word.

Appendix B

Units

SI nomenclature is used throughout this document, with SI units wherever possible. The most common prefixes are:

Prefix	Symbol	Value	Example
nano	n	one billionth	nanosecond
micro	μ	one millionth	micrometre (or micron)
milli	m	one thousandth	millisecond
kilo	k	one thousand	kilobyte
mega	M	one million	megahertz
giga	G	one billion	gigaFLOPS
tera	T	one trillion	terabyte

Unfortunately, computer scientists have traditionally confused the meanings of kilo, mega and and giga. This is because many features of computer architectures are centred around powers of two. Since 2^{10} (1024) is so close to 1000, the prefix "kilo" was appropriated, as in "kilobyte" and by extension, mega has been taken to mean 2^{20} (1,048,576). If this weren't bad enough, once the "giga" prefix is reached, computer scientists stop going up by tenth powers and jump directly to 32 (which is itself a power of 2), so that a "gigabyte" is 2^{32} bytes, rather than 2^{30} (or $\sim 10^9$)

We have adopted both this and the SI convention in this document: where the units are bits, bytes or words the prefix refers to the computer scientists' system, otherwise it is SI.

Appendix C

Glossary

Alvey The UK's strategic program in information technology research, which finished in 1989.

ARA The UK's Atomic Research Authority.

ARE The UK's Admiralty Research Establishment

ARPAnet The US Advanced Research Project Agency network, which was the first large multi-site computer network.

BCS The British Computer Society.

BiCMOS Bi-polar CMOS. BiCMOS is a merger of ECL and CMOS wafer processes allowing both types of circuit to exist on the same chip. This gives the advantage of the small feature size and large scale integration of CMOS with ECL's high power, fast driver circuits.

BLAS Basic Linear Algebra Software: a suite of very basic linear algebra routines, using which almost any other matrix calculation can be built.

blurb Used by our contributors to fill space while waiting for information. If you see any of these, oops.

bus A data path shared by several components in a computer. Typically, several processors will share a bus which connects them to memory, or a processor, some memory, and some I/O devices will share a bus.

C.mmp Carnegie-Mellon University's multiprocessor project, active in the 1970s. Many of today's MIMD machines are descended, at least in spirit, from this pioneering work.

cache A local memory store with very fast access time. If a processor is going to use a particular variable (such as a loop index) or value (such as π) repeatedly, it makes sense to store a copy in a handy place.

CAD Computer-Aided Design: a term which can encompass all facets of the use of computers in manufacturing.

CAE Computer-Aided Engineering: like CAD, but usually applied to the use of computers in fields such as civil and nautical engineering.

CalTech The California Institute of Technology: a pioneer in parallel computing. The hypercube architecture was invented here.

CFD Computational Fluid Dynamics: the simulation or prediction of fluid flow using computers, which has traditionally required roughly twice the computing power available at any given time.

CMOS Complementary Metal Oxide on Silicon: the most popular chip technology today.

co-processor a secondary processor attached to a main processor. Co-processors are usually employed to do arithmetic or to handle I/O or graphics.

CPU Central Processing Unit: in a single processor computer, this is what does all the work. The term is sometimes used as a synonym for processor, so that one speaks of a computer having four CPUs.

CrOS The Crystalline Operating System: developed at CalTech for use on hypercubes, it is the parent (or grandparent) of most operating system software for hypercubes today.

CSP Communicating Sequential Processes: a mathematical notation for describing communicating systems developed by Tony Hoare at Oxford. Also, the philosophy implicit in the notation.

DARPA The Defence Advanced Research Projects Agency: formerly ARPA, this US Government body funds a large portion of the advanced computer research done in the US.

DMA Direct Memory Access: allows devices on a bus to access memory without interfering with the CPU.

DRAM Dynamic RAM: memory which needs periodic refreshing. Usually slower than SRAM.

dusty deck a term applied to old Fortran (or Cobol) programs. (The term comes from the image of a deck of punched cards grown dusty over the years.)

ECL Emitter-Coupled Logic: a high-speed, high-power transistor technology.

EPCC The Edinburgh Parallel Computing Centre: a large parallel computing project at the University of Edinburgh.

EPROM Electronically Programmable ROM: a memory whose contents can be changed using special hardware. This usually involves removed the chips from their environment in order to burn a new pattern into them.

Ethernet A popular Local Area Network technology invented by Xerox.

Eurocard A standard size for printed circuit boards.

Exabyte A high-density tape form utilising video technology.

FDDI Fast Digital Data Interface: a standard for fibre optic communications systems.

FEA Finite Element Analysis: a mathematical technique for modelling solid objects. Traditionally, it has required approximately twice the computing power available at any given time.

FIFO First in, first out: a fancy name for a queue.

FLOPS FLOating Point operations per Second. A traditional measure of computer power in the scientific community. These days, MFLOPS (Millions of FLOPS) or GFLOPS (billions of FLOPS) are usually quoted. A single powerful microprocessor can produce 1 MFLOPS, a typical scientific supermini-computer several tens of MFLOPS, and the most powerful special-purpose machines in the world approximately 5 GFLOPS.

FFT Fast Fourier Transform: a technique used extensively in signal processing.

FPU Floating Point Unit: a chip (or portion of a chip) specialised to do floating point calculations.

GaAs gallium arsenide: an "exotic" semiconductor material. Components made of GaAs can run much faster than silicon-based components, but GaAs fabrication technology is still plagued with problems.

GHC Guarded Horn Clauses: a logical notation which has grown into a logic-based programming language akin to Prolog.

GKS the Graphics Kernel Standard: a graphics standard developed for penplotters, and now supported on a wide variety of pixel-based devices.

HiPPI High Performance Parallel Interface: a point-to-point 100 Mbyte/s interface standard.

iAPX 432 a pioneering multiprocessor project at Intel which spawned the iPSC, Sequent, NCUBE, and BiiN.

Illiac IV Arguably, the first effective large-scale parallel processor. Began operation in 1973.

ISO The International Standards Organisation, which, among other things, sets standards for programming languages.

LAN Local Area Network: any technology for coupling computers together across relatively short distances.

light-weight process a process that executes concurrently with other processes, in the same address space and in an unprotected fashion. Light-weight processes are used by systems such as MACH to reduce the overhead of process start-up.

Linpack a linear algebra software package which has been mounted on a wide range of machines. Also, a set of benchmarks based on that package.

LIW Long Instruction Words: the use of long (64 or more bits) instruction words in a processor to improve its ability to pipeline calculations.

LLL Lawrence Livermore Laboratories: a US Government weapons research laboratory.

MIMD Multiple Instruction/Multiple Data: a type of parallel computer whose processors can run independent programs.

MIPS One Million Instructions Per Second.

minisupercomputer A small (or cheap) supercomputer.

motherboard A printed circuit board on which other boards can be mounted.

MISD Multiple Instruction/Single Data: a machine which applies several instructions to each datum. Either there is no such type of computer, or it wouldn't be useful if it were built, or this term is synonymous with "vector computer".

MOS Metal Oxide on Silicon: the basic technology for fabricating semiconductors.

MS-DOS An operating system for IBM PCs and compatibles, descended from QDOS (Quick & Dirty Operating System).

NFS Network File System: a system, developed by Sun but now widely used, for allowing one machine to access files stored on another.

Occam A computer language based on CSP. Initially, this was the only language available for transputers.

OEM Original Equipment Manufacturer: a company which adds components to someone else's computers and sells the result as a complete product.

OLTP On-Line Transaction Processing: handling transactions (such as deposits and withdrawals) as they occur. OLTP is what lies behind hole-in-the-wall banking machines.

OS Operating System: the basic software which manages the computer.

OSF Open Software Foundation: A organisation established by a number of the major computer manufacturers to set software standards.

parallel computer any computer containing more than one processor.

parallelise convert from serial form to a form suitable for running on a parallel computer.

PC Personal Computer. PC is an IBM brand name, but is also used to mean any similar machine (or clone).

PC-DOS An operating system for IBM PCs and compatibles, descended from QDOS (Quick & Dirty Operating System).

PICT Programme on Information and Communication Technologies: a sociological study of the forces shaping the development of high technology. The research presented in this volume was funded by PICT.

POSIX A standard definition of the interface to the UNIX operating system.

QCD Quantum ChromoDynamics: a model of the behaviour of matter on sub-nuclear scales. Simulating QCD is generally reckoned to require twice as much computing power as will ever be available.

RAE The UK's Royal Aircraft Establishment.

RAM Random Access Memory: computer memory which can be written to and read from in any order.

RARDE The UK's Royal Armaments Research and Development Establishment.

RDMS Relational Database Management System: software to manage a database in which data are stored by attribute.

RGB Red-Green-Blue: the most common form of colour monitor.

RISC Reduced Instruction Set Computer: any computer architecture based on the highly-optimised use of a very small set of instructions.

ROM Read-Only Memory: computer memory which cannot be written to during normal operation.

RSRE The UK's Royal Signals and Radar Establishment.

SCSI Small Computer Systems Interface: a standard for interfacing to devices such as discs.

SIMD Single Instruction/Multiple Data: a type of parallel computer whose processors work in lock-step, carrying out each instruction on large amounts of data.

SISD Single Instruction/Single Data: the traditional computer architecture in which each instruction is applied to a single datum at a time.

SPARC Scalable Processor ARChitecture: a family of chips which can be manufactured using a variety of technologies.

SQL Standard Query Language: a standard for adding data to, or recovering data from, databases.

SRAM Static RAM: memory which stores data in flip-flops, which require no memory refresh and hence have low power consumption. Generally very fast.

superminicomputer A very powerful minicomputer.

transputer a microprocessor developed by Inmos containing memory and communications links as well as a CPU, around which several manufacturers have constructed computers.

UART Universal Asynchronous Receive-Transmit. A standard protocol for device drivers.

UNIX an operating system originally developed by AT&T which, in various incarnations, is now available on most types of computers.

vector computer any computer whose functional units are chained together to carry out the same series of instructions on a long stream (or vector) of data. Vector computers have dominated supercomputing since the 1970s, and are only now being challenged by parallel computers.

Vectorise convert from serial form to a form suitable for running on a vector computer.

VLIW Very Long Instruction Word: the use of extremely long instructions (256 bits or more) in a computer to improve its ability to chain operations together.

VLSI Very Large Scale Integration: an adjective applied to technologies capable of putting hundreds of thousands of components on single chips, or to those chips themselves.

VMS Virtual Machine System: an operating system developed by DEC, and widely used on Vax machines.

Whetstone A standard benchmark for measuring overall computer performance.

wormhole routing A technique for routing messages in a multiprocessor computer in which the "head" establishes a path through the processor network.

Appendix D

Trademarks

Many of the product names used in this report are trademarks belonging to the companies in whose sections those names appear. In addition, the terms given below are also trademarked; we apologise if we have omitted others.

4Sight is a registered trademark of Silicon Graphics Inc..
AdaWorld is a registered trademark of Alsys.
Ada is a registered trademark of the U.S. Government Ada Joint Program Office.
Aion is a registered trademark of Aion Inc..
Ardent is a registered trademark of Ardent Computer Inc..
AVS is a registered trademark of Stardent Computer Inc.
Butterfly is a registered trademark of Bolt Beranek and Newman Inc..
CCLISP is a registered trademark of Goldhill Computers.
CM-1 is a registered trademark of Thinking Machines Corporation.
CM-2 is a registered trademark of Thinking Machines Corporation.
Concurrent FileSystem is a registered trademark of Intel Corporation.
Concurrent Workbench is a registered trademark of Intel Corporation.
Connection Machine is a registered trademark of Thinking Machines Corporation.
CONVERTER/SX is a registered trademark of NEC.
Cray-1 is a registered trademark of Cray Research Incorporated.
Cray-2 is a registered trademark of Cray Research Incorporated.
Cray-3 is a registered trademark of Cray Research Incorporated.
Cray X-MP is a registered trademark of Cray Research Incorporated.
Cray Y-MP is a registered trademark of Cray Research Incorporated.
CTSS is a registered trademark of Cray Research Incorporated.
Cyber-205 is a registered trademark of CDC.
DataPath is a registered trademark of Stellar Computer Corporation.
DataVault is a registered trademark of Thinking Machines Corporation.
Direct-Connect is a registered trademark of Intel Corporation.
DS1000 is a registered trademark of Stellar Computer Corporation.
DS2000 is a registered trademark of Stellar Computer Corporation.
DYL-280 is a registered trademark of Sterling Software.
Ethernet is a registered trademark of Xerox Corporation.
Express is a registered trademark of Parasoft Inc..

FORGE is a registered trademark of Pacific Sierra.
Geometry Engine is a registered trademark of Silicon Graphics Inc..
Geometry Pipeline is a registered trademark of Silicon Graphics Inc..
GFT77 is a registered trademark of Cray Research Incorporated.
GINO is a registered trademark of Bradley Associates.
Gist is a registered trademark of Bolt Beranek and Newman Inc..
GS1000 is a registered trademark of Stellar Computer Corporation.
GS2000 is a registered trademark of Stellar Computer Corporation.
Helios is a registered trademark of Perihelion.
HEX is a registered trademark of Caplin Cybernetics.
i860 is a registered trademark of Intel Corporation.
Idris is a registered trademark of Digital Equipment Corporation.
iLBX is a registered trademark of Intel Corporation.
Intellect is a registered trademark of Artificial Intelligence Corporation.
iPSC is a registered trademark of Intel Corporation.
IRIS WorkSpace is a registered trademark of Silicon Graphics Inc..
IRIX is a registered trademark of Silicon Graphics Inc..
Jade is a registered trademark of Jade Simulations International Corp..
Linda is a registered trademark of Scientific Computing Associates.
Masterflow is a registered trademark of Flomerics Limited.
MegaNode is a registered trademark of Telmat Informatique.
MIMDizer is a registered trademark of Pacific Sierra.
MIPS is a registered trademark of MIPS Computer Systems.
MS-DOS is a registered trademark of Microsoft.
Multibus is a registered trademark of Intel Corporation.
NChannel is a registered trademark of NCUBE Corporation.
NCUBE is a registered trademark of NCUBE Corporation.
NCUBE/4 is a registered trademark of NCUBE Corporation.
NCUBE/7 is a registered trademark of NCUBE Corporation.
NCUBE/10 is a registered trademark of NCUBE Corporation.
NCUBE-2 is a registered trademark of NCUBE Corporation.
NeWS is a registered trademark of Sun Microsystems Inc..
NFS is a registered trademark of Sun Microsystems Inc..
Nomad2 is a registered trademark of Must Software.
nX is a registered trademark of Bolt Beranek and Newman Inc..
NX is a registered trademark of INTEL.
Occam is a registered trademark of the Inmos group of companies.
Oracle is a registered trademark of Oracle Corporation.
Paris is a registered trademark of Thinking Machines Corporation.
PAX is a registered trademark of Alliant Corporation.
Personal IRIS is a registered trademark of Silicon Graphics Inc..

PostScript is a registered trademark of Adobe Systems Incorporated.

Power Fortran Accelerator is a registered trademark of Silicon Graphics Inc..

POWER Series is a registered trademark of Silicon Graphics Inc..

PRISM is a registered trademark of Polyhedron Software Limited.

pSOS is a registered trademark of Software Components Group Ltd..

Q-bus is a registered trademark of Digital Equipment Corporation.

QT is a registered trademark of Caplin cybernetics.

Relational is a registered trademark of DataCache Meiko.

Silicon Graphics is a registered trademark of Silicon Graphics Inc..

SIM++ is a registered trademark of Jade Simulations International Corporation.

Smalltalk is a registered trademark of Xerox.

SPARCstation is a registered trademark of Sun Microsystems, Incorporated.

SPARC is a registered trademark of SPARC International.

Stardent is a registered trademark of Stardent Computer Inc.

Stellar is a registered trademark of Stellar Computer Corporation.

Stellix is a registered trademark of Stellar Computer Corporation.

Strand88 is a registered trademark of SSTL.

Sun-3 is a registered trademark of Sun Microsystems Incorporated.

Sun-4 is a registered trademark of Sun Microsystems Incorporated.

SunOs is a registered trademark of Sun Microsystems, Incorporated.

SuperNode is a registered trademark of Parsys.

SX-2 is a registered trademark of NEC.

SX-3 is a registered trademark of NEC.

SXOS is a registered trademark of NEC.

SXview is a registered trademark of NEC.

Symbolics is a registered trademark of Symbolics Inc..

TC2000 is a registered trademark of Bolt Beranek and Newman Inc..

T-Node is a registered trademark of Telmat Informatique.

Titan is a registered trademark of Ardent Computer Inc..

Totalview is a registered trademark of Bolt Beranek and Newman Inc..

Touchstone is a registered trademark of Intel Corporation.

Transputer is a registered trademark of Inmos.

UltraNet is a registered trademark of Ultra Network Technologies Inc..

Ultrix is a registered trademark of Digital Equipment Corporation.

UNICOS is a registered trademark of Cray Research Incorporated.

Uniform System is a registered trademark of Bolt Beranek and Newman Inc..

UNIX is a registered trademark of AT&T.

VAST is a registered trademark of Pacific Sierra.

VAX is a registered trademark of Digital Equipment Corporation.

VMEbus is a registered trademark of VMEbus Manufacturers Group.

VMS is a registered trademark of Digital Equipment Corporation.

X-Windows is a registered trademark of Massachusetts Institute of Technology.
XENIX is a registered trademark of Microsoft.
XTM is a registered trademark of Cogent.

Index